ENGLISH FURNITURE DESIGNS
of the Eighteenth Century

by

PETER WARD-JACKSON

LONDON
VICTORIA AND ALBERT MUSEUM
1984

© *Crown copyright*
First published by HMSO in 1958
Published by the Victoria and Albert Museum 1984
ISBN 0 905209486
Printed in the UK for HMSO 8219559 3/84

CONTENTS

Preface	v
List of Books referred to in Abbreviated Form	viii
Part 1 General Introduction	
The Purpose of Furniture Designs	1
Furniture Designs in the Seventeenth Century	5
The Furniture of the Palladian Age	7
The Rococo Style	8
Chippendale and the Chinese and Gothic Taste	14
The Neo-Classical Revival	21
Part 2 Catalogue of the Illustrations and Notes on the Artists	31
Index of Designers	69
Part 3 The Illustrations	71
Appendix	335

PREFACE TO THE FIRST EDITION

In this book an attempt is made to illustrate the history of English furniture in the eighteenth century by a new method, using contemporary designs instead of photographs of furniture. The Museum is in a good position to carry out this experiment, because in the Library and in the Department of Engraving, Illustration and Design, it possesses one of the largest collections of English furniture designs in existence. Many of them are engravings, including a number of plates in rare books, which cannot easily be found elsewhere; while others are original drawings, which tend to be scarcer still, because they are apt to be mislaid or destroyed, once they have served their purpose. So rare, indeed, are drawings of this kind that, in order to make the book as complete a guide to the subject as possible, it has been decided to include a number of interesting examples belonging to Sir John Soane's Museum and to the Royal Institute of British Architects. They are by four notable designers, Vardy, Adam, Holland and Soane, whose work in this field is not well represented in this Museum, and we are grateful to the Curator of the Soane Museum and to the Librarian of the Royal Institute of British Architects for kindly allowing us to publish these drawings. We must also thank Mr John Summerson for permitting us to include the design by Nash which belongs to him. Altogether several hundred designs, both prints and drawings, have been reproduced here; and it is hoped that they have been chosen and arranged in a way which will enable the reader to survey the progress of English furniture from a new and enjoyable point of view.

A subsidiary purpose of the book is to provide a bibliographical guide to the furniture pattern books of the period. The Museum possesses copies of most of them, and specimen plates from each are included among the illustrations; while the bibliographical information is set out in the Notes on the Illustrations in Part II. Part I is intended as a general survey of the stylistic trends illustrated in the plates.

The book has been written by Mr Peter Ward-Jackson, Assistant Keeper in the Department of Engraving, Illustration and Design. In dealing with the bibliographical material he has benefited from the work done in this field by the late Mr Fiske Kimball and by Miss Edna Donnell, to whose two indispensable essays frequent reference is made in the text. He also acknowledges his indebtedness to the writings of Mr Ralph Edwards and of the late Miss Margaret Jourdain.

Sir Trenchard Cox
Director,
Victoria and Albert Museum
1955–66

ADDENDA AND CORRIGENDA

compiled by Michael Snodin

2. The drawing is by John Talman (1677–1726).

10, 11, 12. These drawings are now believed to date from the early nineteenth century.

13. A pair of silver chandeliers of this design, made in Hanover, are at Anglesey Abbey, Cambridgeshire.

15. Two of the tables from Chiswick House are at Chatsworth and in the Victoria and Albert Museum.

16. A pair of settees of this design is at Temple Newsam House, Leeds. They were made in 1731 by James Moore for Sir John Dutton. See Christopher Gilbert, *Furniture at Temple Newsam House and Lotherton Hall*, 1978, II, Cat.324. Other examples also survive.

19. The plate is from De la Cour's *Fifth Book of Ornaments, Useful for all manner of furniture and other things*, 1743. A complete set of the eight books of ornaments is at the Cooper-Hewitt Museum, New York. For the painter William De la Cour, who is almost certainly identical with the ornamentalist, see Edward Croft-Murray, *Decorative Painting in England, 1537–1837*, 1970, Vol.II, pp.199–200.

27. For Brunetti's career in England see Edward Croft-Murray, *op. cit.*, pp.176–177. The chair and table designs were used by painters, in particular Charles Phillips (1708–1747) whose portrait of George II, at Marble Hill, includes a chair copied from 27 (see G.L.C., *To Preserve and Enhance*, 1975, cat. 23). The Museum's collection also includes several plates from another set of the *Ornaments*. These are undated, in the opposite direction to the 1736 set and are lettered *G. Brunetti Inv*. In quality they seem to pre-date the 1736 set and may be from the set described in the *Katalog der Ornamentstich Sammlung der Staatlichen Kunstbibliothek Berlin*, 1939, No.587, as the first edition of 1731.

43. A table and pier glass, probably made for the 5th Duke of Bolton, is at Hackwood Park. See Anthony Coleridge, *Chippendale Furniture*, 1968, pls. 78–80. The carving between the front legs is, however, symmetrical in design and adapted from that on the pier glass. The asymmetrical shell and scroll work on the design for the table is copied from a print after J. A. Meissonnier of a design for a sofa. It was published in his collected *Oeuvre* in about 1749 and also very probably at an earlier date. Vardy's architectural work at Hackwood Park was carried out 1761–3.

44. A bed of this design is at Hardwick Hall.

45. This drawing represents a French *bureau-plat* and *cartonnier* of about 1745. The *bureau-plat*, by Bernard van Risenburgh II, is at Temple Newsam House. The Museum's design for a Palladian building dated 1746 is for Richard Arundell's house at Allerton Park. Both pieces of furniture are recorded in the collection of Arundell's heir in 1774. Arundell's letters do not reveal how the pieces were acquired. See C. Gilbert, *op. cit.*, cat. 561.

46, 47. See Christopher Gilbert, 'Early Furniture Designs of Mathias Darly', *Furniture History*, XI, 1975, pp.33–39.

48. A table of this design is at Temple Newsam House. See Christopher Gilbert, *Furniture at Temple Newsam House and Lotherton Hall*, 1978, II, Cat.446.

49–55. See Morrison Hecksher, 'Lock and Copland: A catalogue of the Engraved Ornament', *Furniture History*, XV, 1979, pp.1–23.

61. A table of this design, with a matching pier glass, both from Hinton House, are in the Museum.

70. From the set *A new Book of Ornaments*, 1752. See Geoffrey Beard, 'Babel's A new Book of Ornaments, 1752', *Furniture History*, XI, 1975, pp.31–32.

72–123. See Christopher Gilbert, *The Life and Work of Thomas Chippendale*, 1978, *passim*.

113. This drawing is now believed to have been made c.1755 in the circle of John Vardy.

128–134. See 46, 47 above.

135. See John and Eileen Harris, *Sir William Chambers*, 1970.

137–146. See Helena Hayward, *Thomas Johnson and the English Rococo*, 1964, *passim*.

143. See Christopher Gilbert, *Furniture at Temple Newsam House and Lotherton Hall*, 1978, II, p.355.

147. See Terry Friedman, 'Two Eighteenth-Century Catalogues of Ornamental Pattern Books', *Furniture History*, XI, 1975, p.69.

150. *The Universal System of Household Furniture* was published in facsimile in 1960, with an introduction by Ralph Edwards.

180. See 46, 47 above.

182. See 49–55 above.

189. A set of steps of this form is at Wimpole Hall.

190–201. For John Linnell see Helena Hayward and Pat Kirkham, *William and John Linnell*, 1980, *passim*.

190. *Ibid.*, Fig. 275, p.79.

191. *Ibid*, Fig. 273, p.78.

194. *Ibid*, Figs. 127, 128, pp.62, 80, 104, 117.

195. *Ibid*, Figs. 241–247, pp.21, 111.

197. *Ibid*, Fig. 40, p.78.

198. *Ibid*, Fig. 208, p.77.

200. *Ibid*, Fig. 7, pp.21, 79.

205. The clothes presses from Croome Court are now in the Victoria and Albert Museum and at Temple Newsam House, Leeds.

206. The book case is at the Metropolitan Museum, New York.

237. H. Hayward and P. Kirkham, *op. cit.*, Fig. 20, p.20.

238. *Ibid*, Fig. 24, p.83.

239. *Ibid*, Fig. 118, p.84.

241. *Ibid*, Figs. 87–89, pp.83, 90, 118, 127. Chairs of this design survive at Harewood House and Inverary Castle.

242. *Ibid*, Fig. 83, p.83.

243. *Ibid*, Figs. 68, 71, p.64.

245. *Ibid*, Fig. 255, p.127.

247. *Ibid*, Fig. 214, pp.61, 82, 102. c.1767–8.

249. *Ibid*, Fig. 25, p.25, c.1765.

250. *Ibid*, Figs. 108, 109, p.63. A commode belonging to Lord Howard after this design was made by Christopher Furlogh, who may have been employed by John Linnell.

256. See 49–55 above.

265. This design is now attributed to Thomas Chippendale, c.1769. It is the composite source of the pier suites at Harewood House. See C. Gilbert, *op. cit.*, Figs. 286, 289, 474, 477, 486, p.201.

LIST OF BOOKS REFERRED TO IN ABBREVIATED FORM

CLOUSTON. *English Furniture and Furniture Makers of the Eighteenth Century.* By R. S. Clouston. London, 1906.

COLVIN. *A Biographical Dictionary of English Architects 1660–1840.* By H. M. Colvin. London, 1954.

EDWARDS AND JOURDAIN. *Georgian Cabinet-makers.* By Ralph Edwards and Margaret Jourdain. 3rd edition. London, 1955.

MACQUOID AND EDWARDS. *The Dictionary of English Furniture.* By Percy Macquoid and Ralph Edwards. 3 vols. 2nd edition. London, 1954.

KIMBALL AND DONNELL, vol. I. *The Creators of the Chippendale Style.* By Fiske Kimball and Edna Donnell. In *Metropolitan Museum Studies*, vol. I, pp. 115—154. New York, 1928–29.

KIMBALL AND DONNELL, vol. II. *Chippendale Designs in the Book of the Society of Upholsterers.* [By the same authors.] In *Metropolitan Museum Studies*, vol. II, pp. 41–59. New York, 1929–30.

Part I

GENERAL INTRODUCTION

The Purpose of Furniture Designs

The story of English furniture in Georgian times can be vividly illustrated with a great variety of designs by cabinet-makers, architects and others; and the view we shall thus get of the subject will be different from the usual one, in that the practical and social aspects of furniture, the way it was made, the needs it served in different periods, the woods that were used and other matters of that kind, which have been fully dealt with in several recent books, will occupy our attention less than questions of style and the purely decorative quality of the furniture represented. As revealed in the designs collected together in this book, the history of furniture becomes part of the history of ornament in general, a somewhat specialized study perhaps, but one which has its own interest; for it is not concerned with an accidental or arbitrary phenomenon, but with something more alive, which evolves gradually and may be compared with a biological species, in that it undergoes many modifications, but preserves through them all vestigial traces of an ancestral type, to which it may eventually revert. The ornament of ancient Greece and Rome constitutes the main strain in all the designs reproduced here, and we shall find it nearly always present, even in designs, like those of the rococo age, where its influence is least apparent. But it is often disguised and mingled with other strains, from China and Japan, from Islam, from medieval art; and some of these we hope to unravel as we go along. In this way our survey will acquire a point. But the designs have not been chosen to illustrate a thesis. They are intended primarily to show as fully as possible the different types of furniture which were made during the period, so that the reader may form his own opinions, or simply enjoy the pictures. For many of the designs are attractive works in themselves, while even those which are not may yet provide some entertainment for those who are interested in the taste of our ancestors.

The main drawback of a book composed, as this is, entirely of designs in contemporary prints and drawings, is that the period which it can cover is limited to the eighteenth century and after, owing to lack of material in earlier times. A few designs from the seventeenth century are reproduced here, as an introduction, but very little relevant material survives from that period, and if we go back to the Tudors, we are likely to search for examples in vain. There are several possible reasons for this dearth of early designs. Drawings of this type have only lately begun to interest collectors and museums, and in the past they were not likely to be kept, once they had served their purpose. Nor, until the eighteenth century, were they engraved and thus preserved for posterity. But even if a greater proportion had been spared, the total number would probably still be small; for there is reason to believe that furniture makers under the Tudors and Stuarts were less dependent on drawings of this kind than they afterwards became.

A furniture design, whether it is a rough sketch or a detailed drawing to scale, represents an idea in the designer's mind. If the idea is to be realized, the workman, who may also be the designer, will have to make drawings of a more practical nature, showing exactly how the piece of furniture is to be constructed. These working drawings, as they are called, are usually made full size, because scale drawings are apt to confuse the workman; and, again, a slight error in one of them will be considerably magnified when the work is carried out full size. In addition to working drawings, the cabinet-maker uses templates, or patterns cut out of thin boards, which help him to mark out the required shapes on his wood. If his task is a simple one, to which he is accustomed, he may do without working drawings and use templates only, or he may even dispense with both. But, clearly, no elaborate piece of joinery can be carried out without the aid of working drawings, and this applies to ancient as well as to modern furniture. The design, on the other hand, being an idea, need not necessarily be committed to paper, as long as it is clear in the workman's mind, and he, until comparatively modern times, was a master craftsman quite capable of inventing his own designs, the only guidance he needed being supplied partly by training and tradition and partly by fashion, as revealed in the work of other craftsmen around him. Though such a man might draw a rough sketch to guide an apprentice or to clarify his own thoughts, he was not likely to make carefully finished designs for his own use, when he could express his ideas more accurately and practically in working drawings.

The art of drawing designs began to acquire a greater importance when it became a means of communicating ideas between one man and another. This first happened in the sixteenth century, when artists began to recognize the opportunity which the new art of engraving gave them of selling designs for furniture and other applied arts to a wide public. Among the first in the field were two German artists, Peter Flötner of Nuremberg and the unidentified Augsburg master H.S., who both engraved designs for furniture during the second quarter of the century. The first approach to a comprehensive collection of patterns for household furniture was made in France soon afterwards by Jacques Androuet Ducerceau in a series of about seventy engraved designs; and his plates were soon followed by two books of furniture designs published in the Netherlands, the *Différents Portraicts de Menuiserie* of Hans Vredeman de Vries (1588) and the *Verscheyden Schreinwerck* of his son Paul (1630). Some of these prints were doubtless circulated in England, and there is evidence that they had some influence on Elizabethan and Jacobean furniture. During the seventeenth century designs for furniture were published on the continent in ever increasing numbers, and prints by French artists like Bérain, Boulle and Le Pautre played a part in introducing the baroque style into England. But English artists were slow to make use of engraving as a means of reproducing designs, and the eighteenth century was well advanced before a start was made with the pattern books of William Jones, Batty Langley, Matthias Lock and others.

This backwardness was due not so much to lack of talent as to social conditions in general. Most branches of industry were technically more advanced on the continent than in England at this time, and the wealthy classes there were on the whole more exacting in all that concerned the decoration of their houses than their equals here. A love of magnificence went with political absolutism, and the consequent demand for elaborate furniture taxed the craftsman's invention so heavily that he was forced to accept the help of more sophisticated artists in contriving suitable designs. Thus there came into existence a new kind of artist – the professional designer or ornamentalist. In England an analogous situation did not arise till a century later, at the time of the Restoration, when a sharpened taste for luxury and a desire to emulate the splendour of continental palaces took possession of the rich and extravagant. Here too it became increasingly difficult for the uneducated craftsman to keep abreast with the latest fashions in design, and he began to feel the need for guidance. This want was to some extent satisfied in the eighteenth century by engraved pattern books, which issued from the London printing presses in a steady stream, spreading far and wide over the kingdom an indispensable knowledge of the classical orders and news of the latest fashion.

So many of these handbooks were published that they were made the subject of a parody by the architect Robert Morris, himself the author of several architectural manuals, into one of which[1] he inserted this advertisement: 'There is now in the Press . . . A Treatise on Country Five Barr'd Gates, Stiles and Wickets, elegant Pig-styes, beautiful Henhouses, and delightful Cow-cribs, superb Cart-houses, magnificent Barn Doors, variegated Barn Racks, and admirable Sheep-Folds; according to the Turkish and Persian manner . . . To which is added, some Designs of Fly-traps, Bee Palaces, and Emmet Houses, in The Muscovite and Arabian architecture; all adapted to the Latitude and Genius of England. The whole entirely new, and inimitably designed in Two Parts, on Forty Pewter Plates, under the immediate Inspection of Don Gulielmus De Demi Je ne sai Quoi, chief Architect to the Grand Signor.' The majority of the pattern books thus ridiculed were concerned with architecture and doubtless found their readiest buyers among master builders and carpenters. But a few, more comprehensive in scope, dealt with furniture as well as interior decoration, and during the second half of the century cabinet-makers had at their disposal a regular supply of books devoted exclusively to furniture designs. The authors were mostly cabinet-makers and carvers themselves, and their books served a double purpose in advertising their wares and turning to profitable account their skill as draughtsmen, small though this sometimes was. Some of the larger firms probably retained professional draughtsmen on their staff to make designs, and there is reason to believe, as we shall see, that Matthias Lock was employed by Chippendale for this purpose.

At the same time the whole field of decoration was gradually invaded by architects and other professional designers, who without necessarily possessing any technical knowledge of joinery, cabinet-making, or any other craft, were ready to provide their clients with designs for every article of domestic use. Such a man was William Kent, who was trained as a painter, but in later life devoted most of his attention to architecture and other branches of design. 'He was not only consulted for furniture', wrote Horace Walpole, 'as frames of pictures, glasses, tables, chairs, etc, but for plate, for a barge, for a cradle. And so impetuous was fashion, that two great ladies prevailed on him to make designs for their birthday gowns. The one he dressed in a petticoat decorated with the columns of the five orders; the other like a bronze, in a copper-coloured satin with ornaments of gold.' Such a phenomenon would have been impossible in England a hundred years previously, when

---

[1] *Architecture Improved*, 1755.

designing was still the craftsman's job. But in the eighteenth century, as many instances show, designing and making had to some extent become separate activities. For example, Edward Edwards,[1] the artist, drew patterns for furniture in a cabinet-maker's shop in his early youth. Matthew Darly was both designer and cartoonist, a curious combination, to which he humorously alludes in a caricature of himself seated on a donkey under the title 'Political Designer of pots, pans and pipkins'; and Thomas Sheraton, after he had ceased to practice as a cabinet-maker, informed his clients through his trade card that he 'makes designs for cabinet-makers'. Most notable of all, of course, is the case of Robert Adam who, with no professional knowledge of cabinet-making, made a great number of furniture designs and brought about a fundamental change of style in the furniture of his day. Other architects who turned their attention to furniture were John Vardy, Henry Keene, Sir William Chambers, John Carter, John Yenn, Henry Holland and Sir John Soane; and there were doubtless many others whose drawings have been lost and whose work in this field has remained unidentified. The furniture they designed was mostly made to order for their clients and was intended to form part of a concerted decorative scheme. Being primarily architects, they were not interested in supplying the furniture trade in general with designs, though their more successful ideas were sometimes published in engravings and thus exerted a certain influence on the public taste.

It is not to be supposed, however, that the ordinary eighteenth-century cabinet-maker came to rely entirely on pattern books or drawings by professional artists for his designs. On the contrary, despite the rise of the professional designer, the greater part of the enormous quantity of furniture produced in the period was probably designed by the cabinet-makers themselves. Much of it is plain serviceable furniture based on a generally accepted pattern, and the infinite number of small variations which occur in the decoration doubtless sprang from the cabinet-maker's fancy. Indeed, in some kinds of furniture, in mid-eighteenth-century chair backs for example, the designs vary so greatly in detail, that unless they were invented by the makers, it would be necessary to postulate almost as many designers as cabinet-makers. Again, if cabinet-makers were incapable of making their own designs, it would be hard to explain why they so seldom copied the many suitable engraved patterns which circulated during the second half of the century. Why, for example, have so few existing pieces of furniture been found to correspond with Hepplewhite's admirably practical designs? The reason, no doubt, is that few cabinet-makers of the day were so barren of ideas as to descend to slavish copying. They adapted their style to the latest fashion, as illustrated in pattern books, but they usually invented their own designs instead of taking them ready made; and some of them, like John Linnell, were accomplished draughtsmen, well able to express their ideas on paper.

The furniture of the eighteenth century was therefore designed partly by the makers and partly by architects and other professional artists. The cabinet-makers, inheriting the traditions of an ancient craft, were on the whole more conservative than artists who were not brought up to the trade, and through all the fluctuations of fashion they maintained a certain continuity of style. The more adventurous among them, like Chippendale, might

[1] See the *Account of the Life of Mr. Edwards*, published as an introduction to his *Anecdotes of Painters*, 1808.

strive after modishness, but the majority continued to make plain furniture of proven usefulness, the sort of furniture which it did not need the ingenuity of a professional artist to design. It is therefore well to remember, when looking at some of the more elaborate projects illustrated here, that many of them were probably never carried out. They were, in any case, outnumbered many times by the simpler and more practical products of innumerable obscure cabinet-makers all over the country; and while an architect like Kent was equipping the palaces of his rich patrons with profusely carved and gilt furniture, the ordinary well-to-do householder furnished his rooms with plain walnut or mahogany in a simple style that showed little trace of the baroque fashions affected by the great. It is a pity that more designs of this type cannot be illustrated here beside the more ambitious sort. But they are relatively scarce, because the craftsman could often dispense with them, and they were too homely to find their way into collectors' portfolios or to catch the fancy of the public in a book of patterns. Nevertheless, cabinet-makers like Chippendale and Hepplewhite usually illustrated a few in their trade catalogues to show that they catered for all needs and purses; and some of those illustrated here are interesting because they show how little such furniture varied in style from one age to another despite changes of fashion (cf. Nos. 74 and 282).

Furniture Designs in the Seventeenth Century

The earliest design illustrated here (No. 1) is an eighteenth-century engraving after a drawing by John Webb, the favourite pupil of Inigo Jones. It shows a plain curtained bed standing in an alcove between two palm trees, which grow out of Corinthian columns and meet overhead to form an arch with their branches. It is a charming fancy, and the designer showed a wise restraint in not carrying it too far, allowing the simplicity of the bed to set off the luxuriance of the setting. Though Webb's drawing is dated 1665, and thus falls outside our period, the engraving is included here because it gives some idea of a style which inspired a whole school of designers in the following century. For Webb followed Jones so closely that his numerous drawings, including the one reproduced in this engraving, were mistaken for Jones's in the eighteenth century and were revered accordingly by the architects of the Palladian school. He thus contributed perhaps as much as his master to the formation of their style. No other furniture designs by him have come down to us, nor has any work of this kind by Jones survived.[1] Yet there is no doubt that together they posthumously exerted a considerable influence on furniture design during the Palladian revival; for their admirers adapted their architectural style to furniture; and many a massive architectural bookcase or cabinet, fitted with columns and an entablature, or embellished with large-scale swags and scrolled consoles, can trace back its descent to the doorcases and chimney-pieces of Jones and Webb.

However, more than half a century was to pass before Jones's italianate standards were widely recognized by British architects and designers, and during that interval the predominant influence on furniture was the baroque style of France and Holland.

---

[1] The design for a cabinet in the Ashmolean Museum, Oxford, reproduced in Macquoid and Edwards, under the heading *Jones*, is probably Dutch or Flemish.

The Dutch influence is revealed in No. 2, another architect's drawing, dating from about 1675 and showing various pieces of furniture in their setting. The unknown author has paid close attention to every detail in his scheme, and the furniture has been skilfully planned to harmonize with the architecture. Against one wall he has tried two alternative arrangements with different furniture in each, and it is interesting to observe that in both cases he has taken care to give the frames on the wall exactly the same cornice, with a prominent torus moulding, as the cabinet which stands between them. This device of the recurring motif, which has an analogy in music, later became a favourite method of bringing the different elements of a room into accord and reached its consummation in the work of Robert Adam. In this drawing the ornament is too florid and rotundly baroque to be plausibly attributed to an English hand, and the resemblance which it bears to the decoration of the later rooms at Ham House, largely the work of Dutch craftsmen, suggests that the author was an immigrant from Holland. Only one piece of furniture conforms closely to a pattern generally accepted in England, and that is the writing cabinet with a falling front supported on a chest-of-drawers, a type of furniture commonly found in every large house of the period. The rest of the furniture was clearly specially designed by the architect to match the decoration of the walls, and some of the objects are highly unusual in form. The enormous candlestick, more than eight foot high, holding a single large candle, is an extraordinary thing to find in a secular apartment; and the glazed bookcase, though it belongs to a type of furniture which was beginning to come into use, is exceptional in the style of its decoration, the short thick columns that frame the shelves and the enormous shell-shaped device that crowns the pediment being unusual features.

French influence on English furniture at the turn of the century is illustrated in a number of engraved designs by Daniel Marot. This gifted architect and designer was French by birth, but, forced as a Protestant to flee from his native land to Holland, he came to England for a while in the service of his Dutch patron, William III, for whom he laid out the gardens at Hampton Court Palace and for whom he probably carried out other commissions in this country, though no record of them has been preserved. His stay in England was so short that he can hardly be called an English artist, fond though we are of claiming immigrant talent as our own. It is, nevertheless, convenient to include him in this book, because, in the absence of English designs, his work shows the direction in which the more ambitious English cabinet-makers were tending at the beginning of the eighteenth century; and several of his designs, like the mirror frame in No. 7, incorporate the royal arms of England, showing that they were intended for an English royal palace, at any rate by the artist. Through his personal influence and through his many engraved designs, Marot probably played a greater part than any other artist in introducing into England the classicizing baroque style which flourished in France during the last part of Louis XIV's reign, and the designs reproduced here (Nos. 4–8) illustrate some of its principal features: the shells and masks, the heavy scrolls of C and S form, the human figures used as supports and caryatids, the cornucopias, the festoons and pendants of fruits and flowers, and a particular type of strapwork, composed of narrow bands arranged in a pattern of straight lines and C scrolls interlaced with foliage, which was commonly used to decorate the tops of gilt tables and other flat surfaces. Though some of these motifs can hardly be called classical in any strict sense, they were descended from classical origins and had reached their present form through a gradual process of experiment carried out by several generations of artists on the legacy inherited from the ancient world. Such a style was more alive and, in that important respect, nearer to the spirit of the art which it sought to emulate that one based on close imitation; and that is why it remained an active influence on classicizing designers, like Kent, long after it had been superseded in France.

The Furniture of the Palladian Age

A campaign to purify English architecture and to revive the style of Palladio and Jones was launched in the 1720's by Lord Burlington, who by his ability to fire others with his own enthusiasm and his skill in capturing the leading architectural appointments under the Crown for his own nominees soon succeeded in establishing the Palladian code. His principal lieutenant, William Kent, was keenly interested in furniture design and made interesting attempts to create a type of furniture appropriate to the Palladian style of interior decoration. It was a difficult task, because Vitruvius and Palladio, whose writings the new school of architects consulted on every problem of architecture, had nothing to say about furniture; nor was it possible to form a clear idea of ancient furniture from the scanty evidence then available. Obliged, therefore, to improvise a classical style of their own, Kent and his colleagues tried to solve the problem by reducing the interior architecture of Jones to the scale of furniture. Taking his doorways and chimney-pieces as models (cf. No. 339), they framed cabinets, bookcases and presses between columns or pilasters and crowned them with entablatures and pediments. All their furniture was designed as far as possible on analogous architectural lines and embellished with large-scale sculptural motifs of a monumental character, suggestive of stone rather than wood. Many of these ornaments, such as the massive scrolled console, the human mask, the scallop shell, the floral swags and pendants, the herms and caryatids, were taken straight from Jones and Webb. But devoted though they were to Jones, the Palladian architects would not have been human had they not made some concessions to more modern taste, and they drew largely on the ornamental repertory built up by the great French ornamentalists of Louis XIV's reign. The furniture that resulted was no more like Greek or Roman furniture than Pope is like Homer, but like Pope's heroic couplets, it has an Augustan flavour which evokes the antique. The best examples of the style reproduced here are some designs by Kent himself. The organ (No. 14) illustrates his debt to Jones, as we shall see if we compare it with Jones's design for a chimney-piece (No. 339); while the chandelier (No. 13) owes something to French designers like Marot and Jean Le Pautre. A more idiosyncratic manner is displayed in a table pedantically shaped like an antique vase (No. 15), which makes it easy to believe Walpole's story of the lady Kent dressed in a petticoat decorated with the columns of the five orders. His most characteristic design is the drawing for a side-table at Houghton Hall (No. 18). This truly formidable piece of furniture is supported on mighty scrolled consoles and fluted balusters, which carry an enriched frieze and architrave, while an enormous human mask, flanked by swags and cornucopias, dominates the centre of the apron. Anywhere but in a vast saloon at Houghton, or in some other Palladian palace, the effect would be overpowering, but in its proper setting, in a room of proportionate magnitude decorated in a similar style, the table becomes an appropriate adjunct to the architecture, as Kent intended. His furniture was all conceived in the same spirit. Like Robert Adam in the second half of the century, he sought to impose an ideal harmony on all his creations, and in the pursuit of this aim he strayed beyond the architect's normal field into that of the gardener and the cabinet-maker, designing furniture to complete a room, just as he laid out a landscape to form a perfect setting for a classical building.

An architect closely associated with Kent, and who evidently shared his interest in furniture design, was John Vardy (39–45). His architectural style resembled Kent's and he was one of the two architects who, after Kent's death, carried out his plans for the Horse Guards in Whitehall. Most of the small group of furniture designs by him which survive also recall Kent's style. His design for a table supported by an eagle and by a pair of scrolled consoles in No. 42 is a fine example of the type of furniture which was made for rooms of state in the great Palladian houses; while the handsome bed which he intended for St. James's Palace (No. 44) was clearly inspired by the one which Kent had designed for Sir Robert Walpole at Houghton some seventeen years previously,[1] the dominant feature in each being an enormous shell surmounting the head board. But Vardy's style was more florid than Kent's, and we shall see, when we come to discuss the rococo style, that he sometimes strayed from the narrow path of Palladian orthodoxy and entertained subversive heresies from France.

Two other designers represented here whose work reflects the influence of Kent were William Jones, the author of *The Gentlemen's or Builders' Companion* (1739) (Nos. 20–25), and Batty and Thomas Langley. The Langley brothers compiled a large number of pattern books designed to assist builders, carpenters, joiners, gardeners and other workmen, and their *City and Country Builders and Workman's Treasury of Designs* (1740) contains about twenty-five furniture designs (see Nos. 30–34). They are mostly in the manner we associate with Kent, but the brothers were unscrupulous plagiarists and inserted into their book a whole series of designs by Nicolas Pineau and two others by the contemporary German artists, Johann Jacob Schübler and Johann Friedrich Lauch.[2]

The Rococo Style

Meantime, while English designers like Kent looked backwards to Jones and Palladio, their French contemporaries were advancing in a new direction towards a freer, lighter and more fanciful mode of decoration, which subsequently enjoyed a great vogue in England too. The rococo style, as it was afterwards called, can hardly be described as a complete break with the classical tradition, since many of its characteristics can be traced

[1] Illustrated in Macquoid and Edwards, vol. I, page 61, fig. 44.
[2] For details see page 36.

back ultimately to classical sources, and its evolution was a gradual and continuous process. Moreover, it was primarily an ornamental convention employed within the house for furniture and decoration, while exterior architecture was less subject to its influence and continued, on the whole, to develop on classical lines, at any rate in France and England. The new style nevertheless marks a wide deviation from the principles which had governed designers during the previous two centuries. The classical tradition established at the time of the Renaissance had implanted in all artists and craftsmen a tectonic conception of design. In other words they thought in structural terms. The forms they used served, or seemed to serve, a constructional purpose, and that purpose was usually indicated by the use of appropriate ornament. Thus in a typical Palladian room the ceiling appeared to rest on a system of beams, whose ends were placed on a horizontal entablature, which in its turn was supported by a row of vertical columns, while the various openings for doors, windows and chimney-piece were reinforced by a subsidiary order of columns and architraves. So also, in furniture, the legs of tables and chairs were straight, vertical supports, sharply divided from the horizontal seat rail or table top, and the separate functions of the verticals and horizontals were indicated by the use of motifs borrowed from architecture, by fashioning the former as balusters, consoles or caryatids, and by treating the latter as architraves. On the same principle bookcases and cabinets were fitted with architectural frontispieces, like those used for doorcases and windows.

This type of design was abandoned by the rococo artists in favour of a new kind, which may be called organic rather than tectonic, because it has more affinity with the natural forms of plants and animals than with architecture.

Continuous curves, embracing the whole design, were now used in preference to a logically articulated system of verticals and horizontals. Decoration of constructional origin, like columns and architraves, was banished from the house or relegated to the exterior; and interior walls were henceforth relieved with panels of purely linear ornament devoid of structural significance, and instead of being rigidly separated from the ceiling by an entablature, they were merged into it by means of a rounded cove. Furniture also succumbed completely to the hegemony of the serpentine line. 'How inelegant', exclaimed Hogarth, 'would the shapes of all our moveables be without it!' and he went on in his *Analysis of Beauty* (1753) to discuss and illustrate its application to chair legs. The predominant form in furniture corresponded exactly with what he called 'the line of beauty,' a double curve shaped like an open, elongated S. This sinuous curve, when applied to furniture, bears some resemblance to a quadruped's leg in its general shape and in the way it merges into the body it supports without any distinct joint. It was, in fact, originally derived from a type of animal leg much used by the Romans as a support for tables (cf. Nos. 361 and 362), and Verrocchio had been the first to revive it when he designed the curved profile of his bronze sacrophagus in San Lorenzo at Florence in 1472. During the next century his design was imitated in other tombs and in chests, and at the end of the seventeenth century French designers like Boulle and Jean Bérain adopted the form and applied it to chairs, tables and commodes. Their use of it is an interesting illustration of the influence of technique on design, for they could not have handled it so freely, had it not been possible to conceal the complicated structural framework, often built up of laminated layers of wood, beneath a skin of veneer; and cabinet-makers had only lately acquired the degree of skill necessary for veneering curved surfaces. It may have been some latent animism in the rationalistic eighteenth century mind that asserted itself in this love of animal forms. At any rate, they became increasingly popular as the century advanced, and by 1750 the bowed leg had become the standard support for all types of furniture throughout Western Europe. In commodes and other case furniture it was often combined with an undulating, or *bombé*, surface, accentuating still more the organic nature of the style.

An analogous characteristic of rococo design, reflecting the same predilection for organic forms, was the frequent use of naturalistic ornament. It is impossible to look through the mid-eighteenth century designs in this book without being struck by the profusion of plants, birds, animals and human beings that swarm there. The sconce in No. 57 is only incidentally a piece of furniture. It is primarily a picturesque landscape with a scene from Aesop showing a crafty fox mocking at the goat which he has enticed into the well. We hardly notice that two gnarled branches terminate in candle sockets, so effectively are they disguised as twigs.

In this drawing the informality of the composition is as striking as the naturalism of the detail, and this again was something new in the field of design. Strict axial symmetry was no longer an essential principle of design, as it had been in the sixteenth century. As early as the 1630's certain Italian ornamentalists, notably Stefano della Bella and Agostino Mitelli, had published designs for cartouches in which they infringed this rule and attained a different kind of equilibrium through balance rather than symmetry (see No. 341). In the 1730's these experiments were carried further by Juste Aurèle Meissonnier, who by this means imparted to his designs an air of inconsequence and fantasy which captivated the taste of the age (cf. No. 344); and the convention was soon enthusiastically adopted all over Western Europe, encouraged by the example of Chinese art, which people admired and imitated largely because it offered relief from classical discipline and revealed a new type of beauty in casual and informal arrangements.

Apart from naturalistic motifs like birds, animals, plants, rocks and water, the favourite ornament of the rococo designers, again appropriate to the organic character of the style, was composed of an amorphous-looking substance which could be moulded into any shape the artist's fancy suggested. Its origins may be traced back to the sixteenth-century cartouche, a medallion or armorial shield, to which the mannerist designers had given an elaborate frame resembling cut and rolled paper or leather (No. 340). In the next century the frame lost all semblance of rigidity and acquired a flexible, plastic character, as though modelled in soft clay or wax, which made it an admirable vehicle for the exuberant fancy of artists like della Bella, who loved to display their virtuosity in the manipulation of this tractable material (No. 342). In Northern Europe the cartouche tended to take on a peculiar cartilaginous quality, somewhat like the gristle of the human ear, whence the style is sometimes known as *le style auriculaire* or in German *der Ohrmuschelstil* (No. 343). Other favourite forms for embellishing cartouches were borrowed from those grottoes which, with their stalactites and concretions, their incrustations of shells and their slimy effigies of sea monsters spouting water, had enjoyed a steady vogue as garden ornaments since the sixteenth century. These rockwork and shellwork forms were known in France as *rocailles*, and the term has been used since in a somewhat loose sense to describe rococo ornament in general. Borrowing from these various sources, the French ornamentists of the 1720's and 1730's evolved the characteristic motif of the rococo age: a strange, indeterminate, protean substance, which, like a kind of ectoplasm, was capable of assuming many different forms, sometimes falling into quite abstract patterns of contrasting curves, as in Boilly's page of ornament (No. 345) and in Meissonnier's design for an ink-stand (No. 344), at other times imitating the rim of a fluted scallop shell or taking on fantastic architectural shapes like buildings seen in the flickering embers of a fire. Compositions built up of such motives were usually purposely irregular and asymmetrical, but an effect of harmony and stability was created by the rhythmical interplay of curves.[1]

As these plastic *rocaille* forms were one of the most arresting features in French rococo decoration, they were widely copied in England and other foreign countries, while certain less obvious motifs were neglected. One which played an essential part in the French style, though improperly understood by English imitators, was a type of bandwork ornament used mostly as a frame for wall panels, doors and mirrors. Its origin is to be traced not in the baroque cartouche but in the grotesque, a form of decoration which has played an important part in architecture and the applied arts from the sixteenth to the nineteenth century. The name grotesque was originally given to it because, as Benvenuto Cellini relates in his autobiography, the ancient wall and ceiling decorations which inspired the whole *genre* were to be found in underground caves or grottoes, in reality half buried ruins of Roman tombs, baths and palaces. The specimens which attracted most attention at the time of the Renaissance were frescoes and stucco reliefs of the first century in the so-called 'fourth style', compositions devoid of architectural or structural significance, small in scale and linear in character, sometimes consisting of a system of geometrical compartments filled with conventional ornament (as in No. 347), and sometimes made up of more naturalistic themes, the most characteristic arrangement being a group of small pictures framed in tablets or medallions, suspended in an airy network of scrolls and foliage, and interspersed with a variety of fabulous creatures and other fanciful devices (as in No. 348). The discovery early in the sixteenth century of a whole repertory of such murals in the subterranean galleries of Nero's Golden House on the Esquiline aroused Raphael's interest and, as Vasari recounts, he was so delighted with what he saw that, with the help of his assistant Giovanni da Udine, he made a careful study of the forgotten style and applied it to the embellishment of the Vatican *loggie* (No. 349). Thus launched by a great artist, the grotesque soon became popular, and a knowledge of the style was spread all over Western Europe through engravings and copies. Raphael had employed both types of decoration, the geometrical and the fanciful, in their appropriate places, but what charmed the taste of the age above all was the fantastic element in the style, and this, seized on by a host of imitators, became the hall-mark of the grotesque, and indeed has given the word its normal sense in modern usage. For two hundred years and more the grotesque remained a favourite theme for engravers, ornamentalists and decorators. In the

[1] This and the following paragraph are to a large extent based on Fiske Kimball, *The Creation of the Rococo*, 1943.

course of time it naturally underwent many modifications, and at any early stage it encountered, and tended to coalesce with, the arabesque, a symmetrical ornament, purely linear in character, which, as its name implies, had passed from Islamic into European art through Venice and Spain. One of the consequences of this union between the grotesque and the arabesque was the creation of a peculiar type of bandwork which came into existence in the seventeenth century and served as a framework for the grotesque. In this bandwork ornament, as handled by artists like Jean Bérain at the close of the century, we may discern the origins of the rococo motif which we are considering. If we compare one of Bérain's grotesques (No. 350) with a design for a rococo mirror by J. F. Blondel (No. 351), we shall see that the frame of the looking glass is composed of a type of bandwork very like that employed by Bérain in his grotesque, the pattern in both cases being made up of a series of C and S scrolls joined together by short, straight bars, with sprays of acanthus sprouting from the volutes. There are, of course, great differences between the two designs, corresponding with the difference between the baroque of Louis XIV and the rococo of Louis XV. In Bérain the whole design is surrounded by a rectangular frame, within which the bandwork pattern forms a trellis to support the rest of the decoration; whereas in Blondel the rectangular frame and the spreading surface decoration have both been discarded and the bandwork has been isolated to form a narrow, sinuous frame for the looking glass. This essentially linear ornament was an indispensable component of the rococo style in France; but it was seldom correctly employed in England, as we shall see, if we compare Blondel's mirror with one by Chippendale or Thomas Johnson (e.g. Nos. 96 and 141), or if we place a design for the decoration of a room by the French artist Pineau (No. 352) beside one by an English designer like Thomas Lightoler (No. 353). Lightoler's scheme is basically Palladian in inspiration, but he has sought to create a fashionable effect by planting pseudo-rococo ornament onto architectural features of classical form; whereas in the French engraving every detail of the design is conceived in the same flowing linear terms.

The wide divergence between the French and English styles, illustrated in these examples, is largely due to the fact that in France the rococo movement was a slow and gradual growth, tended in turn by several generations of artists, whereas in England it was only a passing fashion, casually taken up and then laid aside. In these conservative islands it had taken the best part of a century and a half to establish a classical code which the more advanced countries of Europe had meanwhile outgrown; and once established, it was not likely to be hurriedly cast aside in favour of a newfangled mode from France. How widely the two countries differed in their artistic development is suggested by the fact that William Kent, the leading architect of the Palladian school, was an exact contemporary of Nicolas Pineau, one of the more advanced exponents of the rococo style in France. Not only Kent, but a large section of educated opinion in England remained faithful to the classical ideal throughout the century, and few serious architects made any consistent attempt to master the French style. The consequence of this conservatism was that when the rococo eventually crossed the channel, it was transplanted rather than grown from seed, and those who performed the operation were craftsmen and mediocre designers, who from ignorance tended to exaggerate its obvious, and to overlook its more subtle, qualities. One of their commonest mistakes was to lay too much stress on *rocaille* motifs of plastic, asymmetrical character, while neglecting the more delicate and graceful effects which could be obtained by the use of linear patterns and slender bandwork borders.

The rococo fashion began to spread to England in the 1730's. One of Meissonnier's most extravagant *rocaille* designs, representing a silver table centre and two terrines,[1] was carried out for the Duke of Kingston in 1735, and this commission was probably one of the earliest signs of an impending change of taste. Engraved designs for *rocaille* ornament were soon afterwards being printed in England, one of the earliest dated sets being De La Cour's *First Book of Ornament*, 1741[2] (see No. 346). The first furniture designs of rococo tendency published here were those contained in *Sixty Different Sorts of Ornament* published in 1736 by an obscure Italian artist named Gaetano Brunetti (Nos. 27–29); but they are characteristic of a late phase in the Italian baroque style which never found many imitators in England, and there is no evidence that the book had much influence. Among English artists one of the first to publish furniture designs in the French manner was Batty Langley, who, as we have seen, inserted into his *Treasury of Designs* (1740) six projects for tables pilfered without acknowledgment from Nicolas Pineau (see No. 31); and a few years later we find Abraham Swan, a carpenter and joiner who published a number of handbooks for builders, introducing fragments of *rocaille* decoration into some of his designs, as in No. 38, where a square early Georgian mirror frame with classical mouldings is dressed up in an incongruous garb of rococo shellwork. Like many English designers, he tried to produce a modish effect by applying rococo motifs onto furniture of a fundamentally different character, but he woefully misunderstood the nature of the style he was trying to imitate. A more interesting case is that of the architect John Vardy, who, as we have observed, was closely associated with William Kent and faithfully imitated his Palladian style. Yet two of his drawings reproduced here (Nos. 43 and 45) show that he could assume the Gallic manner with surprising readiness; indeed, the writing table with a *cartonnier* in No. 45 is a startlingly successful imitation and approaches the true French style more nearly than any other design in this book.

However, Vardy does not appear to have made any other such drawings, and the first English furniture designer who consistently succeeded in capturing something of the spirit of the French rococo style was a carver and engraver named Matthias (or Matthew) Lock. His first book, published in 1740, under the title *A New Drawing Book of Ornaments*, though not concerned with furniture, was one of the earliest collections of *rocaille* motifs printed in England; while his next three works *Six Sconces* (1744), *Six Tables* (1746) and *A New Book of Ornaments* (which was published in collaboration with an obscure artist named Copland in 1752) are the earliest English furniture designs in which the rococo style is handled with real assurance. Apart from these published works, the Museum possesses a collection of over two hundred original drawings for furniture by Lock. Among them are a few designs in an early Georgian style (cf. No. 48) and a number of later ones

---

[1] The design is engraved in his *Oeuvre*.
[2] Other early authors of rococo pattern books include Lock and Copland (see pages 38 and 53); P. Glazier (designs for metalwork dated 1748 and 1754); Chatelin (*A Book of Ornaments . . . from the drawings of Messrs. Germain, Meissonnier, Si Cattarello &c.*); A. Heckell (*A New Book of Shields*); J. Collins (*A New Book of Shields*).

in the manner of Adam (Nos. 252–256). But the majority are in a full-blooded rococo vein, many of them being rapid sketches executed in pen and ink with a spontaneity and *bravura* admirably suited to the style. Some of his early designs, as illustrated in *Six Sconces* (1744) and *Six Tables* (1746) show that at the outset of his career he studied French engravings with true understanding. Indeed, his projects for tables (Nos. 49 and 50) and another for a mirror (No. 51) may be compared, not unfavourably, with designs by François Cuvilliés (Nos. 354 and 355), one of the few French artists of the period who published patterns specifically for furniture as distinct from ornament in general. Lock's proficiency in interpreting the French style can be still better illustrated by comparing these two examples of his work with an analogous imitation (No. 143) by Thomas Johnson, who may fairly be said to have ruined a design by Cuvilliés (No. 357) in attempting to adapt it. But Lock was not merely an imitator. Having mastered the style through copying French models, he employed it more freely in his later work; and *A New Book of Ornaments*, which he published with Copland in 1752, contains idiosyncrasies which are seldom found in the work of continental artists, though they soon afterwards became essential features of English rococo. A typical motif, first seen in these designs, was a slender shaft or colonnette with a base and capital of concave plan, which served as a prop for part of the design (cf. No. 52). This device, seldom used abroad, became a favourite resource of English carvers, and there is hardly an English mirror in the rococo taste which does not make use of it. In other respects, too, Lock's mirrors and wall lights (or girandoles, as they were called) differ widely from their French counterparts and prepared the way for a characteristic English type. The mirrors are towering structures composed of several frames, one within another, running riot with rockwork, shellwork and vegetation, and haunted by apes, dragons, exotic birds and other denizens of the rococo menagerie, with perhaps an occasional mandarin seated within a pagoda or a shepherd playing the flute in an arbour. Still more original and engaging are the girandoles, which soon became so popular in England, with their miniature scenes of rustic or idyllic life and their episodes from Aesop, enacted in an airy *rocaille* landscape against a background of looking glass, lit by candles supported on extravagantly contorted branches. These are purely English creations, which have no close parallel abroad, and to Lock must be given the credit of having first introduced the type.

Chippendale and the Chinese and Gothic Taste

There is reason to believe that Lock made most of his drawings for Thomas Chippendale, the cabinet-maker, who was probably his employer in the 1750's and 1760's.[1] Chippendale doubtless learnt how to handle the rococo style from him, and recognizing its commercial possibilities, appropriated it with all the enthusiasm of an ambitious young business man in search of a new idea. The use he made of it is abundantly illustrated in the great book of designs which he published as a trade catalogue in 1754 under the title *The Gentleman and Cabinet-Maker's Director*. The designs in this volume, which was widely circulated and played a great part in establishing the rococo fashion in England, diverge more widely from the French style than Lock's and reveal the pervasive influence of the Chinese and

[1] For the evidence see page 39.

the Gothic fashions, two apparently incompatible styles, the one international, the other peculiar to England, which are nevertheless often found fused together in the productions of Chippendale and his contemporaries. Both these influences must be taken into account if Chippendale's contribution to English furniture design is to be properly understood.

The arts of China and Japan had begun to impinge on Europe in the middle ages, when the first imported specimens of porcelain had excited the wonder of craftsmen and collectors. But it was not until the seventeenth century, with the great expansion of far eastern trade, that the manufactures of China and Japan were brought to Europe in sufficient quantities to arouse widespread interest and admiration. Porcelain and lacquer, above all, charmed people through the intrinsic beauty of their materials, the mysterious processes by which they were made and the exquisite paintings with which they were often decorated; and the rich developed a passion for collecting them. One of the uses to which such collections were sometimes applied is illustrated here in a design by Daniel Marot (No. 358). It represents a 'Chinese cabinet', a room in which the walls are lined with panels of lacquer, while the doorcase and the chimney-piece are fitted with innumerable shelves and ledges for china vases. There are several contemporary accounts of such rooms. At Hampton Court Palace, Celia Fiennes about 1695 refers to 'little rooms like closets or drawing rooms, one panell'd all with Japan . . .'[1] and Evelyn, on visiting Mr Bohun's house at Lee on July 30th, 1682, observes that 'in the hall are contrivances of Japan screens instead of wainscot'. The demand for china and lacquer was so insatiable that imitations of both commodities were soon being made in Europe; and the earliest English book specifically concerned with furniture, Stalker and Parker's *Treatise of Japanning* (1688), expounded the various methods of copying oriental lacquer and provided 'above one Hundred distinct Patterns for Japan Work for Tables, Stands, Frames, Cabinets, Boxes, Etc.' (cf. No. 3). Lacquer and Japan work (as the imitations were usually called) remained fashionable materials for decorating furniture all through the eighteenth century; but their use did not necessarily affect the style of the objects to which they were applied, and all kinds of furniture of purely European design, both classical and rococo, were often veneered with lacquer, or japanned, without any sense of incongruity.

At the same time, through the constant use of eastern lacquer, porcelain and wallpaper, English people became familiar with Chinese and Japanese ornament, and certain motifs gradually found their way into the designer's repertory, until by the middle of the century some of them, such as pagodas, mandarins and dragons, had become stock ornaments almost as common as the putto and were as freely used, regardless of the European context in which they were often placed. What the designer called a 'Chinese' design was usually a European one to which a faint Chinese flavour had been imparted by the addition of one or two such ingredients, as in the design for a mirror reproduced here from Edwards and Darly's *New Book of Chinese Designs* (No. 131). This book, published in 1754, was a repository of pseudo-Chinese details useful to designers, japanners, cabinet-makers and other craftsmen, and it also contained a number of designs for furniture (see Nos. 128 to 134). It was followed and, to some extent, plagiarized by the anonymous *Ladies Amusement or Whole Art of Japanning Made Easy* and by P. Decker's *Chinese Architecture*,

---

[1] *The Journies of Celia Fiennes*, edited by C. Morris, 1947, page 59.

Civil and Ornamental (1759). The French artist Jean Pillement, who spent several years in England in the 1750's, also published here several sets of engravings of ornament in the Chinese taste, and some of his designs are plagiarized in *The Ladies Amusement*.

The adoption of this type of ornament was not the only consequence of the Chinese fashion. The arts of China influenced European designers in another direction by constantly presenting to their eyes the example of an art which was the antithesis of Renaissance classicism. Here were porcelain vases and lacquer screens and boxes painted, with a triumphant disregard for symmetry and perspective, by artists whose fancy seemed to be untrammelled by convention and whose sense of balance was, none the less, unerring. The whimsical and fantastic element in such paintings, exaggerated through unfamiliarity, made a strong appeal to artists who wished to relax from classical discipline, and it encouraged them to give their imagination freer rein, to prefer the casual to the formal and to appreciate the charm of irregularity. In this way the Chinese fashion strengthened the anti-classical tendencies in the rococo movement. To what absurd lengths an artist might go in an attempt to capture the wayward spirit of Chinese art is shown in the two preposterous designs for a table and chair made of gnarled roots which Edwards and Darley included in their *New Book of Chinese Designs* (Nos. 133 and 134).

In so far as it provided designers with a fund of new ornament and contributed to the formation of the rococo style, the influence of China was felt all over Western Europe. But its influence on English furniture was even more marked, because English designers and cabinet-makers went further than their foreign contemporaries in trying to reproduce the actual forms of Chinese furniture. As the models available to them were inadequate, being mostly, as William Chambers observed, 'lame representations found on porcelain and paper hangings', their imitations bore little resemblance to the originals. But they seized on certain obvious features of Chinese furniture and joinery neglected by their continental colleagues; and in their attempts to reproduce these, they not only turned out a quantity of furniture somewhat nearer to the true Chinese taste than anything made abroad, but also enriched the native English style with a stock of fresh ideas. The most prevalent of these borrowings from the Chinese was the type of lattice work known as 'Chinese railing' or 'Chinese paling'. The first engraved designs for it are to be found in William Halfpenny's *New Designs for Chinese Temples* (1750); and this book illustrates the many different uses to which it might be applied, from park railings, gates and bridges to staircase balustrades and garden seats (cf. Nos. 126 and 127). Other designs for lattice work are given in Edwards and Darly's *New Book of Chinese Designs* and in Chippendale's *Director*, which both came out in 1754; and both volumes illustrate furniture constructed with lattice work, the most successful being Chippendale's lattice work chairs (cf. No. 82), which are among the most attractive creations of the English rococo and have no close parallels abroad, though they were soon being produced in considerable quantities in this country and are illustrated in most pattern books published in the 1760's. Lattice work was also used for the glazing bars in china cabinets; and in Chippendale's well-known japanned bed from Badminton House, now in the Museum, panels of lattice work employed in conjunction with a pagoda roof contribute more than any other feature to the agreeable oriental effect. Another favourite way of using Chinese railing, on a miniature scale, was to place it as a parapet round the edge of tea-tables, stands and trays, and along the top of cabinets and bookcases; and it was often applied in this way to furniture of purely European design, so completely had it been absorbed into the current repertory of ornament.

A similar motif often used on furniture, in low relief instead of openwork, was the 'Chinese fret': a narrow band or frieze carved with a countersunk repeating pattern based on Chinese lattice work. These frets and lattice work railings soon became an indispensable feature of English furniture, and several pattern books were devoted exclusively to designs of this type, among them the *Joyner and Cabinet-Maker's Darling or Pocket Director* by John Crunden and *The Carpenter's Companion for Chinese Railing and Gates* by J. H. Morris and John Crunden, both published in 1765 (see Nos. 124 and 125). As we shall see, when we come to discuss the Gothic taste, similar frets and railings were made in the 'Gothic' style. These too became so completely naturalized that they were applied indiscriminately to furniture of European or even Chinese design; and in the end the two types of lattice work, the Chinese and the Gothic, became so confounded that it is impossible to distinguish between them (cf. Nos. 122 and 123).

Among the many ignorant attempts made by designers to imitate the Chinese style one book stands out as a well-informed and objective study: Sir William Chambers' *Designs of Chinese Buildings, Furniture, Dresses, Machines and Utensils*, published in 1757. Chambers had made the voyage to China in the service of the Swedish East India Company some eight years previously, and while at Canton he had made a number of drawings which provided him with the material for his book. He expressed a hope in the preface that these designs 'might be of use in putting a stop to the extravagancies that daily appear under the name of Chinese'. He denied that he wished 'to promote a taste so much inferior to the antique', but he allowed the Chinese the merit of originality and was not averse from seeing their style employed with discretion. 'In immense palaces,' he wrote, 'containing a numerous series of apartments, I do not see the impropriety of finishing some of the inferior ones in the Chinese taste.' The two plates from Chambers' book reproduced here (Nos. 135 and 136) doubtless represent drawings of actual Chinese furniture rather than original designs, but it is interesting to compare them with the creations of less learned designers like Chippendale, unlikely though it is that replicas as accurate as these were ever actually carried out.

The Gothic fashion, unlike the Chinese, was at this time peculiar to England. The British had been slow in adapting themselves to the Renaissance style, and notwithstanding the powerful classicizing influence of Inigo Jones, the medieval tradition had persisted all through the seventeenth and well into the eighteenth century, particularly in the provinces, and in the building and decoration of churches, a task largely carried out by master builders and joiners, who kept to the style of their ancestors. A good example of Gothic survival in church furniture may be seen in Durham Cathedral, where Bishop Cosin's choir stalls, dating from about 1670, are carved in the 'perpendicular' style. But the Gothic idiom was not confined to provincial craftsmen, and metropolitan architects of the classical school were prepared to revive it for certain purposes. Wren constructed several church towers, like those of St. Dunstan-in-the-East and St. Michael Cornhill, in a Gothic convention that would have amazed his French contemporaries; and in the next century Kent designed a Gothic castle, while Hawksmoor built a Gothic quadrangle at All Souls College, Oxford. So far, however, the medieval style had survived, or been revived, only in buildings, like churches and colleges, in which its use was hallowed by tradition. A change occurred during the second quarter of the eighteenth century, when Gothic buildings became the object of a sophisticated cult and were admired for their romantic atmosphere, particularly when in a state of ruin. During the 1740's the first sham Gothic ruins were erected, and these follies soon spread among the parks of country gentlemen like an epidemic. Sanderson Miller, an amateur architect who played a leading part in introducing the vogue, went so far as to provide one of his ruined castles with Gothic furniture, as we learn from a letter written to him by his client George Lyttelton, the owner of Hagley Hall, Worcestershire. 'I forget how many chairs are wanting for the castle'; Lyttelton writes, 'but how can I bespeak them without the model you drew for them? You know they are not to be common chairs but in a Gothic form'.[1] This letter was written in 1749, but already mock Gothic had penetrated into private houses some years previously, and Batty Langley in the Preface to his *Gothic Architecture Improved*, published in 1742, recommended the 'Saxon' style, as he liked to call it, for 'all parts of private buildings; and especially in Rooms of State, Dining Rooms, Parlours, Stair-Cases, &c. And in Porticos, Umbrellos, Temples and Pavillions in Gardens, Parks, &c.' This book is probably the earliest collection of Gothic designs published and, though it contains no furniture designs, the Gothic chimney-pieces which Langley provides and his rather absurd garden architecture show that the style was already well on the way to losing its former venerable associations and becoming a fashionable mode of decoration (for a specimen see No. 359). The process was carried a step further by Horace Walpole, who bought his villa, Strawberry Hill, in 1747, and was busy gothicizing it for the next ten years.

The earliest published designs for Gothic furniture were those included in Darly's *A New Book of Chinese, Gothic and Modern Chairs*, which are dated 1750 and 1751 (Nos. 46 and 47). But there is little that is recognizably Gothic, or for that matter, Chinese, in these inept and rudimentary designs; and the first noteworthy examples of the Gothic style applied to furniture were those published by Chippendale in his *Director* in 1754. As Strawberry Hill was at that date still incomplete and known only to a restricted circle, Chippendale's numerous Gothic designs must have charmed the uninitiated public by their novelty, and they were widely imitated for ten years or more.

In these engravings Chippendale was not, of course, concerned with copying the actual furniture of the middle ages; he merely decorated the furniture of his own day with tracery, cusps, crochets, pointed arcades and other late medieval motifs. In some of the plates (cf. No. 94) the ornament is handled with a certain consistency; but in others it is combined with Chinese or rococo features, and sometimes with both. These incongruous mixtures of styles were typical of the age, and some of the plates in books like Halfpenny's *Chinese and Gothic Architecture properly ornamented* (1752) and Over's *Architecture in the Gothic, Chinese and Modern Taste* (1758) are even stranger hotchpotches of Gothic, Chinese and baroque ingredients. As the titles of their books suggest, the more ignorant designers of the day seem to have made little distinction between Gothic and Chinese, perhaps because both satisfied

---

[1] L. Dickins and M. Stanton, *An Eighteenth Century Correspondence*, 1910, page 159.

equally well some obscure romantic craving, one being remote in time, the other in space, and both being anti-classical. With Chippendale the mixture of styles is not always obvious, for his normal manner was by no means a pure rococo, like Lock's, but a highly individual synthesis to which the four main styles of the early Georgian period – the Palladian, the rococo, the Chinese and the Gothic – each contributed a share. There are, of course, a number of designs in which one or other of these styles is used by itself, as for example in the bookcase in No. 72, which is designed on severe architectural lines in the manner of the Palladians. Far more common, however, are the designs in which two or more styles are combined. The juxtapositions occasionally create an effect of obvious incongruity, as in the cabinet illustrated in No. 90, in which the frieze is decorated with a 'Chinese' fret, while above that there is a band of Gothic arcading and a rococo finial. But in many cases the various strands in the design are so inextricably interwoven that the discrepancies tend to disappear and a new style emerges, with a peculiar character of its own, the so-called 'Chippendale' or 'Director' style.

In this highly eclectic style the Gothic element is as pervasive as the Chinese, though often disguised. Its influence can be discerned in Chippendale's handling of the rococo scrollwork ornament, which in his designs tends to fall into patterns abounding in cusps, ogees, lancets and other shapes borrowed from Gothic tracery. There is a striking example of this tendency in the cabinet in No. 89, where the scrolls of the rococo decoration on the doors are cusped along their lower edge in a way which would have been impossible on the continent. The symmetrical four-pointed pattern which embellishes the cupboard door of the writing table in No. 87, though composed of rococo scrolls and shellwork, is likewise alien to the spirit of continental rococo and has a certain affinity with Gothic tracery. The same can be said of many of the pierced bandwork patterns which form the splats of Chippendale's most characteristic type of chair (cf. Nos. 100 and 101).

Another of Chippendale's favourite ornaments, which owes its character largely to Gothic influence, is a species of fretted decoration analogous to the Chinese frets and railings which we have already described, with the difference that the pattern was suggested, ostensibly at any rate, by medieval stonework friezes instead of the lattice work structures of the Chinese. But here again the ornament was seldom used in a pure form, and nearly every designer, including Chippendale, regularly confused Gothic elements with Chinese. The design in No. 123, for example, illustrates three designs for 'Gothic frets' in Chippendale's *Director*, while No. 122 shows two designs for 'Chinese railings'. But a comparison between the lower designs in each plate reveals that they are closely similar patterns with no essential difference between them. These fretted friezes, whether Chinese, Gothic or hybrid, gratified that love of repeating patterns which is deeply rooted in the English race, and they were used regularly by nearly every designer and cabinet-maker in the 1750's and 1760's, though nothing analogous is ever found in continental furniture of the same period. The Chinese and the Gothic vogue each contributed something to the form, but their influence tended to amalgamate, and in many cases it is hard to say which is uppermost.

Apart from the originality of the designs, the idea behind Chippendale's *Director* was new and ingenious, for it was intended largely as a trade advertisement, and this was something that had not been done before on such scale. The numerous furniture designs which had been published on the continent were mostly issued in small sets of a few plates each, and the majority were the work of architects and professional artists rather than cabinet-makers. Boulle, the great French cabinet-maker, had certainly published a number of his own designs, and a few German craftsmen had done likewise. But none of their publications had anything like the scope of Chippendale's work, which contained a choice of designs for almost every piece of furniture that might be needed in a well-appointed house; and there can be little doubt that the variety and freshness of the designs and the accomplished manner in which they were presented must have attracted a great deal of business to the house of Chippendale. Of course, there was nothing to prevent other cabinet-makers from copying his designs, and we must presume that some did so, considering that out of 310 subscribers to the first edition 140 were joiners, carvers and cabinet-makers. But there was no reason why Chippendale should object to this, as long as his name became known; and, in fact, the celebrity he attained through the *Director* has lasted to this day, while cabinet-makers as skilled, like William Vile, are comparatively little known, because they lacked his genius for advertisement.

The success of the *Director* was such that a second edition was published the next year, and in 1762 a third. This was virtually a new book, as only 96 of the original plates were retained, while 105 entirely new ones were added; and the scope of the work was extended to embrace types of furniture which had not been included in the first edition. On the whole, however, there are no substantial changes of style, though one new project for a commode (No. 92) seems to suggest that a revulsion against the rococo style was at hand, for it is clearly inspired by late seventeenth-century French models, which were afterwards much imitated by neo-classical designers like Neufforge in France. It is curious to find Chippendale experimenting on these lines so early.

Apart from the 277 plates contained in the first and third editions of the *Director*, many original drawings from Chippendale's workshop have survived and are preserved in the Victoria and Albert Museum in London and the Metropolitan Museum in New York. Some of these are by Lock and have been described above. The others include a series of original designs for the plates in the *Director*, most of them signed by Chippendale and inscribed in his hand with the legend which he wished the engraver to copy. These drawings are the subject of a detailed study by two American scholars,[1] who advance the theory that the designs for the *Director* and most of the other drawings (apart from those by Lock) were made, not by Chippendale, but by Copland, an obscure artist who published a small book of rococo ornament in 1746, and collaborated with Lock in another. Succeeding writers have adopted this hypothesis and have consequently tended to represent Chippendale as an unscrupulous self-advertiser who arrogated to himself the credit for work done by others. The arguments put forward in support of this opinion are examined in the notes on Chippendale in Part II, and our conclusion is that stronger proof is needed before Chippendale can be convicted of the charge[2]. The drawings are mostly variations on the *Director* themes, but a few, like Nos. 115 and 121 are rather later in date and show signs of

---

[1] The late Mr Fiske Kimball and Miss Edna Donnell, volume I, pages 115–154. For title see page viii.
[2] See pages 42–44.

neo-classic influence. Unfortunately, no designs by Chippendale survive in the fully developed neo-classical style which he used for some of his finest furniture at Harewood House and elsewhere.

Chippendale's originality as a designer cannot easily be assessed. The style illustrated in the *Director* differs sharply from that which prevailed a few years previously, being more rococo than the work of older cabinet-makers and more permeated by Gothic feeling than the designs of an artist like Lock. But after the publication of the *Director*, it so quickly became the accepted style that it is impossible to determine whether Chippendale inaugurated the change or merely followed the latest fashion.

Among the designers who were soon afterwards working in the same style were the rival firm of cabinet-makers, Ince and Mayhew, and the carver Thomas Johnson. Johnson's designs, published between 1755 and 1760, were mostly, as one would expect, for carvers' pieces. That he studied French models is shown by his design for a stand carved with dolphins (No. 143), which was suggested by an engraving after François Cuvilliés (No. 357). There is certainly a great difference between the two designs, but the use of the dolphin motif in both, added to a decided similarity in the shape of the stands, can hardly be accidental, and the differences in handling merely illustrate the divergence between French and English practice. In Cuvilliés' design the framework of the stand is composed of carefully articulated, symmetrical curves, which extend in a continuous movement from the top to the base and which admirably exemplify the type of rococo bandwork described above (page 12). Johnson, on the other hand, in his effort to capture the whimsical spirit of the rococo, has produced an exaggerately asymmetrical and disjointed structure, consisting of a central shaft and a collection of contrasting C scrolls arbitrarily arranged round it. The grace of the original is lost and the object is barely recognizable as a tripod. Many of Johnson's designs are marred by a tendency towards exaggeration and excessive elaboration, and he carried the device of asymmetry to ludicrous lengths. But his vagaries are sometimes entertaining, and those miniature scenes, enacted by animals and human beings, which enliven many of his designs, have a certain charm.

William Ince and John Mayhew, partners in a firm of cabinet-makers, began publishing a trade catalogue in rivalry with Chippendale in 1759. It was brought out in separate numbers, which were eventually collected together in a single volume entitled *The Universal System of Household Furniture*. The general style of the work is similar to Chippendale's, but there are fewer designs in the pure rococo manner, and the authors developed a peculiar ornament of their own which has very little in common with true rococo; it was a kind of flat strapwork decoration arranged symmetrically in loops and scrolls, sometimes applied in countersunk relief and sometimes carved in openwork tracery, the somewhat degenerate issue of a cross between rococo scrollwork and Gothic tracery (cf. No. 152).

The Neo-Classical Revival

In 1754, the year when Chippendale's *Director* was published, the young Robert Adam, who was soon to introduce a style completely opposed to the one illustrated in that book, arrived in Italy to complete his training as an architect. The four years he spent there were a decisive period in his life, because they opened his eyes to certain neglected aspects of classical and renaissance architecture, and the ideas he formed then influenced him in all his subsequent work. Among the ancient remains which made a strong impression on his mind were the grotesques which had formerly delighted Raphael. He studied these attentively, as well as Raphael's experiments in the use of the same convention; and he came to the conclusion that in them he had re-discovered the true classical manner of decorating the interior of a private house. He afterwards criticized the Palladian architects for neglecting these models and for failing to make a distinction between the interior and exterior architecture of the Romans. This error, according to Adam, led them to overload their rooms with large-scale ornament suitable only to the outside of a building; 'whereas with regard to the decoration of their private and bathing apartments, they (the Romans) were all delicacy, gaiety, grace and beauty'. These were the qualities which Adam admired in Roman domestic interiors and sought to emulate in his own. From all except the grandest and most formal compositions, like the marble hall at Kedleston, he banished the heavy columns and entablatures with which Jones and Kent had framed doorcases, windows and chimney-pieces; and in their place he made use of light and slender mouldings, pilasters embellished with floral arabesques, and panels of grotesque work, executed in low relief in plaster. The coffered ceiling, still employed by classicizing architects, he likewise rejected in favour of a flat surface lightly decorated with grotesques or geometrical patterns, often picked out in colours. He also brought into use a repertory of classical ornament more varied and more closely copied from antique prototypes than any hitherto used by English architects, and eschewing the bold and prominent forms favoured by the Palladians, he sought to impart to every motif the utmost refinement of which it was capable: a tendency which he sometimes carried so far that his decoration tended to look too much like lace or filigree.

Adam's ideal in his interiors was to create an effect of perfect harmony and completeness, which could only be achieved if every part were subordinated to a ruling design. In the pursuit of this aim no detail was too insignificant for his consideration, and he often lavished as much care on minutiae, like door handles, lanterns, grates and fire irons as on the architecture itself. As his admirer Sir John Soane observed, 'in his flights of fancy, he descended to trifles, and gave an elegance and an importance to a Sedan chair, or to the key-hole of a lady's Escritoire'; and as though to bear out these words, we find an entry in Lady Shelburne's diary for January 1766 noting that her husband, one of Adam's patrons, had been 'consulting Mr Adam about the chain of my watch'.[1] As furniture must occupy a prominent place in any decorative scheme, it engrossed a large share of Adam's attention. Indeed, he probably designed more furniture than any other architect has ever done, and his work in this field constitutes an impressive monument to his genius as a designer. It consists partly of a substantial quantity of furniture made from his designs in the various houses which he built, and partly of a large number of original drawings, most of which are preserved in the great collection of his designs in Sir John Soane's Museum.

In designing furniture to go with his classical interiors Adam faced the same kind of

---

[1] Quoted by A. T. Bolton, *The Architecture of Robert and James Adam*, 1922, vol. II, page 8.

difficulty as Kent had encountered previously: his architectural decoration was based on classical prototypes, but there were few ancient specimens to guide him in his attempt to create the appropriate furniture. Some advances, it is true, had been made in archaeology since Kent's day, and a certain amount of fresh data had been obtained from the excavations at Herculaneum and Pompeii. Moreover, knowledge of this kind had become more accessible than it had been before in a number of splendidly illustrated books, among which Piranesi's great series of etchings of Roman antiquities was of particular value to a designer in search of material, as it contained accurate illustrations of Roman tripods, altars, candelabra and other small objects in bronze and marble. From such sources as these, as well as from his own observations in Italy, Adam built up a new repertory of small-scale ornament suitable for furniture. Many of his favourite devices, like the anthemion, the patera, the urn, the husk, the ram's head and the sphinx, had long been familiar to designers, but he invested them with a delicacy and an elegance seldom surpassed since the Renaissance, and he took care to avoid introducing into his designs any ornament derived from non-classical sources, which would have marred the purity of effect at which he aimed.

However, the innovations which Adam introduced into furniture design were not concerned with ornament alone, but with form too. At first, it is true, he tried to achieve his purpose by grafting antique ornament onto contemporary forms, as in the design for a sofa, reproduced in No. 202, in which a typical mid-eighteenth-century frame with bowed legs is carved with anthemion and winged sphinxes; while other early designs, like the organ case in No. 204, are in the massive architectural style of the Palladians. But he was equally opposed to the heaviness of the one as to the anti-classical bias in the other, and by degrees he perfected a style which had little in common with either. For certain types of furniture he was able to find approximate analogies in classical marbles, and he had a happy gift for adapting his ancient models to serve a contemporary purpose. His designs for stands and tripods, for example (Nos. 224–226), unmistakably proclaim their classical ancestry; while the pedestals with urns which he liked to place on each side of a side-table in his dining rooms (cf. No. 233) are obviously taken from Roman altars. A particularly ingenious adaptation is illustrated in No. 207, which shows a stool imitated from an antique porphyry cistern (Nos. 363 and 364) and surprisingly little altered in the metamorphosis.

However, there was a limit to what could be achieved in this direction, and for the numerous types of furniture for which no classical model could be found Adam was obliged to work out a system of his own. After a few youthful experiments he rejected for good the flowing curves of the rococo and evolved a more architectonic type of design in which the weight is carried on straight vertical supports and the separate function of each part of the composition is strongly emphasized by ornament of an architectural character. As there are plenty of classical precedents for furniture of curved outline (see Nos. 360–364), Adam's cult of the straight line was doubtless due to a reaction against the extravagances of the rococo, and he employed it most consistently in those parts of the design, notably the supports of chairs, tables and commodes, where the rococo ornamentalists had indulged their passion for the serpentine line most freely. For tables and chairs he invented an entirely new kind of support which was not only straight, but evenly tapered towards the foot. In other respects its shape varied considerably, but it was usually either square in section, with fluted or reeded decoration, or else formed like an attenuated baluster, inverted, with the thicker part uppermost. Such supports look so exactly right for their purpose that it is surprising to find that they had seldom been used before, certainly not by the Greeks and Romans, whose style Adam thus sought to evoke. Commodes and other case furniture he designed on the same simple tectonic lines, always placing the weight on rectilinear uprights and stressing the structural framework by means of pilasters, friezes, enriched mouldings and other architectural motifs. If curved lines were neeeded for the sake of variety, they were introduced into the plan instead of the elevation, as in his numerous semi-circular commodes and tables, which invariably have straight legs or sides. The plain surfaces on his furniture he usually relieved with the same kind of chastened classical ornament that he applied to walls and ceilings: an essentially flat and linear form of decoration, which was more suitably rendered in marquetry than carving and thus led to the revival of a technique which had fallen into neglect.

The furniture designed on these lines bears little resemblance to that of the Greeks and Romans, but it displays to such a high degree the classical virtues of proportion, restraint and fitness that we are almost persuaded to believe the contrary. English furniture has seldom possessed such grace and lightness, and for that reason it is commonly supposed that Adam borrowed the elements of his style from France. In fact, Adam preceded all his foreign contemporaries in the use of the rectilinear neo-classic style. There is no French furniture on these lines which can be dated before 1770, and among the earliest examples are some designs by Neufforge, published about 1771 (cf. No. 366), which are rudimentary compared with the accomplished work carried out from Adam's designs in the 1760's.[1]

Adam's style of decoration rapidly established itself in public favour during the 1770's. Chippendale was among the first cabinet-makers to abandon the rococo, which he himself had done so much to popularize, and between 1771 and 1775 he was busy making furniture in Adam's manner, if not from Adam's designs, for Harewood House; while Lock, Chippendale's employee and the first artist to adopt the rococo idiom in England, again took the lead with a small book of furniture designs in the neo-classical manner, his *New Book of Pier Frames*, published in 1769 (cf. No. 256). In 1770 Matthew Darly, who had already published designs for rococo, Chinese and Gothic furniture, entered the field anew with a fresh book of exercises in the latest fashion entitled *The Ornamental Architect or Young Artist's Instructor*, which contained a few designs for furniture (cf. Nos. 257 and 258). A more varied and interesting repository of designs, mostly neo-classical, with a few in the Gothic taste, was *The Builder's Magazine*, published in numbers between 1774 and 1778. The author of all the plates was the architect and antiquarian draughtsman John Carter. They are mostly concerned with architecture, but a number of furniture

---

[1] See two articles by Fiske Kimball: *Les influences anglaises dans la formation du style Louis XVI* in *Gazette des Beaux Arts*, 6th series, Vol. V, 1931, pages 29–44 and 231–255. England is here shown to have been the main stronghold of the classical tradition in architecture throughout the 18th century, and many practices regarded as neo-classical innovations in France were inspired by earlier English examples.

designs are included and, though they are somewhat awkward and inelegant and were probably never carried out, they possess a certain originality, being less dependent on Adam than most furniture of the period (see Nos. 269–273). They were possibly inspired by the designs of Piranesi, whose *Diverse Maniere di Adornare i Camini*, published in 1769, deserves mention here as the first authoritative collection of neo-classical designs published in Europe, and a work which played an important part in familiarizing artists in all civilized countries with the elements of the new style. This book was the first to illustrate Egyptian ornament, which was to enjoy an extensive vogue at the beginning of the next century. But Piranesi's work was too imaginative to be easily imitated, and the engraved designs which had most influence on taste in Europe were those published by Adam himself in the first two volumes of his *Works in Architecture*, which came out in separate numbers between 1773 and 1779 (a third volume was published posthumously in 1822). The comparatively late date of this work is sometimes used as an argument to prove that Adam was not the first to apply the neo-classical style to furniture and decoration, but we must remember that all the furniture illustrated in the plates had already been carried out, much of it before the publication of Piranesi's designs.

Among the furniture designers who followed in Adam's wake and whose work has survived, one of the most talented was John Linnell, a leading London cabinet-maker during the second half of the century. The Museum possesses a large collection of his drawings, which show him to have been an accomplished and versatile draughtsman. Some of his earliest drawings are in the robust manner of Kent (cf. No. 190), but he also published a set of engraved designs for vases in a flamboyant *rocaille* style inspired by Meissonnier, and some of his most engaging furniture designs, like the one for the well-known sofa with merfolk supports at Kedleston Hall (No. 195), are fresh and lively exercises in the same manner. When he afterwards adopted the neo-classical convention, his best work lost none of its charm or individuality, and in many of his drawings, as in Nos. 235 and 246, a touch of rococo fantasy relieves the severity of the classical form. On the other hand, the numerous drawings by him for picture and mirror frames which the Museum possesses are uninspired hack work of a kind which a busy firm with a large custom must always be in danger of producing.

The last phase of the neo-classical style is illustrated here in the work of four artists of whom two, Holland and Soane, were architects, while the other two, Hepplewhite and Sheraton, were trained as cabinet-makers.

Hepplewhite, though his name has been given to a style, was the least original of the four. His chief merit, shared with countless unremembered cabinet-makers, was that he successfully adapted the neo-classic style to ordinary household furniture, and in many of his designs, which were published in 1788, two years after his death, in a book entitled *The Cabinet-maker and Upholsterer's Guide*, he contrived to impart to plain, useful objects a sober elegance that makes them ideal for modern rooms. Apart from that, he contributed little that was new to the style introduced by Adam, and he displayed small imagination in his use of a formula that was beginning to grow stale. His repertory of ornament was confined to the usual neo-classical stock of urns, medallions, paterae, swags, pendants and similar devices, which recur with monotonous frequency, in a somewhat dry and attenuated form, all through his work. There is no evidence in the form of bills or references to him in contemporary documents to suggest that as a cabinet-maker he enjoyed extensive or fashionable patronage, and his designs, practical, but unenterprising, are such as might have been expected from a modest and conservative firm. The author himself declared in the preface that he had 'designedly followed the latest or most prevailing fashion only, purposely omitting such articles, whose recommendation was mere novelty'. The fashion he followed was certainly not advanced. His design for a clothes press (No. 282) is very similar to one designed by Chippendale more than thirty years previously (No. 74) and illustrates the conservative taste of the ordinary eighteenth-century cabinet-maker. Again, Hepplewhite lags behind the times in some of his designs for chairs. One of those reproduced in No. 274 is surprisingly reminiscent of designs published by Manwaring twenty years earlier, and, like many of his contemporaries, he went on using the bowed leg both for chairs and tables long after it had been discarded by Adam (cf. No. 288).

The obsolete character of some of Hepplewhite's designs was pointed out by Sheraton a few years later in the preface to his *Cabinet-Maker and Upholsterer's Drawing Book*. 'Notwithstanding the late date of Hepplewhite's book', he wrote, 'if we compare some of the designs, particularly the chairs, with the newest taste, we shall find that this work has already caught the decline, and perhaps in a little time, will suddenly die in the disorder.' Hepplewhite's successors were evidently struck by this stricture, for in a third edition of the *Guide*, published in 1794, they made an attempt to bring the book up to date by replacing some of the more old-fashioned designs; and, as though in response to Sheraton's criticism, all the changes (with one exception) were concerned with chairs and sofas. Those which still retained the bowed leg in the first edition were omitted in favour of rectilinear designs; so were the two chairs with backs reminiscent of Manwaring (No. 274). The new type of chair, illustrated by Sheraton and now adopted by Hepplewhite, had a square instead of an oval or shield-shaped back, and, to make up for the previous omission of such designs, Hepplewhite's successors inserted about twenty patterns for chairs of this kind into the new edition. Several sofas with backs of serpentine form were also replaced by a new type with straight horizontal backs, as favoured by Sheraton; while three projects for oval mirrors, a shape often used by Adam, were discarded in favour of others with the more fashionable rectangular frame. These changes illustrate one of the main differences between the styles of Hepplewhite and Sheraton, that is to say between the fashions of the eighties and those of the nineties. The earlier period still made use of certain curved forms like the oval and the shield, and had not even entirely renounced the bowed leg, a relic of the rococo; whereas the later decade preferred the rectangle.

One of the designers responsible for bringing about the change of style was the architect Henry Holland, whose work for the Prince of Wales at Carlton House in the 1780's marks the birth of a new variety of classicism. Holland, like Adam, regarded furniture as a complement to his decorative schemes; indeed, he sometimes went further than Adam and made furniture a part of the architecture. Adam and others had, of course, made occasional use of fitted furniture, especially in libraries, but Holland seems to have made a practice of designing commodes, pier tables and other furniture as architectural fixtures, as we may see in the few specimens of his work reproduced here (Nos. 298 to 302). They show his ideas for the pier tables and bookcases in the library at Woburn and for a pair of low bookcases resembling commodes at Southill, and we can see from them how the furniture, which was all built in, is conceived as an extension of the architecture and so brought into complete accord with it.

These designs possess something of that 'august simplicity' which Horace Walpole praised in Holland's architecture. 'You cannot call it magnificent', Walpole continued; 'it is the taste and propriety that strike.' This was his opinion on Carlton House, which he visited, while it was still incomplete, in 1785. 'How sick one shall be', he went on, 'after this chaste palace, of Mr Adam's gingerbread and sippets of embroidery.' Walpole had once been a great admirer of Adam, but the finicky element in Adam's ornament had begun to pall after more than twenty years of use and mechanical imitation. Holland infused fresh life into a languishing style. He drastically pruned the luxuriant tendrils of ornament which, under Adam's influence, tended to invade every vacant space, and his favourite method of relieving the flat surfaces of his walls and furniture was to break them up into framed panels of simple outline, which, though bare of internal ornament, fulfilled their decorative purpose through their good proportions and skilful placing. His mouldings were neither so lavishly nor so minutely enriched as Adam's, and such ornament as he used was larger in scale and bolder in character. He studied classical models for fresh themes, and his pupil Tatham, whom he helped to maintain for three years in Italy, supplied him with specimens, casts and drawings of antique decoration, which can sometimes be recognized in his work.[1] The winged chimera in No. 299, for example, is obviously related to several similar beasts illustrated in Tatham's drawings and etchings (cf. No. 361). Holland was among the first in England to make use of these large sculptured animal forms, closely modelled on the antique, which became popular in the first decade of the nineteenth century.

As we have seen, a characteristic of the school of design represented by Holland was a marked predilection for rectangular forms. But though Holland seldom allowed curves to intrude into his elevations, he was not afraid of using them to enliven the plan. Thus in his design for the bookcases at Southill (No. 298) the front is composed on strictly rectilinear lines, but in the plan the centre projects forward between two concave quadrants; while in a commode which he designed for the Prince of Wales, now preserved at Buckingham Palace, the ends are convex and fitted with open shelves (No. 310).[2] There is a similar pair at Southill,[3] and they recall a type of commode made in France before the Revolution by Beneman and Weisweiler, the favourite *ébénistes* of Marie Antoinette. Another French device, much favoured by Weisweiler and occasionally copied by Holland, was to insert a pair of slender colonnettes or candelabra of ormolu at the corners of a cabinet or commode between the architrave and the base moulding – a type of ornament illustrated in an ebony rosewood cabinet probably designed by Holland at Southill.[3] These feature suggest that

---

[1] A good example at Southill is given in F. J. B. Watson's article on the furniture in *Southill, A Regency House* (Editor, Major S. Whitbread), 1951, pages 19–41. Part of Tatham's correspondence with Holland is in the Museum, in the Print Room.

[2] Illustrated in H. Clifford Smith, *Buckingham Palace*, plate 267.

[3] Illustrated in *Southill, a Regency House*, by Major S. Whitbread (editor), page 36.

although Holland travelled abroad very little, even in France, he made good use of his opportunity to study the fine examples of contemporary French furniture in the collection of his patron the Prince of Wales; and the style of his decoration in general shows that he was aware of architectural trends in France.

Holland's pupil Sir John Soane, who had spent six years in his office as a young man, seems to have shared to some extent his interest in furniture. At any rate, a few furniture designs by Soane are preserved in the Soane Museum, and they are good enough to make us regret that no more have survived. His fine design for a music table for the Duke of Leeds, dated 1797 (No. 303), is very similar to some of Holland's work at Woburn and Southill, and two other designs reproduced here (Nos. 304 and 305) show that like Holland he aimed at a stringent simplicity of form. The chair with a rushwork seat, decorated with nothing but knops and painted stringing lines, is an admirable example of graceful functionalism and possesses a most engaging sort of rustic elegance. Soane's rival John Nash also took an interest in furniture, if we may judge from the carefully considered design for a chair reproduced in No. 308. The detailed instructions concerning the colour scheme, which was to be green and gold, and the upholstery (the cushion was 'to be stuffed very square'), show that Nash was not above supervising such small points. Drawings like these are tantalizing, because they suggest that architects were responsible for designing more furniture than is generally attributed to them.

The most prolific designer of furniture working at the end of the century was not, however, an architect, but an artist who had been trained as a cabinet-maker and who had given up the trade in order to specialize in writing and designing: Thomas Sheraton. Many of his early designs were made under the influence of Henry Holland, for whose work he appears to have had a great admiration. When he published his first series of designs, *The Cabinet-Maker and Upholsterer's Drawing Book*, which came out in separate numbers between 1791 and 1794, Holland had but lately completed the reconstruction and redecoration of Carlton House, and Sheraton, who had an opportunity of seeing the interior, was so struck by the furniture and decorations that he inserted into his book views and descriptions of the Dining Room[1] and of the Chinese Drawing Room.[2] We gather that he also visited the Duke of York's residence, probably Featherstonehaugh House, Whitehall (now Dover House), which Holland had recently altered and fitted up; and Sheraton states that his design for a drawing room[3] was a composite invention inspired by the Prince of Wales's and the Duke of York's. One of his views of the Chinese Drawing Room shows a commode designed by Holland (No. 310) which, though not strictly an original design, is reproduced here, because it closely resembles some of Sheraton's own work and indicates the source of some of his ideas. In No. 323, for example, he has designed a cabinet on the same lines, with rounded ends fitted with open shelves. The same design illustrates his characteristic use of elongated colonnettes or candelabra placed at the corners of a piece of furniture and extended throughout its entire height, interrupting all the mouldings from the base to the architrave. This was one of his favourite devices and he used it in all kinds of

[1] *Drawing Book*, No. 29. Plate 60.
[2] *Ibid*, No. 41. Plates 2 and 3. See also No. 310 among the illustrations in this work.
[3] *Ibid*, No. 31. Plate 1.

furniture, even in chairs and tables, prolonging the legs upwards to interrupt the seat rail or the table top (cf. Nos. 312, 314 and 327). This form of construction was never employed by Hepplewhite and it constitutes one of the main stylistic differences between the two designers.

Sheraton, in his first book of designs, followed the example of Holland in using square and rectangular forms in all his elevations. Even his mirror frames, sofas and chair backs, objects which had given Adam and his followers welcome opportunities of relieving the severity of a rectilinear design with an oval shield or other curved shape, were usually rectangular; and his only substantial concession was to introduce an occasional dome or elliptical pediment. In his plans, on the other hand, he was even readier than Holland to make bold experiments with curved recesses and projections, with serpentine outlines and rounded or chamfered corners. In his pursuit of variety he provided chairs with circular seats, bent sofas into the shape of a banana, designed a 'Kidney Table' and contrived 'An Eliptic Bed for a Single Lady' ('as fancifulness', he explained, 'seems most peculiar to the taste of females'). Like Holland, he made sparing use of Adam's ornamental repertory, and he usually relieved flat surfaces, not with marquetry arabesques, but with borders of crossbanding and with black or brass stringing lines inlaid in simple geometrical patterns.

Some of the designs in Sheraton's second book, *The Cabinet Dictionary*, published in 1803, reveal a marked deviation from the style used in his first volume. The change was not confined to Sheraton or to furniture designers, but was the consequence of a new and widespread attempt to imitate more accurately the exact forms of ancient art. The number of prints and books illustrating classical remains had greatly increased. Indeed, so much new knowledge was now available about the furniture of the Greeks and Romans that designers tended to become students of archaeology. Thomas Hope, the author of *Household Furniture* (1807), even felt obliged to justify some of his designs by pointing to the classical prototypes on which they were based and provided his readers with a bibliography of books bearing on the classical sources of his work. Though Sheraton was not so learned or so punctilious, his later designs show that he too, and the cabinet-makers whose shops he frequented, had gleaned some new ideas from classical models. One of their discoveries was that the Greeks and Romans had not confined themselves to purely rectangular or rectilinear designs, but had made free use of curves in their furniture, as in the typical Greek chair, or *klismos*, often represented in vase paintings, which had legs raked outward and curved like sabres, a graceful type of support entirely neglected since the dark ages and now revived by Sheraton and his contemporaries, both for tables and chairs (cf. Nos. 332 and 335). The later Roman practice of embellishing furniture with large-scale scrolls and volutes, well illustrated in books like Tatham's *Etchings of Ancient Ornamental Architecture* (cf. Nos. 360–363), was also copied by the new school of designers, who applied it with good effect to the backs of chairs and sofas, as in some of Sheraton's designs reproduced here (Nos. 335–338); and they enthusiastically adopted once again the Roman device of using all sorts of animal forms as supports and terminals. So, in one way and another, the study of classical precedents led to the formation of a style which was the antithesis of Sheraton's earlier manner. Indeed, surprising though it may seem, the new type of furniture had perhaps more in common with the designs of the Palladian architects than with anything that immediately preceded it. The attenuated linear forms introduced by Adam and the severe rectangular designs illustrated in Sheraton's first book now both gave way to more robust compositions characterized by sweeping curves and scrolls and by the use of large-scale sculptural motifs, both animal and human, not unlike those formerly employed by William Kent and his contemporaries. The claw and the paw foot, realistically carved, came back into fashion as a support for furniture, together with the winged sphinx, the dolphin, and the chimera; while the ringed lion's mask reappeared on chair knees and friezes, and the eagle's head once more served as a terminal for the arms of chairs and sofas. All these motifs, dear to the furniture makers of the early Georgian period, can be seen in the plates reproduced here from Sheraton's *Cabinet Dictionary* and from his last work, which he did not live to finish, *The Cabinet-Maker, Upholsterer and General Artist's Encyclopaedia* (Nos. 332–338). The comparison with the earlier style must not be pressed too far. But if we place Sheraton's curious X-framed chairs (No. 331) beside a design by Adam (No. 220), or even next to one of his own earlier engravings, and then compare it with a chair by William Kent (No. 17), there can be no doubt with which they have the closest affinity. The scrolled seats and arms, the paw feet, the medley of human and animal heads, the large key pattern, the X-shape itself, are all features which we should expect to find in a chair designed by Kent, though he would not, of course, have handled them in exactly the same way and there can be no mistaking the later date of Sheraton's designs.

However, this unexpected turn in the evolution of English furniture belongs to the history of the nineteenth century and must be reserved for another volume. A few examples only from Sheraton's last period are reproduced here to show the way in which furniture design was developing at the end of the eighteenth century, and because it is interesting to see the wheel of fashion so nearly describe a complete circle.

Part 2

CATALOGUE OF THE ILLUSTRATIONS
AND
NOTES ON THE ARTISTS

Explanatory Note

An attempt is here made to provide a reasonably full bibliography of the principal eighteenth-century pattern books which contain designs for furniture, and secondly to give some account of the various collections of drawings for furniture which belong to the Museum. The material is arranged under the designers' names approximately in chronological order. Short biographical notes are also given on each artist, but these are not intended to be exhaustive and their purpose is merely to give the general reader some idea of the artist's life and work. Books and articles dealing more fully with a particular artist are mentioned, but most of the information available about the artists can be obtained from five indispensable sources, which it would be tedious and unnecessary to enumerate anew under each heading: they are *The Dictionary of National Biography*; Thieme and Becker, *Allgemeines Lexicon der Bildenden Künstler*, 1907–1950; Percy Macquoid and Ralph Edwards, *The Dictionary of English Furniture*, 2nd edition, revised, 1954; Ralph Edwards and Margaret Jourdain, *Georgian Cabinet-Makers*, 3rd edition, 1955; and H. M. Colvin, *A Biographical Dictionary of English Architects 1660–1840*, 1954. Some of the bibliographical problems are usefully discussed in R. S. Clouston, *English Furniture and Furniture Makers of the 18th century*, 1906; and an essential source of information on the Chippendale drawings and on mid-eighteenth-century engraved designs is to be found in two essays by Fiske Kimball and Edna Donnell, entitled *The Creators of the Chippendale Style*, published in New York in *Metropolitan Museum Studies*, vol. I, 1929, pp. 115–154, and vol. II, 1930, pp. 41–72. The abbreviated forms in which some of these works are mentioned in the text are listed on page viii.

The engravings reproduced in the illustrations are divided between the Library and the Print Room. Those kept in the Print Room have a Museum number, which is quoted in the catalogue, while those belonging to the Library are not numbered. All the drawings reproduced are in the Print Room and, therefore, numbered, except for a few kindly lent by owners whose names are given on page vii. In the description of the plates measurements are given in inches, the height first, then the width.

All numerals referring to plates in this work are printed in heavy type, to avoid confusing them with plates in the various pattern books discussed.

CATALOGUE AND NOTES

JOHN WEBB, 1611–1672

Architect. The favourite pupil, assistant and kinsman of Inigo Jones. His most important surviving work is the 'King Charles's Block' at Greenwich Hospital (then Palace), the designs for which, together with many other drawings by him, were incorrectly ascribed to Inigo Jones in the eighteenth century. The design described below appears to be his only extant design for furniture.

1. An alcove and bed for King Charles II at Greenwich Palace. After an original drawing by Webb dated 1665. Plate No. 4 in John Vardy's *Some Designs of Mr. Inigo Jones and Mr. William Kent*, 1744, where it is wrongly ascribed to Inigo Jones. Engraving. 8¼ in. × 9¼ in.

Note: For a discussion of the correct attribution of the drawing see J. A. Gotch, *Inigo Jones*, 1928, pp. 111–113.

ANONYMOUS

2. Design for a state apartment and its furniture. Inscribed within a panel inside the chimney-piece 'Pierces bassorilievo'. Pen and ink. About 1675. Size of sheet 11½ in. × 7¾ in.   3436.246.

Note: The inscription doubtless refers to Edward Pierce the sculptor (d. 1695), who, according to Vertue, 'was much employed by Sir Christopher Wren in his carvings and designs'. He also carried out carving commissions for the interior and exterior of various private houses, including Wolseley Hall, Staffordshire, and Combe Abbey and Castle Bromwich, Warwickshire. The English origin of the drawing, despite its somewhat Dutch or German character, is further proved by the fact that one of the dimensions of the bas-relief is given in inches in English. The drawing is interesting on account of the idiosyncratic character of the furniture and decoration, and also because it is an early example of furniture designed specifically to fit into an architectural background. The glazed bookcase, for instance, of a type which had not long been in use in England, was clearly conceived on architectural lines to harmonize with the chimney-piece and the elaborate architrave of the window.

JOHN STALKER AND GEORGE PARKER

The authors of a folio book published in 1688 under the title:

A Treatise of Japaning and Varnishing, being a compleat discovery of those arts. With the best way of making all sorts of varnish . . . the method of guilding burnishing and lackering, with the art of guilding, separating and refining metals . . . Also rules for counterfeiting tortoise-shell, and marble . . . Together with above an hundred distinct patterns for Japan-work in imitation of the Indians, for tables, stands, frames, cabinets, boxes, etc. . . . By George Parker and John Stalker, Oxford. . . . In the year MDCLXXXVIII

The same book was issued twice again in the year of publication with different title-pages. Apart from a few minor alterations, the titles read as before, but in the one case the order in which the names are given is reversed and in the other John Stalker is mentioned as the sole author.

The designs for Japan-work were drawn, in the authors' words, 'according to the patterns which the best workmen amongst them have afforded us on their Cabinets, Screens, Boxes, etc. Perhaps,' they add, 'we have helpt them a little in their proportions, where they were lame or defective, and made them more pleasant, yet altogether as Antick. Had we industriously contriv'd prospective, or shadow'd them otherwise than they are; we should have wandred from our Design, which is only to imitate the true genuine Indian work.' The authors, like most of their contemporaries, made no distinction between the products of India, China and Japan, and they strayed further than this declaration would suggest from a faithful imitation of oriental originals, doubtless misled by specimens of Dutch and English Japan-work, as well as by illustrated travel books.

The book contains a full and informative account of the various techniques used by seventeenth-century japanners, and the instructions on gilding were the clearest and most complete since Cennino Cennini's handbook, published in the fifteenth century.

3. Four designs for japanning the drawers of a cabinet. Plate 19 in *A Treatise of Japaning*, 1688. Engraving. 13¾ in. × 8½ in.

DANIEL MAROT, c. 1663–1752

Architect, ornamentalist and engraver. The son of Jean Marot, a gifted designer and engraver, he was born in Paris and had already started on a promising career there, when the Revocation of the Edict of Nantes in 1685 compelled him, as a Protestant, to seek refuge in Holland, where he entered the service of William III, Prince of Orange. When his patron ascended the throne of England as King William III, Marot continued to enjoy his patronage and usually styled himself 'architect to William III, King of Great Britain'. There is evidence that he was working in London in 1695 and 1696, and again in 1698. But apart from the fact that he laid out the gardens of Hampton Court Palace and designed a number of Delft vases for the interior, no exact record of his activities in England has yet come to light. It may be assumed, however, that he was at any rate consulted in the decoration of Hampton Court Palace, where some of the rooms reveal the influence of his style. Some of his engraved furniture designs bear the royal arms of England (cf. No. **7**). Marot published a great number of designs for all kinds of work, including furniture, usually issued in sets of six. The first collected edition of his designs was published in 1702 under the title:

Oeuvres Du Sr D. Marot . . . Contenant plusséurs, penssez utille aux architects, peintres, sculpteurs, orfeures & jardiniers, & autres; le toutes en faveure de ceux qui s'appliquerent aux beaux arts. A La Haye, 1702. Chez Pierre Husson.

A second and enlarged edition was issued in 1712, the title remaining the same, apart from certain changes in the spelling and the deletion of the publisher's name, for which the following imprint was substituted: 'A Amsterdam, Ce vand Chez L'Authuer . . .'

Another collection of his designs, re-engraved, was published without date or publisher's name under a Dutch and Latin title as follows:

Werken van D. Marot, Opperboumeester van Zyne Maiesteit Willem den Derden Koning von Groot Britanje. Behelfende veele vindingen dienstig voor Boumeesters, Schilders, Beelthouwers, Goutsmeden . . . Opera D. Marot . . . Continentia magnam multitudinem inventorum in usum architectorum, pictorum . . .

This is the only edition of which the Museum possesses a complete copy.

Though so little is known of Marot's work for William III in England, there are abundant signs of his influence in all the decorative arts at the turn of the century. A conspicuous example in the Museum is the great Melville bed (W.33-1949) which, in its general design as well as in the details of the embroidered hangings, evokes Marot (cf. Nos. **4** and **5**). Of course, there were other French designers, like Jean Bérain and Pierre Le Pautre, working in a similar style, and their engraved patterns were doubtless studied in England also. But it is with Marot's designs that English furniture and decoration under William III and Queen Anne have the closest affinity. His influence lasted well into the reign of George II and traces of it can even be discerned in the furniture designs of Kent.

See M. H. Destailleur, *Recueil d'estampes relatives à l'ornementation des appartements*, Paris, 1863. vol. I, p. 43.

A. Bérard, *Catalogue de toutes les estampes qui forment l'oeuvre de Daniel Marot*, Brussels, 1865.

P. Jessen, *Das Ornamentwerk des Daniel Marot*, Berlin, 1892.

M. D. Ozinga, *Daniel Marot*, Amsterdam, 1938.

Arthur Lane, on Marot's work at Hampton Court Palace, in *The Connoisseur*, vol. 123, 1949, pp. 19–24.

4. A state bedstead. Plate from the set entitled *Second Livre d'Appartements*. About 1700. Etching. 10⅞ in. × 7½ in.   13672.3

5. A state bedstead. Plate in *Werken van D. Marot*. (n.d.) Copy, in reverse, after a plate in the set entitled *Second Livre d'Appartements*. About 1700. Etching. 10¾ in. × 7⅞ in.

6. Two tables supported by herms. Plate from the set entitled *Nouveau Livre d'Orfeurie*. About 1700. Etching. 10½ in. × 7⅞ in.   13672.13

7. Designs for four mirrors and two brackets. Plate from the set entitled *Nouveaux Livre d'Ornements pour Lutillite des Sculpteurs et Orfèvres*. About 1700. Etching. 10⅞ in. × 7½ in.   15672.14.

Note: On one of the mirrors the arms of King William III are indicated, as in many of Marot's furniture designs.

8. Designs for chairs, stools and valances. Plate in *Werken van D. Marot* (n.d.). Copy after a plate in the set entitled *Second Livre d'Appartements*. About 1700. Etching. 10⅞ in. × 7⅞ in.   E.5919-1905.

SIR JAMES THORNHILL, 1675–1734

Now remembered mainly as a painter, especially of murals and ceilings; but like Kent, who was likewise trained as a painter, he was also an ambitious architect, though political and personal intrigues deprived him of any extensive practice. The only important building he is known to have designed was Moor Park, Herts, often incorrectly attributed to Leoni. The drawing reproduced here, possibly intended for stage scenery rather than for a real room, illustrates a baroque ideal in English furniture design seldom carried out in practice.

9. Design for a state bedroom and its furniture. About 1720. Pen and ink and wash. 10¾ in. × 11 in.   D.28A-1891.

Anonymous

Three designs for furniture. Early eighteenth century. Pen and ink.

10. A mirror frame. Inscribed 'Glass and Room Border'. $4\frac{5}{8}$ in. $\times 2\frac{3}{8}$ in.   D.2319B–1885.

11. A tripod stand. Inscribed 'Wood Tripod'. $7\frac{3}{8}$ in. $\times 2\frac{3}{8}$ in.   D.2316–1885.

12. A mirror frame. 5 in. $\times 2\frac{5}{8}$ in.   D.2319A–1885.

William Kent, ?1685–1748

Painter, architect and designer. After spending ten years studying painting in Italy, he came back to England in 1719 with Lord Burlington, from then on his constant friend and patron, who gradually directed his interest towards architecture and imparted to him his own enthusiastic admiration for the Palladian style. Kent began practicing seriously as an architect from about 1730 and soon became Burlington's principal ally in an attempt to establish the Palladian ideal in England. Among his best known works are Holkham Hall, Norfolk, and the Horse Guards and Treasury Buildings in Whitehall. But it was perhaps in designing interiors that Kent's greatest gift lay, and much of his finest surviving work is to be found in houses planned by others, for example at Houghton Hall, Norfolk, which was built by Campbell and Gibbs, but decorated and largely furnished by Kent. He was, indeed, the first English architect to take a serious interest in furniture, and, like Robert Adam later in the century, he sought to establish a harmonious relation between the architecture of a room and its furniture. His most successful achievements in this field can be seen at Holkham and Houghton in Norfolk, where the original furniture is still in place. There is nothing specifically Palladian about it, but the large-scale sculptural and architectural motives of which it is composed possess a boldness and simplicity appropriate to the heavy classical treatment of the walls. A certain amount of furniture preserved in houses where Kent is known to have worked may be attributed to his pen, but very few actual designs for furniture by him have survived. A few were published by John Vardy in *Some Designs of Mr. Inigo Jones and of Mr. William Kent*, London, 1744.

See also pages 7–8 and M. Jourdain, *The Work of William Kent*, 1948.

13. Design for 'a chandelier for the King'. Plate 23 in *Some Designs of Mr. Inigo Jones and Mr. William Kent*, 1744. Etching by Vardy. $8\frac{3}{4}$ in. $\times 7\frac{1}{4}$ in.

14. An organ case. Plate 47 in *Some Designs of Mr. Inigo Jones and Mr. William Kent*, 1744. Etching by Vardy. $9\frac{3}{8}$ in. $\times 6\frac{3}{4}$ in.

15. A table designed for Lord Burlington's villa Chiswick House. Plate 40 in *Some Designs of Mr. Inigo Jones and Mr. William Kent*, 1744. Etching by Vardy. $8\frac{7}{8}$ in. $\times 6\frac{5}{8}$ in.

16. A design for a settee (with two alternative crestings) and two chairs. Plate 42 in *Some Designs of Mr. Inigo Jones and Mr. William Kent*, 1744. Etching by Vardy. $9\frac{5}{8}$ in. $\times 6\frac{5}{8}$ in.

17. An arm-chair. Plate 43 in *Some Designs of Mr. Inigo Jones and Mr. William Kent*, 1744. Etching by Vardy. $6\frac{1}{2}$ in. $\times 9$ in.

18. A table for Sir Robert Walpole at Houghton Hall, Norfolk. Inscribed on the back in the artist's hand with the title and dated November 1731. Pen and ink and wash. $6\frac{1}{8}$ in. $\times 11\frac{1}{4}$ in.   8156.

Note: Kent was employed to decorate the interior of Houghton, c. 1726–1731. The design was engraved as plate 41 in *Some Designs of Mr. Inigo Jones and Mr. William Kent*, 1744. The table itself is still at Houghton.

De La Cour

An engraver and ornamentalist, presumably of French origin, who worked in England and, between 1741 and 1747, published eight books of ornament in the rococo style. His *First Book of Ornament*, dedicated to Lord Middlesex, with plates dated 1741 (see No. **346**), and his *Eighth Book of Ornament*, 1747, are in the Museum. He may have been identical with the painter William Delacour, who was working in London in 1747 and afterwards settled in Edinburgh.

19. Designs for chairs. About 1745. Etching by R. White. $8\frac{1}{8}$ in. $\times 10\frac{5}{8}$ in.   E.240–1892.

William Jones, d. 1757

Architect and designer. Among his architectural works were Ranelagh Gardens and the Rotunda and various buildings for the East India Company, to which he was appointed surveyor in 1752. He published:

The Gentlemens or Builders Companion containing variety of useful designs for doors, gateways, peers, pavilions, temples, chimney-pieces, slab tables, pier glasses, or tabernacle frames, ceiling pieces, &c. Explained on copper-plates by Wm Jones, architect . . . 1739. London. Printed for the author, and sold at his house near the chapple in King Street Golden Square.

This work contains twenty designs for tables and mirrors which are among the earliest published by an English author. The mirror frames are in a classical architectural style typical of the period and derived from the chimney-pieces of Inigo Jones (Nos. **24** and **25**); and the tables (Nos. **20** and **21**) recall William Kent, though some of them show a lighter French influence, and No. **23** is clearly inspired, like some of Batty Langley's work, by the engraved designs of Nicolas Pineau.

20. A side-table. Plate 29 in *The Gentlemens or Builders Companion*, 1739. Etching. 6 in. × 8 in.

21. A side-table. Plate 27 *ibidem*. 6 in. × 8 in.

22. A side-table. Plate 31 *ibidem*. 6 in. × 8 in.

23. A side-table. Plate 32 *ibidem*. 6 in. × 8 in.

24. A mirror frame. Plate 50 *ibidem*. $7\frac{3}{4}$ in. × 6 in.

25. A mirror frame. Plate 47 *ibidem*. $7\frac{3}{4}$ in. × $5\frac{7}{8}$ in.

Anonymous

26. A mirror flanked by caryatids. Pen and ink and wash. About 1740. 10 in. × $6\frac{7}{8}$ in. 3436.255.

Gaetano Brunetti, d. 1758

A decorative painter from Lombardy who was working in Paris about 1730. It is not known whether he ever came to England, but in 1736 a book was published in London entitled *Sixty Different Sorts of Ornaments invented by Gaetano Brunetti Italian painter. Very useful to painters, sculptors, stone-carvers, wood-carvers, silversmiths etc*. It contains a title-page and 61 plates, engraved by H. Fletcher and J. Roque, all dated June the 25th, 1736. Six of the plates show designs for furniture. They are decidedly Italian in style, and it is unlikely that any furniture was actually made from them in England. The book nevertheless probably played some part in introducing the rococo style to English designers, for much of the ornament is composed of shellwork twisted into characteristic asymmetrical shapes, and no other designs of the kind had so far been published in this country.

27. An arm-chair and mirror frame. Plate from *Sixty Different Sorts of Ornaments*. 1736. Engraved by Henry Fletcher. Etching. $6\frac{3}{4}$ in. × $4\frac{7}{8}$ in.
E.987-1904.

28. Two tables. Plate *ibidem*. Engraved by Fletcher. Etching. $6\frac{3}{4}$ in. × $4\frac{7}{8}$ in. E.991-1904.

29. Two chairs. Plate *ibidem*. Engraved by Fletcher. Etching. $4\frac{7}{8}$ in. × $6\frac{3}{4}$ in. E.989-1904.

Batty Langley (1696–1751) and Thomas Langley (b. 1702)

Batty, the elder brother, was an architect, landscape gardener and designer, while Thomas was mainly an engraver and draughtsman, who collaborated with his brother in some of the numerous pattern books for builders, gardeners and other workmen which he published. One of these works contains some twenty-five designs for furniture and was first published in 1740 under the title:

The City and Country Builder's and Workman's Treasury of Designs: or the art of drawing and working the ornamental parts of architecture . . . By Batty Langley. London. Printed by J. Ilive . . . 1740. (Engraver: Thomas Langley.)

Other editions, with 14 additional plates, were issued in 1741, 1750 and 1756. The Museum's copy is of the 1750 edition, in which the publisher's imprint reads: *Printed for and sold by S. Harding, on the pavement in St. Martin's Lane.*

Most of the furniture designs are dated 1739. Some are by Batty, and others by Thomas, whose small contribution consists mainly of plagiarisms, the dressing table in his plate 156 being pilfered from the contemporary Nuremberg artist Johann Jakob Schübler (plate 27 in his *Vierte Ausgabe seines vorhabenden Wercks*, as Mr R. W. Symonds was the first to point out); while the clock in No. **30** is copied from a design by Johann Friedrich Lauch (No. **365**). Moreover, six of his designs for tables are taken straight from Nicolas Pineau's *Nouveaux Desseins de Pieds de Tables*, which explains why they reveal a more advanced rococo character than anything else in the book. The other designs for furniture are more in accord with the Palladian taste predominant in England at the time.

The only other book by the Langleys which has a bearing on furniture design is the work on Gothic architecture for which they are now best known. It was published in 1742 under the title:

Ancient Architecture restored and improved by a great variety of grand and useful designs, entirely new, in the Gothic mode, for the ornamenting of buildings and gardens . . . 1742. (The plates are dated 1741 and 1742).

The book was afterwards republished under a new title:

Gothic Architecture improved by rules and proportions in many grand designs of columns, doors, windows . . .

(The copy in the Museum is undated, while the British Museum copy is dated 1747.)

The plates are preceded by 'An Historical Dissertation' (dated 1742), in the course of which Batty defines the purpose of the book in these words: 'The Rules by which the ancient Buildings of this Kingdom were erected and adorned, having been entirely lost for many centuries, ... I have therefore ... assiduously employed myself ... in making researches into many of the most ancient buildings now standing, ... and from thence have extracted rules for forming such designs and ornaments in the ancient mode, which will be exceedingly beautiful in all parts of private buildings; and especially in Rooms of State, Dining Rooms, Parlours, Stair-Cases, etc. and in Porticos, Umbrellos, Temples, and Pavillions ...'

The rules propounded by Langley were for 'five new orders of columns' in the Gothic style, which he illustrates in 16 plates (cf. No. **359**), while in the remaining plates he demonstrates their use in composing designs for doors, windows, chimney-pieces, garden houses, etc. The orders were, of course, entirely his own invention and were concocted of Gothic ingredients served up *à la Vitruvius*. But the designs themselves are not lacking in charm, and though there are none for furniture, those for chimney-pieces and other interior fittings are of interest in the present context, because they represent the first attempt to introduce the Gothic style into the ordinary domestic interior. Horace Walpole, who soon afterwards tried to do the same sort of thing in his own villa, was contemptuous of his predecessor's Gothic. 'All that his books achieved', he wrote in his *Anecdotes of Painting*, 'has been to teach carpenters to massacre that venerable species.'

Yet if it was an offence to divert the Gothic style from churches and colleges, in the building of which it was still occasionally used, and to apply it to the more trivial purposes of furniture and decoration, Walpole was hardly less to blame than Langley. Together they were the first in a field soon to be invaded by nearly every joiner and cabinet-maker in the country.

See Kenneth Clark, *The Gothic Revival*, 1928; 2nd edition, 1950.

30. A hanging clock. Plate 140 in the *Treasury of Designs*. Signed: 'Thos. Langley Invent delin and Sculp'. Engraving. $9\frac{3}{8}$ in. × $7\frac{1}{2}$ in.

Note: This design was pilfered from the German artist J. F. Lauch. See No. **365**.

31. A marble table. Plate 143 *ibidem*. Signed: 'Thos. Langley Invent delin and Sculp. 1739'. Engraving. $7\frac{1}{2}$ in. × $9\frac{3}{8}$ in.

Note: The design is copied from plate 3 in Nicolas Pineau's *Nouveaux Desseins de Pieds de Tables*. A table in the Museum (W.12–1952) was clearly inspired by this plate.

32. 'A Dorick Bookcase'. Plate 159 *ibidem*. Signed: 'Batty Langley Invent 1739. T. Langley Sculp'. Engraving. $9\frac{1}{2}$ in. × $7\frac{1}{2}$ in.

33. A cabinet on a stand. Plate 155 *ibidem*. Signed: 'Thos. Langley Invent and Sculp. 1739'. Engraving. $9\frac{1}{4}$ in. × $7\frac{1}{2}$ in.

34. 'A medal case'. Plate 154 *ibidem*. Signed: 'T. Langley Invent' & Sculp. 1739'. Engraving. $9\frac{3}{8}$ in. × $7\frac{1}{2}$ in.

Anonymous

35. A pier table and mirror, with two sconces. About 1740. Pen and ink and wash. $8\frac{7}{8}$ in. × $8\frac{1}{2}$ in.   214.

36. A mirror. About 1740. Pen and ink and wash. $3\frac{5}{8}$ in. × $3\frac{3}{8}$ in.   215.

37. A side-table. About 1745. Pen and ink. $2\frac{1}{8}$ in. × $4\frac{3}{4}$ in.   E.3049–1938.

Abraham Swan, Worked c. 1745–1765

Carpenter and joiner, and the author of several architectural handbooks. Most of his designs are in an academic classical style, but they are often overlaid with misunderstood rococo ornament, as in the specimen reproduced here:

38. Design for a chimney-piece and overmantel mirror. Plate 49 in *The British Architect: or the Builder's Treasury of Staircases ... By Abraham Swan, Carpenter. London. The second edition. 1750.* (First edition 1745. Third edition 1758.) Engraving. $13\frac{3}{4}$ in. × $8\frac{5}{8}$ in.

John Vardy, d. 1765

Architect. He passed most of his career in the Office of Works and was closely associated with William Kent, some of whose designs he published in a book entitled *Some Designs of Mr. Inigo Jones and Mr. William Kent*, 1744. His most prominent surviving building is Spencer House, Green Park, London. He seems to have shared Kent's interest in furniture, and a small number of interesting furniture designs by him is preserved in the Museum and in the R.I.B.A. Some of them are in the manner of Kent, while others show that, despite his Palladian training, he had studied the French rococo style with more understanding than most English architects.

His design for a writing table and *cartonnier* (No. **45**) is particularly interesting, because it approaches more nearly to the true French style than any other design reproduced in this book.

39. A chimney-piece and overmantel mirror. About 1745. Pencil, pen and ink and wash. $7\frac{7}{8}$ in. × $5\frac{1}{2}$ in. 3436.201.

40. An overmantel mirror or picture frame. Inscribed on the back in ink: 'This design for Lady Milton's Dressing Room Frame over the Chimney. J. Vardy. 1761'. Pen and ink and wash. $7\frac{7}{8}$ in. × $7\frac{5}{8}$ in. (Royal Institute of British Architects. K9/6.)

Note: Vardy appears to have been employed by Lord Milton to make designs for Milton Abbey, Dorset, and there are other drawings for the same house in the R.I.B.A.; but they were probably never carried out.

41. A pedestal for a bust or candelabrum. About 1745. Pen and ink and wash. $5\frac{1}{4}$ in. × $1\frac{5}{8}$ in. (Royal Institute of British Architects. K9/23.)

42. A side-table and mirror. About 1745. Pen and ink and wash. $7\frac{1}{2}$ in. × $3\frac{1}{4}$ in. (Royal Institute of British Architects. K9/21.)

43. A side-table and mirror. About 1745. Pen and ink and wash. $17\frac{5}{8}$ in. × $8\frac{3}{4}$ in. (Royal Institute of British Architects. K9/19.)

44. Design for a state bed at St. James's Palace. Signed on the back: 'J. Vardy Invent. et delin 1749' and inscribed with title. Pen and ink and wash. $7\frac{7}{8}$ in. × $4\frac{5}{8}$ in. E.3143-1938.

Note: Vardy was Clerk of the Works at Whitehall and St. James's in 1749, when this drawing was made. The design is clearly inspired by the great bed designed by William Kent for Houghton Hall, Norfolk (illustrated in Macquoid and Edwards, vol. I, p. 61, fig. 44), but the ornament is more florid.

45. A writing table and *cartonnier*. Inscribed on the back in ink: 'J. Vardy delin. at Mr. Arundales'. About 1745. Pen and ink and wash. $6\frac{3}{8}$ in. × $10\frac{5}{8}$ in. (Royal Institute of British Architects. K9/17.)

Note: This drawing is curious, because the furniture represented is a remarkably skilful imitation of the Louis XV style, and it belongs to a type which English cabinet-makers seldom, if ever, attempted to copy. The inscription is ambiguous. It might mean that Vardy made the design for Mr Arundale; or it might mean that he made the drawing at Mr Arundale's house, either from memory or from a French table in Mr Arundale's possession. The word *invenit* which would remove all doubt is missing. The first alternative is probably correct. Closely though the drawing resembles a French writing table and *cartonnier*, it does not look completely convincing, considering how carefully it is executed. We know that Vardy was employed by a man named Arundell from a design for a Palladian house in the Museum, which is inscribed *J.V. 1746. for Mr Arundell*. This was probably Richard Arundell, Surveyor of the King's Works, 1726-1737, and he was probably identical with the 'Mr Arundale' for whom the table was designed. If the drawing is an original design, it is clearly based on a French design or a French table which Vardy had seen.

MATTHEW DARLY, Working *c.* 1750-1778

Engraver, designer, caricaturist and publisher. His earliest work was entitled:

A New Book of Chinese, Gothic and Modern Chairs with the manner of putting them in perspective according to Brook Taylor . . . M. Darly invt et Fect.

The plates are dated 1750 and 1751. The designs are eccentric, and despite the adoption of Brook Taylor's method of linear perspective, something seems to have gone wrong with the proportions of the chairs, which all have short spindly legs and look as though they were made of cast iron. Nor is it easy to distinguish between the three different types of chair – Chinese, Gothic and Modern – which the author set out to illustrate, as the same peculiarities are common to them all. In fact, it is hard to believe that any of them were actually carried out. Yet the whole set was reprinted fifteen years later in Manwaring's *Chair-Maker's Guide* (see page 52).

Darly's next book, published in collaboration with an artist named Edwards, of whom nothing is known, came out in 1754 under the title:

A New Book of Chinese Designs calculated to improve the present taste, consisting of figures, buildings, & furniture, landskips, birds, beasts, flowr^s and ornaments &c. By Messrs. Edwards, and Darly. Published . . . & sold by the authors, the first house on the right hand in Northumberland Court, in the Strand . . . MDCCLIV. (Engravers: Edwards and Darly).

Fanciful Chinese landscapes and figures, useful to painters, japanners and embroiderers, take up most of the book, but there is also a number of designs for utensils and furniture, in which the Chinese style is more successfully imitated than in Darly's first book. Some of them have a whimsical charm, while others, like the table and chair in Nos. **133** and **134**, are merely preposterous.

About the same time Darly engraved the majority of the plates in the first edition of Chippendale's *Director*, and he later did the same for Ince and Mayhew's *Universal System*. In 1758 he published, again with Edwards, *A Collection of Political Prints*, the first of a long series of satirical and comic works. From now on he appears to have divided his time between caricature and ornament – a dual allegiance humorously hinted at in an engraved self-portrait in the British Museum, dated 1771, in which the artist depicts himself seated on an ass holding a scroll with the inscription: 'The Political Designer of Pots, Pans and Pipkins'. Other self-portraits are signed 'M. Darly P.O.A.G.B.' ('Painter of Ornaments to the Academy of Great Britain'). At the Society of Artists, where he exhibited designs for architecture and ornament between 1765 and 1771, he styled himself 'Professor and Teacher of Ornament'. About this time he set up as a publisher at No. 39, The Strand, from which address he issued a very large number of satirical prints. His later works include *A New Book of Ceilings* (1760), *Sixty Vases of English, French and Italian Masters* (1767), *The Ornamental Architect or young Artist's Instructor* (1770), *A Complete Body of Architecture* (1773), and *A New Book of Ornaments in the present (Antique) Taste* (1772). They contain little in the way of furniture, but the last three are of some interest in this context, as they comprise some of the earliest designs printed in England for ornament in the neo-classic style.

See Kimball and Donnell, vol. I, pp. 128–129.

46. Four chairs. Two plates from *A New Book of Chinese, Gothic and Modern Chairs*, 1750–1751. Etchings. Cut to $4\frac{1}{8}$ in. $\times 6\frac{1}{2}$ in. E.221 and 223–1911.

47. Four chairs. Two plates, *ibidem*. Etchings. Cut to $4\frac{1}{8}$ in. $\times 6\frac{1}{2}$ in. E.220 and 222–1911.

For other designs by this artist see also Nos. **128–134**, **180** and **257–258**.

MATTHIAS (or MATTHEW) LOCK,
Worked c. 1740–1770

Carver and furniture designer. Although he was one of the most accomplished English ornamentalists of the century, nothing is known of his life, apart from the few facts which can be gathered from his engravings and drawings. The list of his published works, established mainly by Kimball and Donnell (vol. I, page 116), is as follows:

1740. *A New Drawing Book of Ornaments, Shields, Compartments, Masks, &c, drawn and engrav'd by M. Lock. Printed For J. Williams, Library of Arts, 10 Charles Street Soho Square.*
(Plates dated 1740. Engravers: Lock, E. Vivares, A. Walker. Only the 2nd edition, of 1768, in the Museum.)

1744. *Six Sconces by M. Lock . . . Published . . . March 1744.* (2nd edition, 1768, only in the Museum.)

1746. *Six Tables by Matths. Lock . . . Published . . . April ye 10, 1746.*
(Title-page and 4 plates, showing five tables, in the Museum).

N.D. *A Book of Ornaments, drawn & engrav'd by M. Lock, principally adapted for carvers, but generally useful for various decorations in the present taste. London, Published by John Weale, No. 59, High Holborn, M. Lock, invt.*
(No original title-page found. Title as given is from restrikes published in 1835.)

1746. A single plate showing a *rocaille* cartouche, with urns on a balustrade at lower left, and large urn with flowers on right. Lettered at bottom: *Published according to act of Parliament, ye 9 of Decem. 1746. by Matthias Lock in Nottingham Court, Castle Street near Long acre. pr.6:d.*
(Not in the Museum).

1752. *A New Book of Ornaments, with twelve leaves, consisting of chimneys, sconces, tables, spandle pannels, spring clock cases, & stands, a chandelier & gerandole &c. By M. Lock and H. Copland . . . Published . . . Nov. 13, 1752 & Sold by the proprietors M. Lock near ye Swan Tottenham Court Road & E. Copland Gutter Lane Cheapside.*

1768. *A New Book of Ornaments consisting of tables, chimnies, sconces, spandles, clock cases, candle stands, chandeliers, girondoles &c By Matt. Lock and H. Copeland (sic), inventors and engravers, published . . . Jany 1, 1768 by Robert Sayer at No. 53 Fleet Street. . . .*
(Some of the plates are identical with those in the 1752 edition, others are copies.)

1768. *Six Sconces by M. Lock. Printed for Robt. Sayer . . . 1768.* (2nd edition of the work of 1744, plates unchanged.)

1768. *A Book of Tables, Candle Stands, Pedostals, Tablets, Table Knees, &c, &c by Matt. Lock . . . Published . . . April ye 10: 1768 by R. Sayer at No. 53 in Fleet Street where may be had all the Genuine Works of Lock and Copland.*
(2nd edition of the work of 1746, plates unchanged. Title-page only in the Museum.)

1769. *A New Book of Pier-Frame's, Oval's, Gerandole's, Tables &c. by M. Lock . . . Published . . . A.D. 1769 by Carrington Bowles, No. 69 in St. Paul's Churchyard, London.*

1769. *A New Book of Foliage for the Instruction of Young Artists by M. Lock. 1769 . . . Printed for Webley in Holborn near Chancery Lane . . .*

N.D. *A New Book of Ornaments for Looking Glass*

Frames, Chimney Pieces &c. &c, in the Chinese taste by Matt. Lock. Useful for carvers, &c. London, Printed for Robert Sayer map & printseller At No. 53 in Fleet Street.

(Engravers: J. Taylor, June, Walker. Not in the Museum. From their *rocaille* character these plates, like the other reprints by Sayer, must be a second edition issued about 1768, of an earlier work, of which no copies are now known to exist. Plate 1 inscribed, 'Glazier delin'.)

N.D. *A New Drawing Book . . . Printed for Robert Sayer . . .* (2nd edition of work of 1740, issued about 1768, plates unchanged).

N.D. *The Principles of Ornament, or the Youth's Guide to Drawing of Foliage . . . by M. Lock. London. Printed for Robert Sayer near Serjeant's Inn Fleet Street.*

(Title-page only in Museum. No complete copy recorded.)

In addition to these engravings a considerable number of original drawings by Lock is in existence, a few being preserved in the Metropolitan Museum, while the majority are in the Victoria and Albert Museum. The latter collection was acquired in two separate groups, as follows:

1. Nos. 2547–2624. 78 sheets bought in 1862 from George Lock of Edinburgh, the grandson of Matthias Lock. At the time 46 of these drawings (Nos. 2547–2592) were ascribed to Lock and 32 (Nos. 2593–2624) to Chippendale, including 7 original designs for the third edition of the *Director*. These attributions were doubtless based on those of George Lock, and they are borne out by a very distinct difference in style between the two groups. Moreover, the designs attributed to Lock include a design (No. 2572) for a mirror engraved in *A New Book of Ornaments* by Lock and Copland (1752), and six small sheets covered with rough sketches of various pieces of furniture, accompanied by notes stating the number of days spent on the task by Lock and other craftsmen, and the wages due to them (see Nos. **61** and **62**). These documents suggest that Lock was at the time working for an employer and not on his own account.

2. Nos. 2848/1–168. A folio scrapbook, also acquired, a year later, from George Lock and entitled *Original Designs by Matts. Lock Carver 1740–1765*. It contains 168 drawings, most of them manifestly by Lock. Among the more doubtful drawings are two fragmentary designs for Chippendale's *Director* (see page 43) and a sheet containing two projects for console tables (No. 2848/122), one of which corresponds, though reversed, with the upper part of plate 75 in Ince and Mayhew's *Universal System*. Mr Kimball and Miss Donnell are probably right in considering it to be a copy, possibly by Lock, after the original drawing by Ince or Mayhew. Apart from drawings, the Album contains ten memoranda written by Lock and illustrated with rough sketches, recording small carving commissions carried out between 1742 and 1744 (Nos. 2848/156–157).

The collection of Chippendale drawings bought by the Museum in 1906 (see page 43) also contains one drawing by Lock (D.788–1906): a design for the cartouche in the title-page of his *Six Tables*, 1746.

The fact that Lock's drawings are intermingled with others by Chippendale, or anyhow from his workshop, provides a good reason for supposing that Chippendale was Lock's employer. We know that Lock was employed by someone for part of his career from the illustrated memoranda of wages due to him for carver's work described above. These memoranda are undated, but the high rococo character of the furniture illustrated suggests that they date from the 1750's or early 1760's. If Lock was working for Chippendale during these years, it would account for the curious fact that, after publishing a series of books between 1740 and 1752, Lock then brought out nothing new until 1769. This was the period when Chippendale was working on the three editions of his *Director*; and though it has never been suggested that Lock made any of the designs for this work – a claim which has, however, been made for his collaborator Copland (see page 43) – it is not unlikely that Chippendale derived his idea of the rococo style from Lock, its most gifted exponent in England.

Lock was the first English artist to master the difficult French convention, and for more than ten years before the publication of Chippendale's *Director* his engraved designs for rococo furniture were the only ones of their kind in this country. A comparison between his designs and those of François Cuvilliés suggests that he had studied French models more carefully than most of his fellow artists (compare Nos. **49–51** with Nos. **354–356**). But he was far from being a slavish imitator, and having imbued himself with the spirit of the rococo, he applied the style to serve his own fancy, handling it with assurance and that air of brilliant improvization without which it cannot succeed. His manner of drawing, swift, spontaneous and fluid, was perfectly adapted to his theme. He clearly felt a natural sympathy for the rococo, and when at the end of his career he adopted the neo-classical style, some of the spirit went out of his work. His *New Book of Pier Frames* was one of the first pattern books to illustrate the new manner, but it is insipid stuff compared with the lively *capricci* of his pioneering youth. Some of his later unpublished drawings, a few of which are reproduced here, have more life in them, but not as much as the rococo designs of his heyday.

See also pages 13–14, and Clouston, pages 174–188; Kimball and Donnell, vol. I, pages 115–154.

48. Two side-tables. About 1740. Pencil. $8\frac{3}{4}$ in. × $6\frac{7}{8}$ in. From the George Lock Collection (Lock Album). 2848.98.

Note: A table formerly at Ditchley House and now at Temple Newsam House (Leeds Art Gallery) corresponds with the lower design and may have been made by Lock. It is illustrated in Edwards and Jourdain, plate 82.

49. Two designs (on one plate) from *Six Tables*, 1746. Etching. $10\frac{3}{8}$ in. × 7 in. 27811.5.

50. A design from *Six Tables*, 1746. Etching. 7 in. × $11\frac{3}{8}$ in. 27811.2.

51. A design from *Six Sconces*, 1744 (2nd edition 1768). Etching. $9\frac{1}{4}$ in. × $6\frac{1}{4}$ in. 27811.6.

52. An overmantel mirror with chimney-piece, and a wall mirror. From *A New Book of Ornaments*, 1752 (with H. Copland). Etching. $9\frac{7}{8}$ in. × 7 in. E.5051–1907.

53. Designs for two clock cases, a picture frame and a bracket. From *A New Book of Ornaments*, 1752 (with H. Copland). Etching. $9\frac{7}{8}$ in. × 7 in. E.5058–1907.

54. A candle-stand, a girandole and part of a frieze. From *A New Book of Ornaments*, 1752 (with H. Copland). Etching. $9\frac{7}{8}$ in. × 7 in. E.5054–1907.

55. A pier table and a picture frame. From *A New Book of Ornaments*, 1752 (with H. Copland). Etching. $9\frac{7}{8}$ in. × 7 in. E.5056–1907.

56. A girandole. About 1750. Pen and ink and wash. $10\frac{5}{8}$ in. × $5\frac{1}{4}$ in. From the George Lock Collection (Lock Album). 2848.88.

57. A girandole. About 1750. Pen and ink and wash. 10 in. × $5\frac{3}{8}$ in. From the George Lock Collection. 2553.

58. A girandole. About 1750. Pen and ink and wash. $11\frac{1}{2}$ in. × $4\frac{3}{4}$ in. From the George Lock Collection. 2550.

59. A girandole. About 1750. Pen and ink and wash. $10\frac{1}{2}$ in. × $5\frac{1}{4}$ in. From the George Lock Collection. 2555.

60. A girandole. About 1750. Pen and ink and wash. 12 in. × $5\frac{1}{2}$ in. From the George Lock Collection. 2554.

61. A console table, entitled 'A table in y^e Tapestry Room', with a memorandum of the time spent on the carving and joinery by Lock and other craftsmen, and of the wages due. 89 days were devoted to the job; the joiners' wages amounted to £1.5.0 and the carvers' to £21.0.0. About 1755. Pen and ink. $3\frac{1}{8}$ in. × $2\frac{1}{4}$ in. From the George Lock Collection. 2602.

62. A lantern, entitled 'Lanton in y^e Grand Stare Case', with a memorandum of the time spent on the task by Lock and other craftsmen and of the wages due. About 1755. Pen and ink and wash. $3\frac{3}{8}$ in. × $2\frac{1}{2}$ in. From the George Lock Collection. 2615.

63. A mirror frame. About 1760. Pen and ink and wash. $13\frac{1}{2}$ in. × 4 in. From the George Lock Collection. 2558.

64. A mirror for a royal palace. About 1760. Decorated with a royal crown and the cipher G.R. Pen and ink. $13\frac{5}{8}$ in. × $4\frac{1}{2}$ in. From the George Lock Collection. 2565.

65. A mirror frame. About 1760. Pen and ink and wash. $14\frac{1}{8}$ in. × $5\frac{7}{8}$ in. From the George Lock Collection. 2590.

66. A mirror frame. About 1760. Pen and ink and wash. $14\frac{7}{8}$ in. × $5\frac{7}{8}$ in. From the George Lock Collection. 2583.

67. A pier table and looking glass. About 1760. Pen and ink and wash. $15\frac{1}{2}$ in. × $3\frac{1}{2}$ in. From the George Lock Collection. 2584.

68. An oval mirror. About 1760. Pencil, pen and ink and wash. $8\frac{3}{8}$ in. × $2\frac{5}{8}$ in. From the George Lock Collection (Lock Album). 2848.46.

69. A pier table and looking glass. About 1760. Pen and ink and wash. $14\frac{3}{8}$ in. × 4 in. 2589.

For other designs by Lock see also Nos. **251–256**.

GEORGE BICKHAM, the Elder, c. 1684–1769

Engraver and writing-master. He published a number of portraits and several books on penmanship. The design for a mirror reproduced here is stated in the imprint to be after P. Babel, the French artist, but it bears little resemblance to his work, and is probably a free adaptation by Bickham. It appears to be his only experiment in this field.

70. A mirror frame in the French style. Lettered: 'G. Bickham according to Act of Parliament. P. Babel Invent. 1752'. Etching 9½ in. × 7⅞ in.
29067D.

THOMAS CHIPPENDALE, c. 1718-1779

Chippendale was a native of Otley in Yorkshire and was descended from a family of joiners and carpenters. Nothing is known of his early years until 1748, when he married his first wife in London, where he had presumably established himself as a cabinet-maker. In 1753 he took a house in St. Martin's Lane, where several leading cabinet-makers had their premises; and in that street he remained in business for the rest of his life, at first in partnership with James Rannie, who died in 1766, and afterwards, from 1771, with Thomas Haig. After Chippendale's death Haig carried on the business with Chippendale's son Thomas. Among the firm's most important commissions was the furnishing of Nostell Priory for Sir Rowland Winn (1766-1770) and of Harewood House for Sir Edwin Lascelles (1771-1775). The furniture at Harewood, probably the finest he ever made, is not in the rococo manner usually associated with his name, but in the neo-classical style introduced by Robert Adam.

Chippendale was certainly one of the foremost cabinet-makers of his day, but his fame rests largely on his great book of designs, published in 1754 under the title:

The Gentleman and Cabinet-Maker's Director. Being a large collection of the most elegant and useful designs of household furniture in the Gothic, Chinese and modern taste: including a great variety of book-cases for libraries or private rooms, commodes, library and writing-tables, buroes, breakfast-tables, dressing and china-tables, china-cases, hanging-shelves, tea-chests, trays, fire-screens, chairs, settees, sopha's, beds, presses and cloaths-chests, pier-glass sconces, slab frames, brackets, candle-stands, clock-cases frets, and other ornaments. To which is prefixed a short explanation of the five orders of architecture, and rules of perspective; with proper directions for executing the most difficult pieces, the mouldings being exhibited at large, and the dimensions of each design specified: the whole comprehended in one hundred and sixty copper-plates, neatly engraved, calculated to improve and refine the present taste, and suited to the fancy and circumstances of persons in all degrees of life.
Dulcique animos novitate tenebo. Ovid.
Ludentis speciem dabit & torquebitur. Hor.
By Thomas Chippendale of St. Martin's Lane, cabinet-maker. London, printed for the author, and sold at his house in St. Martin's Lane. MDCCLIV. Also by T. Osborne, bookseller in Gray's Inn; H. Piers, bookseller, in Holborn; R. Sayer, printseller, in Fleet-street; J. Swan, near Northumberland House, in the Strand. At Edinburgh, by Messrs. Hamilton and Balfour: and at Dublin, by Mr. John Smith, on the Blind-Quay.

The book, a large folio, contains a dedication to the Earl of Northumberland, a preface, a list of subscribers, a commentary on the designs and 161 plates, including two which are both numbered 25. They are dated 1753 and 1754, and most of them were engraved by Matthew Darly, with a few by T. and J. S. Müller.

A second edition was published in 1755. There were no changes, apart from a few minor corrections in the numbering of the plates, and three alterations to the title-page, viz: 'The Second Edition' was inserted after 'Cabinet-Maker' and before 'London': 'Printed by J. Haberkorn, in Gerrard-Street' was inserted between 'London' and 'for the Author': 'MDCCLIV' was omitted and MDCCLV added at the bottom of the page.

The third edition was published in 1762, and the title-page reads:

The Gentleman and Cabinet-Maker's Director; being a large collection of the most elegant and useful designs of household furniture, in the most fashionable taste. Including a great variety of chairs, sofas, beds, and couches; china-tables, dressing-tables, shaving-tables, bason-stands, and teakettle-stands; frames for marble-slabs, bureau-dressing-tables, and commodes; writing-tables, and library tables; library book-cases, organ-cases for private rooms, or churches, desks, and book-cases; dressing and writing-tables with book-cases, toilets, cabinets, and cloaths-presses; china-cases, china-shelves, and book-shelves; candle-stands, terms for busts, stands for china jars, and pedestals; cisterns for water, lanthorns, and chandeliers; fire-screens, brackets, and clock-cases; pier-glasses, and table-frames; girandoles, chimney-pieces, and picture-frames; stove-grates, boarders, frets, chinese-railing, and brass-work, for furniture. And other ornaments. To which is prefixed, a short explanation of the five orders of architecture . . . The whole comprehended in two hundred copper-plates, neatly engraved. Calculated to improve and refine the present taste, and suited to the fancy and circumstances of persons in all degrees of life. By Thomas Chippendale, cabinet-maker and upholsterer, in St. Martin's Lane, London.
The third edition. London: printed for the author

and sold at his house, in St. Martin's Lane. Also by T. Becket and P. A. De Hondt, in the Strand. MDCCLXII.

(Engravers: Darly, T. and J. S. Müller; B. Clowes, I. Taylor, J. Hulett, W. Foster, Hemerick, Morris.)

Only 95 out of the 161 plates of the first edition were retained and 105 new plates were added, making 200 in all. Up to 12 alternative plates are found in some copies, numbered 25, 36, 45, 49, 67, 68, 153, 159, 167, 171, 179, 187. Number 68 is the same as number 47 in the first edition, while the other alternatives are mostly dated 1759 and 1760. The plates substituted for them in most copies, on the other hand, are all dated 1762, except two dated 1761 and one with no date. This suggests that the book was revised soon after the first printing and twelve more recent plates inserted in place of the earlier ones.

The 105 new plates reveal no radical change of style. Some of the simpler designs, like Nos. **71–73**, were omitted in favour of more elaborate ones, the most drastically revised section being that concerned with mirrors and girandoles, all of which, with one exception, were renewed. At the same time the scope of the work was enlarged to embrace categories which had not been included in the first edition, such as hall chairs, wash stands and shaving tables, chamber organs, cisterns and pedestals, lanterns and chandeliers, chimney-pieces, grates and overmantel mirrors.

A French edition of the *Director* was published under the title:

Le Guide du Tapissier, de l'Ébéniste et de tous ceux qui travaillent en meubles . . . troisième édition . . . Londres . . . T. A. Becket and P. A. de Hondt 1762. (A copy was sold at Christie's on May 1st, 1907, with the Massey-Manwaring collection.)

In his preface Chippendale states that some of the designs, especially those in the Gothic and Chinese manner, were criticized as 'so many specious drawings impossible to be work'd off by any Mechanic whatsoever'; 'I am confident', Chippendale wrote in reply 'that I can convince all Noblemen, Gentlemen and Others, who will favour me with their Commands, that every Design in the Book can be improved . . . in the execution of it, by their most obedient servant Thomas Chippendale'. His claim could probably have been justified. Yet it is clear from the notes on the plates that not all the designs had actually been carried out by the firm; for of a Gothic bookcase, plate 75 in the first edition, Chippendale observes: 'This design is perhaps one of the best of its kind, and would give me great pleasure to see it executed'; and of the ribband back chairs in plate 16 he writes: 'the Chair on the left hand has been executed from this design, which had an excellent effect . . . I make no doubt but the other two will give the same content, if properly handled in the execution'.

Chippendale also contributed a small number of designs to a book published in 1760 by a Society of Upholsterers (see page 51). Apart from these and the 277 plates contained in the first and third editions of the *Director*, a large number of designs made by or for Chippendale are extant in the shape of original drawings, including many designs for plates in the *Director*. The view generally accepted among recent writers on the subject is that few, if any, of these drawings are by Chippendale himself, but were mostly made by Lock and Copland, two artists whom he is presumed to have employed for the purpose, the theory being that Copland was responsible for the designs for all carver's pieces published in the *Director*, that is to say for the majority of the plates, while Lock's task was to design furniture to order for the firm's private clients.

This theory was originally advanced, in two closely reasoned articles, by Mr Fiske Kimball and Miss Edna Donnell, who were the first to subject the Chippendale drawings to a critical examination, and it is impossible to discuss the authorship of these designs without taking their arguments into account. (See Kimball and Donnell, vol. I, *passim*.)

The drawings involved are divided between the Victoria and Albert Museum and the Metropolitan Museum in New York. Those in the Metropolitan Museum are contained in two folio scrapbooks and comprise 180 designs, including drawings for nearly all the plates of the first edition, with many for the third, and about 25 other sketches, several of which are attributed to Lock.

The material in the Victoria and Albert Museum was acquired in three separate lots as follows:

1. Nos. 2547–2624. 78 sheets bought in 1862 from George Lock of Edinburgh, the grandson of Matthias Lock the carver. This group of designs has already been described above in the section on Lock (page 39), and it will suffice here to recall that 46 of them may confidently be ascribed to Lock, while the remainder, numbering 32 (Nos. 2593–2624), were attributed to Chippendale at the time when they were bought, and they include 7 original designs for the 3rd edition of the *Director* (viz. plate 30, No. 2616: plate 153, No. 2608: plate 155, No. 2601: plate 158, No. 2623: plate 159, No. 2624: plate 173, No. 2598: plate 187, No. 2594).

2. Nos. 2848.1–168. A folio scrapbook, likewise acquired, in the following year, from George Lock. Its contents have also been described above (page 39). Most of the drawings are by Lock, but there are two designs for plates in the *Director* which appear to be by the same hand as the drawings attributed to Chippendale above, namely:

(*a*) 2848.45. Part of the design for plate 150 in the *Director*, 3rd edition. It represents the pedestal in the centre of the top row in the engraving.

(*b*) Part of the original design for plate 194 in the same work, representing a border for paper hangings (top part of the design only). It is inscribed in Chippendale's hand with the title etc, and Lock's name has been added in pencil, possibly in his own hand. The drawing is so slight and fragmentary that it is impossible to come to any firm decision about its authorship.

3. Nos. D.696–839–1906. A collection of 144 drawings, of unknown provenance, bought from a dealer in 1906. The majority are by the same hand as those originally attributed to Chippendale in section 1 above, and eight are original designs for the third edition of the *Director* (viz. plate 14, No. D.696: plate 16, No. D.697: plate 67, No. D.698: plate 111, No. D.699: plate 112, No. D.700: plate 118, No. D.701: plate 152, No. D.702: plate 179, No. D.703.) There are also three inked versions of sketch designs in the Metropolitan Museum, which may indicate that Chippendale began preparing a fourth edition of his *Director*, which was never published. The same collection contains Lock's design in ink (D.788) for the cartouche on the title-page of his *Six Tables*, 1746, and five designs for plates in pattern books compiled by other authors, viz.:

(*a*) *Household Furniture in Genteel Taste for the Year 1760 by a Society of Upholsterers*, plate 32 (No. **108**), and plates 75 and 100. (See page 51.)

(*b*) *Household Furniture* by Ince and Mayhew, plate 32 (No. **149**). This drawing is clearly by William Ince.

(*c*) *One hundred and fifty new designs*, by Thomas Johnson, plate 19 (No. **146**). This drawing, quite different from the others in handling, may confidently be ascribed to Johnson.

Together, these three groups of drawings in the Victoria and Albert Museum provide numerous incontrovertible examples of Matthias Lock's style of drawing; and the fact that his drawings were mingled with others from Chippendale's workshop suggests that Lock was closely associated with Chippendale and perhaps employed by him, a hypothesis more fully discussed above (see page 39).

Lock's work having been separated from the rest, there remains a considerable group of drawings all manifestly by the same hand, including some fifteen original designs for the *Director*. The latter are mostly inscribed in ink in Chippendale's hand with the legends which were afterwards engraved on the plates, that is to say with the title, plate number and engraver's name, and they are signed *T. Chippendale Invent. et delin.* The authenticity of the signatures is not disputed. Moreover, Chippendale gives us clearly to understand in his preface and elsewhere that he was the author of the designs. 'I frankly confess', he writes, 'that in executing many of the drawings, my pencil has but faintly copied out those images that my fancy suggested', and again, in the commentary on the plates in the first edition, he writes of plate 111: 'I had a peculiar pleasure in re-touching and finishing this design'. What reasons are there for doubting Chippendale's statements?

Mr Fiske Kimball and Miss Donnell advance two main arguments against him. In the first place they contend that Chippendale, the busy tradesman, could hardly have found the time to draw with his own hand over 300 designs minutely finished for publication. And, in the second place, they maintain that the hand of Copland, Lock's collaborator in *A New Book of Ornaments*, can be recognized in the designs for the *Director* and in the other similar drawings. This claim is seriously weakened by the fact that there is not a single drawing known which can be attributed to Copland with any confidence. Nor does his engraved work, restricted as it is in quantity and scope, afford a convincing basis for attributing to him a collection of drawings for furniture. For apart from *A New Book of Ornaments*, which he published in partnership with Lock in 1752, Copland's only certain works are the 10 plates of engraved ornament, mainly shields, which he published in a book of the same title in 1746, and this volume contains no furniture designs. For want of more conclusive evidence, Mr Fiske Kimball and Miss Donnell are obliged to compare Copland's engraved ornament with approximately similar ornament in the furniture designs, and they assert that we have only to place a drawing in the Metropolitan Museum, showing festoons of flowers, beside a pendant from Copland's *New Book of Ornaments* to recognize the hand of Copland. They also point to certain 'sprays of spiny grasses' which, they claim, are common to Copland's engraved designs and to the *Director* drawings. This is all the stylistic evidence they offer, and it is unconvincing. Comparing the style of an engraving with that of a drawing must inevitably be an uncertain method of determining authorship. And in this case the comparison has not been carried far enough; for while certain small similarities have been noted, important differences have been overlooked. For example, a prevalent mannerism in the *Director* is the use of 'icicles' or drops of water as a border. This motif was often used by the ornamentalists of the day to indicate water spilling over the rim of a shell or basin – a favourite *rocaille* theme – and is thus correctly employed by Copland in two of his plates. In the *Director*, on the other hand, the ornament, which recurs with mechanical regularity, is handled quite differently, being entirely divorced from its appropriate setting and serving merely as a border for the lower edge of a scroll or band, sometimes even as a foot for a heavy commode (cf. Nos. **75** and **76**). There is nothing like this in Copland's engravings; nor in his designs is there anything analogous to the Gothic and Chinese paling and fretwork which are essential ingredients of the *Director* style. (See pages 16 and 19.)

If comparisons are to be made between Copland's work and the *Director*, six designs which may be attributed to Copland in Manwaring's *Chair-Maker's Guide* ought to be taken into consideration. One of these plates is signed *Copland fecit* and the other five are patently by the same hand. Admittedly, the form of the signature does not make it clear whether Copland was the author of the design or only the engraver. But the plates in his *New Book of Ornaments* are signed in the same way, and there is therefore a good reason for ascribing the designs to him. They are the only furniture designs which can be attributed to him with a fair degree of probability, and the two examples reproduced here (Nos. **181** and **182**) show that they are utterly unlike anything in the *Director*. Yet they are not discussed by Mr Kimball and Miss Donnell.

The evidence of style is thus on the whole against Copland. Nor is there any external evidence in his favour, beyond the fact that Copland, after publishing a small book of ornament under his own name in 1746 and another with Lock in 1752, published no other books after that date; from which it might be inferred that, like Lock, he was working for Chippendale. This assumption can neither be proved nor disproved, for the simple reason that absolutely nothing is recorded of Copland after 1752, and for all we know, he may have been dead.

As to the argument that Chippendale was too busy to make three hundred minutely finished drawings with his own hand, that is a pure supposition. The large collection of drawings by Linnell which the Museum possesses proves that an eighteenth-century cabinet-maker might well be an accomplished draughtsman and even find the time to exercise his gift; and there is no reason to suppose that Chippendale was professionally less well qualified than Linnell. Indeed, evidence that Chippendale was capable of making his own designs has lately been published; for in a letter to his client Sir Rowland Winn, dated July 19th, 1767, Chippendale writes: 'As soon as I had got to Mr Lascelles and looked over the whole of ye house (i.e. Harewood House) I found that I should want a many designs. I knowing that I had time enough I went to York to do them, but before I could get all don I was taken very ill of a Quinsey...' (From an article by R. W. Symonds entitled *Chippendale Furniture* at *Nostell Priory* in *Country Life*, October 3rd, 1952, p. 1028). The grammar may be weak, but the sense is plain and goes far to dispose of the notion that Chippendale could not make his own designs, particularly when it is remembered that the furniture which Chippendale made for Harewood House is outstanding for the excellence of the design.

To sum up, we have on the one hand Chippendale's own assertion that he drew the designs himself, his autograph signatures and inscriptions on the original drawings, and the proof that he was capable of designing furniture for a house like Harewood. On the other hand, we have an obscure artist of whom nothing is known except that he published a small book of ornament in 1746, collaborated in another in 1752, and engraved six designs for chairs in a style which has nothing in common with the *Director*. On the scanty evidence brought forward against Chippendale and in favour of Copland, it seems as impossible to convict the one of deliberate deceit as to credit the other with the authorship of several hundred furniture designs. We have, therefore, retained the traditional attribution of the drawings concerned to Chippendale, who thus emerges as a gifted and original designer instead of the unscrupulous exploiter of other men's ideas, which has been the part assigned to him by most modern authorities.

See also pages 14–21.
Oliver Brackett, *Thomas Chippendale*, 1924.
Kimball and Donnell, *passim*.

71. 'A cloths press' and a 'cloths chest'. Plate 96 in the *Director*, 1st edition, 1754. (Not in the 3rd edition.) Engraved by J. S. Müller. $8\frac{7}{8}$ in. × $13\frac{3}{4}$ in.

72. 'A library book-case'. Plate 60 in the *Director*, 1st edition, 1754. (Not in the 3rd edition.) Dated 1753. Engraving. $8\frac{7}{8}$ in. × $13\frac{3}{4}$ in.

73. A chest of drawers in two stages, or tallboy. Plate 86 in the *Director*, 1st edition, 1754. (Not in the 3rd edition.) Engraving. $8\frac{7}{8}$ in. × $13\frac{3}{4}$ in.

CATALOGUE AND NOTES

74. A 'cloaths press'. Plate 102 in the *Director*, 1st edition, 1754, and plate 129 in the 3rd edition. Dated 1753 and engraved by M. Darly. 8⅜ in. × 13¾ in.

75. 'A side-board table'. Plate 40 in the *Director*, 1st edition, 1754. (Not in the 3rd edition.) Dated 1753 and engraved by J. S. Müller. 8¾ in. × 13¾ in.

76. 'A French commode table'. Plate 46 in the *Director*, 1st edition, 1754. (Not in the 3rd edition.) Dated 1753 and engraved by M. Darly. 8⅞ in. × 13¾ in.

77. Two long case clocks. Plate 135 in the *Director*, 1st edition, 1754. (Not in the 3rd edition.) Engraved by M. Darly. 8⅞ in. × 13¾ in.

78. Two 'pier glass frames'. Plate 141 in the *Director*, 1st edition, 1754. (Not in the 3rd edition.) Engraved by M. Darly. 8⅞ in. × 13¾ in.

79. Two 'pier glass frames'. Plate 146 in the *Director*, 1st edition, 1754. (Not in the 3rd edition.) Engraved by M. Darly. 8⅞ in. × 13¾ in.

80. Two 'table clock cases'. Plate 138 in the *Director*, 1st edition, 1754, and Plate 165 in the 3rd edition, 1762. Engraved by M. Darly. 8⅞ in. × 13¾ in.

81. Two 'breakfast tables'. Plate 33 in the *Director*, 1st edition, 1754, and plate 53 in the 3rd edition, 1762. Engraved by M. Darly. 8⅞ in. × 13¾ in.

82. Three 'Chinese chairs'. Plate 23 in the *Director*, 1st edition, 1754. (Not in the 3rd edition.) Dated 1753 and engraved by M. Darly. 8⅞ in. × 13¾ in.

83. Three 'ribband back chairs'. Plate 16 in the *Director*, 1st edition, 1754, and plate 15 in the 3rd edition, 1762. Engraved by M. Darly. 8⅞ in. × 13¾ in.

Note: Of these ribband back chairs Chippendale observes that they, 'if I may speak without vanity, are the best I have ever seen (or perhaps have ever been made)'. He states that the one on the left 'has been executed from this design, which had an excellent effect'. A set of chairs in the Museum (W.65A–C–1935) and another single chair (W.64–1926) have backs closely modelled on the two left-hand designs.

84. Three 'Gothick chairs'. Plate 21 in the *Director*, 1st edition, 1754. (Not in the 3rd edition.) Engraved by M. Darly. 8⅞ in. × 13¾ in.

85. Three 'Gothick chairs'. Plate 22 in the *Director*, 1st edition, 1754, and plate 25 in the 3rd edition, 1762. Engraved by M. Darly. 8⅞ in. × 13¾ in.

86. Two 'French chairs'. Plate 17 in the *Director*, 1st edition, 1754. (Not in the 3rd edition.) Engraved by M. Darly and dated 1753. 8⅞ in. × 13⅞ in.

87. Two 'buroe tables'. Plate 42 in the *Director*, 1st edition, 1754. (Not in the 3rd edition.) Engraved by M. Darly and dated 1753. 8⅞ in. × 13¾ in.

88. 'A desk and bookcase'. Plate 80 in the *Director*, 1st edition, 1754, and plate 109 in the 3rd edition. Engraved by M. Darly and dated 1753. 13½ in. × 8⅞ in.

Note: Chippendale states that this design is 'in the Chinese taste', but there is little that is Chinese about it apart from the 'pagoda' finial, hung with bells.

89. 'A chest of drawers with sliding shelves for cloaths'. Plate 88 in the *Director*, 1st edition, 1754, and plate 113 in the 3rd edition, 1762. Engraved by J. S. Müller and dated 1753. 8⅞ in. × 13⅝ in.

90. A cabinet 'in the Gothic style'. Plate 94 in the *Director*, 1st edition, 1754, and plate 124 in the 3rd edition, 1762. Engraved by M. Darly. 8⅞ in. × 14 in.

91. 'A library table'. Plate 58 in the *Director*, 1st edition, 1754, and plate 85 in the 3rd edition, 1762. Dated 1753 and engraved by J. S. Müller. 8⅞ in. × 13¾ in.

92. Two 'French commodes'. Plate 68 in the *Director*, 3rd edition, 1762. Engraved by M. Darly. 8⅞ in. × 13¾ in.

Note: Chippendale observes that 'the ornaments may be brass'. The right-hand commode was clearly designed under the influence of the Louis XIV style.

93. Shelves for china. Plate 141 in the *Director*, 3rd edition, 1762. Dated 1761 and engraved by M. Darly. 8⅞ in. × 13⅞ in.

94. 'A Gothic library bookcase'. Plate 89 in the *Director*, 3rd edition, 1762. Dated 1760 and engraved by I. Taylor. 8⅞ in. × 13⅞ in.

Note: A bookcase in the Museum (W.29–1951) was made from this design.

95. 'A toilet table', i.e. a dressing table. Design for plate 118 in the *Director*, 3rd edition, 1762. Signed *T. Chippendale* and inscribed in Chippendale's hand with title and plate number. Pen and ink and wash. 13¼ in. × 5⅞ in. D.701–1906.

96. Two alternative designs for pier glasses. Design for plate 173 in the *Director*, 3rd edition, 1762. Signed *T. Chippendale* and inscribed in Chippendale's hand with title and plate number. Pen and ink and wash. $13\frac{1}{4}$ in. × $7\frac{1}{2}$ in. From the George Lock Collection. 2598.

97. Two fire screens. Part of the design for plate 158 in the *Director*, 3rd edition, 1762. Inscribed in Chippendale's hand with plate number and title. Pen and ink and wash. Size of sheet $8\frac{1}{2}$ in. × $8\frac{1}{4}$ in. From the George Lock Collection. 2623.

98. A picture frame. Design for plate 187 in the *Director*, 3rd edition, 1762. Signed and inscribed in Chippendale's hand with plate number and title. Pen and ink and wash. 9 in. × $12\frac{7}{8}$ in. From the George Lock Collection. 2594.

99. 'A desk and bookcase'. Design for plate 111 in the *Director*, 3rd edition, 1762. Signed and inscribed in Chippendale's hand with title, etc. Pen and ink and wash. $12\frac{1}{8}$ in. × $5\frac{3}{8}$ in. D.699–1906.

100. Three chairs. Design for plate 14 in the *Director*, 3rd edition, 1762. Pen and ink and wash. $6\frac{1}{8}$ in. × $11\frac{1}{4}$ in. D.696–1906.

101. Six chair backs. Design for plate 16 in the *Director*, 3rd edition, 1762. Signed and inscribed in Chippendale's hand with title, etc. Pen and ink and wash. $6\frac{3}{8}$ in. × $10\frac{3}{8}$ in. D.699–1906.

102. A sofa. Pen and ink and wash. About 1760. $6\frac{3}{4}$ in. × $9\frac{7}{8}$ in. From the George Lock Collection. 2597.

103. An arm-chair. About 1760. Pen and ink and wash. $6\frac{3}{4}$ in. × $4\frac{3}{4}$ in. 2599.

104. A glazed china cabinet. About 1760. Pen and ink and wash. $11\frac{1}{2}$ in. × $6\frac{1}{4}$ in. D.708–1906.

105. A bedstead. About 1760. Pen and ink and wash. $11\frac{3}{4}$ in. × $6\frac{3}{4}$ in. D.711–1906.

106. Two commodes. About 1760. Pen and ink and wash. Size of sheet 11 in. × $7\frac{1}{2}$ in. D.720–1906.

107. A commode in the French style. About 1760. Pen and ink and wash. $3\frac{1}{8}$ in. × $3\frac{3}{4}$ in. D.728–1906.

108. A library table. Design for plate 10 in *Household Furniture in Genteel Taste for the year 1760 by a Society of Upholsterers, Cabinet-Makers, etc.* (plate 32 in the 2nd edition) (see page 51). Pen and ink and wash. $3\frac{5}{8}$ in. × $4\frac{5}{8}$ in. D.721–1906.

109. A chandelier. About 1760. Pen and ink and wash. $9\frac{3}{4}$ in. × $10\frac{1}{4}$ in. From the George Lock Collection. 2606.

110. A cabinet or bookcase. About 1760. Pen and ink and wash. $6\frac{5}{8}$ in. × $7\frac{3}{8}$ in. D.709–1906.

111. A mirror with Chinese motifs. About 1760. Pen and ink and wash. $10\frac{1}{2}$ in. × $2\frac{5}{8}$ in. D.763–1906.

112. A mirror with Chinese figures. About 1760. Pen and ink and wash. $8\frac{3}{8}$ in. × $2\frac{3}{8}$ in. D.775–1906.

113. A console table and mirror. About 1760. Pen and ink and wash $16\frac{3}{4}$ in. × $7\frac{3}{8}$ in. D.831–1906.

114. A console table and mirror. About 1760. Pen and ink and wash. $12\frac{5}{8}$ in. × $4\frac{3}{8}$ in. D.704–1906.

115. A mirror. About 1765–1770. Pen and ink and wash. $9\frac{7}{8}$ in. × 4 in. D.738–1906.

116. A mirror. About 1750. Pen and ink and wash. $6\frac{5}{8}$ in. × $3\frac{1}{4}$ in. D.757–1906.

117. A mirror. About 1765–1770. Pen and ink and wash. $7\frac{3}{4}$ in. × $3\frac{1}{2}$ in. D.741–1906.

118. A candle-stand. About 1760. Pen and ink and wash. $6\frac{7}{8}$ in. × 4 in. From the George Lock Collection. 2609.

119. A candle-stand. Pen and ink and wash. About 1760. $7\frac{1}{4}$ in. × $2\frac{7}{8}$ in. From the George Lock Collection. 2603.

120. A candle-stand. Pen and ink and wash. About 1760. $6\frac{1}{2}$ in. × $2\frac{1}{4}$ in. From the George Lock Collection. 2612.

121. A pedestal and urn. About 1770. Pen and ink and wash. $6\frac{7}{8}$ in. × 4 in. From the George Lock Collection. 2605.

Note: This is the only design by Chippendale in the Museum collection which has a pronounced neo-classical bias.

122. Two designs for 'Chinese railing'. Plate 157 in the *Director*, 1st edition, 1754. (Not in the 3rd edition, 1762.) Engraved by M. Darly. $8\frac{7}{8}$ in. × $13\frac{3}{4}$ in.

Note: Chippendale describes these designs as 'very proper for gardens and other places, and may be converted (by the ingenious workman) to other uses'. Among these other uses were railings round the tops of tea tables, trays, cabinets, etc, and lattice work doors for breakfast tables (cf. No. **81**), etc. Like the 'Gothic fret' illustrated in No. **123**, this type of Chinese railing was a common and characteristic feature of mid-eighteenth century English furniture and is not found elsewhere in Europe. See also pages 16 and 17.

123. Three designs for 'Gothick frets'. Plate 156 in the *Director*, 1st edition, 1754, and plate 196 in the 3rd edition, 1762. Engraved by M. Darly. $8\frac{7}{8}$ in. $\times 13\frac{3}{4}$ in.

Note: These frets were used to enrich friezes, etc. See also page 19.

For another design by Chippendale see also no. **170**.

John Crunden, c. 1740–1828

Architect. He is believed to have been a pupil or assistant of Henry Holland the Elder, and for a time he was District Surveyor for the Parishes of Paddington, St. Pancras and St. Luke, Chelsea. He was the architect of Boodle's Club, St. James's Street, London. He published a number of handbooks for builders and carpenters, including:

(i) *The Joyner and Cabinet-Maker's Darling or Pocket Director, containing sixty different designs . . . forty of which are Gothic, Chinese, mosaic, and ornamental frets, proper for friezes, . . . book-cases, tea tables, tea stands, trays . . . The whole designed and engraved by John Crunden, architect. London: . . . sold by Henry Webley, in Holborn . . . MDCCLXV.*

(ii) *The Carpenter's Companion for Chinese Railings and Gates. Containing thirty-three . . . designs, very proper to be executed at the entrance or round Chinese temples, summer houses . . . on sixteen copper plates, from the original drawings of J. H. Morris, carpenter, and J. Crunden. London: Printed for Henry Webley, in Holborn. MDCCLXV.*

(For an account of 'Gothic frets', etc., see pages 16–19.)

124. Two 'frets proper for tea stands, trays and fenders'. Plate 9 in *The Joyner and Cabinet-Maker's Darling*, 1765. Etching. $4\frac{1}{2}$ in. $\times 7\frac{3}{8}$ in.

125. A 'Gothic' and a 'Chinese' fret. Plate 11 in *The Joyner and Cabinet-Maker's Darling*, 1765. Etching. $4\frac{1}{2}$ in. $\times 7\frac{3}{8}$ in.

William Halfpenny, d. 1755
(alias Michael Hoare)

Architect and carpenter. He was also the author of many architectural pattern books designed to assist the carpenter and the master builder, published between 1722 and 1755. The majority are concerned with buildings on a modest scale, such as parsonages, farm houses, inns, etc, rather than with architecture in the grand style. Some of his designs in the Chinese and Gothic taste are among the earliest published. There are a few designs for garden furniture among them.

See Colvin for a list of his published works.

126. 'A garden seat in the Chinese taste'. Plate 39 in *New Designs for Chinese Temples*, part I, 1750. Engraved by Parr. 7 in. $\times 7\frac{5}{8}$ in.

127. 'A chair in the Chinese taste'. Plate 46 in *New Designs for Chinese Temples*, part I, 1750. Engraving. 7 in. $\times 3\frac{3}{4}$ in.

Matthew Darly, Working c. 1750–1778

See also page 37 and Nos. **46–47**, **180** and **257–258**.

128. Two candle-stands. Plate 27 in *A New Book of Chinese Designs*, 1754. Signed 'Edw^{ds} et Darly Inv^t et Sculp . . . 1754'. Etching. $10\frac{1}{8}$ in. $\times 7\frac{1}{2}$ in.
E.6528–1905.

129. Three wall brackets. Plate 67 *ibidem*. Signed and dated as No. **128**. Etching. $7\frac{1}{2}$ in. $\times 10\frac{1}{8}$ in.
E.6566–1905.

130. A 'Chinese' bedstead. Plate 10 *ibidem*. Signed and dated as No. **128**. Etching. $10\frac{1}{8}$ in. $\times 7\frac{1}{2}$ in.
E.6511–1905.

131. A mirror with decoration in the 'Chinese' taste. Plate 68 *ibidem*. Signed and dated as No. **128**. Etching. $10\frac{1}{8}$ in. $\times 7\frac{1}{2}$ in. E.6567–1905.

132. A fire-side stool and set of chimney furniture in the 'Chinese' taste. Plate 64 *ibidem*. Signed and dated as No. **128**. Etching. $7\frac{1}{2}$ in. $\times 10\frac{1}{8}$ in.
E.6563–1905.

133. A garden table with an umbrella. Plate 66 *ibidem*. Signed and dated as No. **128**. Etching. $10\frac{1}{8}$ in. $\times 7\frac{1}{2}$ in. E.6565–1905.

134. A garden chair made of roots of trees. Plate 86 *ibidem*. Etching. $10\frac{1}{8}$ in. $\times 7\frac{1}{2}$ in. E.6585–1905.

Sir William Chambers, 1723–1796

One of the leading British architects of the century. He was born into a Scottish family settled in Sweden, and he began earning his living as a cadet in the service of the Swedish East Company, which sent him on a voyage to China. In 1749 he gave up the sea and devoted himself to architecture, studying for six years in Paris and Italy. He began practicing in England in 1755 and soon rose to the top of his profession, holding at different times various posts under the Crown. His best known public building is Somerset House, London (1776–1786). He was one of the few European artists of his day who had the opportunity of making a first-hand study of Chinese art, and the drawings which he made in Canton in his youth he afterwards published in a folio book entitled:

Designs of Chinese Buildings, Furniture, Dresses, Machines and Utensils . . . From the originals drawn in China by Mr. Chambers, Architect . . . To which is annexed a description of their temples, houses, gardens, &c. London . . . 1757.

(Engravers: P. Fourdrinier, P. Sandby, C. Grignion.)

A French edition was published in London the same year.

The book contains two plates showing various types of Chinese furniture, more accurately represented than in any other work of the period. They can hardly be considered original designs, but it is curious to compare them with the *chinoiseries* of other designers, and we have reproduced them here for that reason.

135. Designs of Chinese chairs and tables. Plate 13 in *Designs of Chinese Buildings, Furniture, etc*, 1757. Engraving. 18⅛ in. × 11 in.

136. Designs of Chinese furniture, including a sofa, tables, stands, etc. Plate 14 *ibidem*. Engraving. 18¼ in. × 11 in.

Thomas Johnson, Working c. 1755

'Carver, Teacher of Drawing and Modelling and author of a Book of Designs for Chimney pieces and other ornaments; and of several other pieces'. So he is described in Mortimer's *Universal Director* (1763). His first book was entitled:

Twelve Gerandoles. Published and sold by Thos. Johnson carver, in Queen Street, near 7 Dials, London . . . 1755.

(Engraver: W. Austin).

The following year he began publishing another series of designs for carver's pieces in monthly parts; and these were issued bound together in one volume in 1758. There was no title and the first page bears instead a dedication *To the Right Hon:ble Lord Blakeney, Grand President of the Antigallican Associations and the rest of the Brethren of that most Honourable Order*, and the legend *Sold by T. Johnson carver, At the Golden Boy, in Grafton St, St. Ann's Westminster . . . 1758.* (Engravers: B. Clowes and Jas. Kirk). The lettering is contained within a frame on which Britannia is seated, while, above, a winged genius sets fire with a torch to a fragment of *rocaille* and a scroll inscribed *French Paper Machee*. Some of the plates are dated 1756, others 1757.

A second edition was published in 1761 under the title:

One Hundred and Fifty New Designs, By Thos Johnson carver. Consisting of ceilings, chimney pieces, slab, glass & picture frames, stands for china &c, clock & watch cases, girondoles, brackets, grates, lanthorns, &c. &c. The whole well adapted for decorating all kinds of ornamental furniture, in the present taste. Engraved on 56 copper plates . . . Sold by Robert Sayer, at the Golden Buck, near Serjeants Inn, in Fleet Street, London, 1761.

It was issued in four parts with separate title-pages; and the plates were re-arranged and augmented by one (No. 48).

In 1760 Johnson apparently published another book of designs under the title:

A New Book of Ornaments by Thos. Johnson . . . 1760. Sold by the Proprietor at ye Golden Boy in Grafton Street . . . T. J. fecit.

But only the title-page appears to be extant. A few of the plates were republished by John Weale in 1835 and 1858 in a miscellaneous collection of eighteenth century designs entitled *Old English and French Ornaments*. Weale also reprinted Johnson's plates for *150 New Designs* in a book fraudulently entitled *Chippendale's One Hundred and Thirty-three Designs of Interior Decorations* (1834), deleting Johnson's name from every plate and substituting that of Chippendale.

According to Mr Kimball and Miss Donnell (vol. II, pp. 41–46) Johnson contributed eight designs to *Household Furniture in Genteel Taste . . . by a Society of Upholsterers* (described on page 51). The plates which they attribute to him, on stylistic grounds, are Nos. 60 and 93–99.

In the preface to his second collection of designs Johnson makes the usual declaration that 'the designs may all be performed by a Master of his Art: This again I assert with greater Confidence as I am well satisfied they can be executed by myself'. Some of the more elaborate designs involve carving of almost incredible intricacy. Nevertheless, there are still in existence a few objects carved after them, possibly by Johnson himself, and they go some way to substantiate his claim. Examples from Corsham Court and Hagley Hall are illustrated in Edwards and Jourdain, plates 74–77. There is also in the Museum a stand based on the right-hand design in No. **143**. This design is interesting because it shows that Johnson, despite his professed abhorrence of French fashions, was not above taking a hint from a French designer, François Cuvilliés, whose design for a stand carved with dolphins (No. **357**) was obviously the source of Johnson's idea. In fact, little of his work is free from Gallic influence, though he was not a close imitator and liked to add touches of his own. He was fond of introducing naturalistic scenes with human figures or animals into his compositions, and some of these, like the miller bearing a sack of corn up a ladder into his windmill (No. **138**), have a whimsical charm. The only drawing by him which survives (No. **146**) shows him to have been a fluent draughtsman.

See Kimball and Donnell, vols. I and II, *passim*.

137. A girandole. Plate from *Twelve Gerandoles*, 1755. Etching. 7½ in. × 4¼ in. E.3774-1903.

138. Another girandole. *ibidem*. Etching. 7½ in. × 4½ in. E.3778-1903.

139. A bracket with shelves for china. Plate 49 in the collection of designs dedicated to Lord Blakeney (1758). (Plate 46 in *150 New Designs*, 1761). Dated 1756. Etching. 9¾ in. × 6⅞ in. E.3767-1903.

140. A table clock. Plate 46 *ibidem*. (Plate 16 in *150 New Designs*, 1761). Dated 1756. Etching. 9¾ in. × 7 in. E.3764-1903.

141. A mirror. Plate 6 *ibidem*. (Plate 21 in *150 New Designs*, 1761). Etching. 9¾ in. × 6⅞ in. E.3724-1903.

142. Three mirrors. Plate 9 *ibidem*. (Plate 33 in *150 New Designs*, 1761). Etching. 6⅞ in. × 9⅝ in. E.3727-1903.

143. Three candle-stands. Plate 18 *ibidem*. (Plate 39 in *150 New Designs*, 1761). Etching. 7 in. × 9¾ in. E.3731-1903.

Note: The right-hand stand is based on a design by François Cuvilliés (see No. **357** and page 14). A somewhat similar design was later published by Chippendale (*Director*, 3rd edition, plate 145, dated 1760). A candle-stand carved with dolphins in the Museum (W.9-1950) was inspired by Johnson's engraving and was perhaps carved by Johnson himself. It was originally at Hagley Hall, Worcestershire, where there were also two girandoles made from designs by Johnson. See Edwards and Jourdain, plates 74-77.

144. Six designs for wall brackets. Plate 43 *ibidem*. (Plate 38 in *150 New Designs*, 1761). Etching. 9¾ in. × 6⅞ in. E.3761-1903.

145. A frame for a table with human supports. Plate 23 *ibidem*. (Plate 44 in *150 New Designs*, 1761). Dated 1757. Etching. 6⅞ in. × 9¾ in. E.3741-1903.

146. Two console tables. Original design for plate 19 *ibidem*. (Plate 40 in *150 New Designs*, 1761). Pen and ink and wash on yellow tinted paper. 3⅞ in. × 6½ in. D.731-1906.

Note: This drawing is among the Chippendale drawings bought by the Museum in 1906 (see page 43).

FRANÇOIS VIVARES, 1709–1780

An engraver of French origin who came to England at the age of eighteen and spent the rest of his life here. He is best known for his engravings of landscapes after Claude and other artists. He also engraved a small number of ornamental designs, some of his own invention and some after other artists. The series of brackets, of which one plate is reproduced here, does not appear to be recorded.

147. A bracket. Entitled 'Bracketts No. 1' and dated September 1759. Etching. Cut to 7⅜ in. × 4¾ in. 23107.9.

CHARLES OVER

The author of a book published in 1758 entitled: *Ornamental Architecture in the Gothic, Chinese and Modern Taste, being above fifty intire new designs . . . (Many of which may be executed with roots of trees) for gardens, parks, forests, woods, canals, etc. . . . From the designs of Charles Over, architect. London. Printed for Robert Sayer . . . at the Golden Buck, near Serjeant's Inn, Fleet Street.*

It contains a few designs for garden furniture, of which a specimen is illustrated.

148. A garden seat. Plate 5 in *Ornamental Architecture*, 1758. Described in the index as 'in the Chinese Taste, of small Expence, genteel and durable'. Engraving. 4 in. × 6½ in.

WILLIAM INCE and JOHN MAYHEW

A leading firm of cabinet-makers in London during the second half of the eighteenth century. An announcement in the *Public Advertiser* for January 27th 1759 stated that 'Messrs. John Mayhew, who served his time with Mr. Bradshaw, and William Ince, who served his time with the Late Mr. West', had taken a house opposite Broad Street, Carnaby Market, and were ready to execute orders for cabinet work. The wording suggests that the two partners were young men who had but lately served their apprenticeship. Encouraged, no doubt, by Chippendale's success with the *Director*, they at once began advertising their goods in a similar manner, and in a list of new books published in the *Gentleman's Magazine* for July 13th, 1759 (vol. XXIX, p. 338), the following entry occurs: 'A general system of useful and ornamental furniture. By Mess. Ince and Mayhew, publishing in numbers 1s. each'. The publication of the 16th number was announced in the Public Ledger for February 13th, 1760. The designs were afterwards collected together and published in a large folio dedicated to the Duke of Marlborough. The date is not stated on the title-page, but R. S. Clouston (p. 158) deduces that it was probably 1762 from the fact that in certain copies an insertion has been made into the dedication describing the Duke as Lord Chamberlain, a post to which he was appointed in that year.

The book is entitled:

The Universal System of Household Furniture. Consisting of above 300 designs in the most elegant taste, both useful and ornamental. Finely engraved, in which the nature of ornament and perspective, is accurately exemplified. The whole made convenient to the nobility and gentry, in their choice, and comprehensive to the workman, by directions for executing the several designs, with specimens of ornament for young practitioners in drawing. By Ince and Mayhew cabinet-makers and and upholders, in Broad Street, Golden Square, London. Where every article in the several branches, treated, of, is executed on the most reasonable terms, with the utmost neatness and punctuality. Sold by Robt. Sayer, map and printseller near Serjeants Inn, Fleet Street. (Engraver: Matthew Darly. All except the last 12 plates.)

The copy in the Museum contains 101 plates apart from the title and dedication. The last 12 plates, which comprise a metalwork section with designs for stoves, fenders, railings, etc, appear to have been added as an afterthought, since they are in a different style and smaller in size, two being printed on a page. They bear no artist's or engraver's name, whereas 11 of the other plates are signed *Mayhew* and the remainder are all signed *Ince*. The title-page and part of the text are printed in French as well as English, showing that the firm hoped to receive orders from abroad.

The book was clearly conceived in rivalry with Chippendale's *Director*, being of a similar format and arranged in the same way, with a preface and a commentary on the plates, the latter being intended 'to render the Explanation as easy as possible to the Capacity of every Workman', though in fact it contains little practical advice. The style of the designs is likewise influenced by the *Director*, but they possess certain characteristics of their own, the most marked being the frequent use of elaborate symmetrical patterns, half gothic and half rococo, executed in fretwork and applied blind to panels or used as an openwork filling for a frame (cf. No. **152**). Sheraton, though he considered the work 'a book of merit in its day', pronounced it 'much inferior to Chippendale's, which was a real original, as well as more extensive and masterly in design'.

Apart from the *Universal System*, Ince and Mayhew contributed a certain number of designs to *Household Furniture in Genteel Taste for the year 1760 by a Society of Upholsterers* (see page 51). They are easily recognized, because several of them are variants of designs published in the *Universal System*, while the others are in a very similar style. Nos. **160** and **165** are examples. Mr Fiske Kimball and Miss Donnell (vol. 2, p. 45) attribute to them plates 12, 13, 21, 25, 36, 53, 71, 76, 82, 83, 85 to 91, 103, 104 and 107. (The plate numbers refer to the 2nd edition.)

In their commentary on the plates in the *Universal System* the authors specifically declare that certain designs have been 'executed from the plate'; and a certain amount of such furniture may still be in existence, though few pieces have so far been recognized. Indeed, it is surprising how little furniture extant today can be assigned to the firm. Among the few attributions based on conclusive evidence are a cabinet in the Museum of Decorative Arts at Copenhagen, which contains the firm's label, and a set of mahogany chairs made in 1795 for the Westminster Fire Office and still in the company's possession, together with a minute recording the directors' decision to order the goods from Ince and Mayhew.

Only one drawing, reproduced here as No. **149**, has been identified as the work of Ince or Mayhew. See Kimball and Donnell, vols. I and II, *passim*.

149. A bedstead. Part of the design by William Ince for plate 32 in the *Universal System of Household Furniture*, 1759–1762. Pen and ink and wash. 9½ in. × 6½ in. D.838–1906.

Note: This drawing was among the Chippendale drawings bought by the Museum in 1906 (see page 43).

150. Alternative designs for a bed. Plate 82 in *The Second Edition of Genteel Furniture in the Present Taste by a Society of Upholsterers, Cabinet-Makers, etc.* (1st edition 1760). Etching. 7⅞ in. × 4⅞ in.

Note: The design is convincingly attributed to Ince and Mayhew on grounds of style by Kimball and Donnell, vol. II, page 45.

151. A 'china case'. Plate 48 in *The Universal System of Household Furniture*, 1759–1762. Signed: 'Ince.' Engraving. 14 in. × 9 in.

Note: The authors suggest that the exterior should be japanned and 'the inside all of looking-glass, in that manner it has been executed'.

152. Two 'corner shelves or ecoineurs' (i.e. *encoignures*). Plate 47 *ibidem*. Signed: 'Ince'. Engraving. 14 in. × 9 in.

Note: The authors state that the second one 'has been executed from the Plate; the sides or back part to the shelves were lined with Glass silver'd'.

CATALOGUE AND NOTES

153. Two designs for 'Lady's Toiletta's' or dressing tables. Plate 36 *ibidem*. Signed: 'Ince'. Engraving. 9 in. × 14 in.

154. Three 'night tables'. Plate 33 *ibidem*. Engraving. 9 in. × 14 in.

Note: 'The middle one is intended to be lined with Silk, to show the Frets'.

155. Six designs for 'stair-case lights'. Plate 7 *ibidem*. Engraving. $8\frac{3}{4}$ in. × 14 in.

Note: The authors state that the lights 'are mostly designed to fix on the Hand Rail'.

156. Designs for 'reading or music desks'. Plate 26 *ibidem*. Engraving. 9 in. × 14 in.

157. Two sets of library steps. Plate 22 *ibidem*. Engraving. 9 in. × 14 in.

158. 'An alcove ornamented in the Gothic Taste; with a sofa adapted to the whole side of a room'. Plate 63 *ibidem*. Signed: 'Ince'. Engraving. $8\frac{3}{4}$ in. × 14 in.

159. Four 'dressing chairs'. Plate 35 *ibidem*. Signed: 'Mayhew'. Engraving. 14 in. × $8\frac{3}{4}$ in.

160. Two arm-chairs. Plate 21 in *The Second Edition of Genteel Furniture in the Present Taste by a Society of Upholsterers, etc.* (1st edition 1760) and in Manwaring's *Chair-Maker's Guide*, 1766. Engraving. $5\frac{1}{2}$ in. × 8 in.

Note: The designs can confidently be attributed to Ince and Mayhew on grounds of style (cf. No. **159**).

161. Three hall chairs. Plate 4 in *The Universal System of Household Furniture*, 1759–1762. Engraving. $8\frac{3}{4}$ in. × 14 in.

Note: The authors suggest that 'the ornaments, if thought too expensive, may be painted and have a very good effect'.

162. Two 'Burjairs', or *bergère* chairs. Plate 60 *ibidem*. Signed: 'Mayhew'. Engraving. 14 in. × 9 in.

163. Four designs for 'trays or voiders'. Plate 15 *ibidem*. Engraving. 14 in. × 9 in.

164. Eight designs for 'tea-kettle stands'. Plate 14 *ibidem*. Engraving. $8\frac{3}{4}$ in. × 14 in.

165. 'A lady's desk'. Plate 53 in *The Second Edition of Genteel Furniture in the present Taste by a Society of Upholsterers* (1st edition 1760). Etching. $7\frac{3}{4}$ in. × 5 in.

Note: The design resembles plate 18 in *The Universal System* and is clearly by Ince and Mayhew.

SOCIETY OF UPHOLSTERERS

A book of designs was published in 1760 under the title:

Household Furniture in Genteel Taste for the year 1760. By a Society of Upholsterers, Cabinet-Makers, etc. containing upwards of 180 designs on 60 copper plates. Consisting of china, breakfast, side-board, dressing, toilet, card, writing, claw, library, slab, and night tables, chairs, couches, French-stools, cabinets, commodes, china shelves and cases, trays, chests, stands for candles, tea kettles, pedestals, stair-case lights, bureaus, beds, ornamental bed-posts, corniches, brackets, fire-screens, desk, book and clock-cases, frames for glasses, sconce & chimney-pieces, girandoles, lanthorns, chandalears &c. &c. London Printed for Robt. Sayer, map and printseller, at the Golden Buck, in Fleet Street. (Engraver: J. Couse [on one plate].)

A second edition, undated, bears the title:

The II^d. Edition of Genteel Household Furniture in the Present Taste with an addition of several articles never before executed, by a Society of Upholsterers, Cabinet-Makers, &c containing upwards of 350 designs on 120 copper plates . . . London. Printed for Robt. Sayer map and printseller, at the Golden Buck in Fleet Street.

Copies of the first edition are rare and the only recorded one appears to be in the Metropolitan Museum, New York. The Victoria and Albert Museum has a copy of the second edition, which is divided into four parts, sold separately with separate title-pages; and all the plate numbers cited here refer to this edition. The Kunst-Bibliothek, Berlin, has a later edition entitled *Household Furniture for the year 1763*.

Some of the cabinet-makers who contributed designs to the book have been identified as follows [See Kimball and Donnell, vol. II, page 41]:

1. Robert Manwaring. The first 28 plates in the Society's Book were reprinted in 1766 in the *Chair-Maker's Guide* by Manwaring and others (see page 52). Most of them are probably after designs by Manwaring, except plates 12 and 13, which are obviously adapted from plates 60 and 57 in Ince and Mayhew's *Universal System*.

2. Ince and Mayhew (see page 49). In addition to the two plates mentioned above Mr Kimball and Miss Donnell also assign to them plates 21, 25, 36, 53, 71, 76, 82, 83, 85–91, 103, 104 and 107, several of them being simplified variants of plates in the *Universal System*.

3. Chippendale. Three original designs for plates in the Society's Book are in the Museum among the Chippendale drawings acquired in

1906. They are 721-1906 (No. **108**) for plate 32; 717-1906 for plate 75; and 725-1906 for plate 100. Moreover, the design for plate 30 (No. **170**) is among the Chippendale drawings in the Metropolitan Museum. These drawings are by the same hand as the *Director* drawings. Mr Kimball and Miss Donnell also attribute to the same hand on grounds of style plates 29, 31, 44, 72-74.

4. Thomas Johnson, to whom the same authors for stylistic reasons assign plates 60 and 93-99.

The designs in the Society's book are mostly for rather plain and modest furniture, and they are somewhat dull and lacking in originality. The indifferent quality of the engraving does not improve the mediocre effect.

See Clouston, pages 189-205 and, especially, Kimball and Donnell, vol. II, pages 41-46, the most thorough discussion of the subject published.

166. 'A toilet table'. Plate 35 in *The Second Edition of Genteel Furniture in the Present Taste by a Society of Upholsterers, Cabinet-Makers, etc.* (1st edition 1760). Engraving. 7⅞ in. × 5 in.

167. Two alternative designs for a library table. Plate 62 *ibidem*. Engraving. 5 in. × 7⅞ in.

168. 'A gothic bookcase'. Plate 68 *ibidem*. Engraved by J. Couse. 6½ in. × 4 in.

169. 'An embattled bookcase'. Plate 69 *ibidem*. Engraving. 6½ in. × 4 in.

170. 'A side-board table' designed by Thomas Chippendale. Plate 30 *ibidem*. Engraving. 7⅞ in. × 5⅛ in.

Note: The original drawing is in the Metropolitan Museum (illustrated in Kimball and Donnell, vol. II, page 41).

See also Nos. **108**, **150**, **160**, **165**, **171**, **172** and **178**.

ROBERT MANWARING. Worked c. 1765

A chair-maker and cabinet-maker, now remembered as the author (or part author) of three books of designs:

(1) *The Carpenter's Compleat Guide to the Whole System of Gothic Railing, consisting of twenty-six entire new designs for paling, and gates of different kinds etc. . . . Printed for A. Webley, in Holborn, near Chancery Lane, 1765.*

(2) *The Cabinet and Chair-Maker's Real Friend and Companion, or, the whole system of chair-making made plain and easy; containing upwards of one hundred new and useful designs for all sorts of chairs . . . Also some very beautiful designs, supposed to be executed with the limbs of yew, apple or pear trees, ornamented with leaves and blossoms, which if properly painted will appear like Nature; these are the only designs of the kind that ever were published . . . The whole invented and drawn by Robert Manwaring, cabinet-maker; and beautifully, and correctly engraved on forty copper plates by Robert Pranker London: Printed for Henry Webley, in Holborn, near Chancery Lane, 1765.* (Engraver: Pranker.)

A second edition was brought out in 1775 with the title unaltered, apart from the date and the name of the new publisher 'I. Taylor'.

(3) *The Chair-Maker's Guide; being upwards of two hundred new and genteel designs . . . for Gothic, Chinese, ribbon and other chairs, couches, settees, burjairs, French, dressing and corner stools . . . Many of the rural kind may be executed with rude branches, or limbs of trees etc. By Robert Manwaring, cabinet-maker and others . . . on seventy-five copper plates. Printed for Robert Sayer . . . at the Golden Buck, near Serjeants-Inn, Fleet St. MDCCLXVI.* (Engravers: Darly, Copland and others.)

The first 28 plates in the *Chair-Maker's Guide* are reprints of the first 28 plates in the Society of Upholsterers' book published in 1760 (see page 51); but most of them are probably by Manwaring, except plates 12 and 13, which are clearly by Ince and Mayhew (q.v. page 50). Of the remaining plates eleven (viz. Nos. 33, 34, 37, 39-45 and 58) may be assigned to Matthew Darly (q.v. page 37), at least six (Nos. 33, 34, 37, 39, 40, 43) being after designs published by him in 1750 in *A New Book of Chinese, Gothic and Modern Chairs*. Plate 55 is lettered *Copland fecit* and may be attributed to that artist, together with a number of other similar designs (see under Copland, page 53).

'I have made it my particular study', Manwaring wrote in the preface to his first book of chairs, 'to invent such Designs as may be easily executed by the hands of a tolerable skilful Workman', and he went on to assert that 'there are very few Designs advanced, but what he has either executed himself, or seen completely finished by others'. Most of the designs are, in fact, reasonably practical, despite the weak drawing and the faulty perspective, and some, like No. **176**, are very simple. He never mastered the rococo style and his attempts at it are for the most part laboured and graceless. Sheraton mentions Manwaring's two books of furniture designs in the Preface to his *Drawing Book*, only to dismiss them as worthless 'as all his chairs are nearly as old as Chippendale's and seem to be copied from them'.

171. Two 'hall and lobby chairs'. Plate 18 in *The*

CATALOGUE AND NOTES

Second Edition of Genteel Furniture in the Present Taste by a Society of Upholsterers, Cabinet-Makers etc. (1st edition 1760) and in Manwaring's *Chair-Maker's Guide*, 1766. Engraving. 5¼ in. × 7⅞ in.

172. Two 'Gothic chairs'. Plate 15 in *The Second Edition of Genteel Furniture* and in Manwaring's *Chair-Maker's Guide*, 1766. Engraving. 5¼ in. × 7⅞ in.

173. Two 'Gothic chairs'. Plate 31 in the *Chair-Maker's Guide*, 1766. Engraving. 5¼ in. × 8 in.

174. Two 'dressing chairs'. Plate 16 in *The Cabinet and Chair-Maker's Real Friend and Companion*, 1765. Etching. 5⅛ in. × 8 in.

175. Three backs for parlour chairs and three brackets for chairs. Plate 33 *ibidem*. Etching. 5¼ in. × 8 in.

176. Two parlour chairs. Plate 9 *ibidem*. Etching. 5¼ in. × 8 in.

177. Two 'rural chairs for summer houses'. Plate 26 *ibidem*. Etching. 5¼ in. × 8 in.

Note: These are some of the 'very beautiful designs supposed to be executed with the limbs of yew, apple or pear trees, ornamented with leaves and blossoms, which, if properly painted will appear like Nature' (see the wording of the title of the book above). A set of chairs in the Museum (W.61–66–1952) bears some resemblance to the designs.

178. 'A chair with a frett back'. Plate 23 in *The Second Edition of Genteel Furniture* and in Manwaring's *Chair-Maker's Guide*, 1766. Engraving. 6⅞ in. × 4½ in.

179. Two 'parlour chairs'. Plate 5 in *The Cabinet and Chair-Maker's Real Friend and Companion*, 1765. Etching. 5¼ in. × 8 in.

See also Nos. **180–183**.

MATTHEW DARLY. Working c. 1750–1778

See also page 37 and Nos. **46–47, 128–134** and **257–258**.

180. Two 'parlour chairs'. Plate 41 in *The Chair-Maker's Guide* by Robert Manwaring and others, 1766. Etching. 4 in. × 6¼ in.

Note: If the designs are compared with the chairs in Darly's *New Book of Chinese, Gothic and Modern Chairs*, 1750/51 (Nos. **46** and **47**), it will be obvious that he is the author. Chairs of this type, with backs composed of bandwork, are nevertheless often described as 'in the style of Robert Manwaring'.

H. COPLAND

The author of a small book of rococo designs entitled:

A New Book of Ornaments by H. Copland . . . Published . . . by Copland and Bucksher in Gutter Lane Cheapside, London.

The plates are inscribed *H. Copland Fecit 16 Ap: 1746*. In the copy in the Metropolitan Museum the words 'and Bucksher' are omitted from the title and none of the plates is signed or dated (see Kimball and Donnell, vol. I, p. 117). The book contains no furniture designs proper, and consists mainly of cartouches and fragments of ornament.

Copland collaborated with Lock in another book also entitled *A New Book of Ornaments*, published in 1752 (see under Lock, page 38, for full title and illustrations).

Copland's only other known contribution to furniture design is a series of 6 plates illustrating chairs which were published in Manwaring's *Chair-Maker's Guide* in 1766. One of these designs (No. **181**) is lettered *Copland Fecit*, a form of inscription which does not make it clear whether he was the author of the design or merely the engraver. In normal practice the engraver's, or rather etcher's, name is indicated by the word *fecit*, while the terms *invenit* or *delineavit* are used to denote the author of the design. In this case the author's name is not stated separately, and it is therefore reasonable to assume that Copland was here acting as his own engraver, as in his *New Book of Ornaments*, where the plates are likewise all signed *Copland Fecit*, though here he was definitely the author as well as the engraver. We therefore attribute this design to Copland and with it five others in a closely similar style published in Manwaring's *Chair-Maker's Guide* (viz. plates 56, 57 and 66–68). Plates 60–65 (see No. **183**) are also sufficiently similar in manner to justify a tentative attribution to Copland. The question is of some interest, because since Mr Fiske Kimball and Miss Donnell published their article on Chippendale's drawings (in Metropolitan Museum Studies, vol. I, 1928/29, p. 115), Copland has generally been credited with most of the designs for Chippendale's *Director*. The arguments in favour of this view are discussed in our notes on Chippendale, and our conclusion is that they are unconvincing (see pages 43–44). If these designs for chairs are, in fact, by Copland, they bear out our opinion, for they are utterly different in style and character from anything that Chippendale ever published; and, what is more, they are the only designs for furniture which can be ascribed to Copland, there being no way of distinguishing between his work and Lock's in their joint *New Book of Ornaments*.

181. A hall chair. Plate 55 in *The Chair-Maker's Guide* by Robert Manwaring and others, 1766. Lettered: 'Copland Fecit'. Etching. $7\frac{1}{4}$ in. × $4\frac{3}{8}$ in.

182. A hall chair. Plate 68 in *The Chair-Maker's Guide*, by Robert Manwaring and others, 1766. Etching. $7\frac{1}{4}$ in. × $4\frac{3}{8}$ in.

Note: The attribution to Copland is justified by the close resemblance of the design to No. **181**.

183. A dining-room chair. Plate 64 *ibidem*. Etching. 6 in. × $3\frac{7}{8}$ in.

Note: The design is attributed to Copland on account of its resemblance to No. **181**.

ANONYMOUS

184. A pier table and mirror. About 1760. Pen and ink and wash. $11\frac{7}{8}$ in. × $5\frac{3}{8}$ in. 3436.389.

185. A glazed cabinet on a stand. About 1760. Inscribed with notes and measurements. Pencil. 7 in. × $4\frac{1}{4}$ in. D.1356-1897.

186. A glazed bookcase. About 1765. Pen and ink and wash. $8\frac{5}{8}$ in. × $9\frac{1}{2}$ in. 7757.4.

HENRY KEENE, 1726–1776

Architect. Apart from three years in Ireland, he spent most of his life in London as Surveyor to the Dean and Chapter of Westminster and to the Fabric of Westminster Abbey. His long connection with the Abbey encouraged his interest in Gothic architecture, and he used the medieval style in some of his own buildings, notably at Arbury Hall, Warwickshire. He also designed classical buildings, the Guildhall at High Wycombe being an elegant example. The Museum acquired a collection of his drawings in 1921, and these include a number of furniture designs. The earliest are in the manner of Kent, while the later ones reveal the influence of Robert Adam.

187. Design for 'Musaeum Cabinets'. Inscribed with the title and a note. About 1760. Pen and ink and water-colour. $6\frac{1}{4}$ in. × $11\frac{1}{2}$ in. E.917-1921.

188. Sketch design for a set of library steps. Inscribed with a note and measurements and, in pencil: 'Museum Library Steps'. About 1750. Pencil and pen and ink. $10\frac{3}{4}$ in. × $4\frac{3}{8}$ in.
E.918-1921.

189. A set of library steps. Inscribed in ink with measurements and: 'Library Steps, at Ld. Hardwickes at Wimple. Wains'. About 1750. Pen and ink. $9\frac{1}{2}$ in. × 7 in. E.919-1921.

Note: Wimpole Hall, Cambridgeshire, was bought by the 1st Earl of Hardwicke in 1740.

For another design by Keene, see also No. **259**.

JOHN LINNELL, d. 1796

Carver, cabinet-maker and furniture designer. He succeeded in 1763 to the business of the late William Linnell, a carver and cabinet-maker, who was presumably a near relation. In the same year he received a large order for furniture and upholstery from William Drake of Shardeloes, and his bills for work there suggest that in the course of the next three years he furnished the whole house. Other bills and the names of his clients written on his drawings show that he had many other wealthy customers. He supplied Sir Nathaniel Curzon, afterwards Lord Scarsdale, with furniture for Kedleston Hall, Derbyshire, and one of his designs for a sofa supported by merfolk, which is still in the house, is reproduced here (No. **195**). He was also employed by the Childs at Osterley Park over a long period, and some of his work there is still in existence. The design for a rococo chimney-piece and overmantel mirror in one of the bedrooms is reproduced here (No. **194**). A later design connected with Osterley is the lyre back chair shown in No. **243**. Though it does not correspond exactly with the handsome set of chairs in the library, it is of a similar type, fitted with a splat in the form of a lyre surmounted by a small portrait medallion. This combination of motifs occurs in three other designs for chairs among Linnell's original drawings, which suggests that he was the maker of the set at Osterley. Two bills preserved in the house show that he was still making furniture there as late as 1782 and 1784.

The Museum has a large collection of original drawings by Linnell, which may be divided into three groups, as follows:

1. E.59–414–1929. A large album containing designs for furniture, etc. on 356 separate sheets. It was compiled by the architect Charles Heathcote Tatham and is entitled in ink:

A miscellaneous collection of original designs, made, and for the most part executed, during an extensive practice of many years in the first line of his profession, by John Linnell, Upholsterer, Carver and Cabinet Maker. Selected from his portfolios at his decease, by C. H. Tatham, Architect, A.D. 1800 . . .

The album was bought by the Museum from a dealer in 1929. It had some time previously belonged to Tatham's daughter Julia, the wife of

George Richmond, the portrait painter, and she had inherited it from her father.

Two of the drawings in it are by Henry Holland and several are signed by Tatham himself, but the majority are by Linnell and consist of designs for a great variety of objects, including furniture, ceilings, architectural fittings, state coaches, etc. The style likewise varies widely from rococo to neoclassic.

2. E.3680–3739–1911. A set of 60 sheets of tracings after drawings by Linnell, mainly after those in Tatham's album. They were originally bound together in a volume with the same title as Tatham's album and an inscription stating that the tracings were the work of J. H. Chance. They were evidently made as a preparation for engraving. It was doubtless Tatham's intention to publish his collection of Linnell's drawings, and Story, in his *Life* of John Linnell the painter (not to be confused with John Linnell the carver, though probably a relative), states that a book was actually published under the title which Tatham inscribed on his album.

3. E.3466–3679–1911. 214 sheets with designs for furniture, chiefly mirror frames, originally bound in two volumes. They were doubtless extracted from the firm's order books and most of the designs are inscribed with the client's name, a serial number, a date and the price in cipher. The dates range from 1773 to 1781.

The most interesting drawings are those collected together by Tatham, who doubtless was in a position to choose the best. Tatham cherished a great admiration for the artist, judging by a letter which he wrote to Henry Holland on receiving the news of Linnell's death. 'His memory', he wrote, 'as often as I reflect upon it, will ever produce the warmest tribute of gratitude', and he goes on to announce that he is at work upon the design of 'a monument very symbolic and ornamental, dedicated to the Genius of John Linnell'. (The letter, dated May 13th, 1796, is in the Print Room, No. D.1479/25–1898). Linnell's best drawings certainly justify Tatham's high opinion and they prove, what in the case of Chippendale has been disputed, that the head of a large firm of cabinet-makers might have the time and the capacity to make his own designs. Linnell drew with great fluency, and his rapid free hand sketches are among the most accomplished and attractive designs illustrated here (cf. **196** and **239**). He employed a number of different styles with success. The first design reproduced (No. **190**) is an exercise in the early Georgian style, still under the influence of Kent. He later became a skilful exponent of the rococo manner, and the Museum possesses a set of engraved designs by him for vases, which reveal the influence of Meissonnier. The margins have been cut above the date, but a set sold at Sotheby's on November the 18th, 1914, was dated 1760. Many of his furniture designs are spirited fantasies in the same vein, and a comparison between his work and that of François Cuvilliés (Nos. **354–356**) suggests that, like Lock, he had studied French models with more understanding than most English artists (cf. Nos. **192** and **193**). Before adopting the neo-classical style in all its rigour, as he eventually did, he passed through an intermediate phase, in which a chastened type of rococo ornament was combined with classical forms to produce a charming and individual synthesis (cf. Nos. **235** and **246**). His only dull drawings are those described in Group 3 above, where there is little variety either in the objects illustrated (they are mostly mirror frames) or in the style, which is based on a somewhat mechanical manipulation of stereotyped neo-classical themes.

190. A side-table with a lion mask and lion legs. About 1750. Pen and ink and wash. $2\frac{1}{4}$ in. × $4\frac{1}{2}$ in.   E.240–1929.

191. Two tea tables. About 1760. Pen and ink and water-colour. Size of sheet $5\frac{1}{4}$ in. × $7\frac{1}{8}$ in.   E.238–1929.

192. A side-table decorated with a parrot. About 1760. Pen and ink and watercolour. $2\frac{3}{4}$ in. × $3\frac{5}{8}$ in.   E.239–1929.

193. A side-table decorated with dragons. About 1760. Pen and ink and watercolour. 3 in. × $5\frac{7}{8}$ in.   E.237–1929.

Note: cf. a table decorated with dragons by Cuvilliés, (No. **354**).

194. Design for a chimney-piece and overmantel mirror for Osterley Park. About 1760. Pen and ink and watercolour. 8 in. × $4\frac{5}{8}$ in.   E.281–1929.

Note: The chimney-piece and mirror executed from this design are temporarily exhibited in the Museum in Room 125.

195. Design for a gilt sofa for Lord Scarsdale of Kedleston. About 1765. Signed: 'J. Linnell'. Pen and ink and watercolour. $4\frac{7}{8}$ in. × $13\frac{1}{4}$ in.   E.129–1929.

Note: The sofa made from this design is still at Kedleston Hall, Derbyshire. It is illustrated in Edwards and Jourdain, fig. 162. Robert Adam designed a somewhat similar sofa for Kedleston (see No. **203**).

196. A chair. About 1765. Pen and ink and wash. $8\frac{3}{8}$ in. × $5\frac{1}{8}$ in.   E.60–1929.

197. An arm-chair upholstered in black. About 1760. Pen and ink and watercolour. $4\frac{3}{8}$ in. × $4\frac{5}{8}$ in.   E.94–1929.

198. A console table and mirror decorated with an eagle. About 1760. Pen and ink and watercolour. $8\frac{7}{8}$ in. × $5\frac{3}{4}$ in.   E.185–1929.

199. A side-table and mirror decorated with animals and mythological figures. About 1760. Pen and ink and watercolour. $11\frac{5}{8}$ in. × $6\frac{1}{2}$ in.   E.247–1929.

200. A bedstead supported by herms. About 1760. Pen and ink and watercolour. $7\frac{7}{8}$ in. × $6\frac{5}{8}$ in.   E.152–1929.

For other designs by Linnell, see also Nos. **235–250**.

Anonymous

201. A state bedstead surmounted by an earl's coronet. About 1760. Inscribed: 'A. Lalande'. Pen and ink and watercolour. $11\frac{3}{4}$ in. × $7\frac{1}{8}$ in.   8448F.

Note: The signature does not look genuine and no likely artist of that name is recorded. The inscription may refer to the French designer Lalonde, but the drawing is clearly English, and reminiscent of Linnell.

Robert Adam, 1728–1792

Architect and designer. He was the son of a successful Scottish architect, and his two younger brothers practised the same profession and were his partners in business. After spending four years studying in Italy, Adam settled in London in 1758 and soon obtained a large practice, partly through the influence of his fellow Scot, Lord Bute, the Prime Minister, through whom, in 1761, he was appointed Architect of the King's Works, in company with Sir William Chambers. His architectural works were numerous, but many have been pulled down, like the Adelphi, or mutilated like Lansdowne House in Berkeley Square. Among the best examples of his work still standing in London are the Admiralty screen in Whitehall and No. 20 St. James's Square. He was seldom given the opportunity to build a country house, but he was constantly employed to remodel or decorate existing houses, and his skill in this kind of work can still be admired in a number of famous mansions like Harewood, Kedleston, Kenwood, Osterley and Syon, though they grow fewer every year through demolitions.

Adam's originality found greatest scope in his interiors, where he attempted to revive the light and elegant style of decoration which the Romans had used in their smaller private apartments. His version of the style was based on a fresh study of the original models and of the experiments made by Raphael and his followers in the use of the same convention. His ideal was to establish a complete harmony between the architectural decoration of a room and its contents. In pursuit of this aim he designed furniture for many of his houses and gradually evolved an entirely new classicizing style, which was much imitated in the 1770's and 1780's. The best witnesses to his genius in this field are the small number of private houses, like Osterley Park and Syon House, near London, where the furniture still stands in the rooms for which he designed it. He also left behind him a considerable quantity of drawings for furniture, most of which are preserved among his other drawings in Sir John Soane's Museum. Thirty-five examples from that collection are reproduced here by the kind permission of the Curator.

Adam himself began publishing a series of splendid engravings illustrating his architecture and furniture. The earliest sets came out in five separate numbers dated 1773, 1774, 1775, 1776 and 1778: and in 1778 they were brought together in one volume under the title:

The Works in Architecture of Robert and James Adam, Esquires, Volume I . . . London: Printed for the authors; and sold by Peter Elmsley, opposite Southampton Street in the Strand . . . MDCCLXXVIII.

A second volume was brought out in 1779, consisting of five more numbers, though in this case they do not appear to have been published previously, as they are without separate title-pages. A third volume was published in 1822, after Adam's death, by Priestley and Weale, No. 5 High Street, Bloomsbury. The text throughout and the various titles are in French as well as English, and Mr Fiske Kimball has suggested that the early numbers exerted a certain influence on furniture design in France (see the footnote on page 24).

A facsimile reprint of the work was published in 1901 by E. Thézard Fils, Dourdan, France.

See pages 21–24; A. T. Bolton, *The Architecture of Robert and James Adam*, 2 vols, 1922 (with index of Adam drawings); and J. Lees-Milne, *The Age of Adam*, 1947.

202. 'A sopha for Sir Laurence Dundass Baronet'. Inscribed with title and dated 1764. Pen and ink and water-colour. $12\frac{3}{4}$ in. × $24\frac{5}{8}$ in. (Sir John Soane's Museum, *Adam*, vol. 17, No. 74).

Note: Adam was making additions to Moor Park, Herts, for Dundas between 1763 and 1764. The sofa executed from this design is illustrated in Bolton, vol. II, p. 293, and in Macquoid and Edwards, vol. III, p. 96, fig. 58. Four arm-chairs were also made *en suite* and one of these

(W.1-1937) is in the Museum (illustrated in R. Edwards, *English Chairs*, 1951, plate 81). The set was probably made by Samuel Norman.

203. 'A sofa for Lord Scarsdale and also executed for Mrs. Montagu in Hill Street'. Inscribed with title and signed and dated 1762. Pen and ink and water-colour. 6 in. × 14⅛ in. (Sir John Soane's Museum, *Adam*, vol. 17, No. 69.)

Note: Kedleston Hall, Derbyshire, was completed by Adam for Lord Scarsdale c. 1762–70, after James Paine had erected the central block. The house contains no sofa corresponding exactly with this design, but the sofa executed from John Linnell's design (No. **195**) has certain features in common with Adam's drawing, notably the curved back and the medallion in the centre of it. Linnell may have been asked to improve on Adam's design or, if Adam's design was carried out, he may have been commissioned to make another sofa in a similar style. The sofa at Kedleston is illustrated in Bolton, vol. II, p. 292: in Macquoid and Edwards, vol. III, p. 96, fig. 57: and in Edwards and Jourdain, fig. 163.

204. An organ case for the Earl of Bute. Inscribed with title and dated 1763. Pen and ink and water-colour. 12 in. × 8¼ in. (Sir John Soane's Museum, *Adam*, vol. 25, No. 4.)

Note: Probably for Lansdowne House, Berkeley Square (now the Lansdowne Club), which was begun about 1762 for Lord Bute, who sold it unfinished to Lord Shelburne, afterwards Marquis of Lansdowne. Other designs for Lansdowne House are reproduced in Nos. **207, 208** and **234**. (See Bolton, vol. II, pp. 1–17.)

205. 'A Cloaths Press for the Earl of Coventry'. Inscribed with title and dated 2 Oct. 1764. Pen and ink and water-colour. 9¾ in. × 8½ in. (Sir John Soane's Museum, *Adam*, vol. 17, No. 213.)

Note: Probably for Croome Court, Worcs, where Adam designed various interiors for Lord Coventry from 1760 onwards (see Bolton, vol. I, pp. 178–192 and his index of Adam drawings, pp. 7 and 67).

206. A bookcase for the Right Honourable Lord Frederick Campbell. Inscribed with title and dated 1767. Pen and ink and water-colour. 13 in. × 9¾ in. (Sir John Soane's Museum, *Adam*, vol. 17, No. 215.)

Note: Presumably for Coombank, Sutton Lathe, Kent, altered and redecorated by Adam, c. 1767 (see Bolton, index, pp. 6 and 65).

207. 'A stool for the Hall at Shelburne House'. Inscribed with title and dated 1768. Pen and ink and wash. 13¾ in. × 10 in. (Sir John Soane's Museum, *Adam*, vol. 17, No. 76.)

Note: See note under No. **204**. Other designs for furniture for the same house are illustrated in Nos. **204, 208** and **234**. This design was inspired by the antique cistern shown in Nos. **363** and **364** and admirably illustrates Adam's skill in adapting ancient forms to contemporary furniture.

208. 'A Glass Frame for the Earl of Shelburne'. Inscribed with title and dated 1768. Pen and ink and water-colour. 9 in. × 5 in. (Sir John Soane's Museum, *Adam*, vol. 20, No. 21.)

Note: Presumably for Shelburne, afterwards Lansdowne House (see note under no. **204**.) Other designs for the same client are reproduced in nos. **204, 207** and **234** (see Bolton, vol. II, pp. 1–17, and index pp. 34 and 87).

209. 'A Glass frame for Lady Coventry's Dressing Room'. Inscribed with title and dated 1768. Pen and ink and water-colour. 14¾ in. × 11¼ in. (Sir John Soane's Museum, *Adam*, vol. 20, No. 62.)

Note: This was for No. 29, Piccadilly (now No. 106 and the St. James's Club), where Adam designed various interiors for the Earl of Coventry between 1765 and 1768 (see Bolton, index, pp. 44 and 67).

210. A table and pier glass for Robert Child's house in Berkeley Square, London. About 1770. Pen and ink and water-colour. 1½ in. × 9½ in. (At Osterley Park.)

211. 'Design of a Commode for Sir George Colebrooke, Bart.' Inscribed with title and dated 1771. Pen and ink and water-colour. 4½ in. × 8 in. (Sir John Soane's Museum, *Adam*, vol. 17, No. 17.)

Note: Adam was decorating parts of Colebrooke's house in Arlington Street, since demolished, in 1771 (see Bolton, index, pp. 34 and 66).

212. 'A commode for His Grace The Duke of Bolton'. Inscribed with title and dated 'Adelphi 16 Janry 1773'. Pen and ink and water-colour. 8 in. × 12 in. (Sir John Soane's Museum, *Adam*, vol. 17, No. 18.)

Note: Adam's designs for decoration and furniture at Bolton House, Russell Square (formerly No. 26, Southampton Row) are dated 1770–1777 (see Bolton, index, pp. 48 and 63).

213. 'A bookcase for Lady Wynn's Dressing Room'. Inscribed with title and dated 'Adelphi 9th Febry 1776'. Pen and ink and water-colour. (Sir John Soane's Museum, *Adam*, vol. 17, No. 222.)

Note: For no. 20 St. James's Square, built by Adam for Sir Watkin Williams-Wynne, 1772–1774 (see Bolton, vol. II, pp. 54–64, and index, pp. 50 and 91). See also Nos. **226** and **232**.

214. 'A Glass and Commode for George Keate Esqr.' Inscribed with title and dated 1778. Pen and ink and water-colour. 14⅛ in. × 4⅛ in. (Sir John Soane's Museum, *Adam*, vol. 20, No. 110.)

Note: Adam carried out alterations for George Keate at 8 Charlotte Street, Bloomsbury, between 1772 and 1778. Other designs for the same client are reproduced in Nos. **215** and **230** (see Bolton, index, pp. 36 and 77).

215. A casket or cabinet on a stand. Inscribed: 'For George Keate Esqr' and dated 'Adelphi 1777'. Pen and ink and water-colour. (Sir John Soane's Museum, *Adam*, vol. 17, No. 33.)

Note: See note under No. **214**. Other designs for the same client are reproduced in Nos. **214** and **230** (see Bolton, index, pp. 36 and 77).

216. 'Design of a table frame and top for Lady Bathurst's Dressing Room'. Inscribed with title and dated 19 June 1779. Pen and ink and water-colour. Size of sheet 12 in. × 10½ in. (Sir John Soane's Museum, *Adam*, vol. 17, No. 48.)

Note: Most of Adam's architectural work at Apsley House for the Earl Bathurst was completed about 1775, but some of the designs are dated 1778 and 1779. There is no furniture corresponding with this design in the house today. For another design for the same client see No. **225** (see Bolton, index, pp. 43 and 62).

217. 'Plan and elevation of two tables for the Salon the tops to be of Scagliola'. Inscribed with title and dated Adelphi 10 June 1775. (Sir John Soane's Museum, *Adam*, vol. 17, No. 28.)

Note: Scagliola was a hard, smooth composition resembling marble, much used for decorating floors, table tops, etc. in the eighteenth century. The client's name is not known.

218. 'A bed for Robert Child Esqr' Inscribed with title and dated 'Adelphi Octr 1775'. Pen and ink and water-colour. 17½ in. × 10¾ in. (Sir John Soane's Museum, *Adam*, vol. 17, No. 156.)

Note: Osterley Park, Middlesex, was reconstructed by Adam for Robert Child, 1761–1780. The bed was carried out from the design and is still in the house. Horace Walpole commented on it after his visit to Osterley in 1778. 'Too theatric, and too like a modern head-dress', he wrote, 'for round the outside of the dome are festoons of artificial flowers. What would Vitruvius think of a dome decorated by a milliner?' (see Bolton, vol. I, pp. 279–302, and P. Ward-Jackson, *Guide to Osterley Park*, 1954). For other designs for Osterley, see Nos. **220**, **221**, **224** and **233**.

219. 'Glass and table frames and tripods for the Drawing Room at Luton'. Inscribed with title and dated Adelphi Octr. 27th, 1772. Pen and ink and water-colour. 23¾ in. × 19 in. (Sir John Soane's Museum, *Adam*, vol. 20, No. 116.)

Note: Luton Hoo, Beds, was built by Adam for Lord Bute between about 1768 and 1775. It has since been reconstructed (see Bolton, vol. I, pp. 65–71, and index, pp. 21 and 64).

220. Design for an arm-chair with sphinx supports at Osterley Park, Middlesex. Dated 24 April 1777. Pen and ink and water-colour. 7⅞ in. × 4⅝ in. (Sir John Soane's Museum, *Adam*, vol. 17, No. 97.)

Note: A set of chairs was faithfully executed from this design and is still in the state bedroom at Osterley. For an illustration see R. Edwards, *English Chairs*, 1951, fig. 82. For other designs for Osterley, see Nos. **218**, **221**, **224** and **233**. See also note under No. **218**.

221. 'A Chair for Robert Child Esqr.' Inscribed with title. About 1775. Pen and ink. (Sir John Soane's Museum, *Adam*, vol. 20, No. 93.)

Note: A set of mahogany chairs was made from these designs and is now in the Eating Room at Osterley Park, Middlesex (see note under No. **218**). One of the chairs is illustrated in R. Edwards, *English Chairs*, 1951, No. 87. See also Bolton, vol. I, pp. 279–302. For other designs for Osterley, see Nos. **218**, **220**, **224** and **233**.

222. 'A chair for the Right Honble Lord Stanley'. Inscribed with title and dated 'Adelphi. Jany. 19. 1775'. Pen and ink and water-colour. 11½ in. × 7⅝ in. (Sir John Soane's Museum, *Adam*, vol. 17, No. 94.)

Note: For 23 Grosvenor Square, reconstructed by Adam for Lord Stanley, afterwards Earl of Derby, 1773–74. The house was demolished in 1862. See also No. **227**. (See Bolton, vol. II, pp. 65–71.)

223. A sofa. Pen and ink and water-colour. Probably about 1770. 6 in. × 15¼ in. (Sir John Soane's Museum, *Adam*, vol. 20, No. 78.)

224. 'A Tripod for the Tapestry Room at Osterley'. Inscribed with title and dated November 13th, 1776. Pen and ink and water-colour. 11½ in. × 4¼ in. (Sir John Soane's Museum, *Adam*, vol. 17, No. 62.)

Note: A pair of tripods made from these designs is still in the Tapestry Room at Osterley Park (see note under No. **218**). They are illustrated in Macquoid and Edwards, vol. III, p. 161, fig. 12. For other designs for Osterley, see Nos. **218**, **220**, **221** and **233**.

225. 'Tripod for the Niches in the First Drawing Room at Apsley House'. Inscribed with title and dated January 14th, 1779. Pen and water-colour. 8 in. × 4½ in. (Sir John Soane's Museum, *Adam*, vol. 17, No. 64.)

Note: See note under No. **216**. There is no furniture corresponding with this design in the house today. For another design for the same client, see No. **216** (see Bolton, index, pp. 43 and 62).

CATALOGUE AND NOTES

226. 'A tripod for the Drawing Room at Sir W. Wynn's in St. James's Square'. Inscribed with title and dated Adelphi 24 August 1773. Pen and ink and water-colour. (Sir John Soane's Museum, *Adam*, vol. 17, No. 60.)

Note: For no. 20 St. James's Square, built by Adam for Sir Watkin Williams-Wynne, 1772–1774. Other designs for the same house are reproduced in Nos. **213** and **232**. (See Bolton, vol. II, pp. 54–64, and index, pp. 50 and 91).

227. Designs for furniture and fittings for Lord Derby's house in Grosvenor Square. Plate 8 in volume II, part I, of the *Works in Architecture*, 1779. Dated 1774 and engraved by Pastorini.

Note: See also No. **222**.

228. Designs for lamps and clock cases, Plate 8 in the fourth number (1776) of *The Works in Architecture* (republished in vol. I, 1778). Engraved by P. Begbie. $23\frac{3}{8}$ in. $\times 17\frac{1}{2}$ in.

229. Designs for furniture for Kenwood House, Hampstead, Middlesex. Plate 8 in the second number (1774) of *The Works in Architecture* (republished in vol. I, 1778). Engraved by P. Begbie. $23\frac{3}{8}$ in. $\times 17\frac{1}{2}$ in.

230. Designs for furniture for various clients. Plate 8 in the first number (1773) of *The Works in Architecture* (republished in vol. I, 1778). Engraved by B. Pastorini. $23\frac{3}{8}$ in. $\times 17\frac{1}{2}$ in.

Note: According to the text the bracket on the left was for James Bourdieu, the one on the right for George Keate; the two tripods were for the Earl of Coventry; the vase-shaped candelabra on the table were executed for Sir Laurence Dundas and the Duke of Bolton.

231. A harpsichord for Catherine, Empress of Russia. Part of plate 8 in the fifth number (1778) of *The Works in Architecture* (republished in vol. I, 1778). Dated 1774 and engraved by P. Begbie. $23\frac{3}{8}$ in. $\times 17\frac{1}{2}$ in.

Note: According to the text, the harpsichord was made in London and the inlaid decoration was carried out in coloured woods. The 'design was considerably altered by the person who executed the work'.

232. An organ for Sir Watkin Williams-Wynne, for the music room at 20, St. James's Square. Plate 8 in the second number of the second volume of *The Works in Architecture*, 1779. Dated 1773 and engraved by D. Cunego. $17\frac{1}{2}$ in. $\times 23\frac{3}{8}$ in.

Note: See also Nos. **213** and **226**.

233. Furniture for Osterley Park. Plate 8 in the third volume of *The Works in Architecture*, 1822. Engraved by P. Begbie. $17\frac{1}{2}$ in. $\times 23\frac{3}{8}$ in.

Note: The left-hand lamp was carried out for the staircase. The table and a pair of urns on pedestals, corresponding with the design on the right, were made for the eating room, where they still are. A drawing for the table alone (at Osterley) is dated 1767. This dining-room furniture was probably made by John Linnell (see page 54). The evidence is in a bill for furniture made by Linnell for William Drake of Shardeloes in 1767, one of the items being 'two coopers, the tops in the form of vases and large brass handles like Mr. Child's . . .' (Quoted in Edwards and Jourdain, p. 77). In the text accompanying the plate, doubtless written after Adam's death, it is incorrectly stated that these designs were for furniture at Syon House. For other designs for Osterley, see Nos. **218**, **220**, **221** and **224**.

234. A hall table for Shelburne House, Berkeley Square (see note under No. **204**). Part of plate 8 in the third number of the second volume of *The Works in Architecture*, 1779. Dated 1768 and engraved by Caldwall. $12\frac{1}{2}$ in. $\times 17\frac{1}{2}$ in.

Note: See also Nos. **204, 207** and **208**.

JOHN LINNELL, d. 1796
See also page 54 and Nos. **190–200**.

235. A hanging cabinet. About 1770. Pen and ink and water-colour. 5 in. $\times 2\frac{1}{2}$ in.   E.301–1929.

236. A bookcase. About 1775. Pen and ink and water-colour. 7 in. $\times 3\frac{1}{2}$ in.   E.298–1929.

237. A cabinet or press. About 1770. Pen and ink and water-colour. $5\frac{3}{8}$ in. $\times 3$ in.   E.297–1929.

238. A glazed cabinet or show case on a stand. About 1775. Pen and ink and water-colour. 6 in. $\times 3\frac{5}{8}$ in.   E.305–1929.

Note: This design is interesting, as it shows that such cases were made in the eighteenth century, though most of those found today are of later date.

239. Two rough sketches for commodes. About 1780. Pen and ink and wash. $8\frac{1}{2}$ in. $\times 5\frac{7}{8}$ in.   E.288–1929.

240. Rough sketch for a china cabinet. About 1775. Pen and ink over pencil. $8\frac{1}{2}$ in. $\times 5$ in.   E.295–1929.

241. A gilt arm-chair. About 1775. Pen and ink and water-colour. $4\frac{1}{2}$ in. $\times 3\frac{1}{2}$ in.   E.82–1929.

242. A gilt arm-chair. About 1775. Pen and ink and water-colour. $4\frac{1}{2}$ in. $\times 3\frac{7}{8}$ in.   E.78–1929.

243. An arm-chair with a lyre-shaped back. Part of a design for the side of a room. About 1775. Pen and ink and water-colour. 2⅝ in. × 1⅝ in. E.336–1929.

Note: There are a number of similar designs among Linnell's drawings. A set of chairs in the library at Osterley Park is characterized by the same lyre-shaped splat and medallion and was probably made by Linnell. Horace Walpole noticed them on one of his visits to the house. 'The chairs are taken from antique lyres' he observed, 'and make a charming harmony'. They are illustrated in Ralph Edwards, *English Chairs,* 1951, plate 89.

244. A chair. About 1770. Pen and ink and water-colour. 4¼ in. × 3½ in. E.103–1929.

245. A gilt sofa. About 1775. Pen and ink and water-colour. 4¾ in. × 13 in. E.141–1929.

246. A gilt sofa and mirror. About 1780. Pen and ink and water-colour. 9⅜ in. × 12 in. E.118–1929.

247. Drawing of a side-table and mirror, headed: 'Design for the glass frames in Drawing Room at Shardeloes for W^{m}. Drake Esq'. An alternative cresting is shown on an attached flap. About 1770. Pen and ink and water-colour. 10⅞ in. × 7 in. E.241–1929.

248. A cabinet on a stand. About 1775. Pen and ink and water-colour. Size of sheet 7¼ in. × 5⅛ in. E.303–1929.

249. A glazed cabinet or bookcase. About 1775. Pen and ink and water-colour. 7⅜ in. × 6⅛ in. E.290–1929.

250. A commode in the French style, with brass mounts. About 1775. Pen and ink and water-colour. 2⅞ in. × 4⅝ in. E.292–1929.

Matthias or Matthew Lock, Working *c.* 1740–1770

See also page 38 and Nos. **48–69**.

251. Two designs for a side table. About 1770. Pen and ink and water-colour. 4⅜ in. × 9⅝ in. From the George Lock Collection. 2551.

252. A gilt arm-chair. About 1770. Pen and ink and water-colour. 7½ in. × 4⅞ in. From the George Lock Collection (Lock Album). 2848.148.

253. A gilt arm-chair. About 1770. Pen and ink and water-colour. 8½ in. × 5¼ in. From the George Lock Collection (Lock Album). 2848.145.

254. A side-table and mirror. About 1770. Pen and ink and wash. 15¼ in. × 4 in. From the George Lock Collection. 2575.

255. A gilt mirror frame. About 1770. Pen and ink and water-colour. Cut to 13⅜ in. × 5¾ in. From the George Lock Collection. 2556.

256. Designs for two side-tables. Plate 2 in *A New Book of Pier-Frames, Ovals, etc,* 1769. Etching. 5⅝ in. × 8⅞ in. E.4262–1906.

Matthew Darley, Working *c.* 1750–1778

See also page 37 and Nos. **46–47**, **128–134** and **180**.

257. 'Frames for pictures, glasses, etc. to be done in carving or stucco'. Lettered with title and dated 1770. Etching. 14½ in. × 8⅞ in. E.2290–1908.

258. Designs for two mirrors and a hanging clock. Etching. Dated 1771. 8 in. × 12¼ in. E.298.91.

Henry Keene, 1726–1776

See also page 54 and Nos. **187–189**.

259. Design (front and side elevation) for a cabinet. About 1770. Pen and ink and wash. 17 in. × 11¼ in. E.911–1921.

Note: On the back a sketch design in pencil of another cabinet inscribed: 'Ld Chesterfield'.

Michaelangelo Pergolesi, Working *c.* 1760–1801

An engraver and designer of Italian origin who came to England at Robert Adam's invitation in the 1760's and collaborated with Adam in decorating interiors. He was the author of a series of designs, mainly for ornamental panels, entitled *Designs for Various Ornaments,* which appeared in numbers between 1777 and 1801.

260. Design for a table, 'for the Duke of Northumberland'. Inscribed with title and 'M. A. Pergolesi'. About 1780. Pen and ink and gouache. 4½ in. × 7 in. D.229–1890.

John Yenn, 1750–1821

Architect. He was the pupil and faithful follower of Sir William Chambers. He succeeded the latter as Treasurer of the Royal Academy and held various appointments under the Crown, but his actual works in architecture are not numerous or important. The Museum has a number of drawings by him for furniture, chimney-pieces, etc.

261. A semi-circular console table supported by winged figures. About 1780. Pen and ink and water-colour. $11\frac{1}{2}$ in. × $7\frac{1}{2}$ in. E.5035–1910.

262. A semi-circular side-table. Signed: 'John Yenn Invt. A° 1780'. Pen and ink and water-colour. 7 in. × $7\frac{1}{2}$ in. E.4967–1910.

263. A mirror with two candelabra. About 1780. Pen and ink and water-colour. $12\frac{1}{2}$ in. × $10\frac{7}{8}$ in. E.4981–1910.

Anonymous

264. A semi-circular side-table (plan and elevation). About 1780. Pen and ink and wash. $8\frac{3}{8}$ in. × $12\frac{1}{8}$ in. D.59–1885.

265. Design for a console table and mirror. About 1780. Pen and ink and water-colour. $13\frac{3}{8}$ in. × $5\frac{5}{8}$ in. E.1740–1912.

Note: The table is very similar to one designed by Adam for Sir Laurence Dundas in 1765 (illustrated in A. T. Bolton, *The Architecture* of *Robert and James Adam*, vol. II, 1922, p. 291), and to another table at Harewood House, Yorkshire, attributed to Chippendale (illustrated in Edwards and Jourdain, fig. 146). These tables, however, have rams' heads instead of satyrs' heads surmounting the legs.

266. A gilt semi-circular side-table. About 1775. Pen and ink and water-colour. $10\frac{5}{8}$ in. × $14\frac{1}{4}$ in. E.11–1921.

267. A picture or mirror frame with heraldic cresting lettered 'In Cruce Glorior'. About 1780. Pen and ink and wash. $10\frac{1}{4}$ in. × $5\frac{1}{2}$ in. E.781–1935.

Note: By the same hand as No. **268**.

268. Two mirror frames. Pen and ink and wash. About 1780. $16\frac{1}{2}$ in. × $5\frac{1}{4}$ in. and $16\frac{1}{2}$ in. × 7 in. E.785 and 786–1935.

Note: By the same hand as No. **267**.

John Carter, 1748–1817

Architect and antiquarian draughtsman. He practiced little as an architect and his principal occupation was drawing medieval antiquities to illustrate books. Among his own works were *Specimens of Ancient Sculpture and Painting* (1780–1794) and *Views of Ancient Buildings in England* (1786–1793). He also published a large number of his own architectural drawings, which have a certain originality, as illustrations to *The Builder's Magazine*, which came out in monthly numbers between 1774 and 1778. Among them are a few furniture designs in a personal neo-classical style.

269. A girandole. Plate 82 in *The Builder's Magazine*, 1774–1786. Dated 1776. Etching. $7\frac{3}{8}$ in. × $5\frac{5}{8}$ in.

270. A mirror frame. Plate 157 in *The Builder's Magazine*, 1774–1786. Dated 1778. Etching. $6\frac{3}{8}$ in. × $3\frac{5}{8}$ in.

271. A chandelier. Plate 118 in *The Builder's Magazine*, 1774–1786. Etched by Royce and dated 1777. $5\frac{7}{8}$ in. × 6 in.

272. A clock case. Plate 149 in *The Builder's Magazine*, 1774–1786. Etching. 5 in. × $4\frac{7}{8}$ in.

273. A chair. Plate 123 in *The Builder's Magazine*, 1774–1786. Dated 1777. Etching. 6 in. × $4\frac{1}{2}$ in.

George Hepplewhite, d. 1786

Cabinet-maker and designer. In 1788, two years after his death, a book of designs was published by his widow Alice under the title:

The Cabinet-Maker and Upholsterer's Guide; or, repository of designs for every article of household furniture, in the newest and most approved taste: displaying a great variety of patterns . . . In the plainest and most enriched styles; with a scale to each, and an explanation in letterpress. Also the plan of a room, shewing the proper distribution of the furniture. The whole exhibiting near three hundred different designs, engraved on one hundred and twenty-six plates: from drawings, by A. Hepplewhite and Co. cabinet-makers. London. Published by I. and J. Taylor . . . 1788.

All the plates are dated 1787. No engraver's name is given.

In 1789 a second edition was published with one additional plate and a few small alterations. 'The third edition, improved', which came out in 1794, contained another new plate and some substantial alterations, mainly affecting the designs for chairs, new designs being substituted for the old in the following plates:

(1) Right side. (3) Left side. (5) Entire plate.
(6) Left side. (8) Entire plate. (9) Left side.
(10) Left side. (11) Left side.
(12) Entire plate replaced by one showing six chair-backs in the style of Sheraton.
(13) Ditto. (21) Entire plate. (23) Ditto.
(25) Ditto. (118) Ditto.

The new designs, with the exception of plate 118,

are all for square-backed chairs and sofas in the manner of Sheraton and were clearly prompted by Sheraton's criticism in *The Cabinet-Maker and Upholsterer's Drawing Book*, part I, 1791, in which he observed that Hepplewhite's designs, particularly the chairs, 'had already caught the decline'.

There are 6 plates signed 'Hepplewhite' in the *Cabinet-Maker's London Book of Prices*, 1788 (second edition 1793. See under Thomas Shearer, page 63).

Little is known of Hepplewhite's career, apart from the fact that he was apprenticed to the firm of Gillow's in Lancaster and afterwards opened a cabinet-making shop in London in Redcross St., Cripplegate. No bills for his furniture are known and very little furniture corresponds with his plates in the *Guide*. It is not even certain that he was the author of the designs. The absence of any reference to him on the title-page and the interval of two years between his death and the publication of the book suggests that another hand may have been responsible for part or all of the work.

See also pages 25–26 for a discussion of Hepplewhite's style; and Clouston, pp. 258–302; J. M. Bell, *Chippendale, Sheraton and Hepplewhite furniture designs*, 1900; R. Edwards, *Hepplewhite Furniture Designs*, 1947. A facsimile reprint of the third edition of the *Guide* was published by Messrs Batsford in 1897.

274. Two chairs. Plate 5 in *The Cabinet-Maker and Upholsterer's Guide*, 1788. Dated 1787. Engraving. $6\frac{7}{8}$ in. $\times 9\frac{1}{4}$ in.

275. Two 'state chairs'. Plate 13 *ibidem*. Engraving. Dated 1787. $6\frac{7}{8}$ in. $\times 10$ in.

Note: In the 3rd edition of the *Guide*, 1794, these two outmoded chairs were replaced by six rectangular chair-backs in the manner of Sheraton, who had criticized Hepplewhite's chairs as out of date.

276. Two chairs. Plate 8 *ibidem*. Dated 1787. Engraving. $10\frac{7}{8}$ in. $\times 9\frac{1}{8}$ in.

Note: Hepplewhite writes of these chairs that, being light, they are particularly suitable for decorating 'with painted or japanned work, which gives a rich and splendid appearance to the minuter parts of the ornaments, which are generally thrown in by the painter'. He states that 'japanned chairs should always have linen or cotton cases to accord with the general hue of the chair'.

277. Two chairs. Plate 4 *ibidem*. Dated 1787. Engraving. $6\frac{7}{8}$ in. $\times 9\frac{7}{8}$ in.

Note: According to Hepplewhite, 'this kind of chair in general is called banister back chair' and he states that they are usually made of mahogany 'with seats of horse hair, plain, striped, chequered, etc. at pleasure'.

278. 'A Bar Back Sofa'. Plate 26 *ibidem*. Dated 1787. Engraving. $6\frac{3}{4}$ in. $\times 9\frac{3}{4}$ in.

Note: Hepplewhite writes that 'this kind of Sofa is of modern invention; and the lightness of its appearance has procured it a favourable reception in the first circles of fashion'.

279. 'A Duchesse', or *chaise longue*. Plate 28 *ibidem*. Dated 1787. Engraving. $6\frac{3}{4}$ in. $\times 9\frac{3}{4}$ in.

280. Two 'Window Stools'. Plate 19 *ibidem*. Dated 1787. Engraving. $9\frac{3}{4}$ in. $\times 6\frac{3}{4}$ in.

Note: Hepplewhite writes that 'the upper one is applicable to japan work, with striped furniture (i.e. upholstery); the under one of mahogany, carved, with furniture of an elegant pattern festooned in front'.

281. 'An Easy Chair' and 'A Gouty Stool'. Plate 15 *ibidem*. Dated 1787. Engraving.

Note: Hepplewhite also refers to the chair as 'A Saddle Check Chair' and recommends covering it with leather or horse hair or providing it with a linen case to fit over the canvas stuffing.

282. A wardrobe. Plate 86 *ibidem*. Dated 1787. Engraving.

283. A Bed. Plate 96 *ibidem*. Engraving. Hepplewhite suggests that 'the cornice will look well japanned'.

284. Three 'Pole Fire Screens', Plate 93 *ibidem*. Engraving.

Note: Hepplewhite writes that 'the Screens may be ornamented variously, with maps, Chinese figures, needlework, etc', and that the frame 'may be made of mahogany, but more frequently of wood japanned'.

285. Two 'Cellerets' or wine cases, also known as *gardes de vin*, according to Hepplewhite. Plate 37 *ibidem*. Engraving.

Note: Hepplewhite informs us that 'they are usually made of mahogany, and hooped with brass hoops lacquered; the inner part is divided with partitions, and lined with lead for bottles'.

286. Four lamps. Plate 112 *ibidem*. Engraving. Hepplewhite states that 'the ornaments are of brass-work – the square one may be wrought in mahogany'.

287. Four knife cases. Plate 39 *ibidem*. Engraving.

Note: According to Hepplewhite, 'they are usually made of satin or other light-coloured wood, and may be placed at each end on the sideboards, or on a pedestal'.

288. Two pier tables. Plate 65 *ibidem*. Dated 1787. Engraving. 10 in. $\times 7\frac{7}{8}$ in.

289. Two 'Pembroke Tables'. Plate 62 *ibidem*. Engraving.

Note: According to Sheraton, they are named after 'the

lady who first gave orders for one of them, and who probably gave the idea of such a table to the workmen'– possibly a Countess of Pembroke.

290. 'A Tambour Writing Table'. Plate 67 *ibidem*. Engraving.

291. A Commode. Plate 78 *ibidem*. Engraving.

Note. Hepplewhite recommends satinwood, 'enriched with painted or inlaid work'.

292. 'A Gentleman's Social Table' and 'A Kidney Knee-hole Writing Table'. Plate 22 in *The London Book of Prices*. 2nd edition, 1793. Lettered: 'Heppelwhite del. Elbon sc' etc. and dated 1792. Etching. 9¾ in. × 6¾ in.

293. 'A Serpentine Cabinet'. Plate 24 *ibidem*. Same lettering and size. Etching.

THOMAS SHEARER, fr. c. 1788

Cabinet-maker. He and the firm of Hepplewhite were responsible for most of the furniture designs in a book published in 1788 under the title:

The Cabinet-Makers' London Book of Prices, and Designs of Cabinet Work, calculated for the convenience of cabinet makers in general, whereby the price of executing any piece of work may be easily found.

A second edition, from which the plates reproduced here are taken, was issued in 1793. It contains 29 plates, of which 17 are by Shearer, 6 by Hepplewhite, 3 by W. Casement and 3 unsigned.

The book is not primarily a collection of designs, but, as the title states, a table of prices for the use of cabinet-makers, setting out the cost of labour and materials needed to make certain typical pieces of furniture. Most of the book is taken up with information of this kind, and the plates only occupy a small space at the end. Nevertheless, Sheraton in the Preface to his *Drawing Book* compared the book favourably with Hepplewhite's *Guide*, observing that 'the designs are more fashionable and useful than his in proportion to their numbers'. He had evidently forgotten that Hepplewhite had contributed to both books, and he was clearly referring to the work of Shearer which, though it has no more merit than Hepplewhite's to modern eyes, is certainly a little more advanced in style and occupies a place midway between Hepplewhite and Sheraton. It has been stated that Shearer's designs were published separately in 1788 under the title *Designs for Household Furniture*, but though there is a volume of his designs bound separately in the Museum Library, it has no title-page and there appears to be no record of a copy with one.

294. A library bookcase. Plate 1 in *The London Book of Prices*, 2nd edition, 1793. Lettered: 'Shearer delin. Jowes sculp' etc. and dated 1788. Etching. 6¾ in. × 9¾ in.

295. A sideboard. Plate 6 *ibidem*. Same lettering and size. Etching.

Note: This is the earliest published design for a sideboard with pedestals all in one piece.

296. Two bureau bookcases. Plate 7 *ibidem*. Same lettering and size. Etching.

297. A wardrobe. Plate 3 *ibidem*. Same lettering and size. Etching.

HENRY HOLLAND, 1745–1806

Architect. Trained by his father, a well-known master builder of Fulham, Holland began his career as the partner and assistant of 'Capability' Brown, the landscape gardener, whose daughter he married. At the age of thirty-one he was employed to design Brooks's Club in St. James's Street, and this commission made him known to the Whig leaders, some of whom afterwards became his patrons; it also brought him to the notice of the Prince of Wales, for whom he rebuilt Carlton House, Pall Mall. Through his association with the Prince and his Whig friends he acquired an interest in French architecture and decoration which was reflected in his furniture designs as well as his buildings. Like Adam, he was interested in furniture as a complement to his architectural schemes, but his style is simpler and bolder. His furniture is enriched with a minimum of ornament, the plain surfaces being relieved by well-proportioned panels devoid of internal decoration. Some of the furniture which he designed for the Prince of Wales is preserved at Buckingham Palace (see H. Clifford Smith, *Buckingham Palace*, 1931); and at Southill, Bedfordshire, some of the rooms are still to a great extent arranged and furnished according to his designs (see Major S. Whitbread (editor), *Southill, A Regency House*, 1951). Few of his designs have been preserved, apart from two sketchbooks in the library of the Royal Institute of British Architects.

For a discussion of Holland's style in furniture design, see pages 26–28. See also Dorothy Stroud, *Henry Holland*, 1950.

298. 'Design for the two Bookcase tables . . .' in the Library at Southill. About 1796–1800. Pen and ink. Size of sheet 14½ in. × 10 in. (R.I.B.A. Holland *Sketch Book*, p. 60.)

Note: Holland's notes show that the bookcase was to be painted white to match the rest of the room, and the mirror frame and ornaments above were to be gilt. For photographs of the bookcases as carried out, see Dorothy Stroud, *Henry Holland*, 1950, p. 95, and Major S. Whitbread (editor), *Southill, A Regency House*, 1951, fig. 13.

299. 'An ornamental stand to support a lamp'. About 1800. Pen and ink. Size of sheet 14½ in. × 10 in. (R.I.B.A. Holland *Sketch Book*, p. 54.)

Note: The drawing is a third of real size, the plinth being 2 ft. 7 in. long and 4 in. high.

300. A wardrobe. About 1800. Pen and ink. Size of sheet 14½ in. × 10 in. (R.I.B.A. Holland *Sketch Book*, p. 73.)

301. Design for the bookcases in the library at Woburn Abbey, Beds. Pen and ink. Size of sheet 14½ in. × 10 in. (R.I.B.A. Holland *Sketch Book*, p. 20.)

Note: Holland carried out various alterations at Woburn between 1787 and 1788.

302. Design for 'pier tables with glass over in library' at Woburn Abbey, Beds. Pen and ink. Size of sheet 14½ in. × 10 in. (R.I.B.A. Holland *Sketch Book*, p. 20.)

Sir John Soane, 1753–1837

Architect. At the age of fifteen he entered the office of George Dance, an architect of originality, whose experiments in unusual structural devices, like the top-lighted dome, made a lasting impression on Soane and helped to form his highly personal style. After four years with Dance, Soane became the assistant of Henry Holland (see page 63), with whom he remained six years. His position became assured in 1788, when he was appointed Surveyor to the Bank of England and was entrusted with the rebuilding of the Bank, an important commission, which occupied him for more than forty years and made him known to other wealthy clients. At his death he left his house in Lincoln's Inn Fields and his valuable collection of architectural drawings and works of art to the nation as a museum for 'the study of Architecture and the Allied Arts'. Whether he regarded the designing of furniture as an 'Allied Art' is uncertain. He mildly reproved Adam for having attached too much importance to such trifles as 'the key-hole of a lady's Escritoire'. On the other hand, there are a few designs for furniture among his drawings in his own museum, and these show that he had a decided gift for this kind of work. The design for a chair for Shotesham Park, Norwich (No. **305**), is particularly interesting, because it is in no sense a reflection of Soane's architectural style, but a purely objective and functional conception, foreshadowing the ideals of craftsmen like William Morris.

See page 28. Also John Summerson, *Sir John Soane*, 1952.

303. 'A Music Table for the Duke of Leeds'. Inscribed with title and dated August 8th, 1797. Pen and ink. 7 in. × 6 in. (Sir John Soane's Museum. *Soane*, Drawer 7. Set 4.)

Note: A note on the doors shows that they were to be lined with blue silk behind brass wire. Soane completed No. 21 St. James's Square for the Duke of Leeds in 1795.

304. A mirror for Henry Peters of Bletchworth Castle, Dorking, Surrey. Inscribed with the client's name and notes. About 1799. Pen and ink and wash. 13 in. × 16½ in. (Sir John Soane's Museum. *Soane*, Drawer 7. Set 4.)

Note: Soane designed the stables at Bletchworth Castle in 1799, and this drawing was probably made about the same time.

305. A chair for Robert Fellowes of Shotesham Park, Norwich. Dated August 12th, 1790. Pen and ink and wash. 9 in. × 6¾ in. (Sir John Soane's Museum. *Soane*, Drawer 7, Set 4.)

Note: Soane's plans for Shotesham Park are dated 1785–1788. No chairs have been traced corresponding with this design, but there are some chairs still at Shotesham in a very similar style, probably made from designs by Soane. (Information kindly supplied by Mrs Fellowes through Miss Dorothy Stroud.)

306 and **306A.** Designs for the stove in the new hall at Bentley Priory, Stanmore, Middlesex, for the Marquis of Abercorn. Inscribed with the title and dated August 31st, 1799. Pen and ink and wash. (Sir John Soane's Museum. *Soane*, Drawer 7. Set 4.)

Note: Soane was responsible for alterations and additions to Bentley Priory between 1789 and 1799.

Charles Heathcote Tatham, 1772–1842

Architect. He was a pupil of Henry Holland, who sent him to Italy to study and who employed him there as his agent to buy specimens of classical ornament and contemporary Italian bronzes in the neo-classical style. In this way Tatham played a small part in the formation of the Regency style, which was to some extent inspired by the study of such material. He published *Etchings of*

Ancient Ornamental Architecture (1799) and *Etchings Representing fragments of Grecian and Roman Architectural Ornaments* (1806), which were both of some use to the classicizing designers of the day (cf. Nos. **360–364**). Tatham was a friend and admirer of John Linnell (see page 54), some of whose designs he collected together in an album now in the Museum. It includes a few of his own designs, one of which illustrated here. Some of the letters which he wrote to Henry Holland from Italy are also in the Museum (in the Print Room).

307. Design for a papal chair. Signed with the initials CHT and dated Rome 1794. Pencil and water-colour. 7 in. × 7⅝ in.   E.372-1929.

John Nash, 1752–1835

Architect. He rose to prominence during the early years of the nineteenth century through the patronage of the Prince Regent, afterwards George IV, for whom his most important works were the planning of the Regent's Park, the building of Regent Street and the rebuilding of Buckingham Palace and the Brighton Pavilion. Up to 1800 he was known mainly as a country house architect, and judging from the style, the furniture design reproduced here dates from that period of his career.

308. Designs for an arm-chair. Inscribed: 'This chair will do in point of form but the wood must be green and the lines gold – the fringe A gold – the flutes B to be formed by gold lines . . . the line or frame H will be the chord or binding of the cushion which is to be stuffed very square. I have no objection to the front of the cushions having a gimp'd face as sketched in I . . .' About 1790. Pen and ink and wash. (By kind permission of Mr John Summerson.)

Thomas Sheraton, 1751–1806

Cabinet-maker and designer. According to an obituary in the *Gentleman's Magazine* for November 1806, he was a native of Stockton-on-Tees and 'for many years a journey-man cabinet-maker, but who since the year 1793 has supported himself, a wife and two children by his exertions as an author'. His works consist of several religious and philosophical tracts and three books on furniture.

His first book of designs appears to have been published in 42 separate numbers, the plates being dated from 1791 to 1793 (see paragraph (*b*) below). The first complete edition was published in 1793 and 1794 under the title:

The Cabinet-Maker and Upholsterer's Drawing-Book. In Three Parts. By Thomas Sheraton, Cabinet-Maker. London: Printed for the author, by T. Bensley; and sold by J. Mathews, No. 18, Strand; G. Terry, No. 54 Paternoster-Row; J. S. Jordan, No. 166, Fleet-Street, L. Wayland, Middle-Row, Holborn; and by the author, No. 41, Davies-Street, Grosvenor Square. (Engravers: G. Terry, J. Newton, J. Barlow, Thornwaite, J. J. Caldwell, J. Cooke and others.)

The work consists of three parts, with an Appendix and an Accompaniment. The Museum copy is in two volumes (bound together), the first volume containing part I, while the second, dated 1794, comprises parts II and III. The Appendix and the Accompaniment have separate title-pages, which read:

(a) *Appendix to the Cabinet-Maker and Upholsterer's Drawing-Book. Containing a variety of original designs for household furniture, in the newest and most elegant style; also, a number of plain and useful pieces, suitable either for town or country; together with a description and explanation to each piece. By Thomas Sheraton . . . Printed for the author by T. Bensley; and sold by . . . and by the author, No. 106 Wardour-Street, Soho. 1793.*

(b) *An Accompaniment to the Cabinet-Maker and Upholsterer's Drawing-Book. Containing a variety of ornaments useful for learners to copy from, but particularly adapted to the cabinet and chair branches: exhibiting original and new designs of chair legs, bed pillars, window cornices, chair splads and other ornaments . . . By Thomas Sheraton . . . Printed by T. Bensley, for the author, No. 106, Wardour-Street, Soho. Of whom may be had, separate, in forty-two numbers . . . The Cabinet-Maker and Upholsterer's Drawing-Book . . .*

The plates in the first three parts and Appendix are dated variously 1791, 1792 and 1793, while in the Accompaniment they are all dated 1794.

A second edition was brought out in 1794, with 7 new plates added to the Appendix.

A third edition, published in 1802, was entitled:

The Cabinet-Maker and Upholsterer's Drawing-Book. In four parts . . . recommended by many workmen of the first abilities in London . . . The third edition, revised, and the whole embellished with 122 elegant copper-plates. London . . . Printed by T. Bensley . . . for W. Baynes (successor to G. Terry) . . . 1802.

(The Appendix was here counted as part IV; there is no substantial addition to the text or the plates).

The first two parts of the *Drawing-Book* are devoted to an elaborate treatise on geometry and another on perspective, which Sheraton evidently regarded as the most important section of the book.

He criticized his predecessors for giving too little advice on this part of the designer's work and observed of Hepplewhite that he gives 'no direction for drawing in any form, nor any pretensions to it. The whole merit of the performance rests on the designs', and these, he pointed out, were already obsolete, 'a fate which all books of the same kind will ever be subject to'. He acknowledged the transitoriness of his own designs, but was confident that his exposition of the principles on which they were drawn would endure, and this belief he expressed in an allegorical frontispiece above the legend: 'Time alters fashions and frequently obliterates the works of art and ingenuity; but that which is founded on Geometry and real Science, will remain unalterable'. In this he was mistaken, for his tract on perspective is probably never studied now, whereas his designs (like those of Hepplewhite) are likely to interest people for many years to come. Nevertheless, his system served his own purpose well, and most of his designs are admirably drawn and presented.

Part III of the *Drawing-Book* 'is intended', in Sheraton's words, 'to exhibit the present taste of furniture, and at the same time, to give the workman some assistance in the manufacturing part of it'. His practical instructions are, indeed, fuller than those in any other book of the kind, and he devotes twelve pages of text to a technical account of a 'Harlequin Pembroke Table'.

His handling of such problems proves that he had a thorough practical knowledge of cabinet-making. But it is clear that he had by this time given up the profession and had no workshop of his own. His trade card (illustrated in Edwards and Macquoid, vol. 3, p. 120, and in A. Heal, *The London Furniture Makers*, 1953, p. 167), makes no reference to any activity of that kind, merely stating that he 'teaches perspective, architecture and ornaments, makes designs for cabinet-makers and sells all kinds of drawing books, etc.' Nor does the copious text which accompanies all his furniture designs contain any allusion to his own activities as a cabinet-maker; indeed, in some cases, he supplies the name and address of firms from which certain types of furniture could be procured, which suggests that he had no business of his own. Unlike most authors of pattern books, he makes no claim to originality in his designs, and in several cases acknowledges his indebtedness to others, as in his description of the Harlequin Pembroke Table, where he writes: 'In this . . . I assume very little originality or merit, except what is due to the manner of showing and describing the mechanism of it; the rest is due from a friend, for whom I received my first ideas of it'.

(*Drawing-Book*, part III, p. 417). This attitude is consistent with his statement in the introduction to part III of the *Drawing Book* that he had made it his business to apply to the best workmen in different shops for advice. Nevertheless, though he borrowed some of his ideas from others and worked in the fashionable style of the day, each of his books displays throughout a firm consistency of style which indicates that most of the designs were his own inventions; and his skill in handling new ideas suggests that he was among those who led rather than followed the fashion.

A German edition of the *Drawing-Book* was published at Leipzig under the title:

Modell-und Zeichnungsbuch für Ebenisten, Tischer, Tapezirer, und Stuhlmacher . . . Aus dem Englischen übersetzt, und mit einigen Anmerkungen versehen von G. T. Wenzel. (The preface is dated 1794).

Sheraton's next book of designs was entitled:

The Cabinet Dictionary, containing an explanation of all the terms used in the cabinet, chair and upholstery branches; with directions for varnish-making, polishing, and gilding. To which is added a supplementary treatise on geometrical lines, perspective and painting in general. The whole illustrated on eighty-eight handsomely engraved copper-plates, including a very great variety of the most fashionable pieces of cabinet furniture . . . By T. Sheraton . . . London. Printed by W. Smith, King Street, Seven Dials . . . 1803.

Some of the articles, like those on gilding and on the various woods used in cabinet-making, contain useful technical information, but others, like the lengthy article on Botany, have virtually no bearing on the subject of the work. The plates reveal that a radical change had taken place in furniture fashions since the publication of the *Drawing-Book*. The new style was based on a more literal interpretation of classical models and made a greater use of large-scale sculptural motifs, such as lions' legs and paw feet. The slender forms of the 1790's gave way to a more solid and monumental handling, and bold sweeping curves and volutes took the place of straight lines. These designs are the first published examples of the so-called Regency style.

The same tendency is illustrated in the plates of Sheraton's last work, of which he completed only one volume before his death in 1806. The plates are dated from 1804 to 1807 and some must, therefore, have been engraved posthumously. The title is:

The Cabinet-Maker, Upholsterer, and General Artist's Encyclopaedia.

Most of the book is taken up with articles on a wide variety of subjects, from Astronomy to Canada, but none to do with furniture or cabinet-making. At the end there are over fifty plates showing furniture designs, accompanied by a 'Description' but they have no apparent connection with the rest of the book. In fact the choice of the articles and the general arrangement of the work plainly show that the author's mind had begun to give way. He did not live to carry the encyclopaedia beyond the word *Capstan*.

In 1812 a number of Sheraton's plates were reprinted in a book entitled *Designs for Household Furniture by the late Thomas Sheraton*.

A facsimile reprint of the third edition of the *Drawing-Book* was issued in 1895. A selection from the plates is reproduced in J. M. Bell, *Chippendale, Sheraton and Hepplewhite furniture designs reproduced and arranged*, 1900 and in R. Edwards, *Sheraton Furniture Designs*, 1945.

For a discussion of Sheraton's style in furniture design see pages 28–30.

309. Design for a mirror. Inscribed: 'Thos. Sheraton'. About 1790. Pen and ink and water-colour. 6 in. × 2⅞ in.   D.228–1890.

Note: There are no other drawings by Sheraton extant, and the authenticity of the signature on this one cannot be proved. The style is not unlike Sheraton's.

310. Pier table. Plate 31 in the *Appendix* to the *Drawing-Book* showing a view of the south end of the Prince of Wales's Chinese Drawing Room in Carlton House. Engraved by J. Barlow and dated 1793. Engraving. Size of plate 7¼ in. × 11 in.

Note: The pier table itself is now at Buckingham Palace (illustrated in H. Clifford Smith, *Buckingham Palace*, 1931, p. 220, fig. 267). It was presumably made from a design by Henry Holland, the architect of Carlton House. Sheraton's impression of it is somewhat inaccurate and he has falsified the scale of the ornament. But the engraving, though not strictly an original design, is of some interest because it reveals the source of some of Sheraton's ideas.

311. A commode. Plate 66 in the *Appendix* to the *Drawing-Book*, second and third editions. Engraved by G. Terry and dated 1794. 7½ in. × 9½ in.

312. Two dressing chests. Plate 15 in the *Appendix* to the *Drawing-Book*, *1793*. Engraving. 10 in. × 7½ in.

313. 'A kidney table'. Plate 58 in the *Drawing-Book*, part III. Engraved by G. Terry and dated 1792. 9½ in. × 7½ in.

314. Two card tables. Plate 11 in the *Appendix* to the *Drawing-Book*. Engraved by G. Terry and dated 1793. 7⅛ in. × 9½ in.

315. Two 'ladies' work tables'. Plate 26 in the *Appendix* to the *Drawing-Book*. Engraved by J. Barlow and dated 1793. 7½ in. × 9½ in.

316. A library book-case. Plate 3 in the *Appendix* to the *Drawing-Book*. Engraved by G. Terry and dated 1793. 7½ in. × 9½ in.

317. 'A side board with vase knife cases'. Plate 21 in the *Appendix* to the *Drawing-Book*. Engraved by G. Terry and dated 1793. 7½ in. × 9½ in.

318. 'A summer bed in two compartments'. Plate 41 in the *Drawing-Book*, part III. Engraved by Barlow and dated 1792. 9½ in. × 7½ in.

319. Three 'corner bason stands'. Plate 42 in the *Drawing-Book*, part III. Engraved by Barlow and dated 1792. 7½ in. × 9½ in.

320. 'A lady's cabinet dressing table'. Plate 49 in the *Drawing-Book*, part III. Engraved by G. Terry and dated 1792. 9½ in. × 7½ in.

321. Two knife-cases and a 'lady's travelling box'. Plate 39 in the *Drawing-Book*, part III. Engraved by G. Terry and dated 1792. 9½ in. × 7½ in.

Note: Of the knife cases Sheraton observes that as they 'are not made in regular cabinet shops, it may be of service to mention where they are executed in the best taste by one who makes it his main business, i.e. John Lane, No. 44, St. Martin's-le-Grand . . .'

322. A lady's drawing and writing table. Plate 60 in the *Drawing-Book*, part III. Engraved by Barlow and dated 1793. 9½ × 7½ in.

Note: Tables of this type were sometimes known as 'Carlton House tables', presumably because the Prince of Wales had ordered one for his London residence.

323. A lady's cabinet. Plate 16 in the *Appendix* to the *Drawing-Book*. Engraved by J. Barlow and dated 1793. 7 in. × 9½ in.

Note: Sheraton states that 'the marble shelves with frets at each end are for a tea equipage'.

324. 'A Pembroke Table'. Plate 61 in the *Cabinet Dictionary*, 1803. Dated 1803. Engraved by J. Caldwall. 4¼ in. × 7 in.

Note: Sheraton states that the name was 'given to a kind of breakfast table, from the name of the lady who first gave orders for one of them', presumably a Countess of Pembroke. The term was in use by the middle of the eighteenth century.

325. Four 'quartetto tables'. Plate 78 in the *Cabinet Dictionary*, 1803. Dated 1803 and engraved by J. Caldwall. 4⅞ in. × 9¼ in.

Note: In his text Sheraton defines the quartetto table as

'a kind of small work table made to draw out of each other, and may be used separately, and again inclosed within each other, when not wanted'.

326. A sofa and two conversation chairs. Plate 10 in the *Appendix* to the *Drawing-Book*. Engraved by J. Caldwell and dated 1793. $9\frac{1}{2}$ in. $\times 7\frac{1}{2}$ in.

Note: Of the conversation chairs Sheraton observes that 'the parties who converse with each other sit with their legs across the seat, and rest with their arms on the top rail . . .'.

327. Two drawing room chairs. Plate 32 in the *Drawing-Book*, part III. Engraved by Thornwaite and dated 1792. $7\frac{1}{2}$ in. $\times 9\frac{1}{2}$ in.

328. Six chair backs. Plate 36 in the *Drawing-Book*, part III. Engraved by Terry and dated 1792. $7\frac{1}{2}$ in. $\times 9\frac{1}{2}$ in.

329. Two parlour chairs. Plate 33 in the *Drawing-Book*, part III. Engraved by J. Barlow and dated 1792. $7\frac{1}{2}$ in. $\times 9\frac{1}{2}$ in.

330. Three designs for chair legs. Plate 14 in the *Accompaniment* to the *Drawing-Book*. Engraved by J. Caldwell and dated 1793. $15\frac{1}{2}$ in. $\times 9$ in.

331. Two drawing-room chairs. Plate 45 in the *Cabinet Dictionary*, 1803. Dated 1803. Engraved by J. Caldwall. $4\frac{1}{8}$ in. $\times 7\frac{1}{8}$ in.

332. Two 'Herculaneums', or arm-chairs, so named 'on account of their antique style of composition'. Plate 7 in the *Cabinet Dictionary*, 1803. Dated 1802. Engraved by J. Barlow. $4\frac{1}{4}$ in. $\times 7\frac{1}{4}$ in.

333. Two 'library tables'. Plate 54 in the *Cabinet Dictionary*, 1803. Dated 1802. $7\frac{1}{4}$ in. $\times 4\frac{1}{8}$ in.

334. A library table. Plate 37 in the *Encyclopaedia*, c. 1806. Etching coloured by hand. $9\frac{5}{8}$ in. $\times 15\frac{7}{8}$ in.

335. 'A Grecian Dining Table'. Plate 47 in the *Cabinet Dictionary*, 1803. Engraved by Warner. $7\frac{1}{8}$ in. $\times 12\frac{1}{8}$ in.

336. 'A Grecian Squab'. Plate 49 in the *Cabinet Dictionary*, 1803. Dated 1802. Engraving. $4\frac{1}{4}$ in. $\times 7\frac{3}{4}$ in.

337. A sofa. Plate 6 in the *Encyclopaedia*, c. 1806. Etching coloured by hand. $9\frac{5}{8}$ in. $\times 15\frac{7}{8}$ in.

338. 'A Grecian bedstead' and footstool. Plate 3 in the *Encyclopaedia*, c. 1806. Etching coloured by hand. Cut to $15\frac{5}{8}$ in. $\times 9\frac{7}{8}$ in.

Note: The illustrations in the Appendix (Nos. **339–366**), which are included for purposes of comparison, are described in the captions under the pictures.

INDEX OF DESIGNERS

The numerals in roman type refer to pages, those in italic type to illustrations.

ADAM, ROBERT. 21–24, 56–59, *202–234*

ANONYMOUS. 32, 35, 36, 54, 56, 61, *10–12, 26, 35–37, 184–186, 201, 264–268*

BICKHAM, GEORGE, THE ELDER. 40, *70*

BRUNETTI, GAETANO. 13, 35, *27–29*

CARTER, JOHN. 24–25, 61, *269–273*

CHAMBERS, SIR WILLIAM. 17, 47, *135–136*

CHIPPENDALE, THOMAS. 14–21, 41–47, *71–123, 170*

COPLAND, H. 42–44, 53–54, *181–183*

CRUNDEN, JOHN. 47, *124–125*

DARLY, MATTHEW. 15, 16, 37–38, *46–47, 128–134, 180, 257–258*

DE LA COUR. 34, *19, 346*

HALFPENNY, WILLIAM. 16, 18, 47, *126–127*

HEPPLEWHITE, GEORGE. 25–26, 61–62, *274–293*

HOLLAND, HENRY, 26–28, 63–64, *298–302*

INCE, WILLIAM (and MAYHEW, JOHN). 21, 49–50, *149–165*

JOHNSON, THOMAS. 21, 48–49, *137–146*

JONES, WILLIAM. 8, 34–35, *20–25*

KEENE, HENRY. 54, *187–189, 259*

KENT, WILLIAM. 7–8, 34, *13–18*

LANGLEY, BATTY AND THOMAS. 8, 13, 35–36, *30–34*

LINNELL, JOHN. 25, 54–56, *190–200, 235–250*

LOCK, MATTHIAS (or MATTHEW). 13–14, 38–40, *48–69, 251–256*

MANWARING, ROBERT. 52–53, *171–179, 180–183*

MAROT, DANIEL. 6–7, 32–33, *4–8, 358*

MAYHEW, JOHN (and INCE, WILLIAM). 21, 49–50, *149–165*

NASH, JOHN. 28, 65, *308*

OVER, CHARLES. 49, *148*

PERGOLESI, MICHAELANGELO. 60, *260*

SHEARER, THOMAS. 63, *294–297*

SHERATON, THOMAS. 28–30, 65–68, *309–338*

SOANE, SIR JOHN. 28, 64, *303–306*

SOCIETY OF UPHOLSTERERS. 51–52, *108, 150, 160, 165–170, 171, 172, 178*

SWANN, ABRAHAM. 13, 36, *38*

TATHAM, CHARLES HEATHCOTE. 54–55, 64, *307*

THORNHILL, SIR JAMES. 33, *9*

VARDY, JOHN. 8, 13, 36–37, *39–45*

VIVARES, FRANÇOIS. 49, *147*

WEBB, JOHN. 5, 32, *1*

YENN, JOHN. 60, *261–263*

Part 3

THE ILLUSTRATIONS

1. John Webb: An alcove and bed for Charles II. Engraving, after a drawing dated 1665.

2. Anonymous drawing: Furniture for a room. About 1675.

3. Stalker and Parker: Designs for japanning. Engraving, 1688.

4. Daniel Marot: A state bed. Engraving, about 1700.

5. Daniel Marot: A state bed. Engraving, about 1700.

6. Daniel Marot: Two tables. Engraving, about 1700.

7. Daniel Marot: Mirrors and brackets. Engraving, about 1700.

8. Daniel Marot: Chairs and stools, etc. Engraving, about 1700.

9. Sir James Thornhill: A state bedroom with furniture. Drawing, about 1720.

10, 11, 12. Three anonymous drawings for a tripod and mirrors. About 1715.

13. William Kent: A chandelier. Engraving, 1744.

14. William Kent: An organ case. Engraving, about 1744.

15. William Kent: A table for Chiswick House. Engraving, 1744.

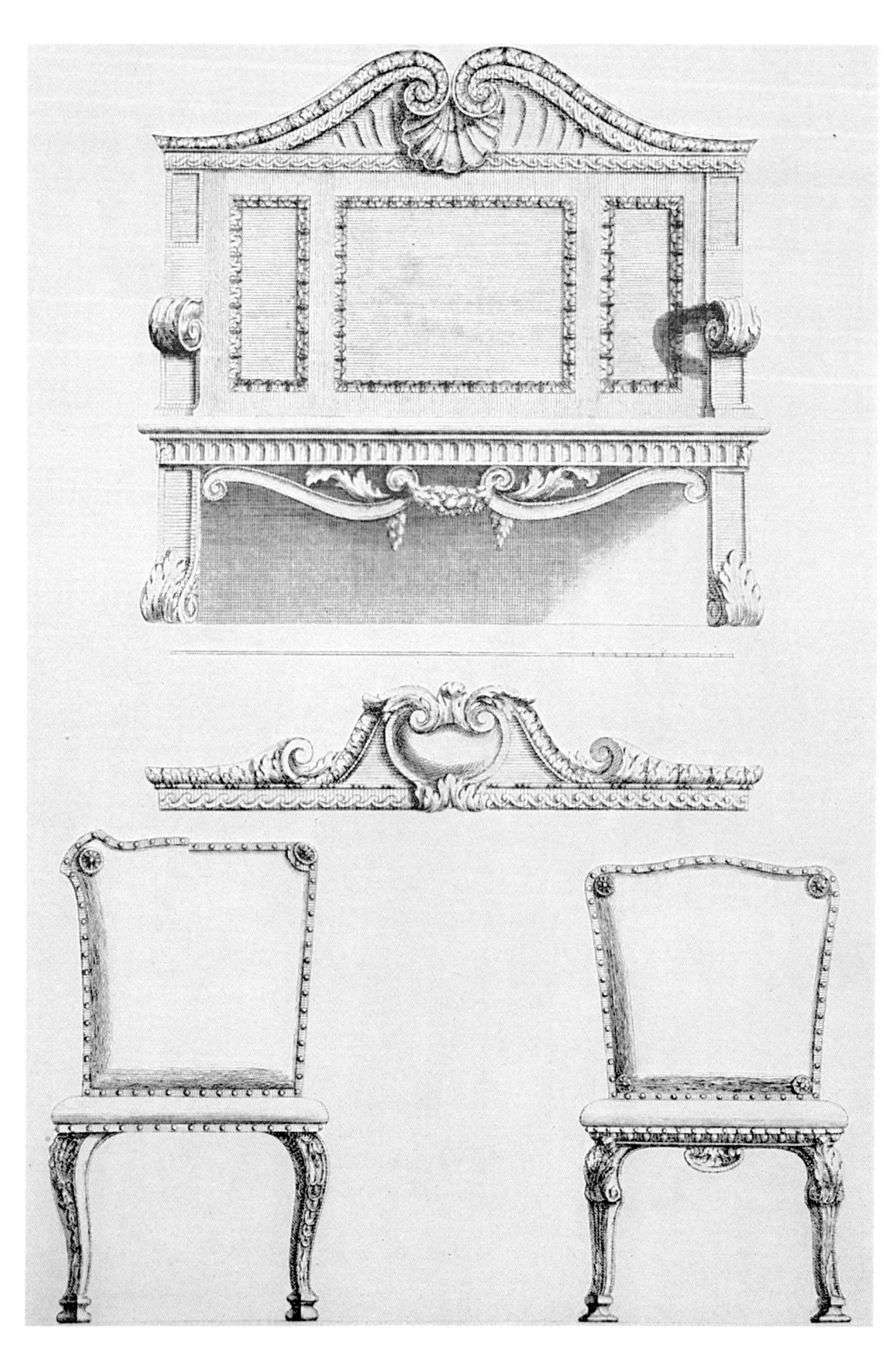

16. William Kent: A settee and two chairs. Engraving, 1744.

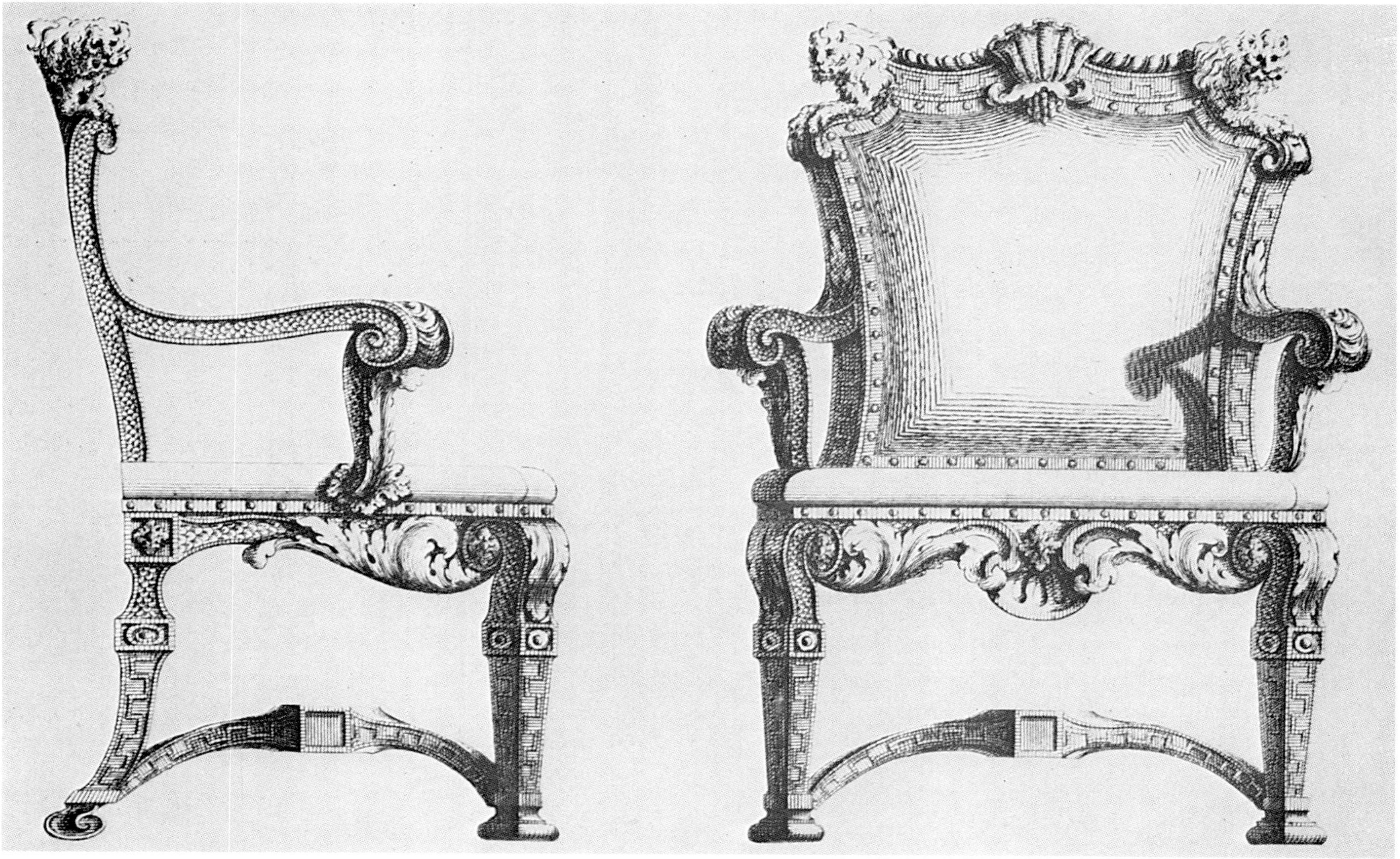

17. William Kent: An arm-chair. Engraving, 1744.

18. William Kent: A table for Houghton Hall. Drawing, 1731.

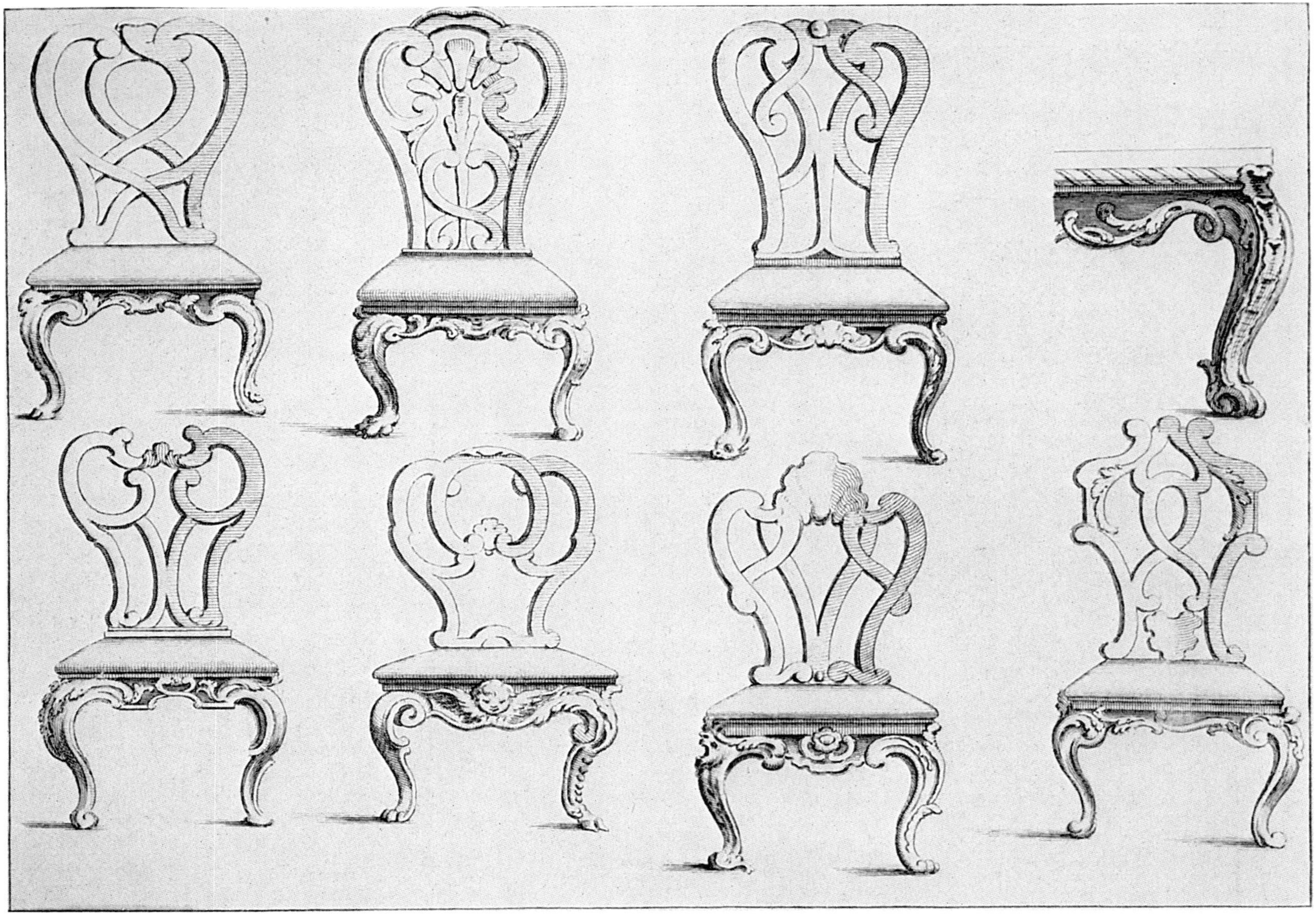

19. De La Cour: Chairs. Engraving, about 1745.

20. William Jones: A side-table. Etching, 1739.

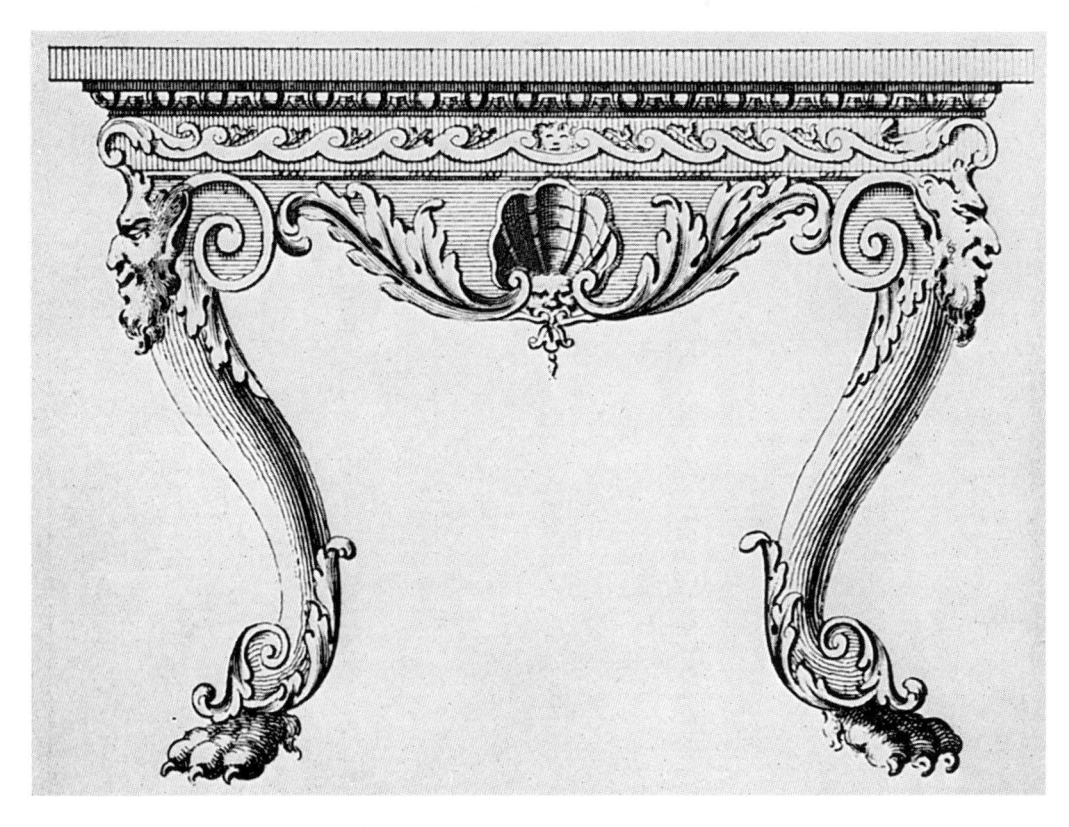

21. William Jones: A side-table. Etching, 1739.

22. William Jones: A side-table. Etching, 1739.

23. William Jones: A side-table. Etching, 1739.

24. William Jones: A mirror. Etching, 1739.

25. William Jones: A mirror. Etching, 1739.

26. Anonymous drawing: A mirror. About 1740.

27. Gaetano Brunetti: An arm-chair and mirror. Etching, 1736.

28. Gaetano Brunetti: Two tables. Etching, 1736.

29. Gaetano Brunetti: Two chairs. Etching, 1736.

Thoˢ Langley Invent delin and sculp

30. Thomas Langley (after J. F. Lauch): A clock. Engraving, 1740.

31. Thomas Langley (after Pineau): A table, Engraving, 1739.

32. Batty Langley: A bookcase. Engraving, 1739.

33. Thomas Langley: A cabinet. Engraving, 1739.

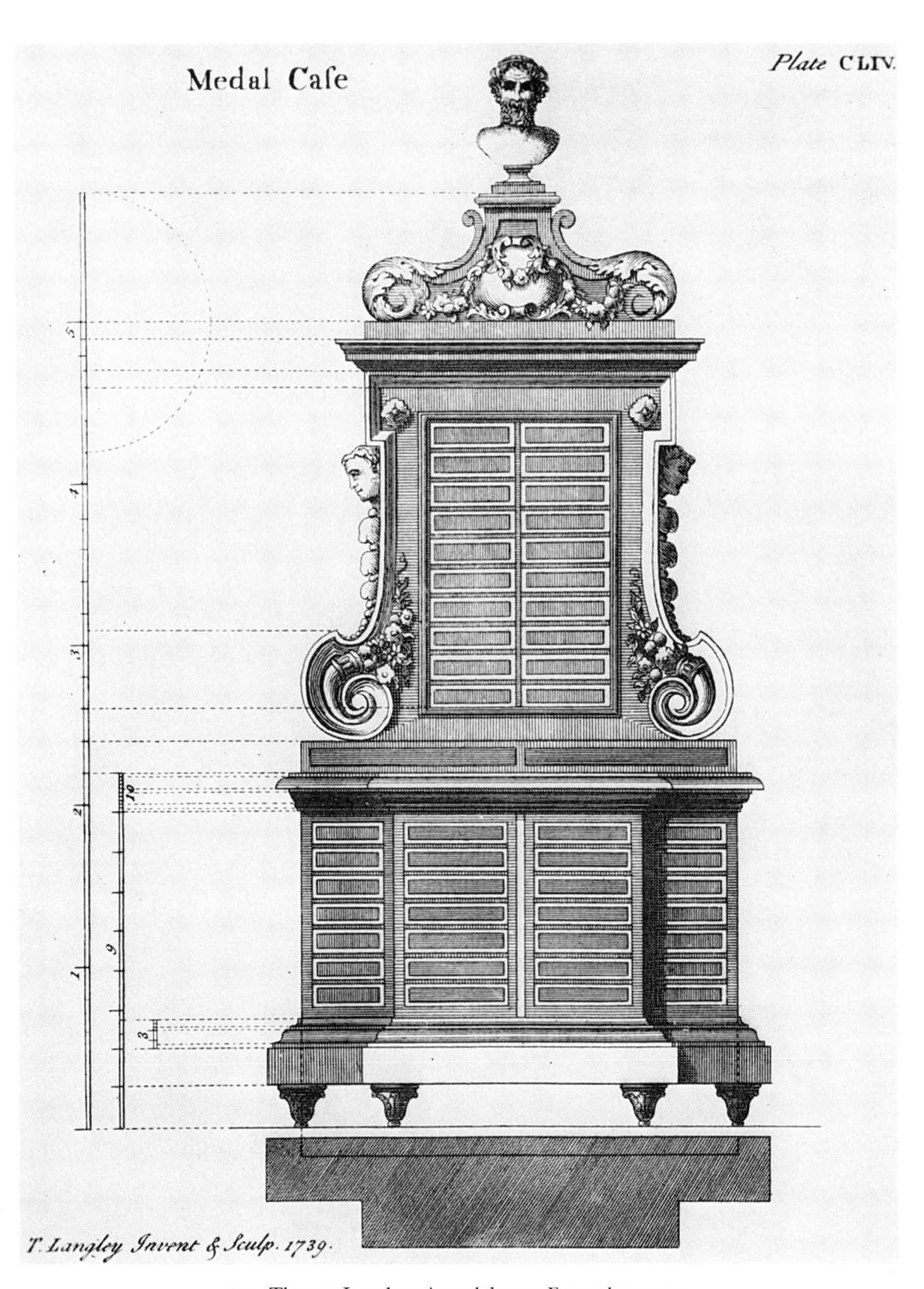

Medal Case

Plate CLIV.

T. Langley Invent & Sculp. 1739.

34. Thomas Langley: A medal case. Engraving, 1739.

35. Anonymous drawing: Pier table and mirror etc. About 1740.

36. Anonymous drawing: A mirror. About 1740.

37. Anonymous drawing: A table. About 1745.

38. Abraham Swan: Mirror and chimney-piece. Engraving, 1745.

39. John Vardy: Mirror and chimney-piece. Drawing, about 1745.

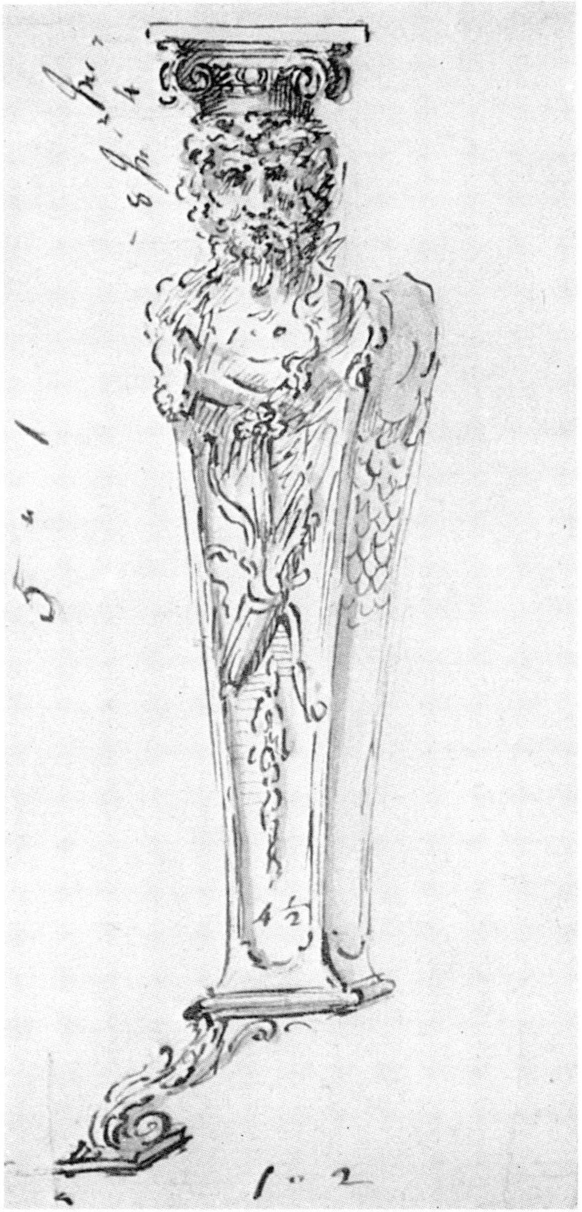

41. John Vardy: A pedestal. Drawing, about 1745.

40. John Vardy: Mirror or picture frame. Drawing, 1761.

42. John Vardy: Pier table and mirror. Drawing, about 1745.

43. John Vardy: Pier table and mirror. Drawing, about 1745.

44. John Vardy: A royal bed. Drawing, 1749.

45. John Vardy: Writing table and *cartonnier*. Drawing, about 1745.

46. Matthew Darly: Four chairs. Etching, 1750.

46. Matthew Darly: Four chairs. Etching, 1750.

47. Matthew Darly: Four chairs. Etching, 1750.

48. Lock: Two tables. Drawing, about 1740.

49. Lock: Two tables. Etching, 1746.

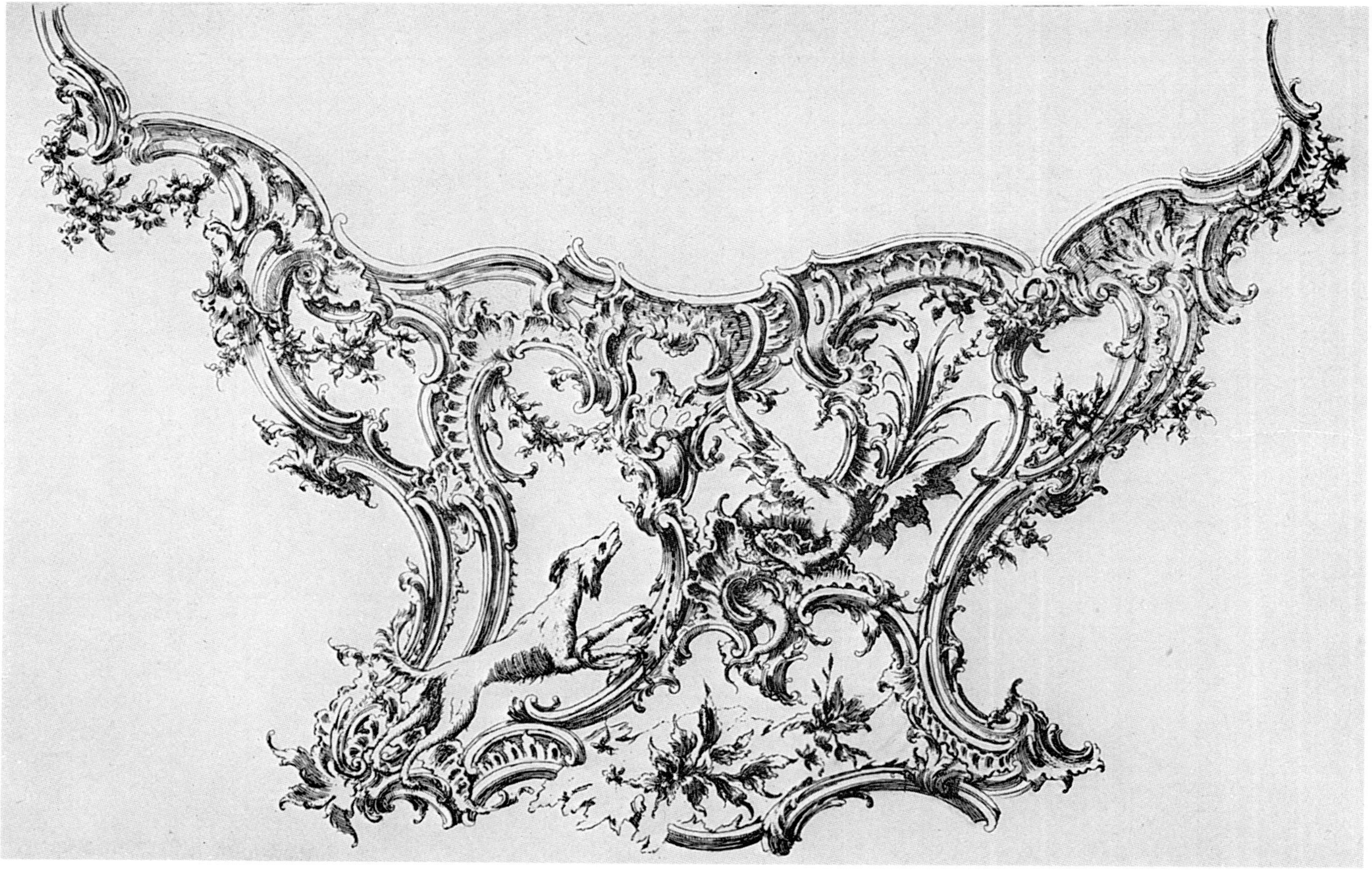

50. Lock: A table. Etching, 1746.

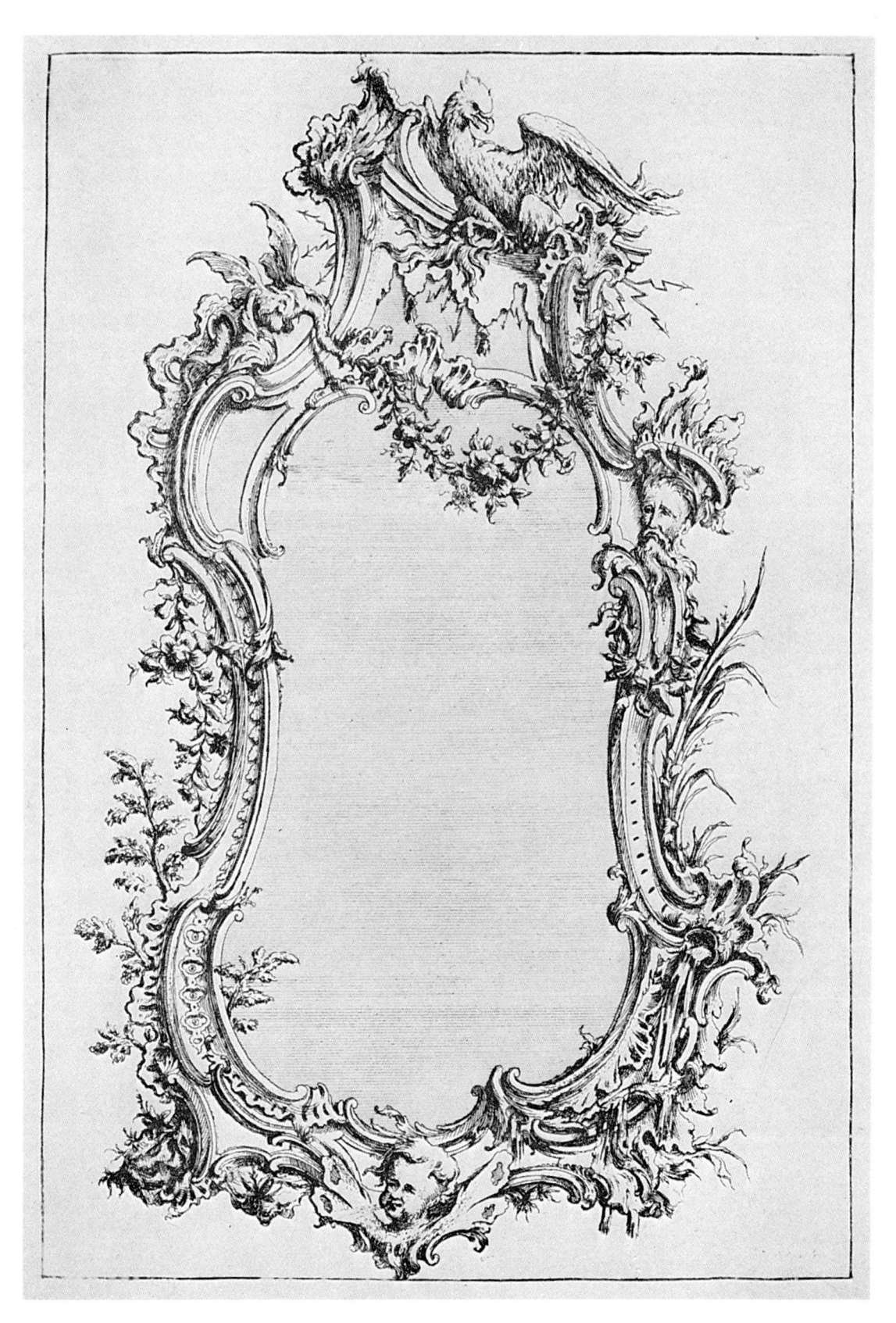

51. Lock: A mirror. Etching, 1744.

52. Lock and Copland: Two mirrors. Etching, 1752.

53. Lock and Copland: Two clocks, etc. Etching, 1752.

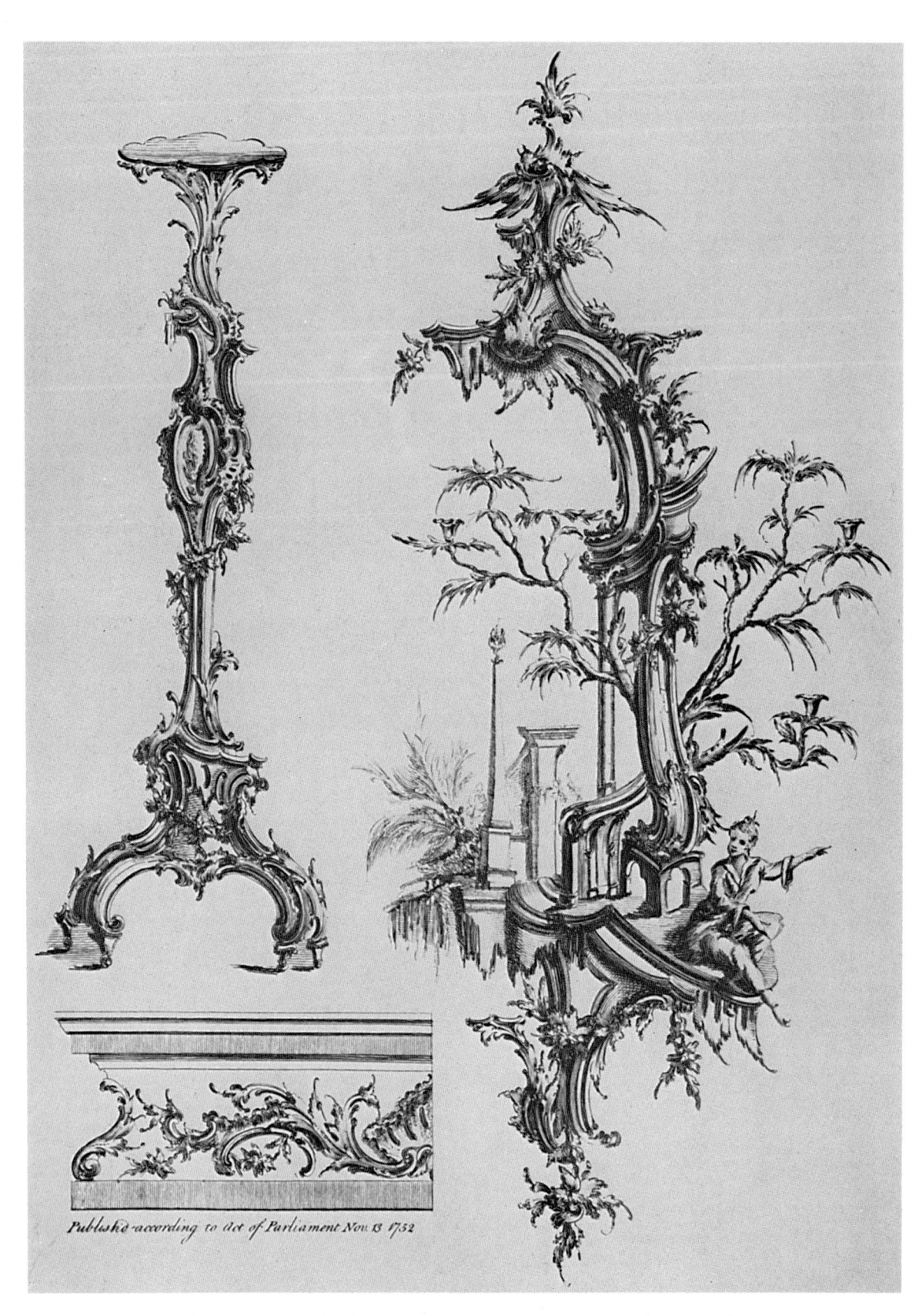

54. Lock and Copland: A sconce and stand, etc. Etching, 1752.

55. Lock and Copland: A table and picture frame. Etching, 1752.

56. Lock. A girandole. Drawing, about 1750.　　　　57. Lock: A girandole. Drawing, about 1750.

58. Lock: A girandole. Drawing, about 1750.   59. Lock: A girandole. Drawing, about 1750.

60. Lock: A girandole. Drawing, about 1750.

61. Lock: A console table, with memorandum of wages. About 1755.   62. Lock: A lantern. Drawing: with memorandum, about 1755.

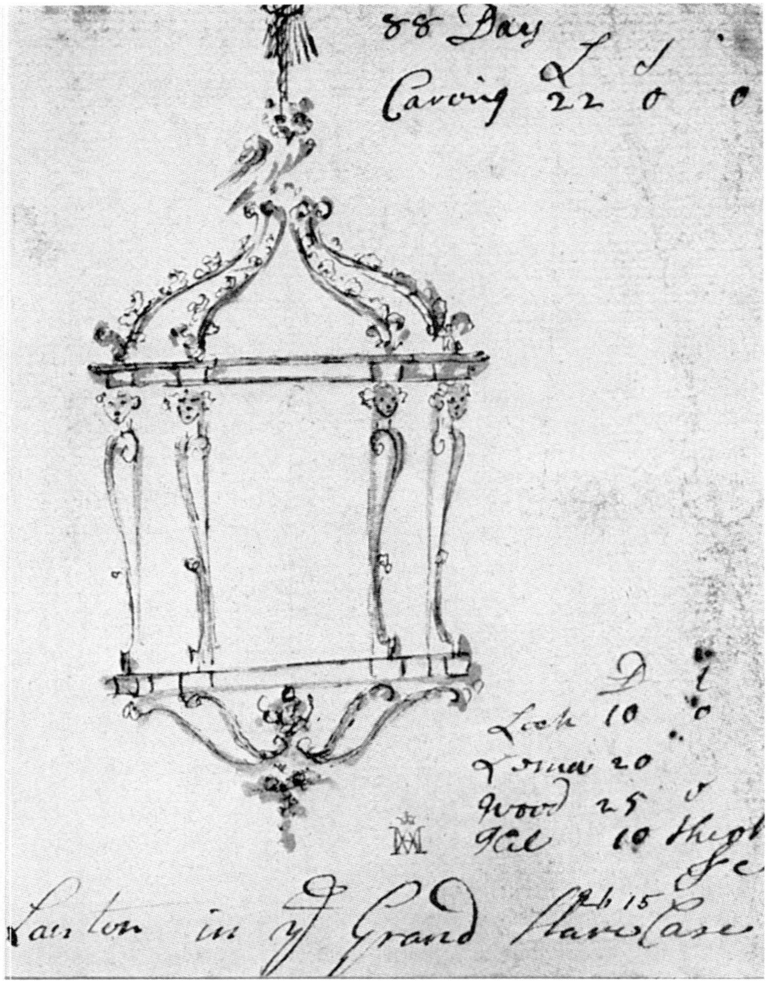

Lock: A mirror. Drawing, about 1760.   64. Lock: A mirror. Drawing, about 1760.

65. Lock: A mirror. Drawing, about 1760.   66. Lock: A mirror. Drawing, about 1760.

67. Lock: Pier table and mirror. Drawing, about 1760.

68. Lock: A mirror. Drawing, about 1760.

69. Lock: Pier table and mirror. Drawing, about 1760.

70. George Bickham: A mirror. Etching, 1752.

71. Chippendale: A clothes press and chest. Engraving, 1754.

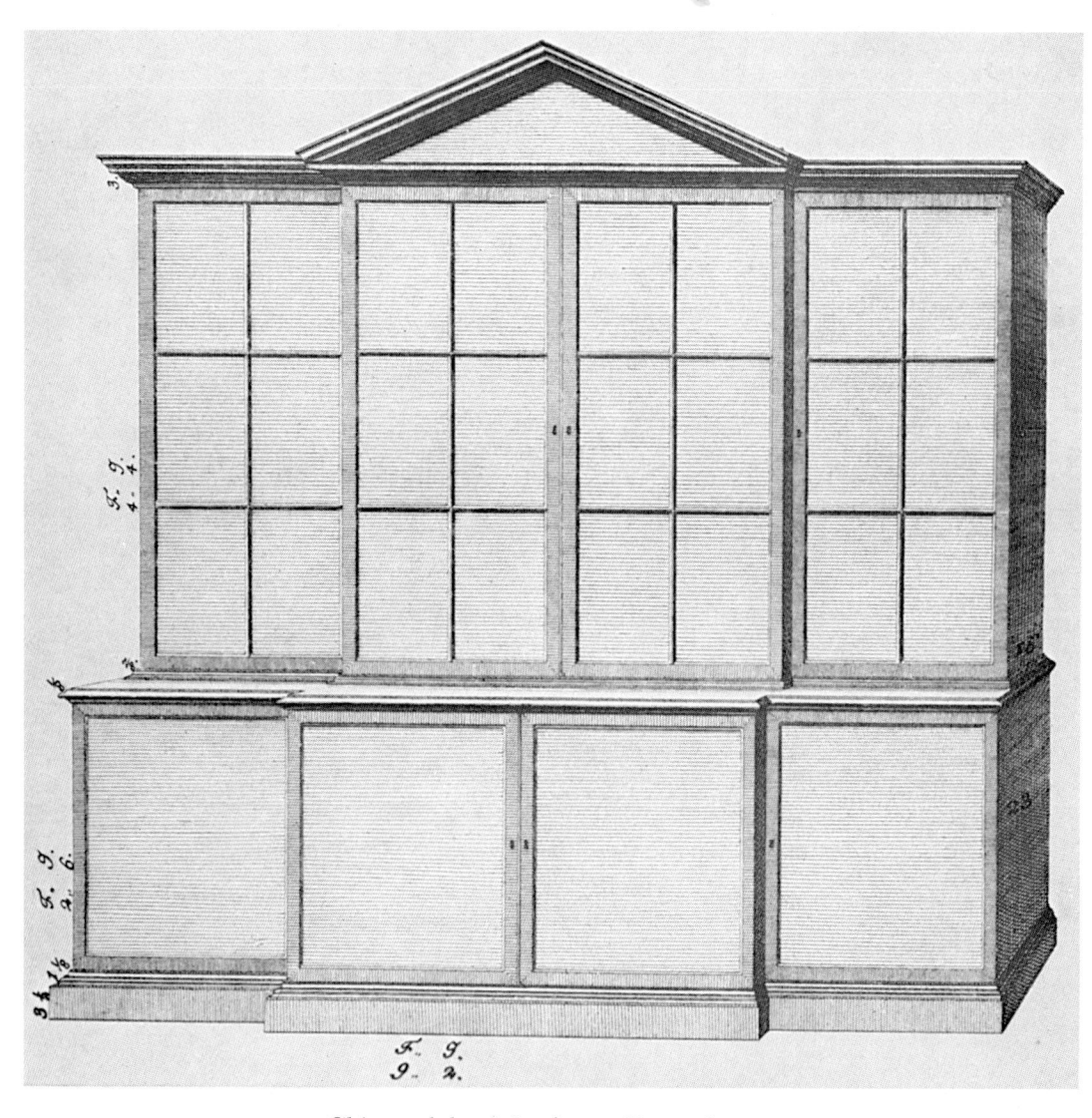

72. Chippendale: A bookcase. Engraving, 1753.

74. Chippendale: A clothes press. Engraving, 1753.

73. Chippendale: A tallboy. Engraving, 1754.

75. Chippendale: A side-board table. Engraving, 1753.

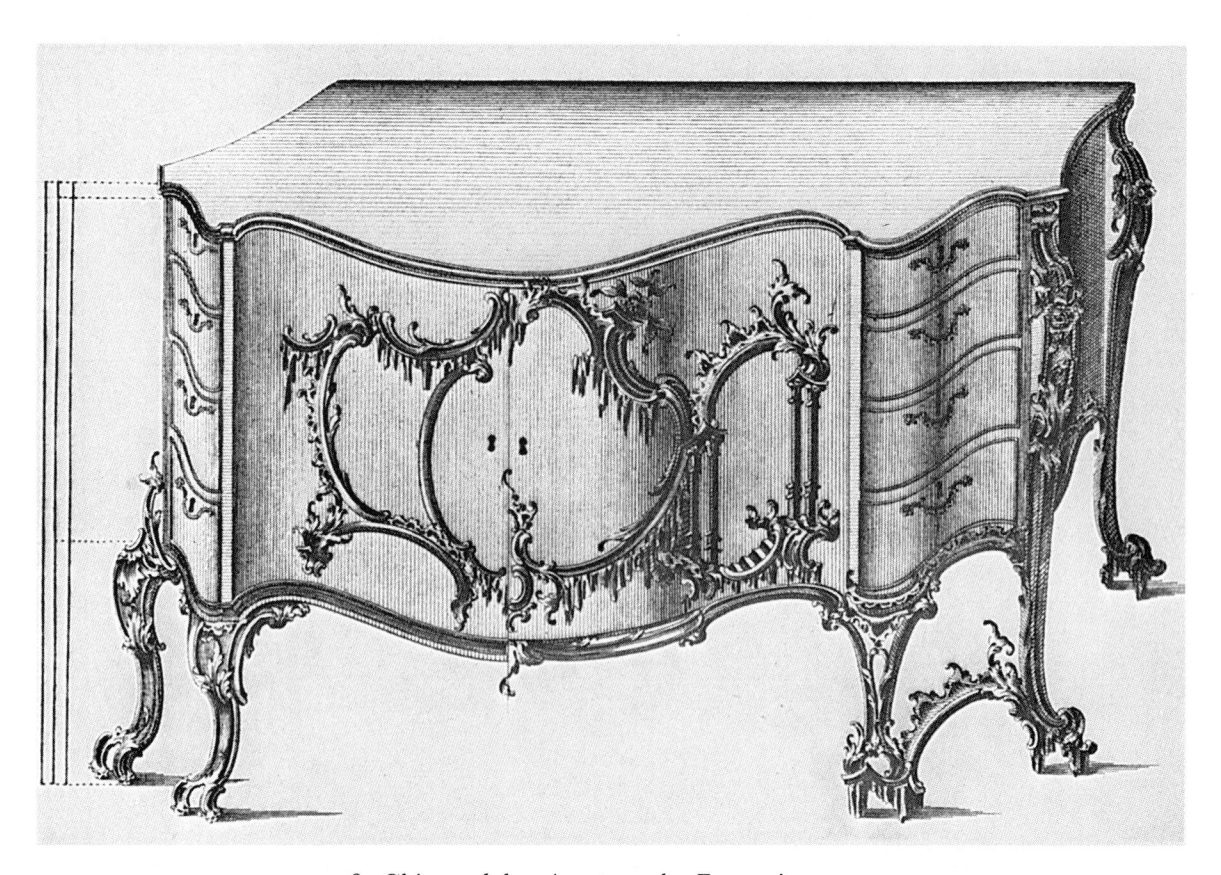

76. Chippendale: A commode. Engraving, 1753.

77. Chippendale: Two clock cases. Engraving, 1754.

79. Chippendale: Two pier glasses. Engraving, 1754.

78. Chippendale: Two pier glasses. Engraving, 1754.

80. Chippendale: Two table clocks. Engraving, 1754.

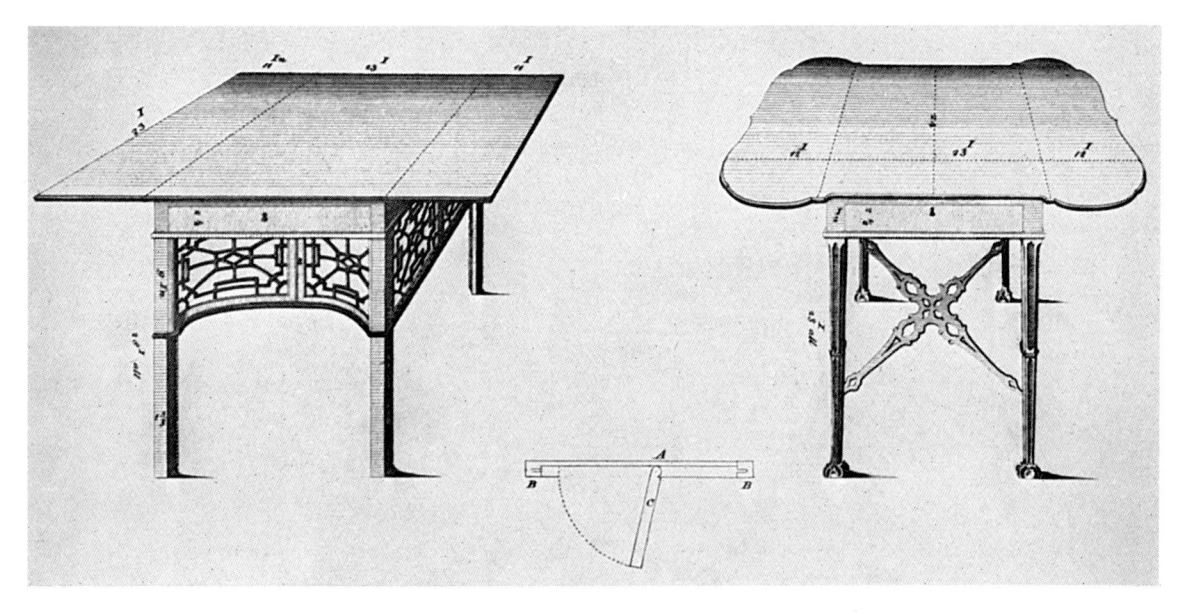

81. Chippendale: Two breakfast tables. Engraving, 1754.

82. Chippendale: 'Chinese' chairs. Engraving, 1753.

83. Chippendale: Ribband-back chairs. Engraving, 1754.

84. Chippendale: 'Gothic' chairs. Engraving, 1754.

85. Chippendale: 'Gothic' chairs. Engraving, 1754.

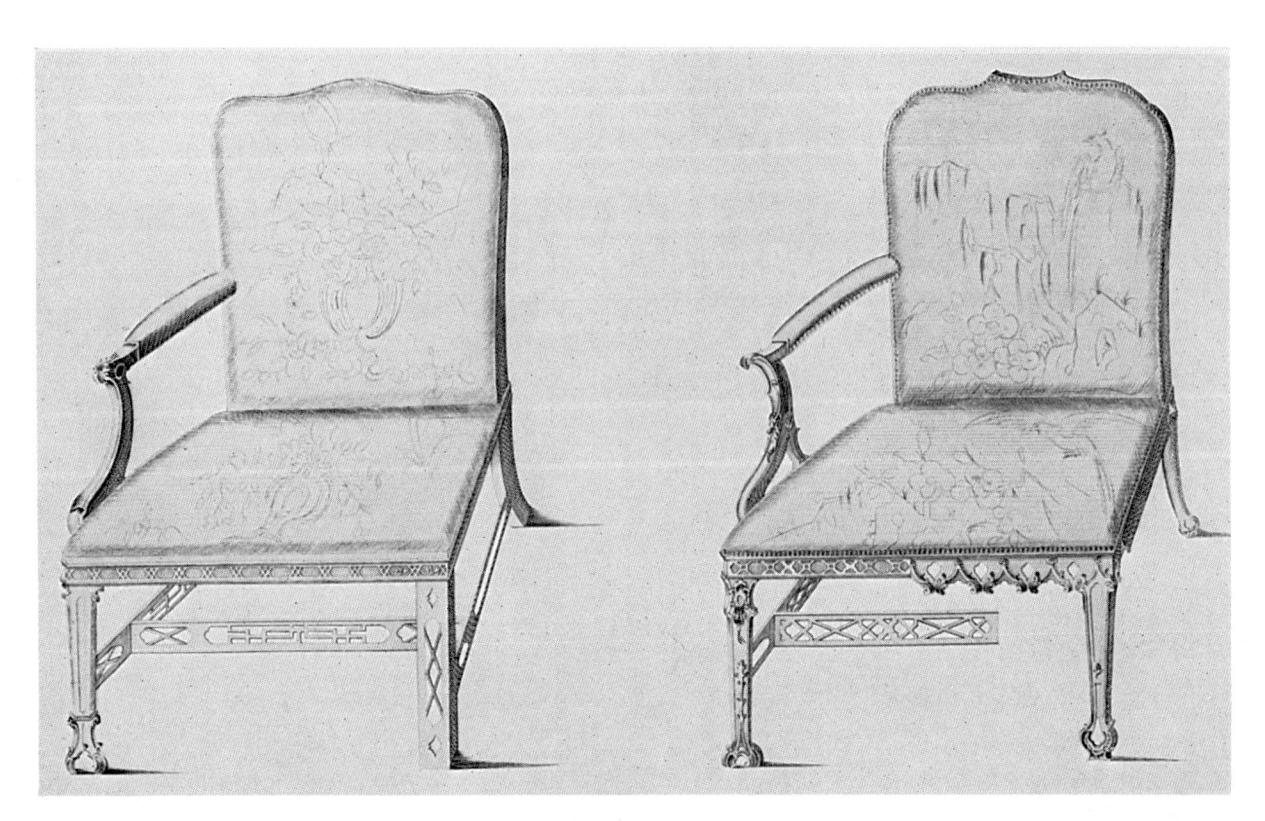

86. Chippendale: Two 'French' chairs. Engraving, 1753.

87. Chippendale: Two writing tables. Engraving, 1753.

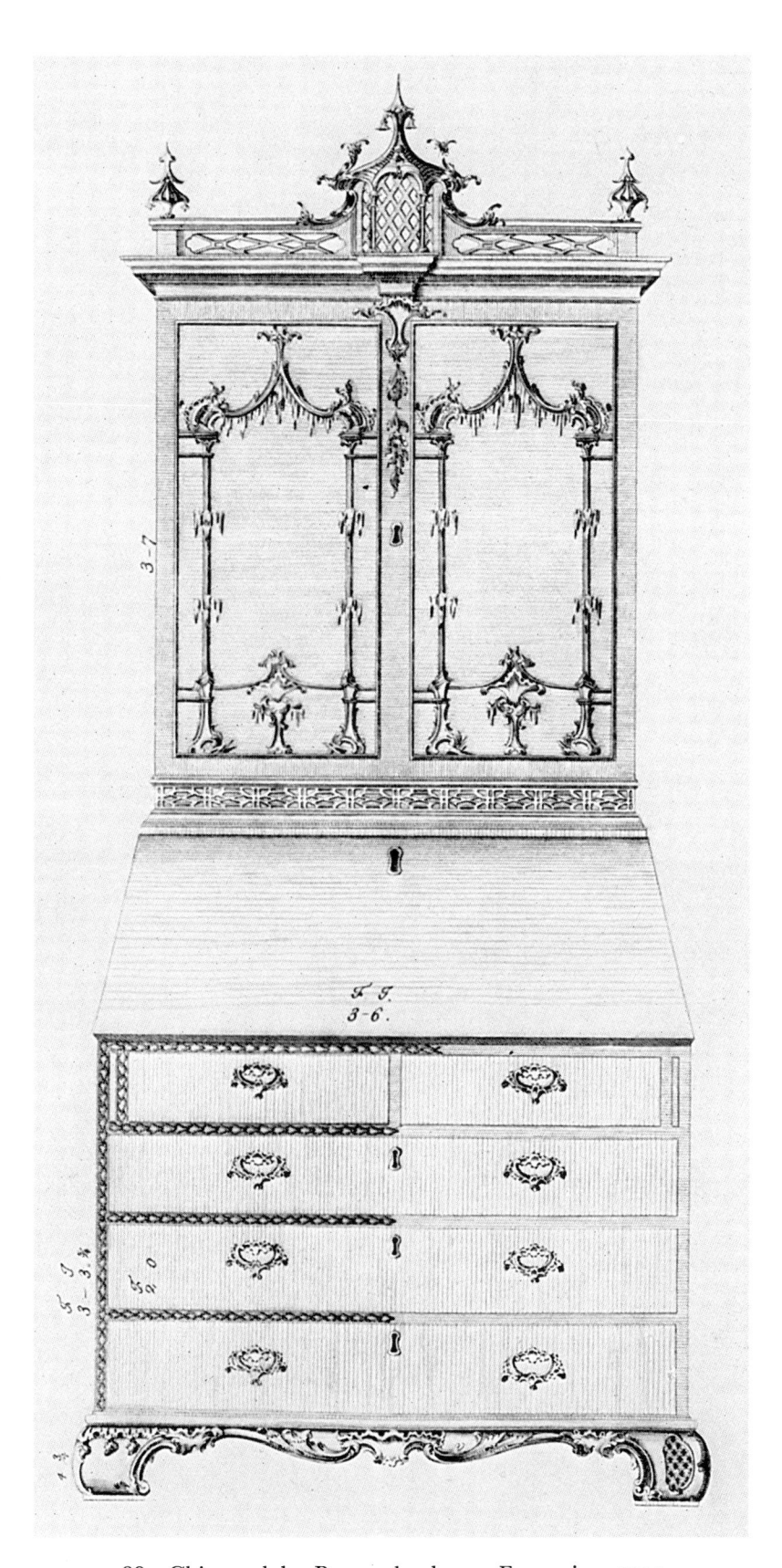

88. Chippendale: Bureau bookcase. Engraving, 1753.

90. Chippendale: A 'Gothic' cabinet. Engraving, 1754.

89. Chippendale: A chest-of-drawers. Engraving, 1753.

91. Chippendale: A library table. Engraving, 1753.

92. Two 'French' commodes. Engraving, 1762.

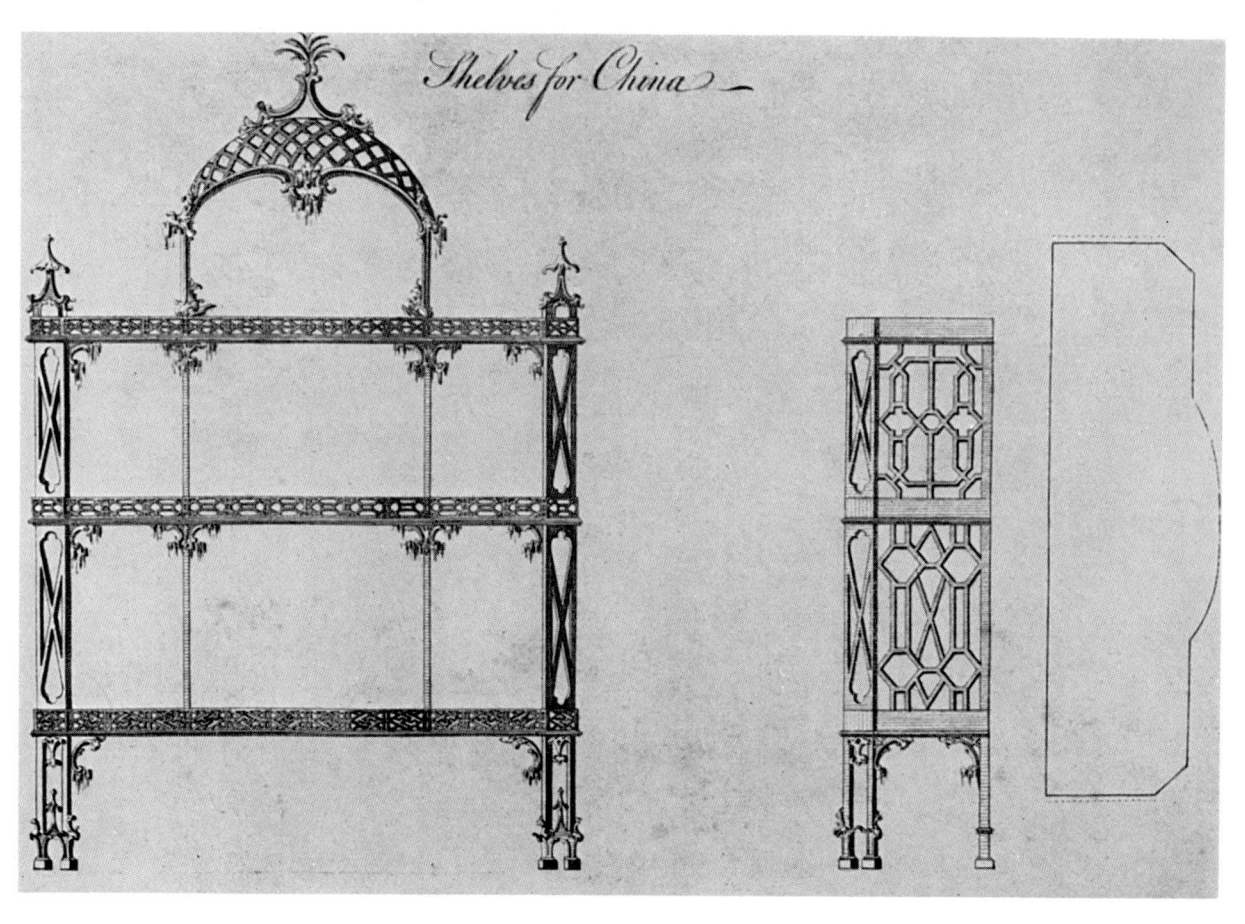

93. Hanging shelves. Engraving, 1761.

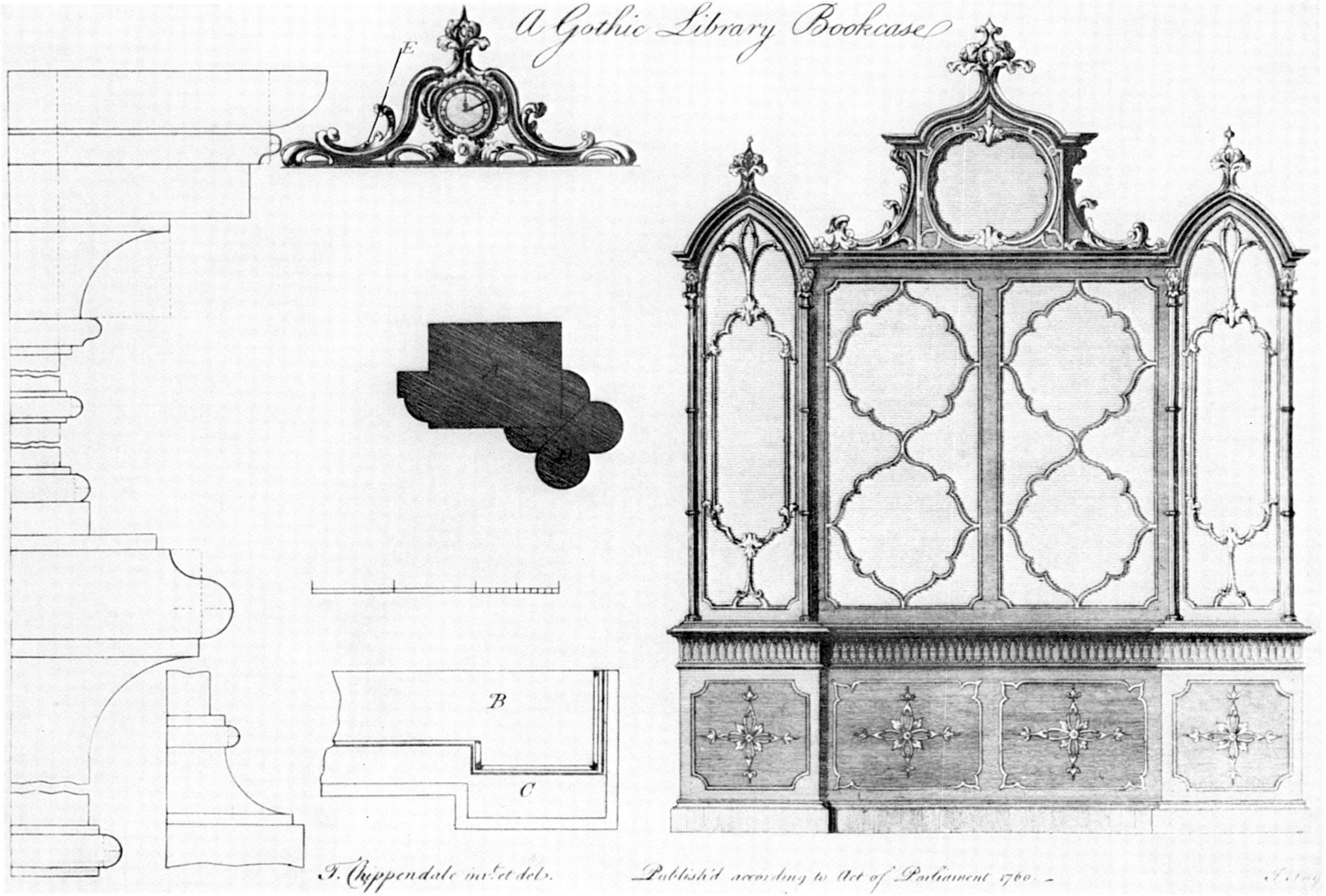

94. Chippendale: A 'Gothic' bookcase. Engraving, 1760.

95. Chippendale: A dressing table. Drawing for the *Director*, 1762.

96. Chippendale: Two pier glasses. Drawing for the *Director*, 1762.

97. Chippendale: Two firescreens. Drawing for the *Director*, 1762.

98. Chippendale: A picture frame. Drawing for the *Director*, 1762.

99. Chippendale: A bureau bookcase. Drawing for the *Director*, 1762.

100. Chippendale: Three chairs. Drawing for the *Director*, 1762.

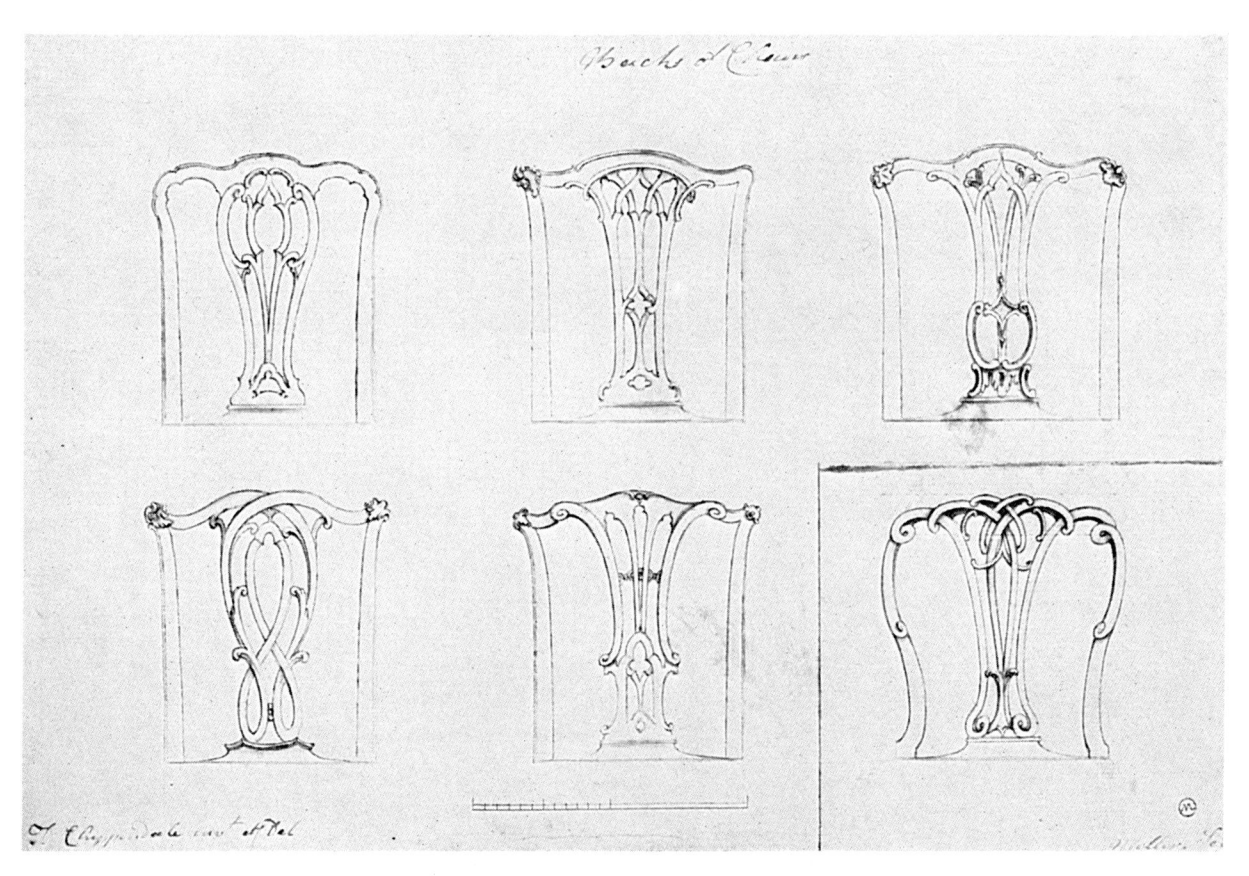

101. Chippendale: Six chair backs. Drawing for the *Director*, 1762.

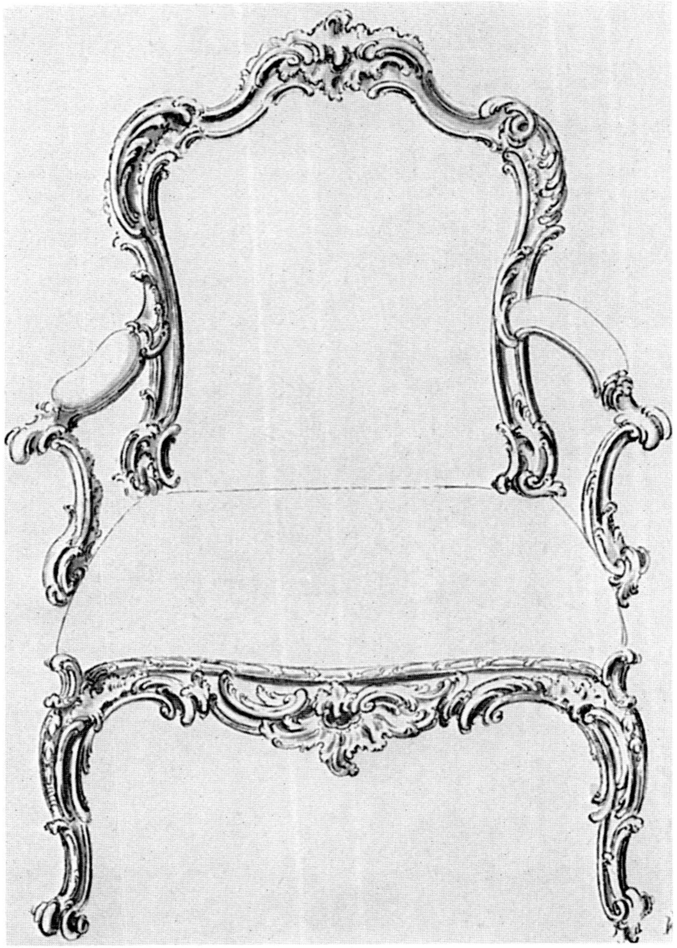

103. Chippendale: An arm-chair. Drawing, about 1760.

102. Chippendale: A sofa. Drawing, about 1760.

105. Chippendale: A bed. Drawing about 1760.

104. Chippendale: A china cabinet. Drawing, about 1760.

106. Chippendale: Two commodes. Drawing, about 1760.

107. Chippendale: A commode. Drawing, about 1760.

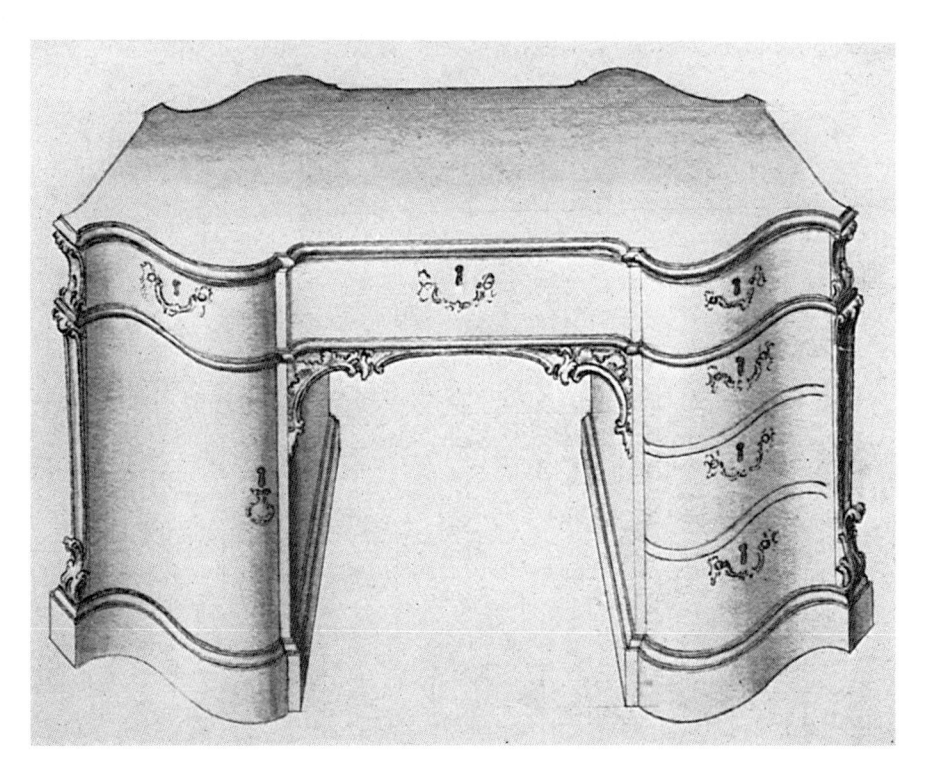

108. Chippendale: A library table. Drawing, 1760.

109. Chippendale: A chandelier. Drawing about 1760.

110. Chippendale: A cabinet or bookcase. Drawing, about 1760.

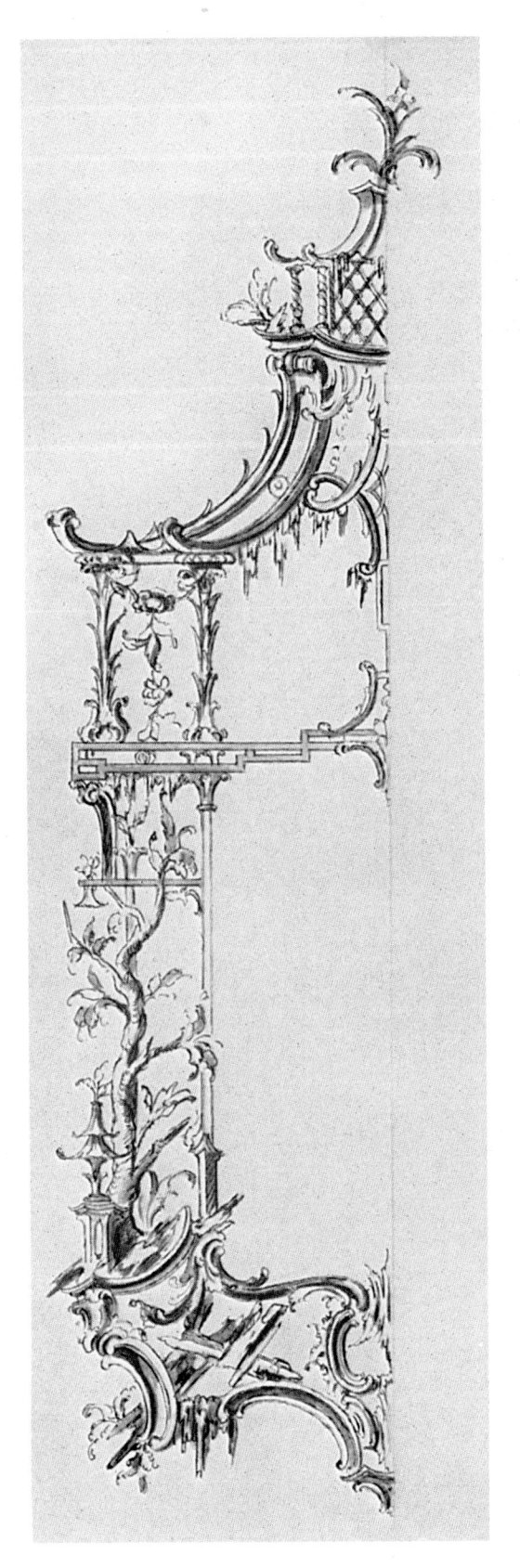

111. Chippendale: Mirror with 'Chinese' motifs. Drawing, about 1760.

112. Chippendale: Mirror with 'Chinese' figures. Drawing, about 1760.

114. Chippendale: A console table and mirror. Drawing, about 1760.

113. Chippendale: A pier table and mirror. Drawing, about 1760.

117. Chippendale: A mirror. Drawing, about 1765-70.

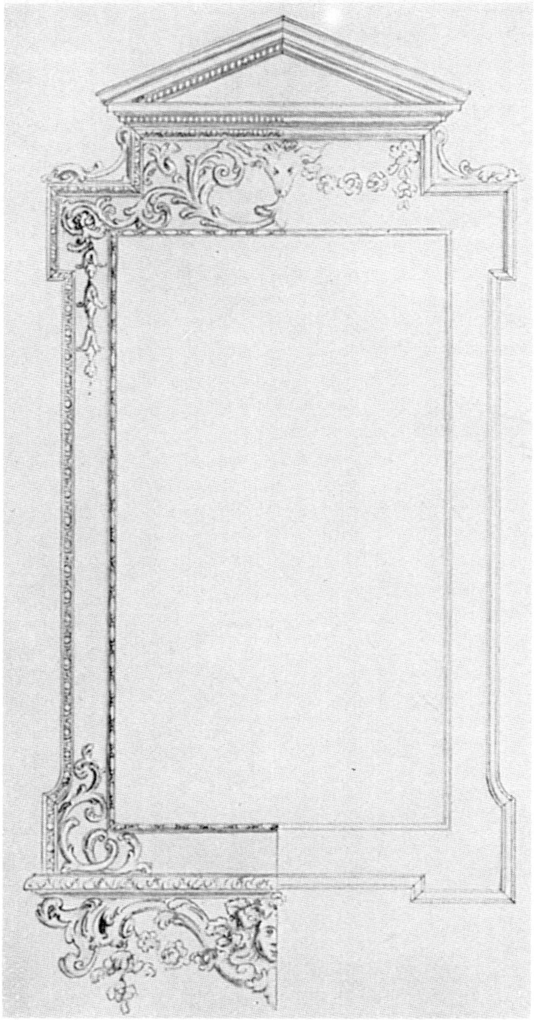

116. Chippendale: A mirror. Drawing, about 1750.

115. Chippendale: A mirror. Drawing, about 1765-70.

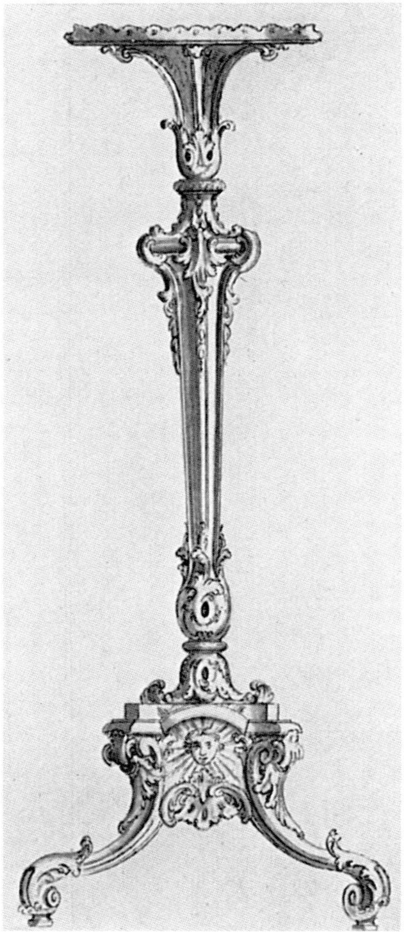

118–121. Chippendale: Four drawings for stands. No. 121 about 1770. The other three about 1760.

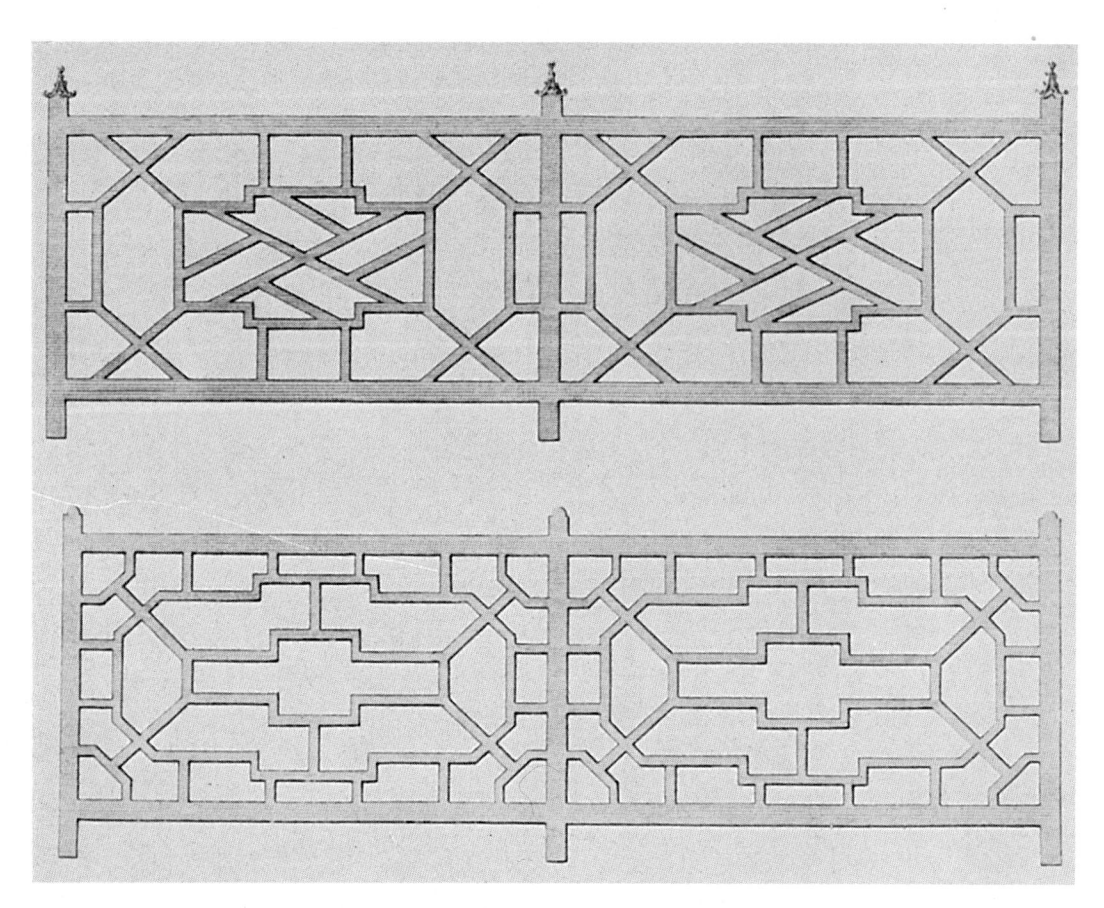

122. Chippendale: 'Chinese railing'. Engraving, 1754.

123. Chippendale: 'Gothic frets.' Engraving, 1754.

124. John Crunden: Frets for tea-trays, etc. Etching, 1765.

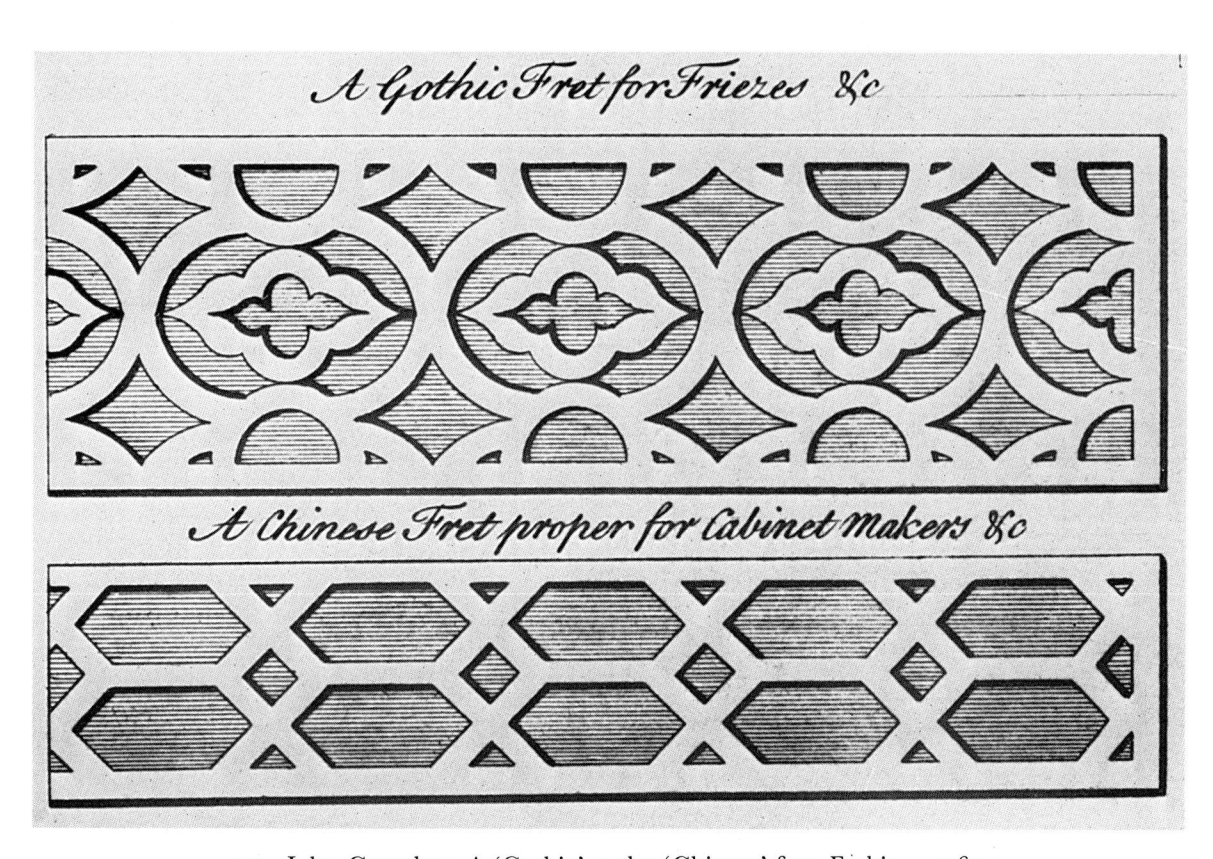

125. John Crunden: A 'Gothic' and a 'Chinese' fret. Etching, 1765.

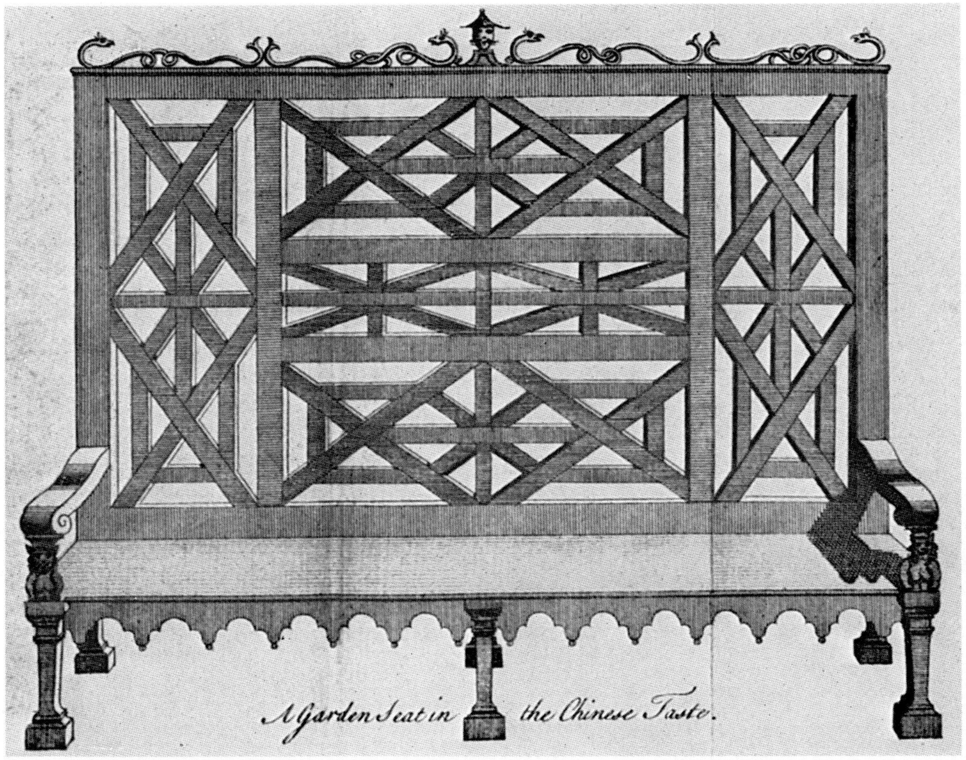

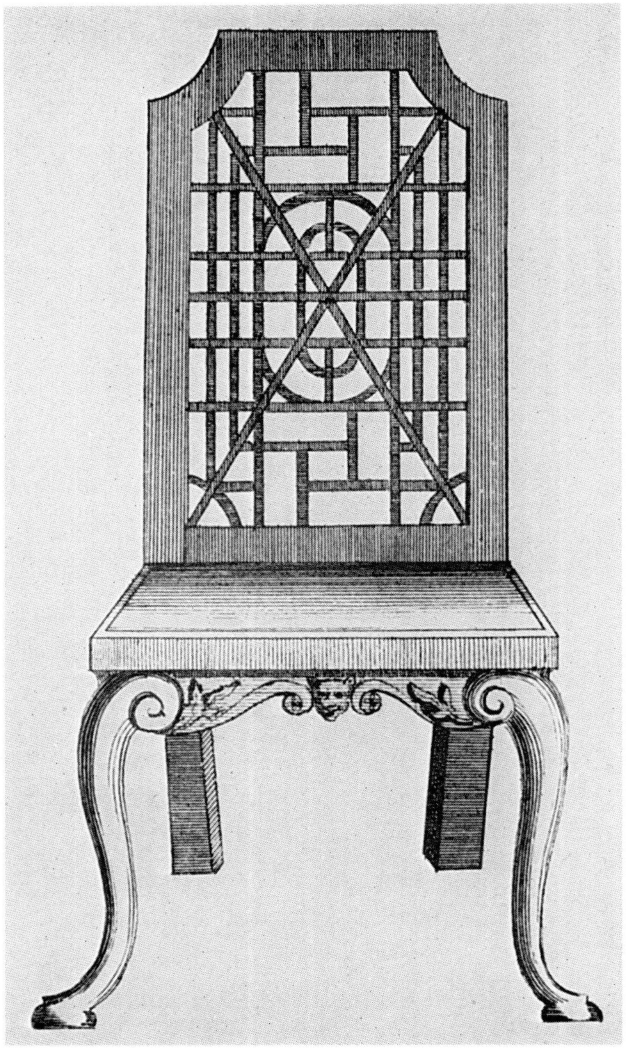

127. William Halfpenny: A chair in the 'Chinese' taste. Engraving, 1750.

126. William Halfpenny: A garden seat in the 'Chinese' taste. Engraving, 1750.

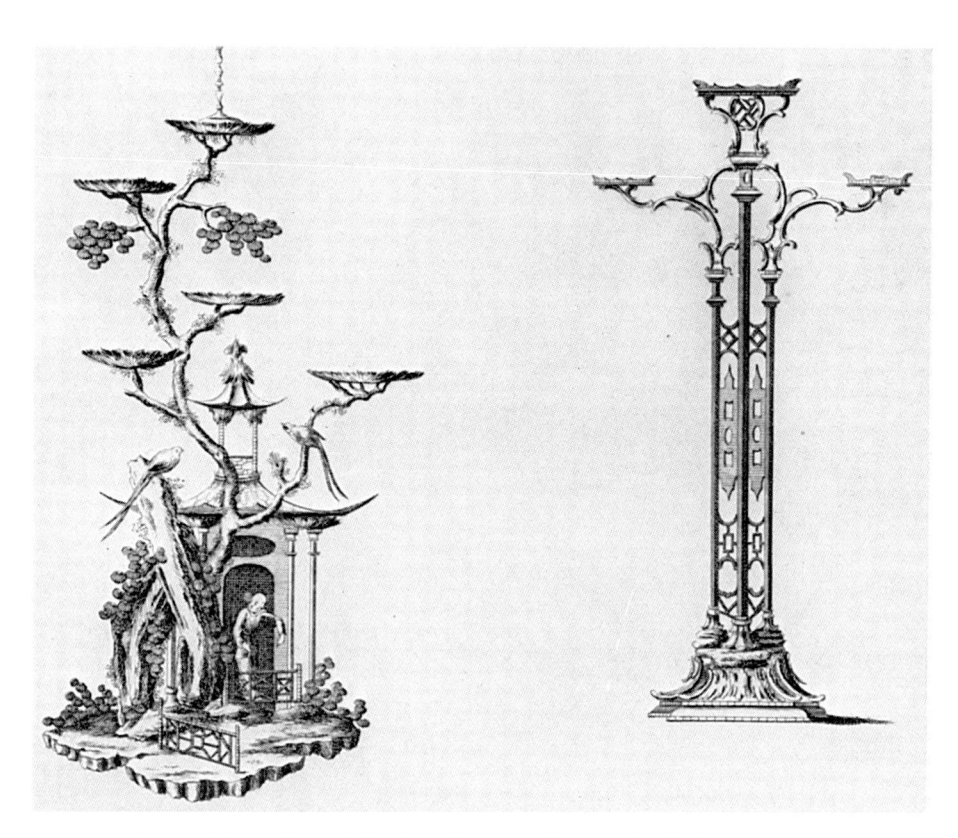

128. Edwards and Darly: Two candle-stands. Etching, 1754.

129. Edwards and Darly: Three wall brackets. Etching, 1754.

131. Edwards and Darly: A mirror in the 'Chinese' style. Etching, 1754.

130. Edwards and Darly: A 'Chinese' bed. Etching, 1754.

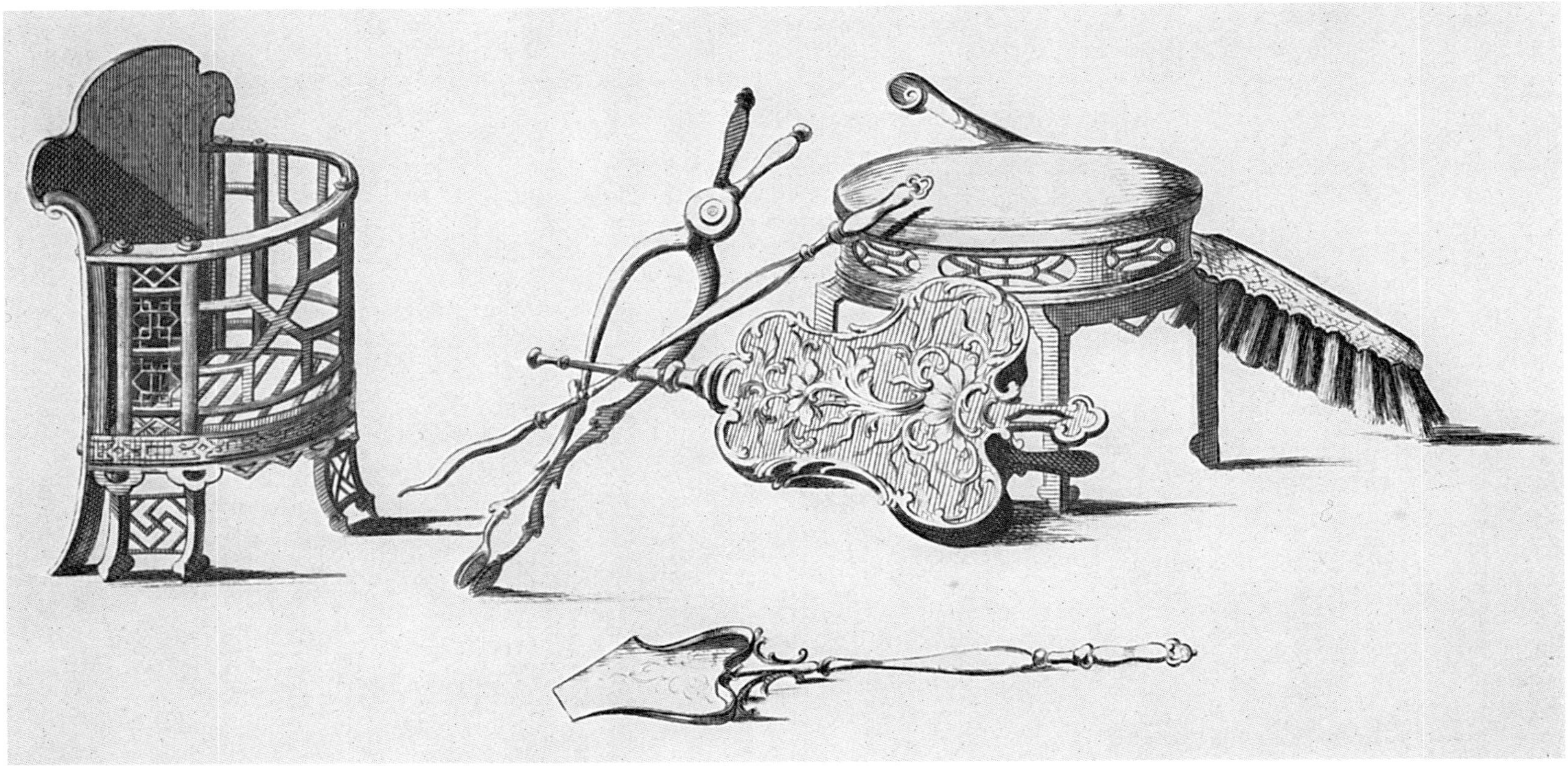

132. Edwards and Darly: Stool and chimney furniture. Etching, 1754.

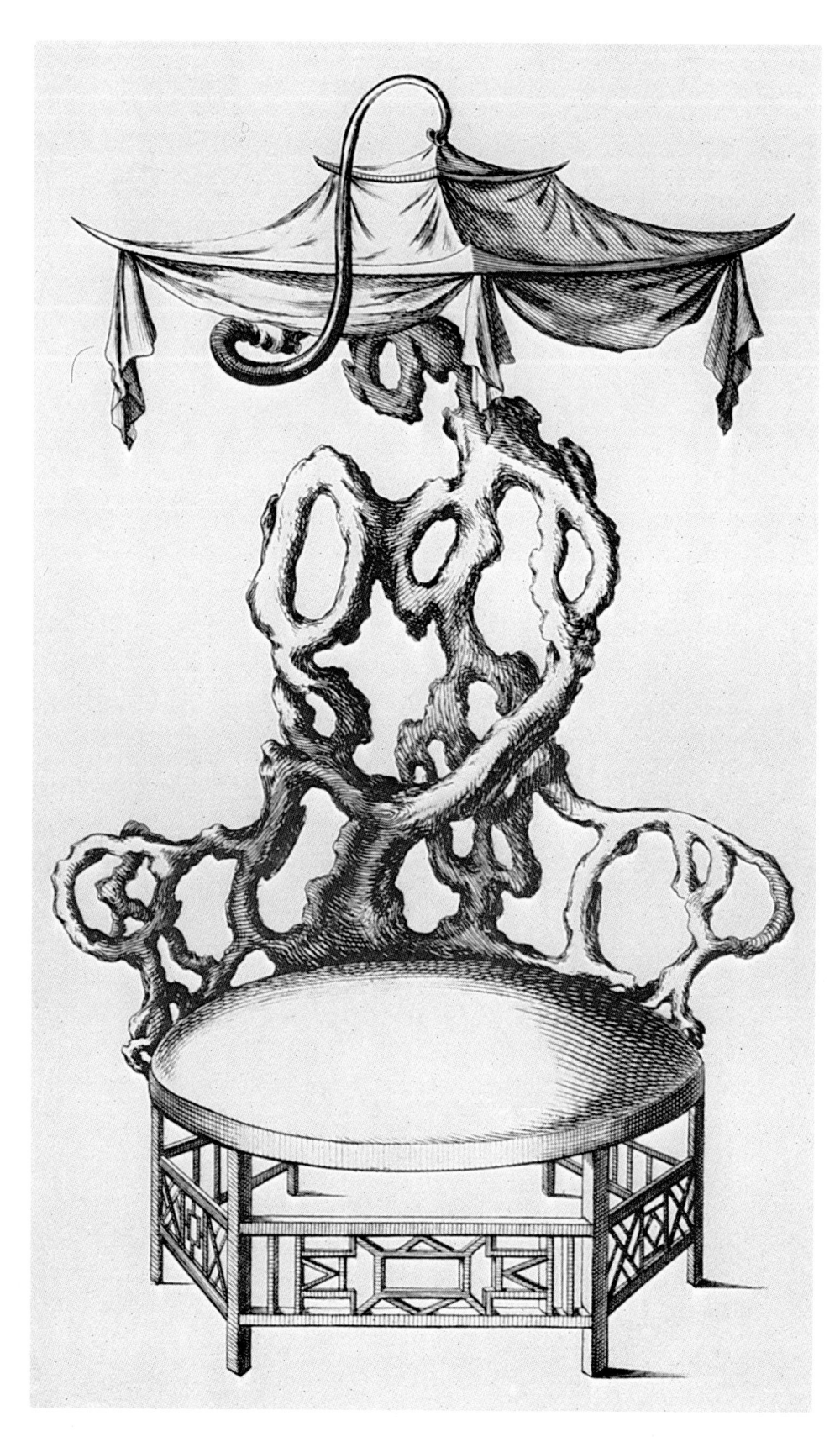

133. Edwards and Darly: A garden table. Etching, 1754.

134. Edwards and Darly: A garden chair made of roots. Etching, 1754.

135. Sir William Chambers: Chinese furniture. Engraving, 1757.

136. Sir William Chambers: Chinese furniture. Engraving, 1757.

137. Thomas Johnson: A girandole. Etching, 1755.

138. Thomas Johnson: A girandole. Etching, 1755.

139. Thomas Johnson: A bracket for china. Etching, 1756.

140. Thomas Johnson: A table clock. Etching, 1756.

141. Thomas Johnson: A looking glass. Etching, 1758.

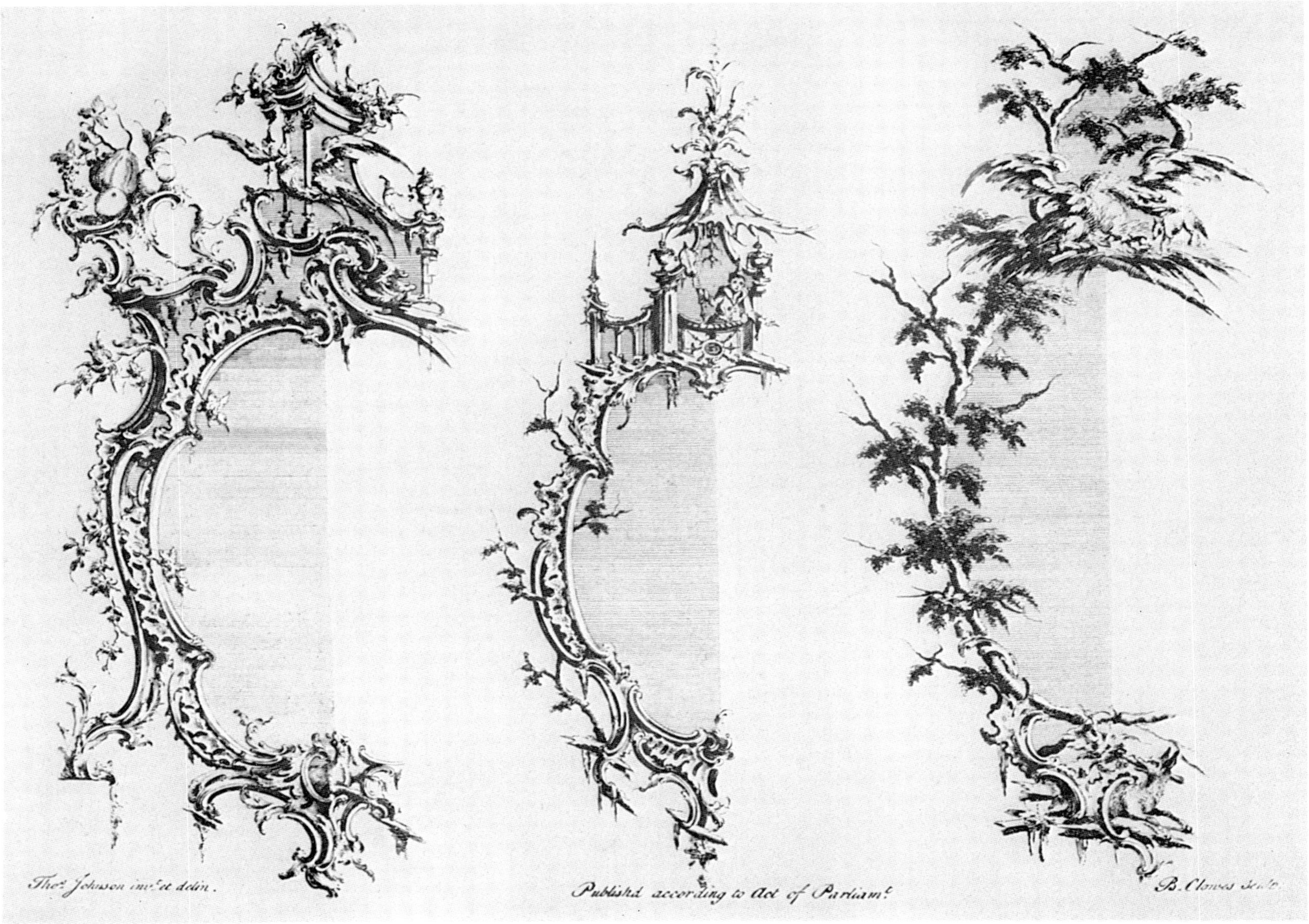

142. Thomas Johnson: Three mirrors. Etching, 1758.

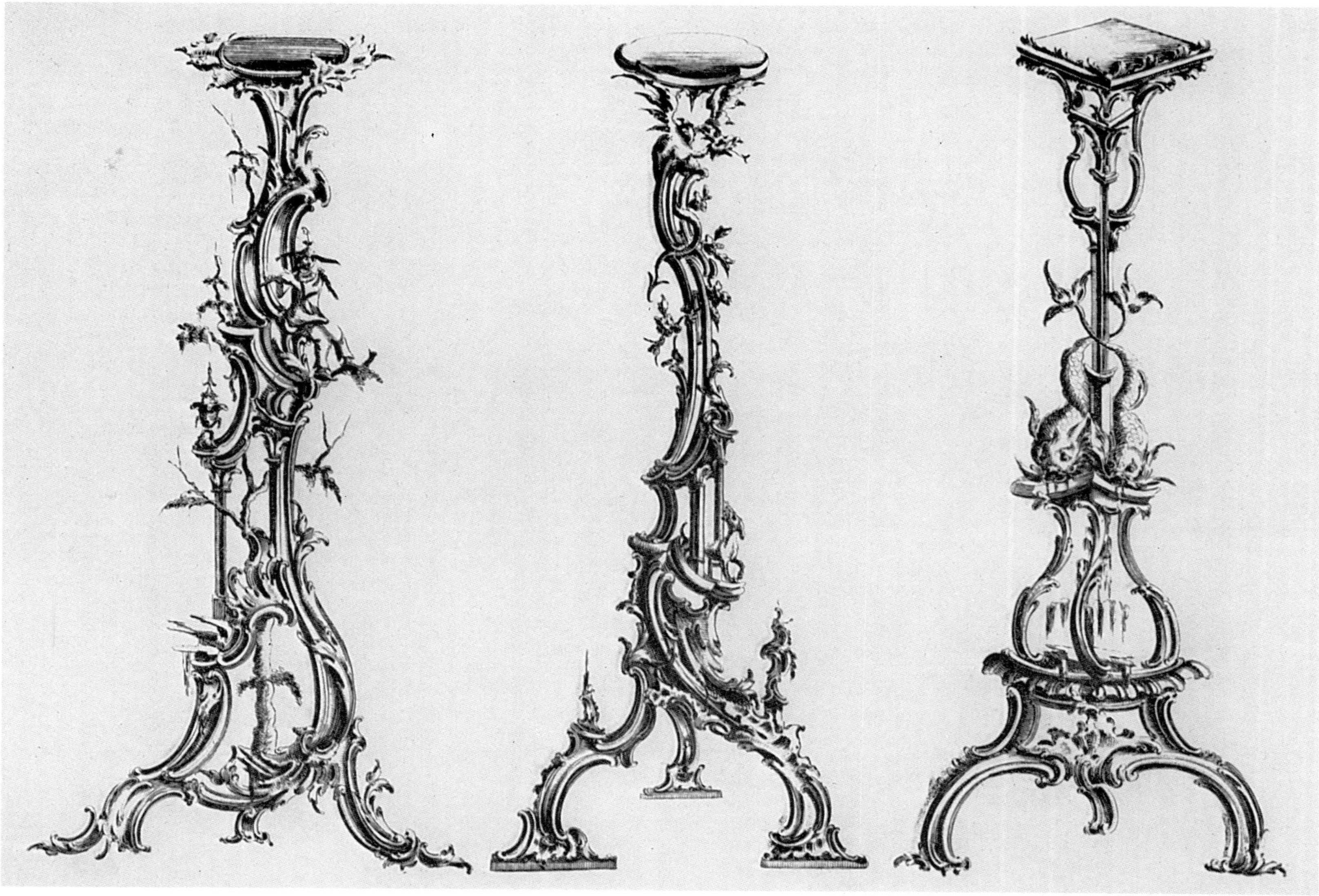

143. Thomas Johnson: Three candle-stands. Etching, 1758.

144. Thomas Johnson: Six wall brackets. Etching, 1758.

145. Thomas Johnson: A table. Etching, 1757.

146. Thomas Johnson: Two console tables. Drawing, about 1758.

147. François Vivares: A bracket. Etching, 1759.

148. Charles Over: A garden seat. Etching, 1758.

149. William Ince: A bed. Drawing, about 1759.

150. Ince and Mayhew: A bed. Etching, 1760.

151. William Ince: A china case. Engraving, about 1760.

152. William Ince: Two corner shelves. Engraving, about 1760.

153. William Ince: Dressing tables. Engraving, about 1760.

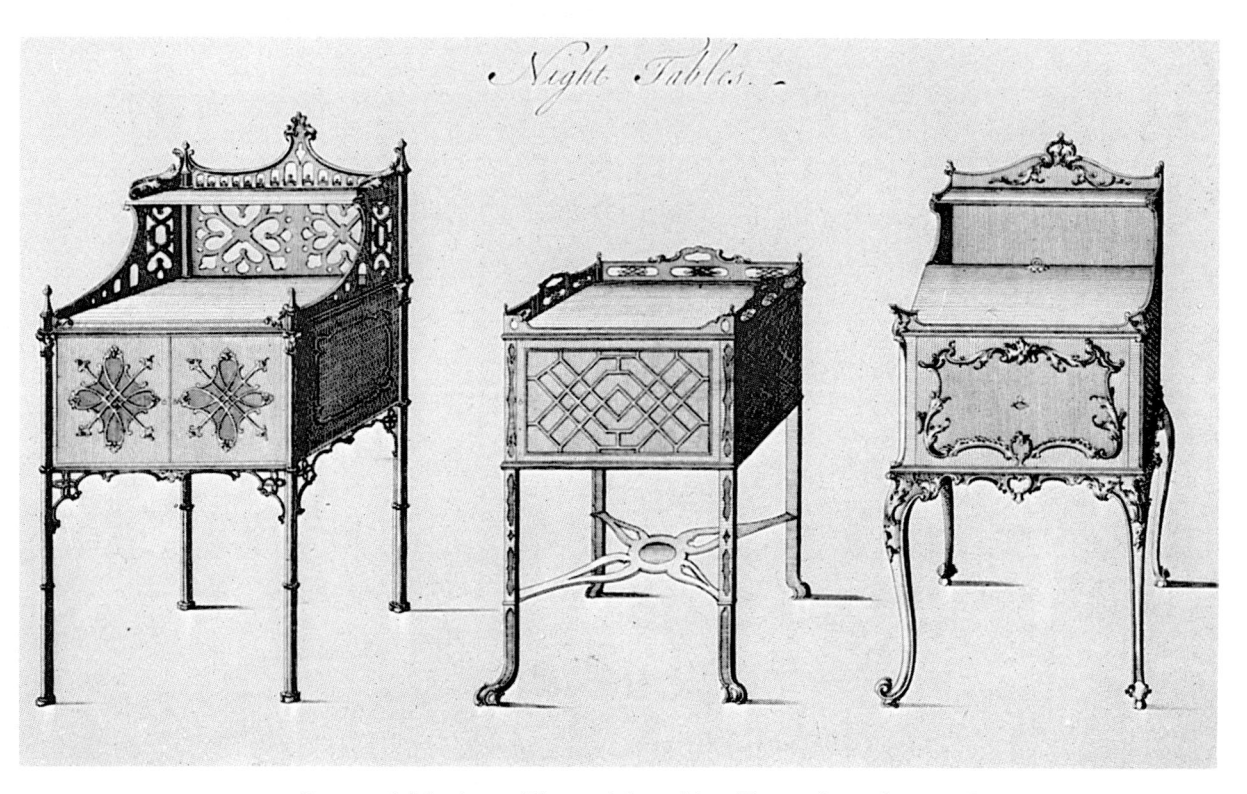

154. Ince and Mayhew: Three night tables. Engraving, about 1760.

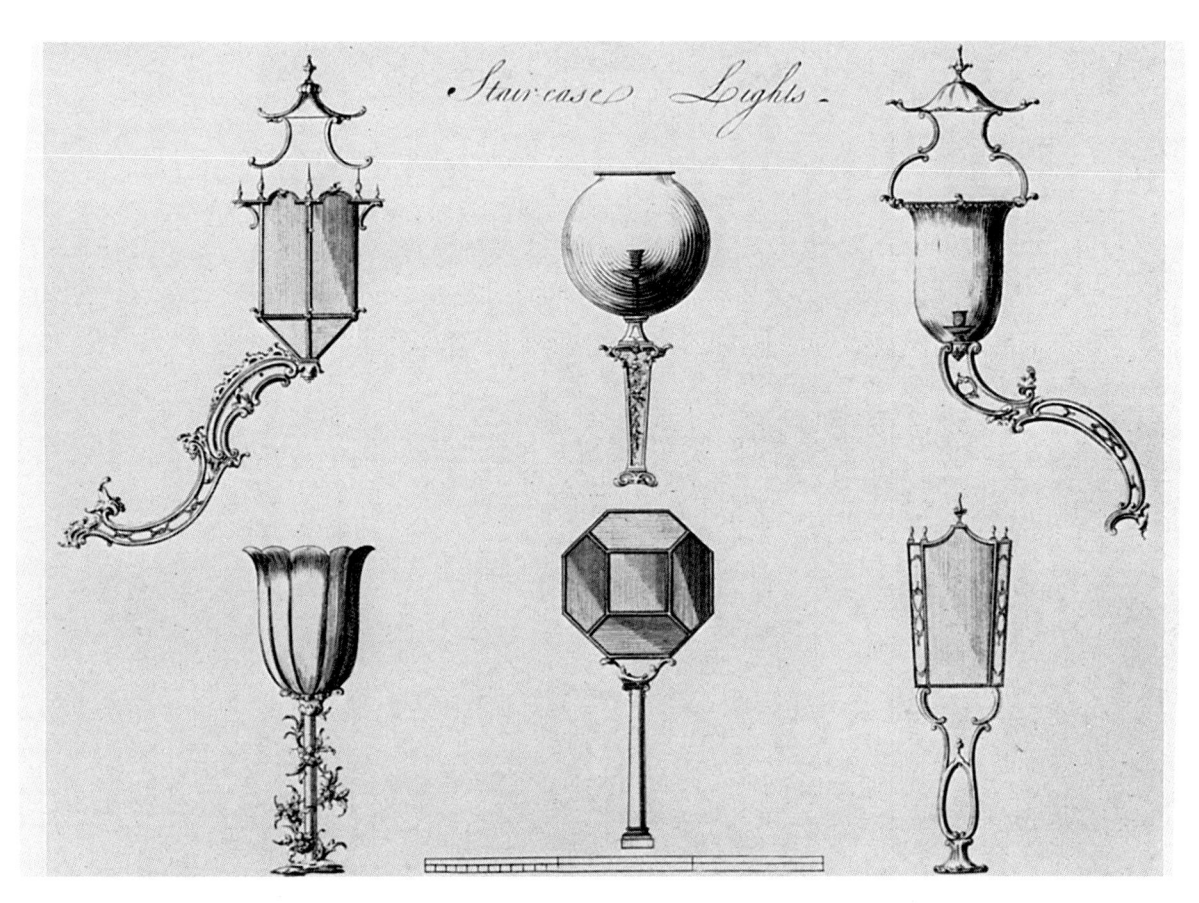

155. Ince and Mayhew: Staircase lights. Engraving, about 1760.

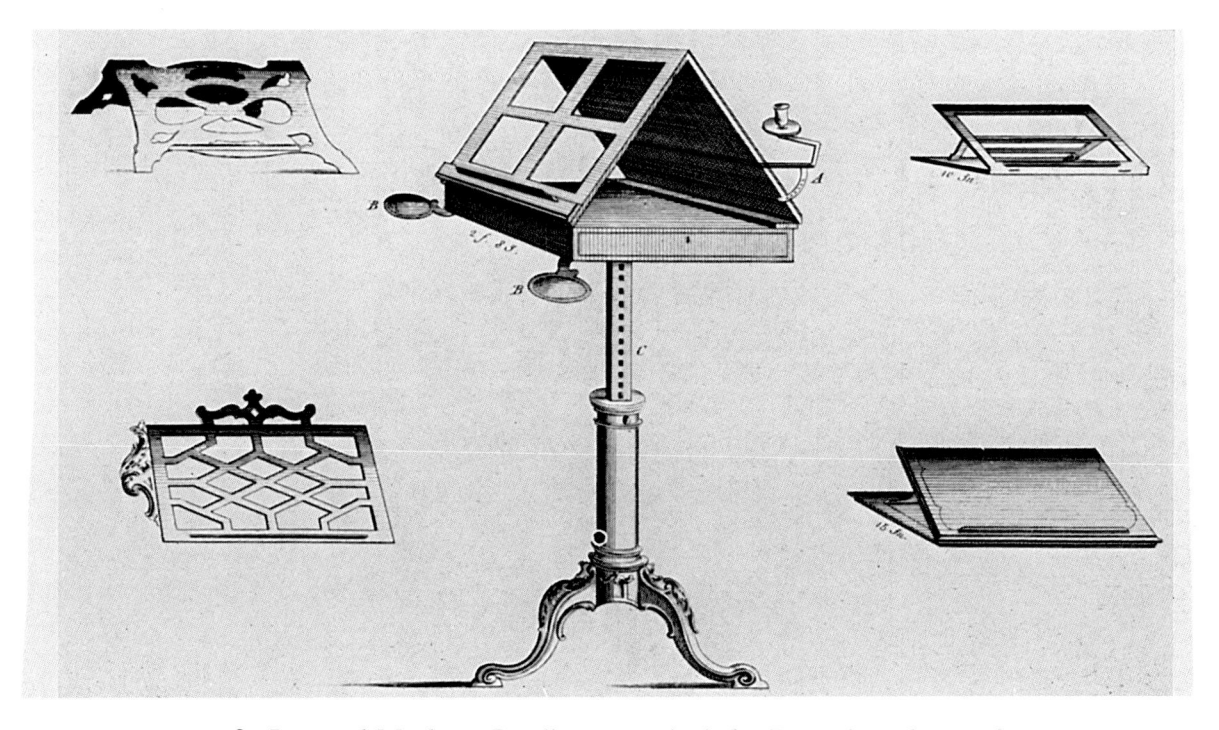

156. Ince and Mayhew: Reading or music desks. Engraving, about 1760.

157. Ince and Mayhew: Library steps. Engraving, about 1760.

158. William Ince: A sofa in an alcove. Engraving, about 1760.

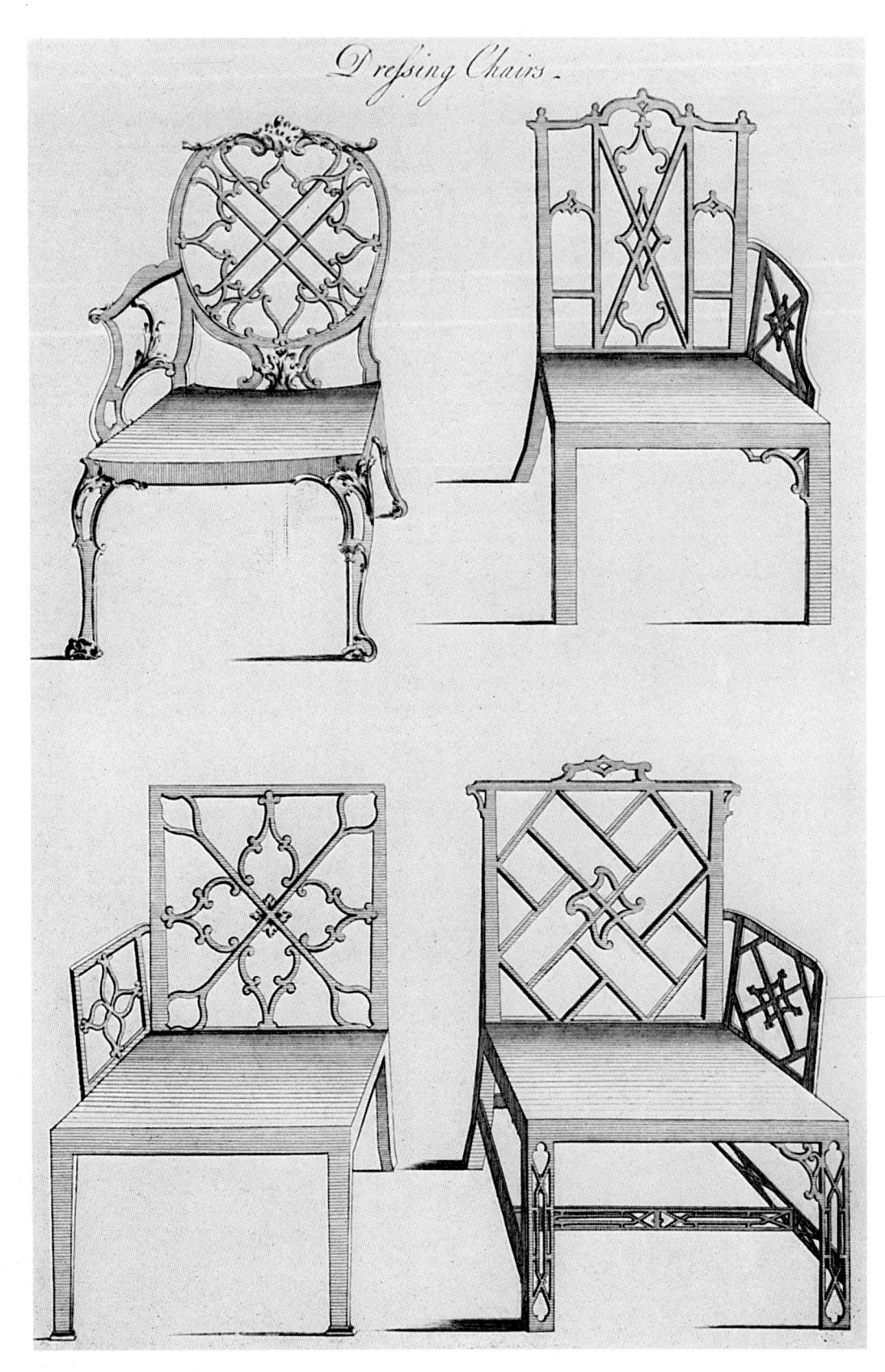

159. John Mayhew: Dressing chairs. Engraving, about 1760.

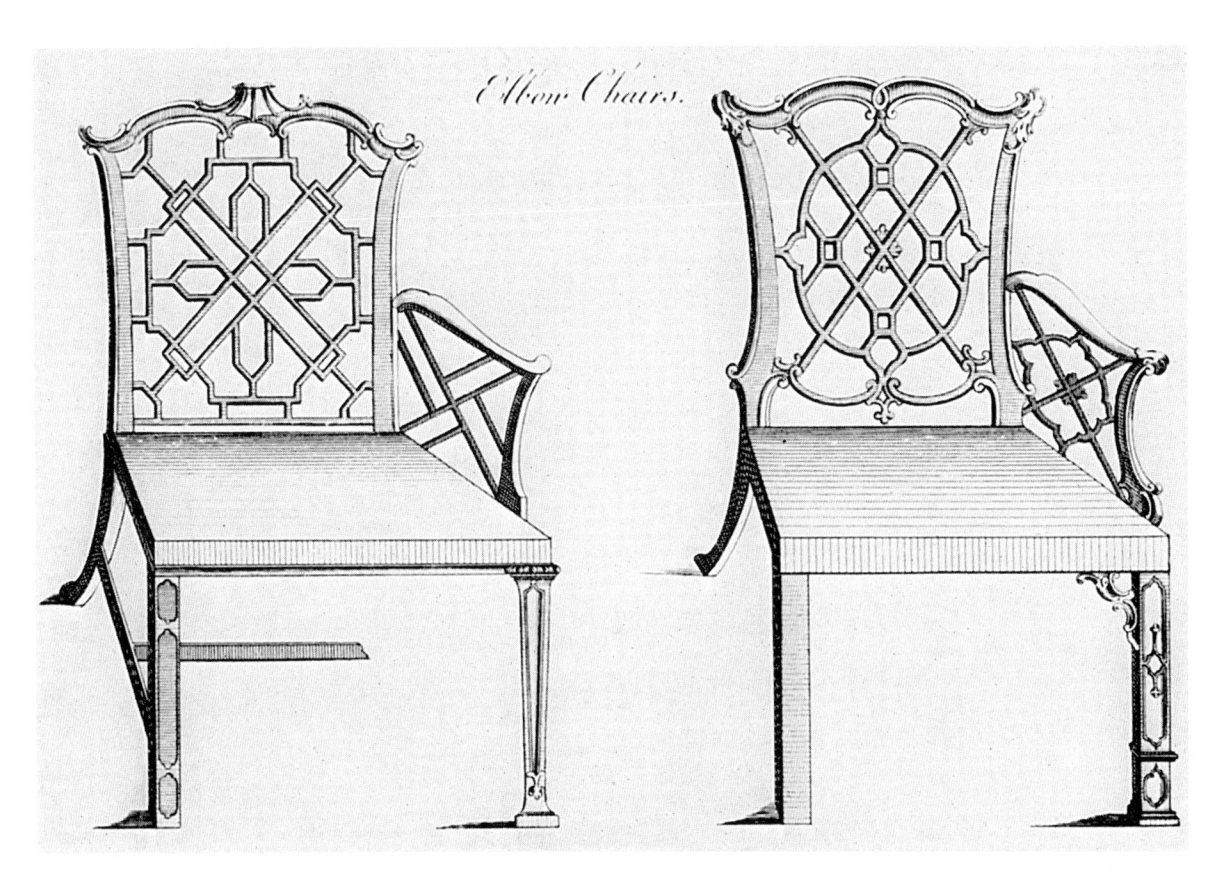

160. Ince and Mayhew: Two arm-chairs. Engraving, about 1760.

161. Ince and Mayhew: Three hall chairs. Engraving, about 1760.

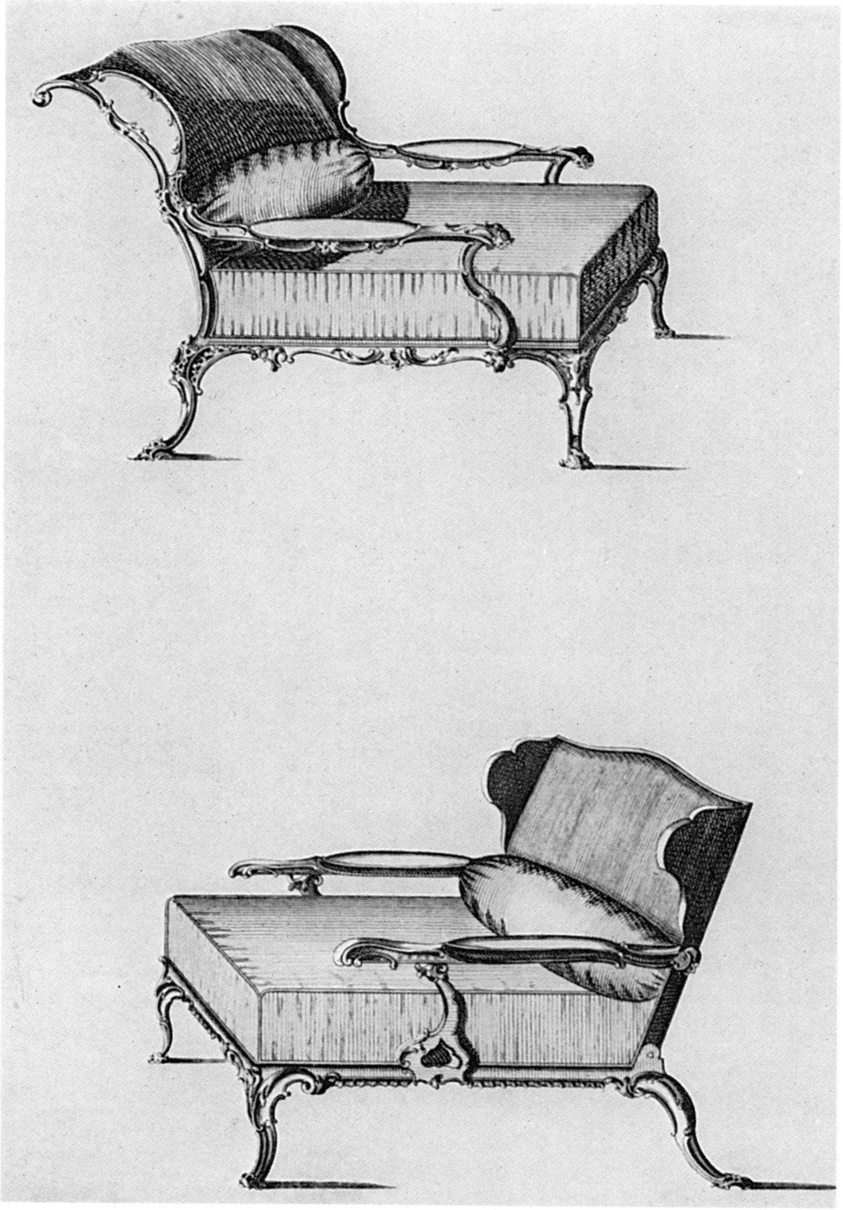

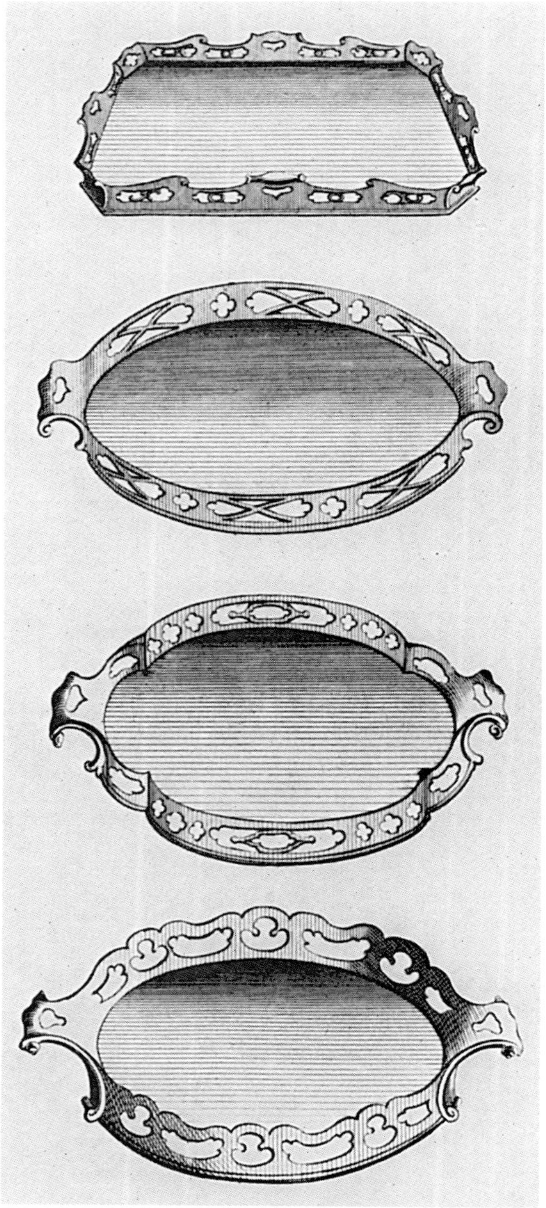

163. Ince and Mayhew: Four trays. Engraving, about 1760.

162. John Mayhew: Two Bergère chairs. Engraving, about 1760.

164. Ince and Mayhew: Tea-kettle stands. Engraving, about 1760.

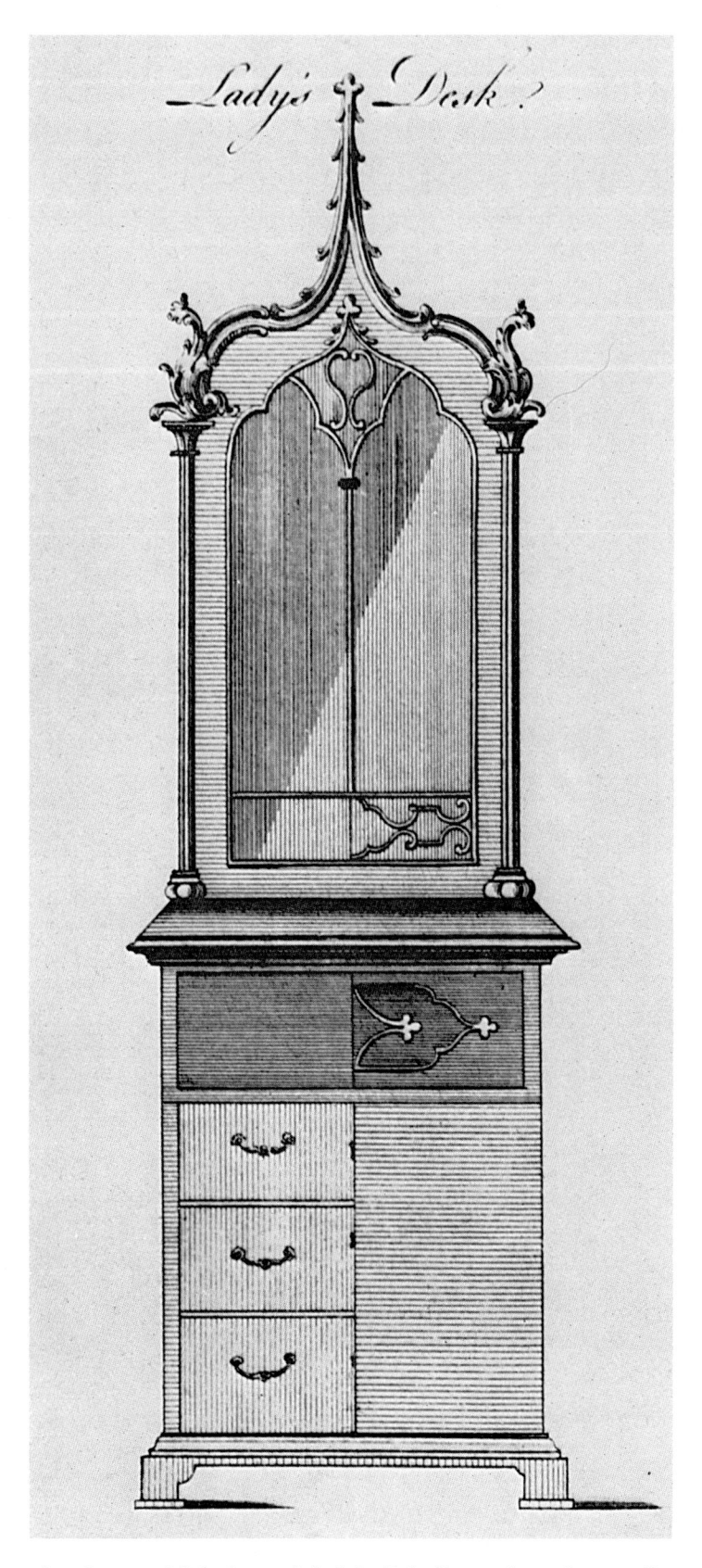

165. Ince and Mayhew: A lady's desk. Engraving, about 1760.

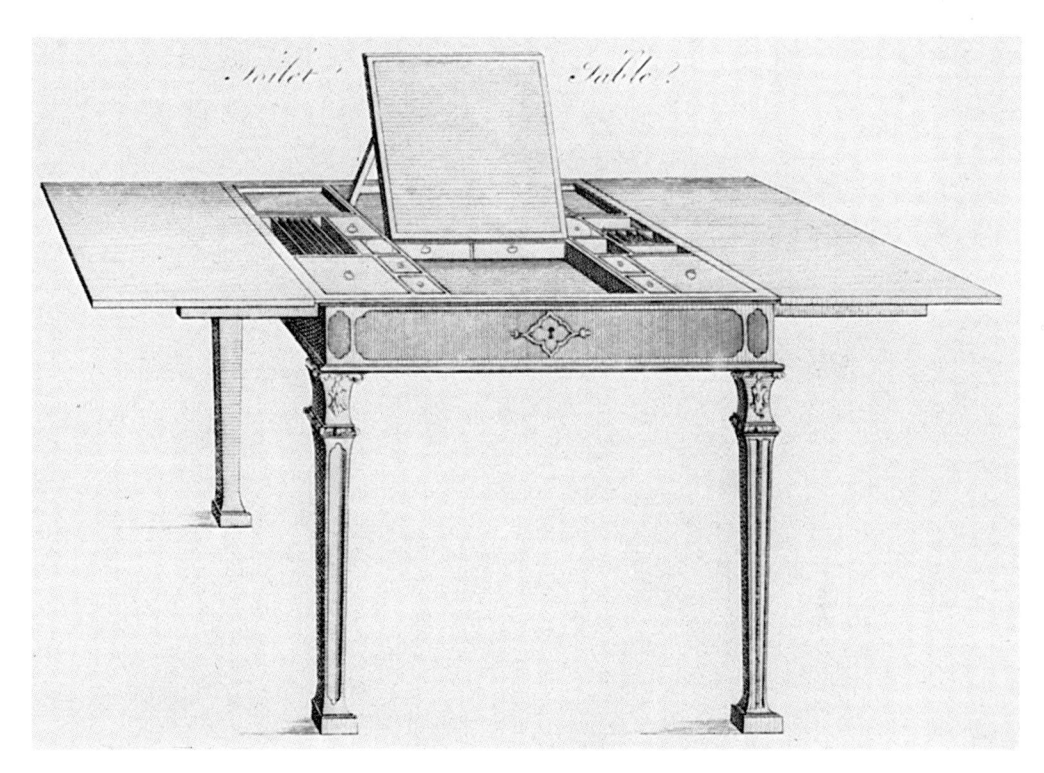

166. Society of Upholsterers: A dressing table. Engraving, 1760.

167. Society of Upholsterers: A library table. Engraving, 1760.

168. Society of Upholsterers: A 'Gothic' bookcase. Engraving, 1760.

169. Society of Upholsterers: 'An embattled bookcase.' Engraving, 1760.

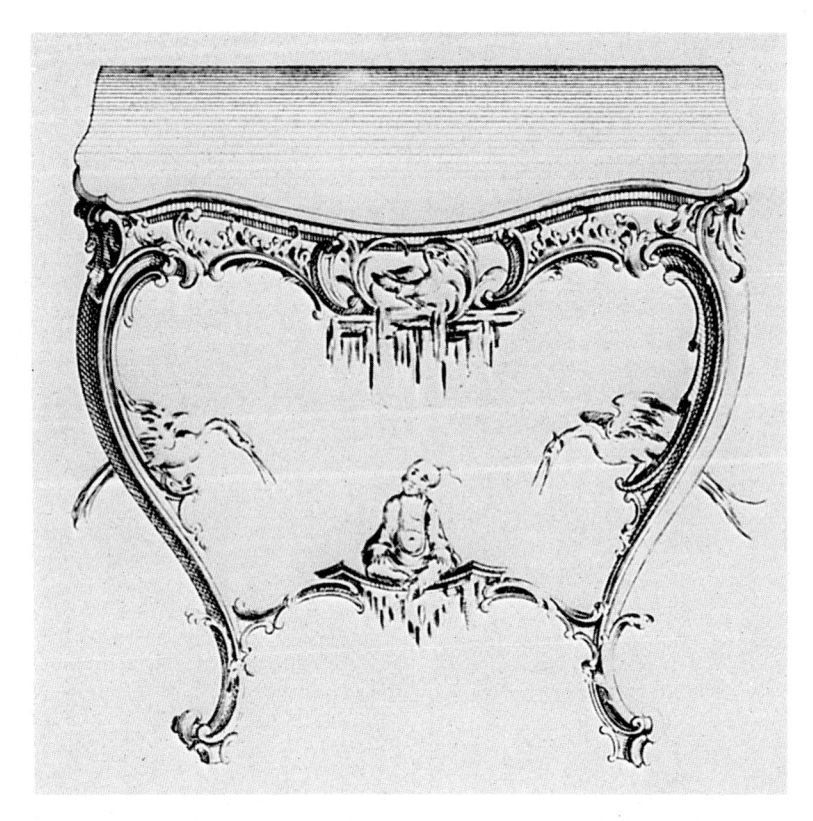

170. Society of Upholsterers: 'A 'side-board table' designed by Chippendale. Engraving, 1760.

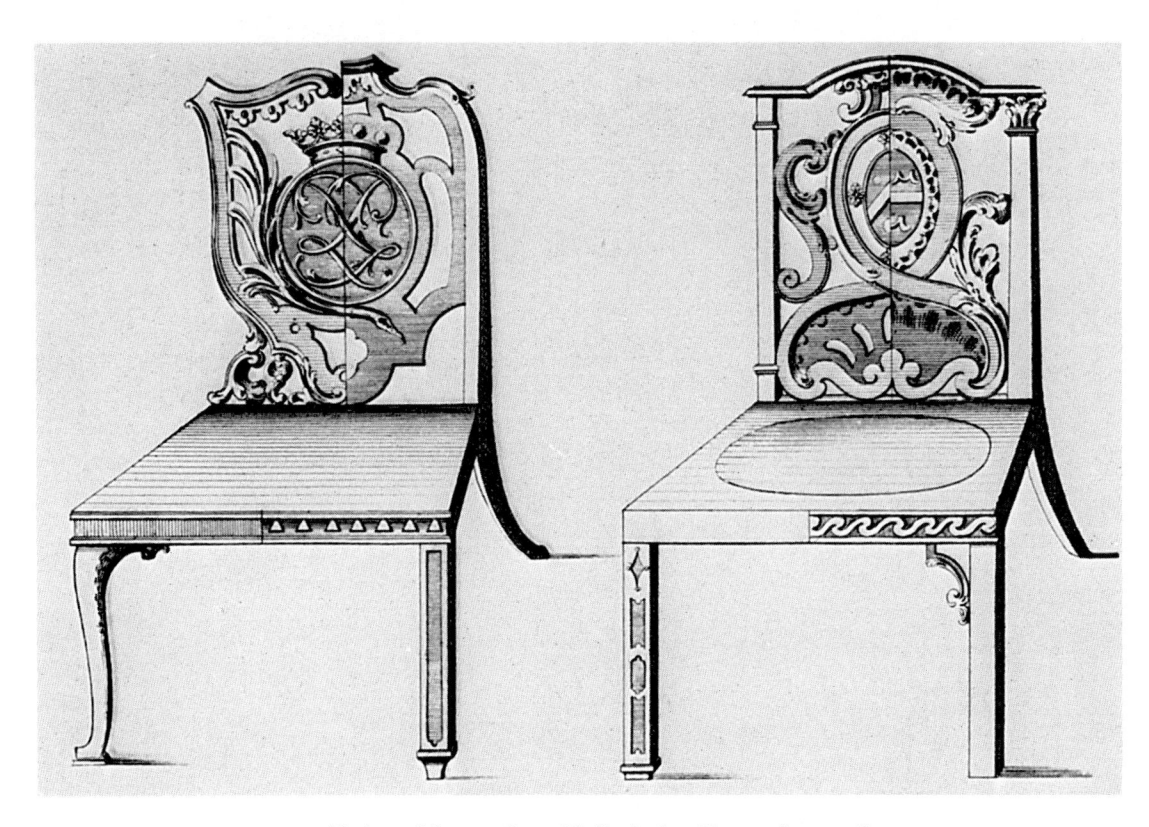

171. Robert Manwaring: Hall chairs. Engraving, 1760.

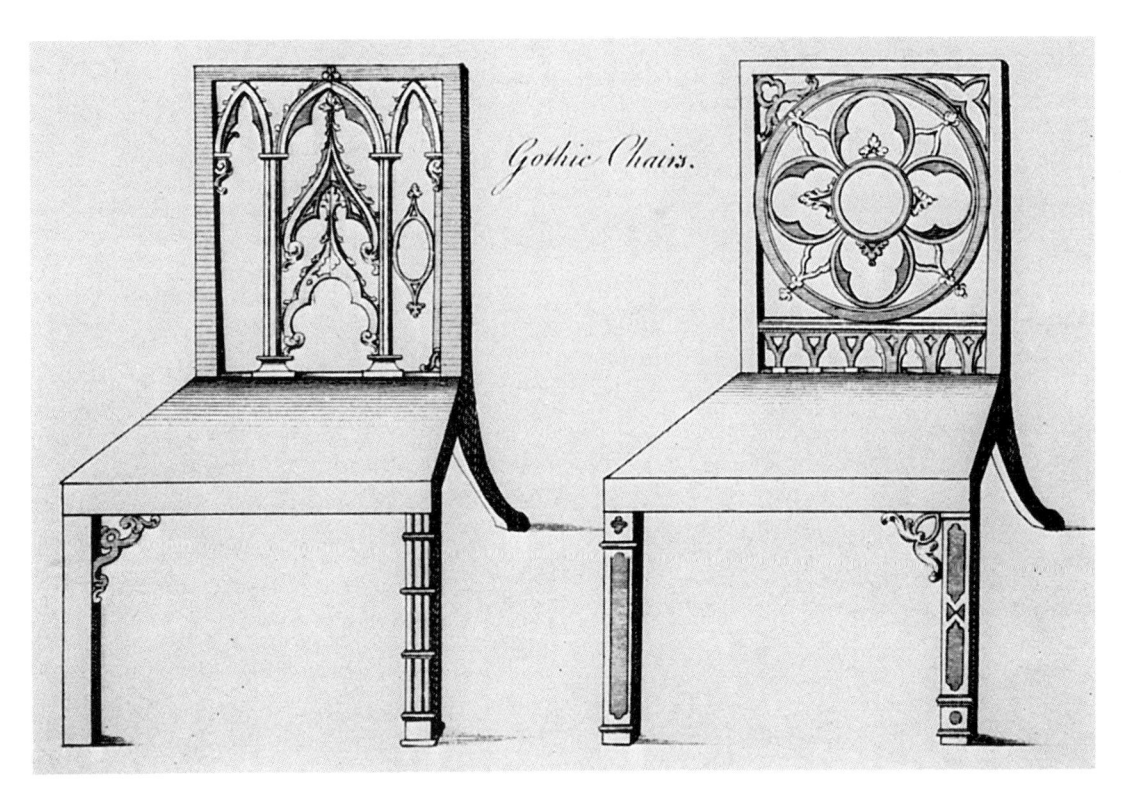

172. Robert Manwaring: Two 'Gothic' chairs. Engraving, 1760.

173. Robert Manwaring: Two 'Gothic' chairs. Engraving, 1766.

174. Robert Manwaring: Two dressing chairs. Etching, 1765.

175. Robert Manwaring: Three chair backs, etc. Etching, 1765.

176. Robert Manwaring: Parlour chairs. Etching, 1765.

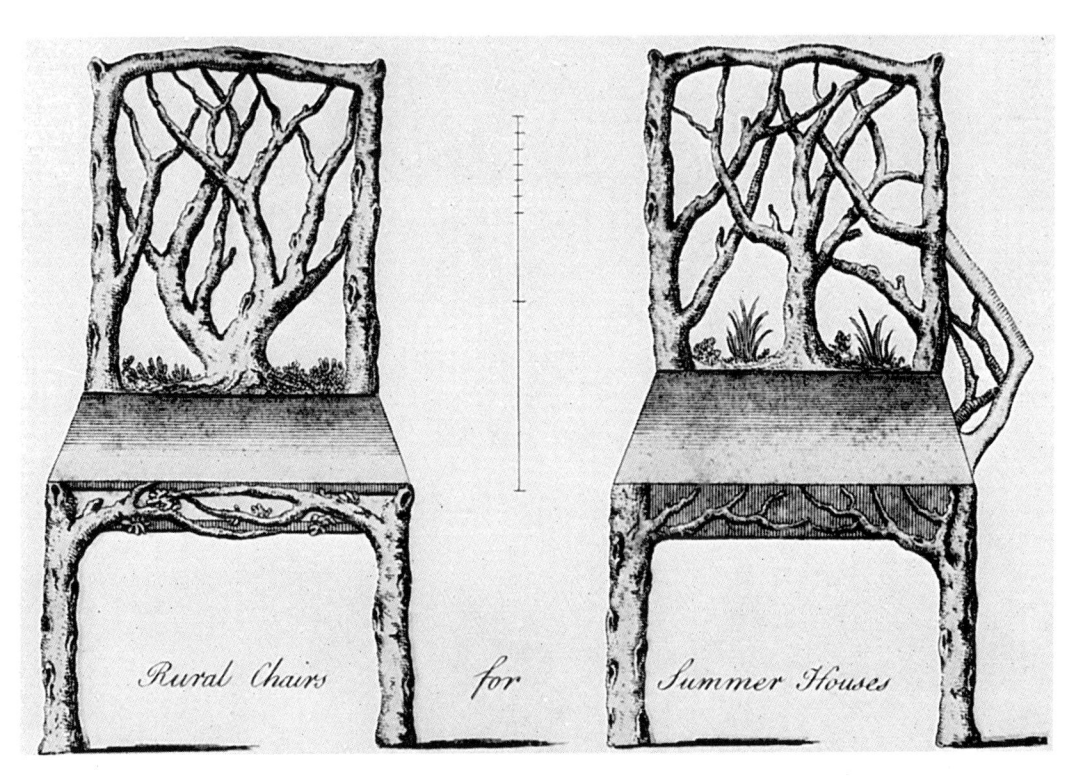

177. Robert Manwaring: 'Rural chairs for summer houses.' Etching, 1765.

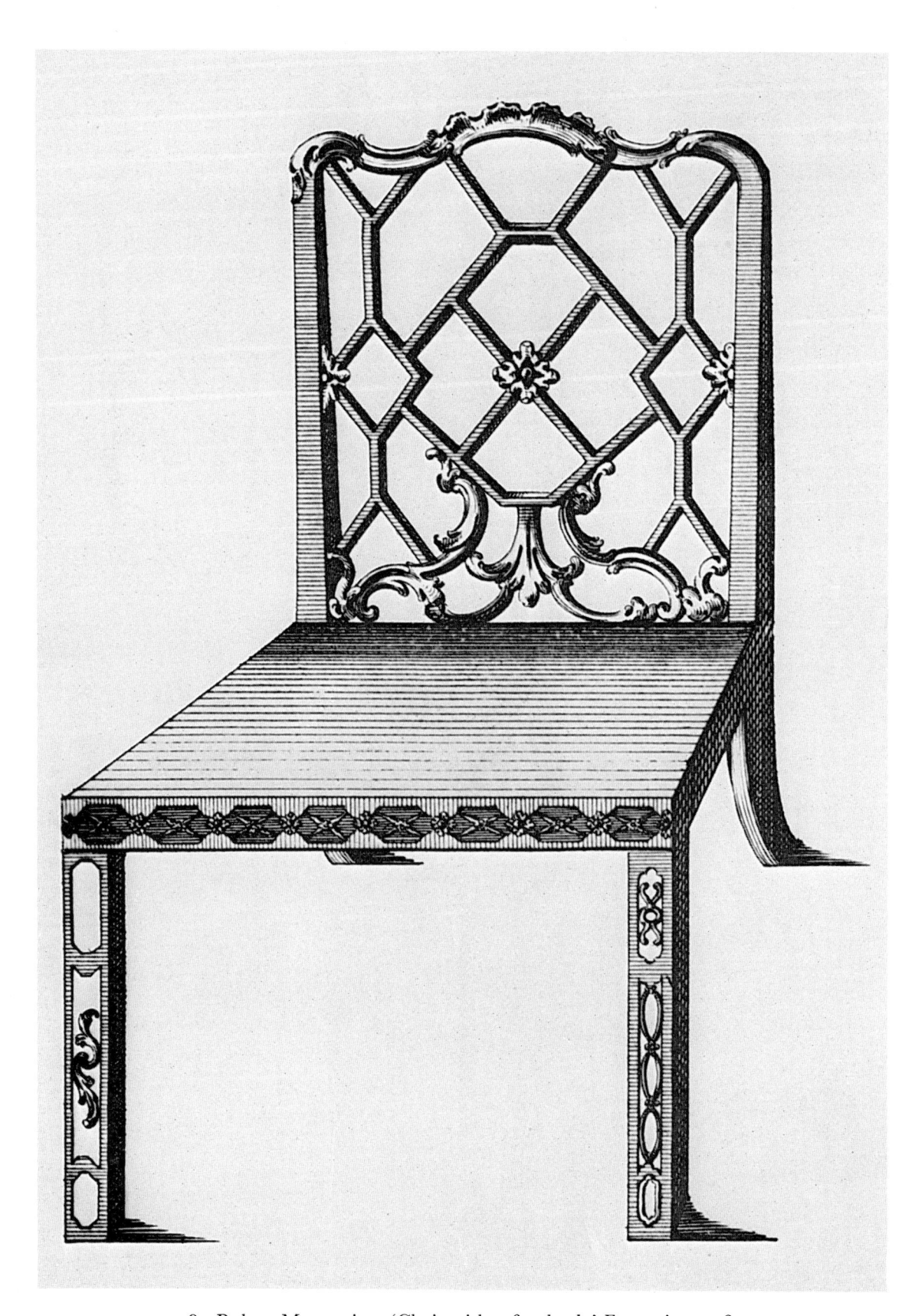

178. Robert Manwaring: 'Chair with a fret back.' Engraving, 1760.

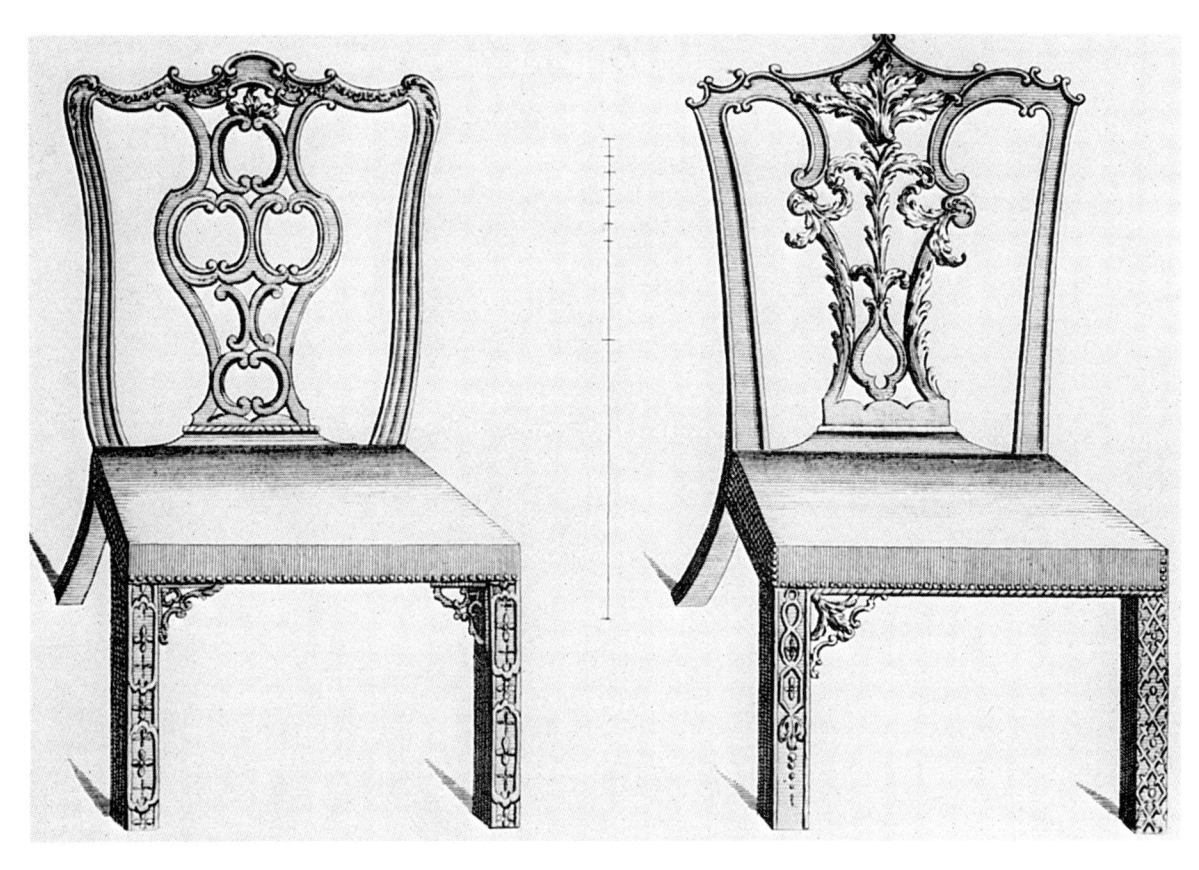

179. Robert Manwaring: Two parlour chairs. Etching, 1765.

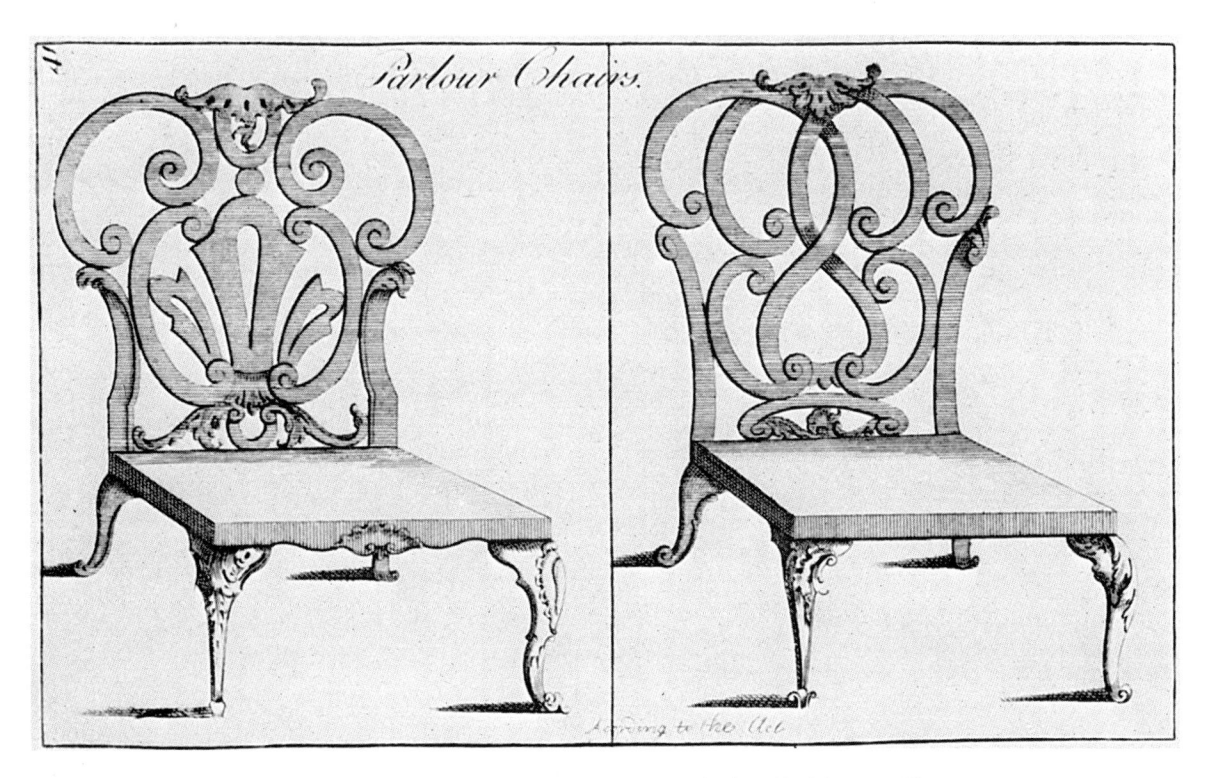

180. Matthew Darly: Two parlour chairs. Etching, 1766.

181. Copland: A hall chair. Etching, 1766.

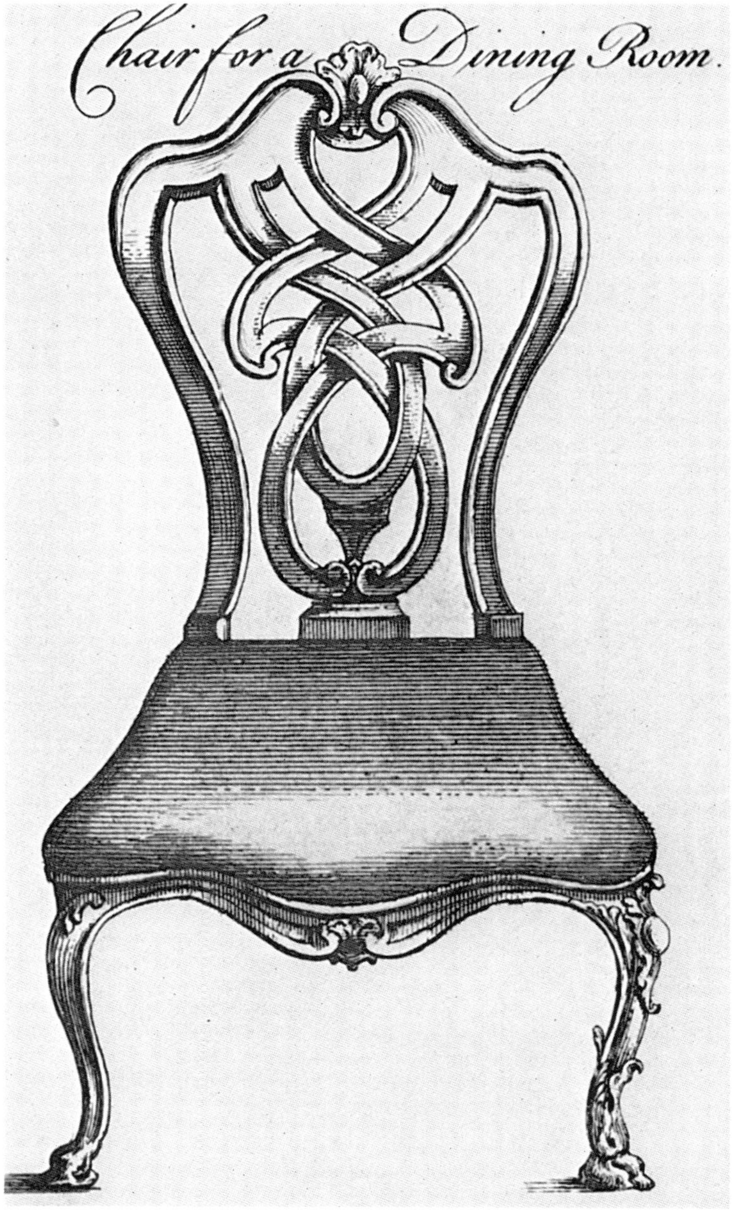

183. Attributed to Copland: A dining-room chair. Engraving, 1766.

182. Copland: A hall chair. Etching, 1766.

184. Anonymous drawing: Pier table and mirror. About 1760.

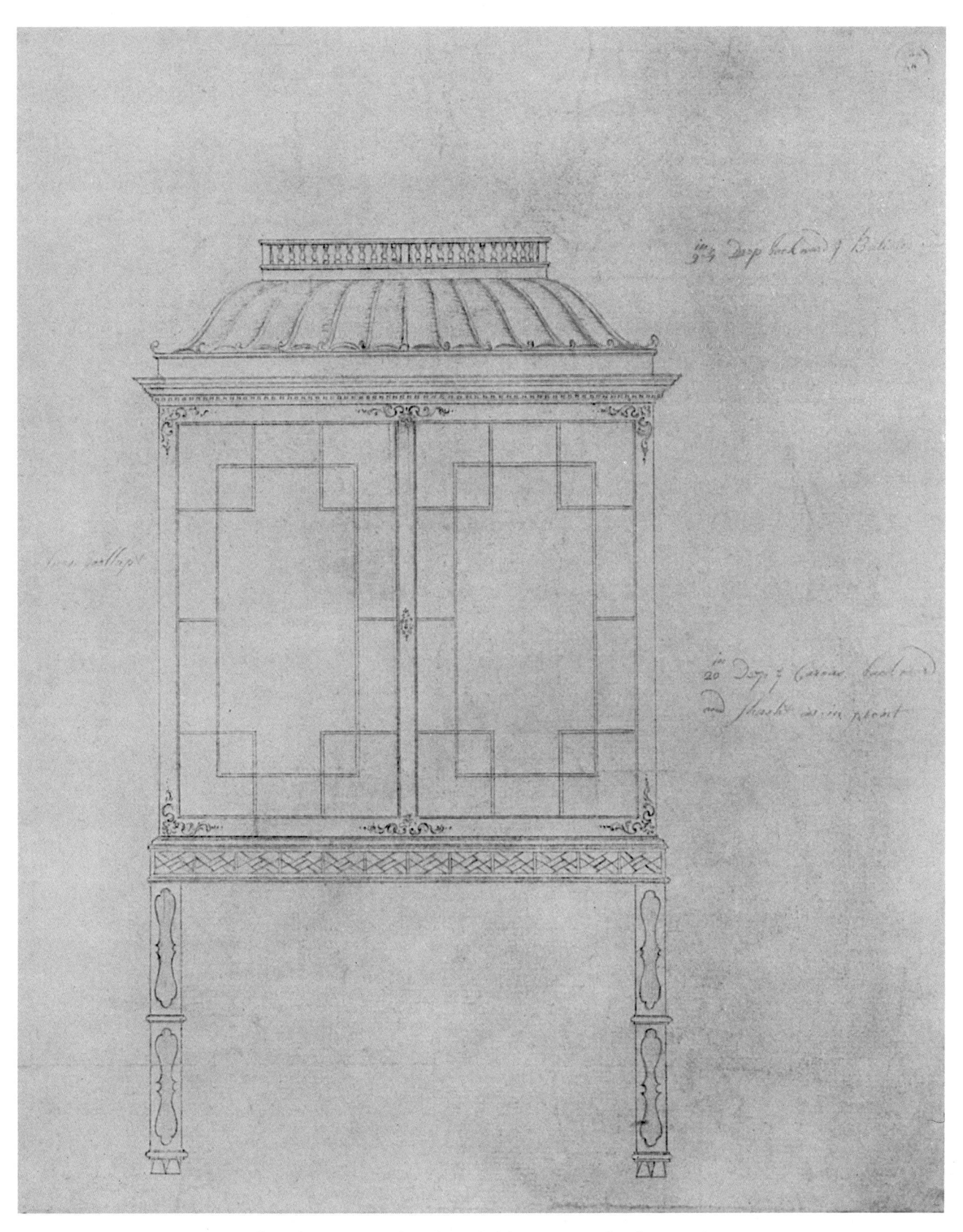

185. Anonymous drawing: Cabinet on stand. About 1760.

186. Anonymous drawing: A glazed bookcase. About 1765.

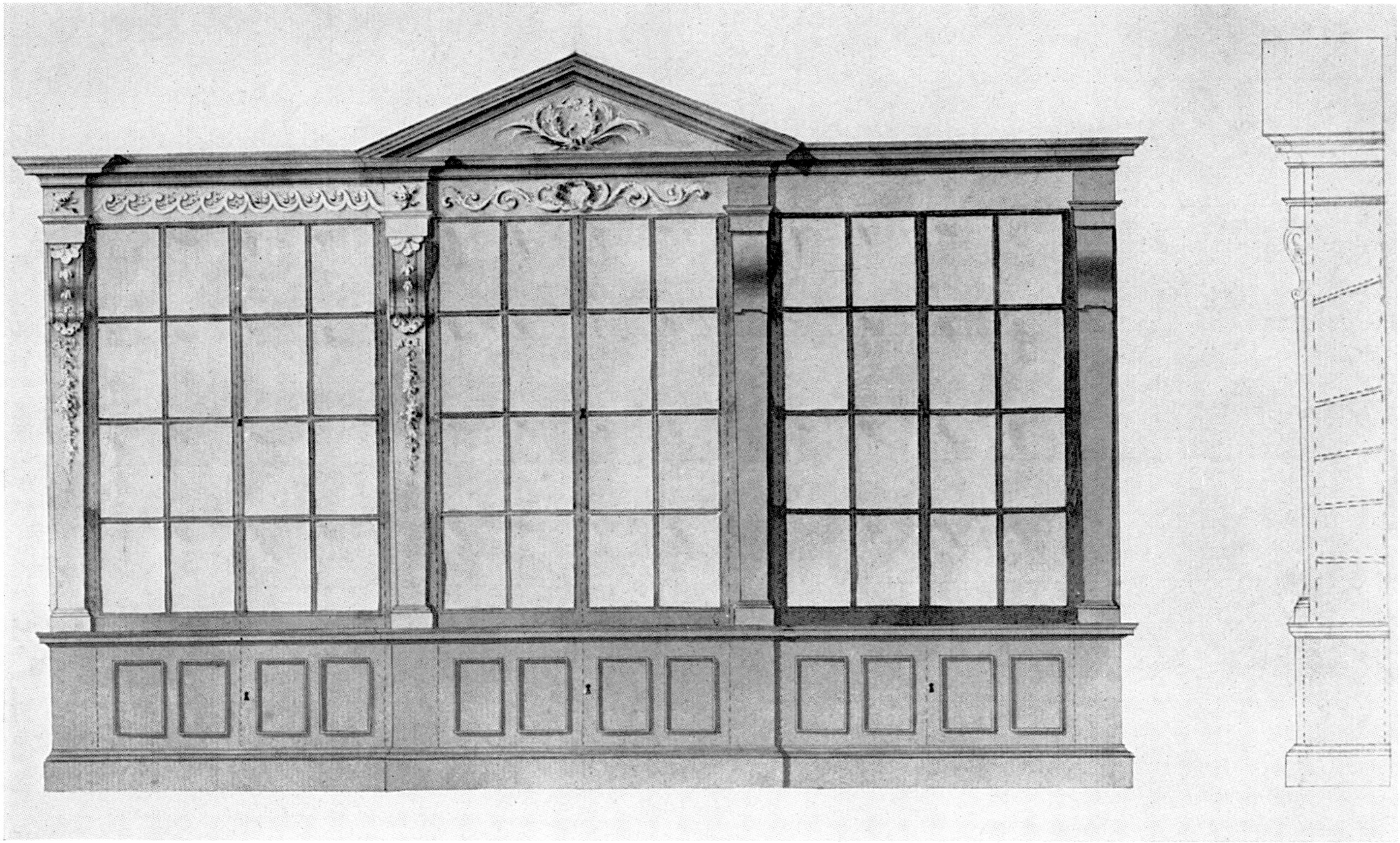

187. Henry Keene: Design for a museum cabinet. Drawing, about 1760.

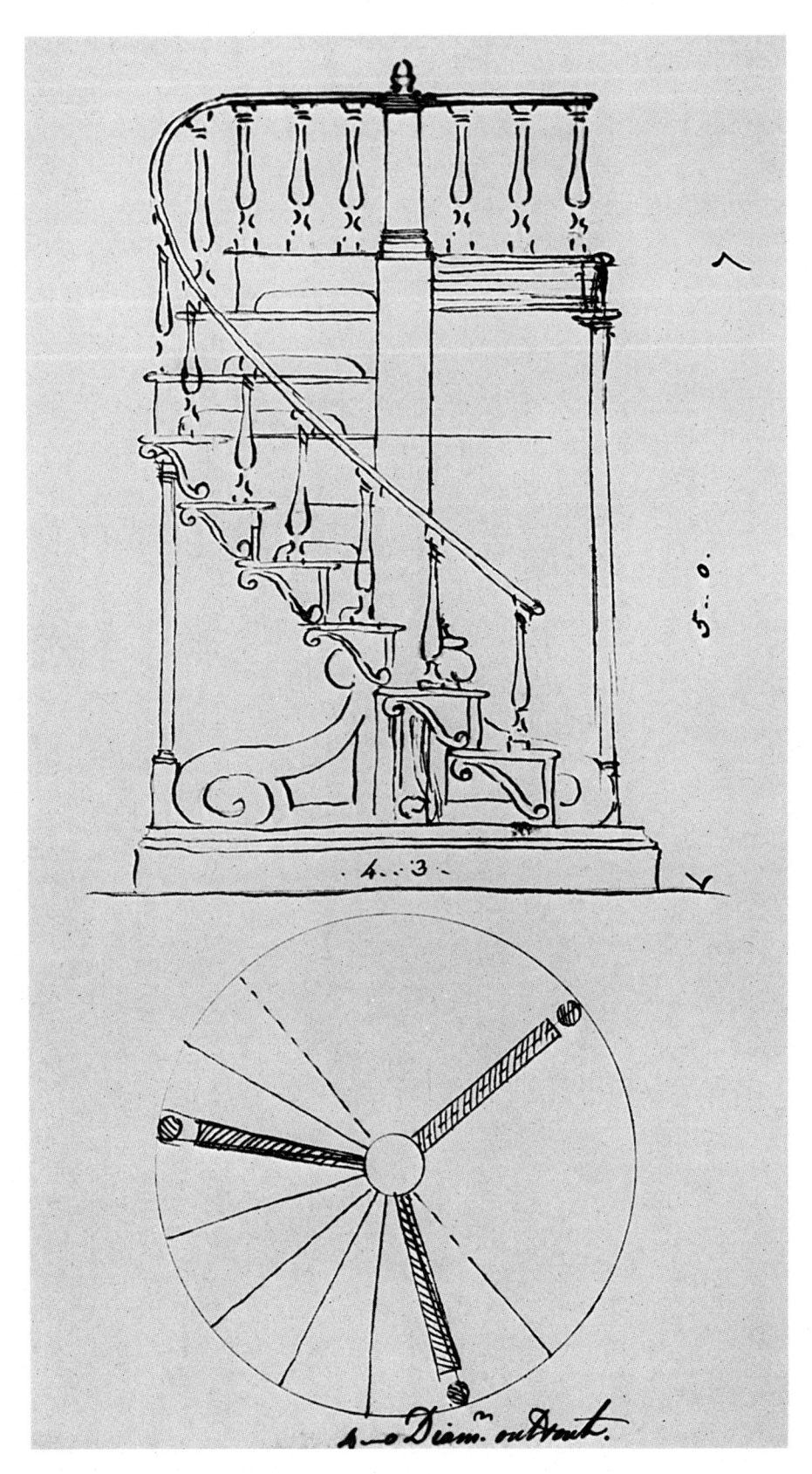

188. Henry Keene: Library steps. Drawing, about 1750.

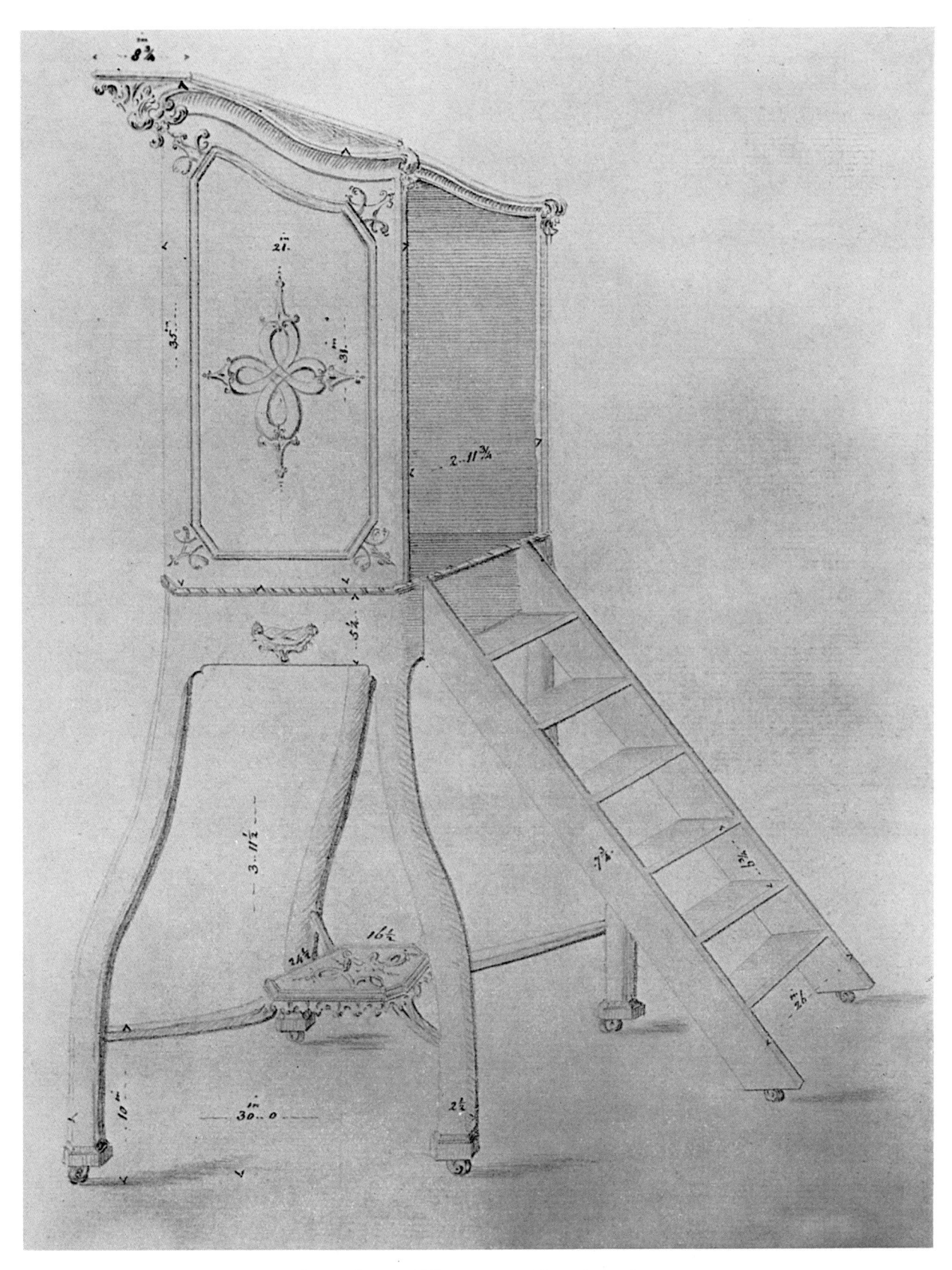

189. Henry Keene: Library steps. Drawing, about 1750.

190. John Linnell: Side-table. Drawing, about 1750.

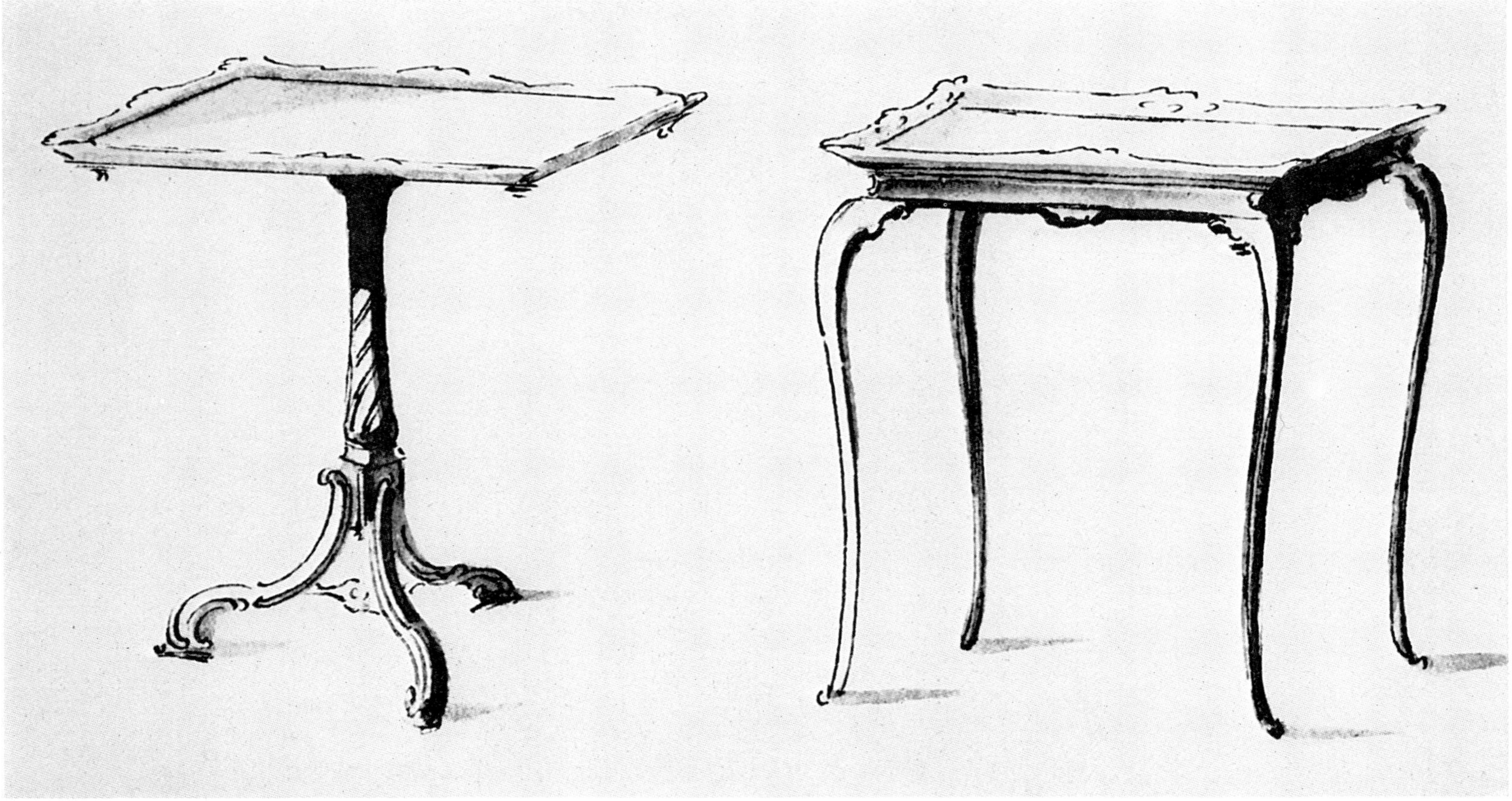

191. Linnell: Two tea tables. Drawing, about 1760.

192. Linnell: A console table. Drawing, about 1760.

193. Linnell: A console table. Drawing, about 1760.

194. Linnell: Overmantel mirror and chimney-piece. Drawing, about 1760.

195. Linnell: A sofa for Lord Scarsdale. Drawing, about 1765.

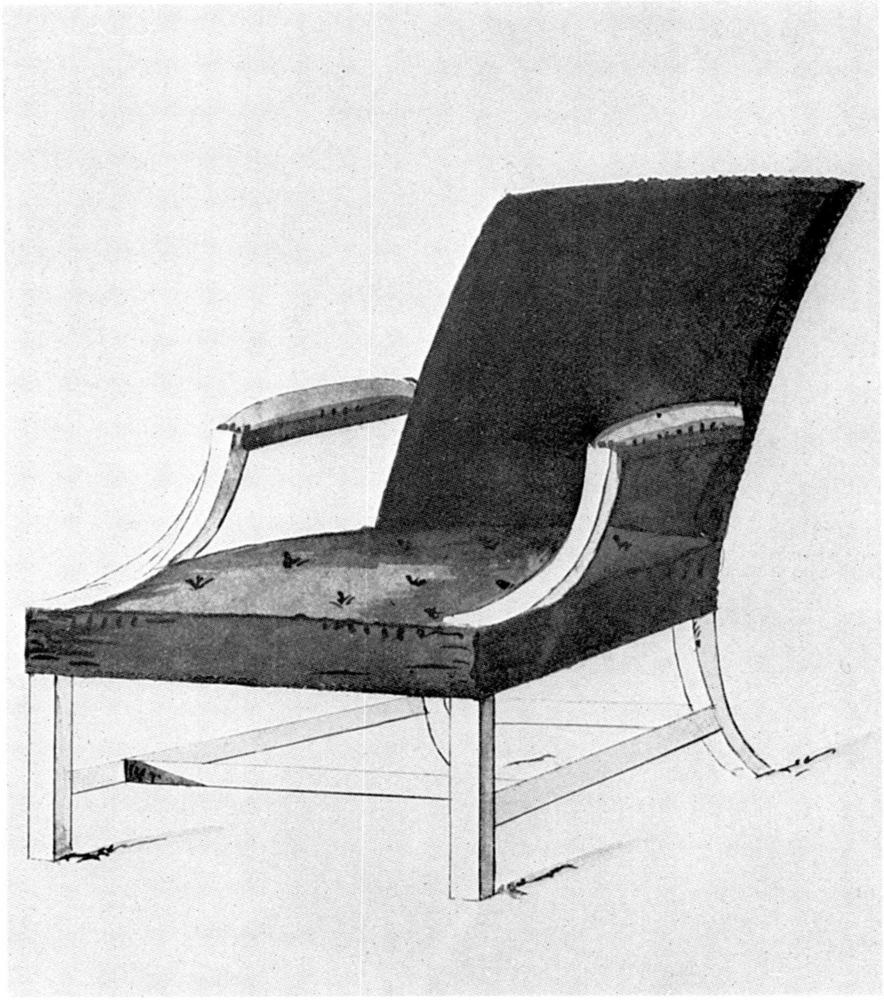

197. Linnell: An arm-chair. Drawing, about 1760.

196. Linnell: A chair. Drawing, about 1760.

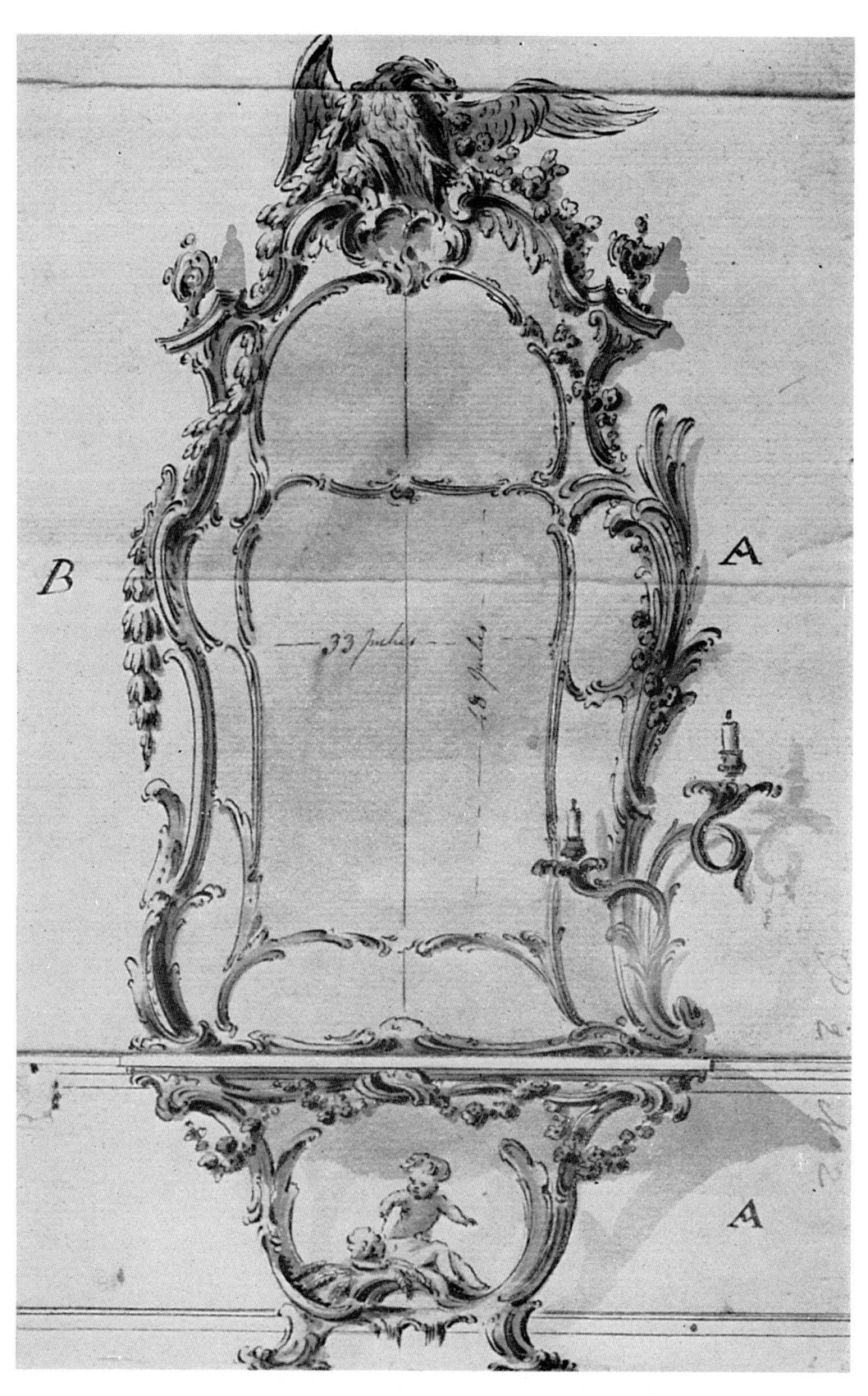

198. Linnell: A console table and mirror. Drawing, about 1760.

199. Linnell: A console table and mirror. Drawing, about 1760.

200. Linnell: A bed. Drawing, about 1760.

201. Anonymous drawing of a bed in the style of Linnell. About 1760.

202. Robert Adam: A sofa for Sir Laurence Dundas. Drawing, 1764.

203. Adam: A sofa for Lord Scarsdale. Drawing, 1762.

204. Adam: An organ for Lord Bute. Drawing, 1763.

205. Adam: A clothes press for Lord Coventry. Drawing, 1764.

206. Adam: A bookcase. Drawing, 1767.

207. Adam: A stool modelled on an antique cistern. Drawing, 1768. *cf.* nos. 363 and 364.

209. Adam: A mirror for Lady Coventry. Drawing, 1768.

208. Adam: A mirror for Lord Shelburne. Drawing, 1768.

210. Adam: A side-table and mirror. Drawing, about 1770.

211. Adam: A commode for Sir George Colebrooke. Drawing, 1771.

212. Adam: A commode for the Duke of Bolton. Drawing, 1773.

213. Adam: A bookcase for 20 St James's Square. Drawing, 1776.

214. Adam: A mirror and commode for George Keate. Drawing, 1778.

215. Adam: A casket on a stand for George Keate. Drawing, 1777.

216. Adam: A table for Lady Bathurst. Drawing, 1779.

217. Adam: A table with a scagliola top. Drawing, 1775.

218. Adam: A bed for Osterley Park. Drawing, 1775.

219. Adam: Table, mirror and tripods for Luton Hoo. Drawing, 1772.

220. Adam: An arm-chair for Osterley Park. Drawing, 1777.

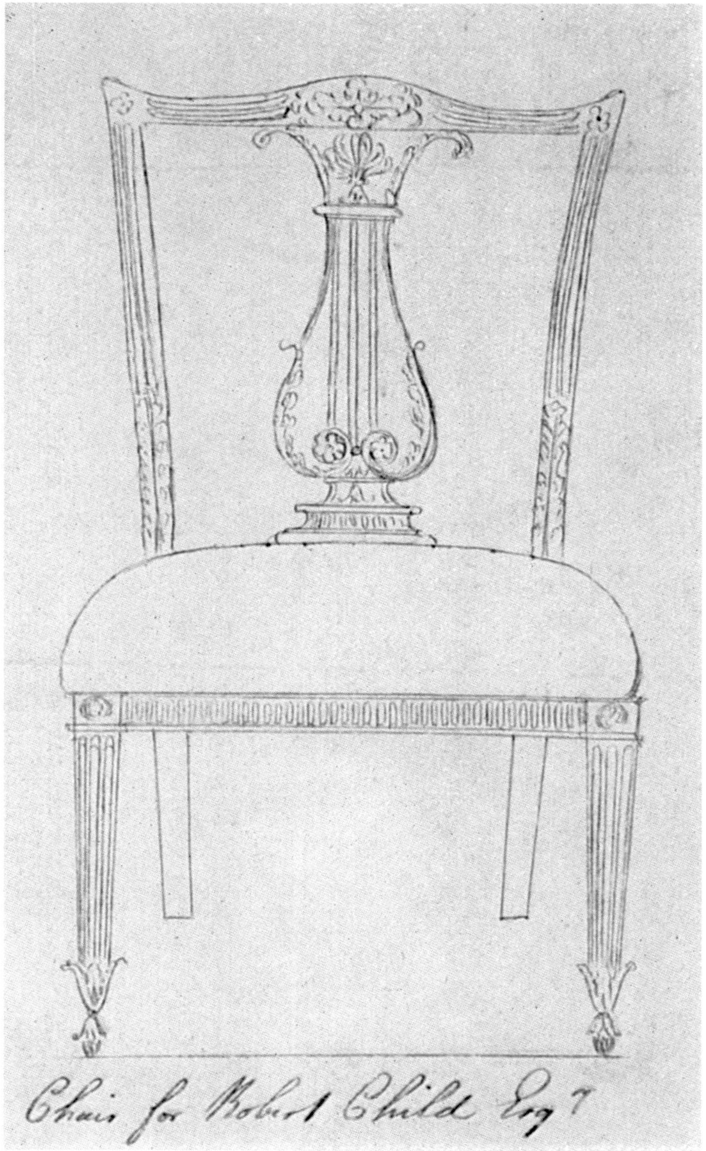

222. Adam: A chair for Lord Derby. Drawing, 1775.

221. Adam: A chair for Osterley Park. Drawing, about 1775.

223. Adam: A sofa. Drawing, about 1770.

226. Adam: A tripod for 20 St James's Square. Drawing, 1773.

225. Adam: A tripod for Apsley House. Drawing, 1779.

224. Adam: A tripod for Osterley Park. Drawing, 1776.

227. Adam: Furniture and fittings for Lord Derby. Engraving, 1774.

228. Adam: Designs for lamps and clock cases. Engraving, 1776.

229. Adam: Furniture for Kenwood House. Engraving, 1774.

230. Adam: Furniture for various clients. Engraving, 1773.

231. Adam: A harpsichord for Catherine, Empress of Russia. Engraving, 1774.

232. Adam: An organ for 20 St James's Square. Engraving, 1773.

233. Adam: Furniture for Osterley Park. Engraving, about 1780.

234. Adam: A hall table for Shelburne House. Engraving, 1768.

235. John Linnell: A hanging cabinet. Drawing, about 1770.

236. Linnell: A bookcase. Drawing, about 1775.

237. Linnell: A cabinet or press. Drawing, about 1770.

238. Linnell: A glazed cabinet on a stand. Drawing, about 1775.

239. Linnell: Two commodes. Drawing, about 1780.

240. Linnell: A china cabinet. Drawing, about 1775.

241. Linnell: An arm-chair. Drawing, about 1775.

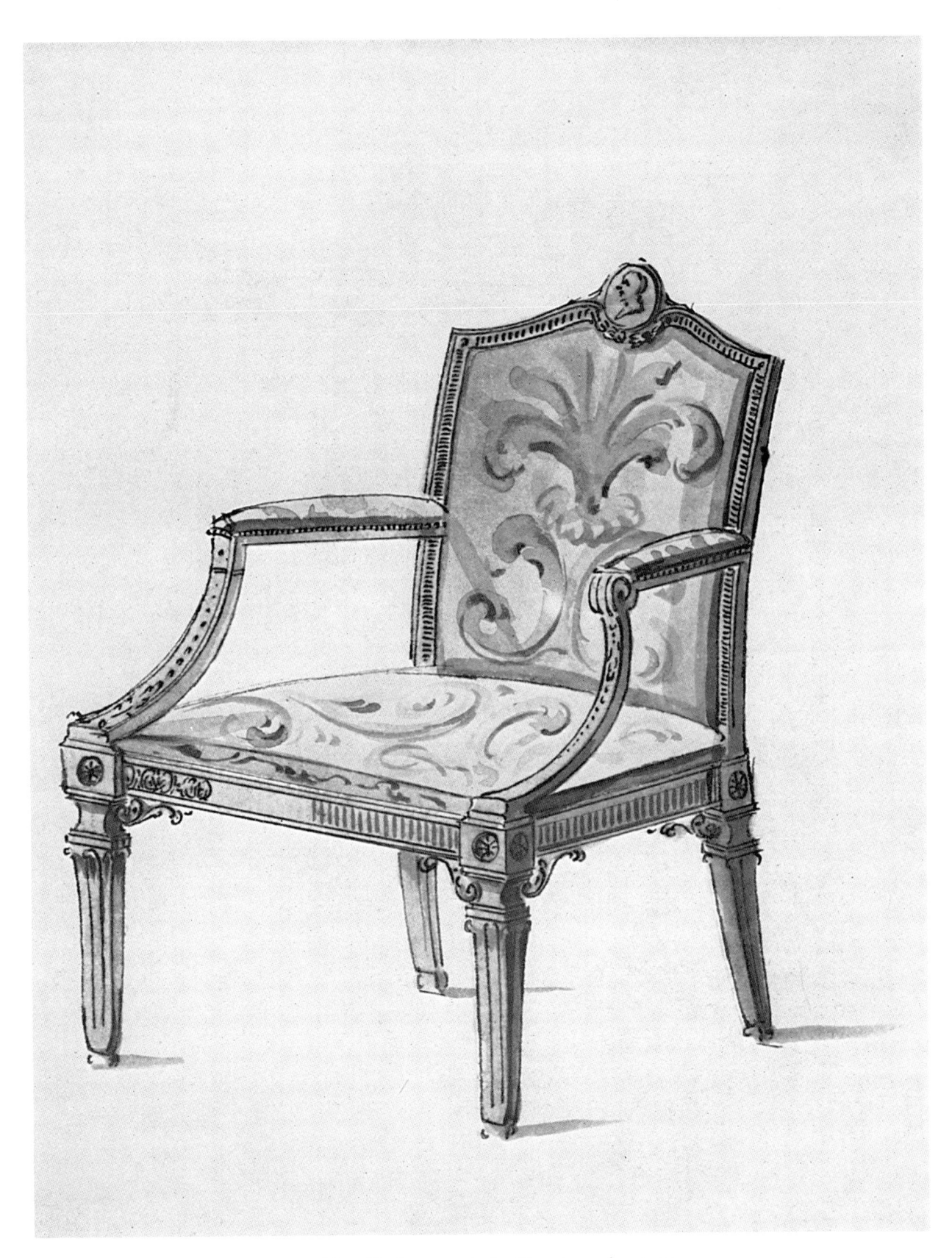

242. Linnell: An arm-chair. Drawing, about 1775.

244. Linnell: A chair. Drawing, about 1770.

243. Linnell: A chair with a lyre-shaped back. Drawing, about 1775.

245. Linnell: A sofa. Drawing, about 1775.

246. Linnell: A sofa and mirror. Drawing, about 1780.

247. Linnell: A side-table and mirror for Shardeloes House. Drawing, about 1770.

248. Linnell: A cabinet on a stand. Drawing, about 1775.

249. Linnell: A glazed cabinet or bookcase. Drawing, about 1775.

250. Linnell: A commode in the French style. Drawing, about 1775.

251. Matthias Lock: Two designs for a table. Drawing, about 1770.

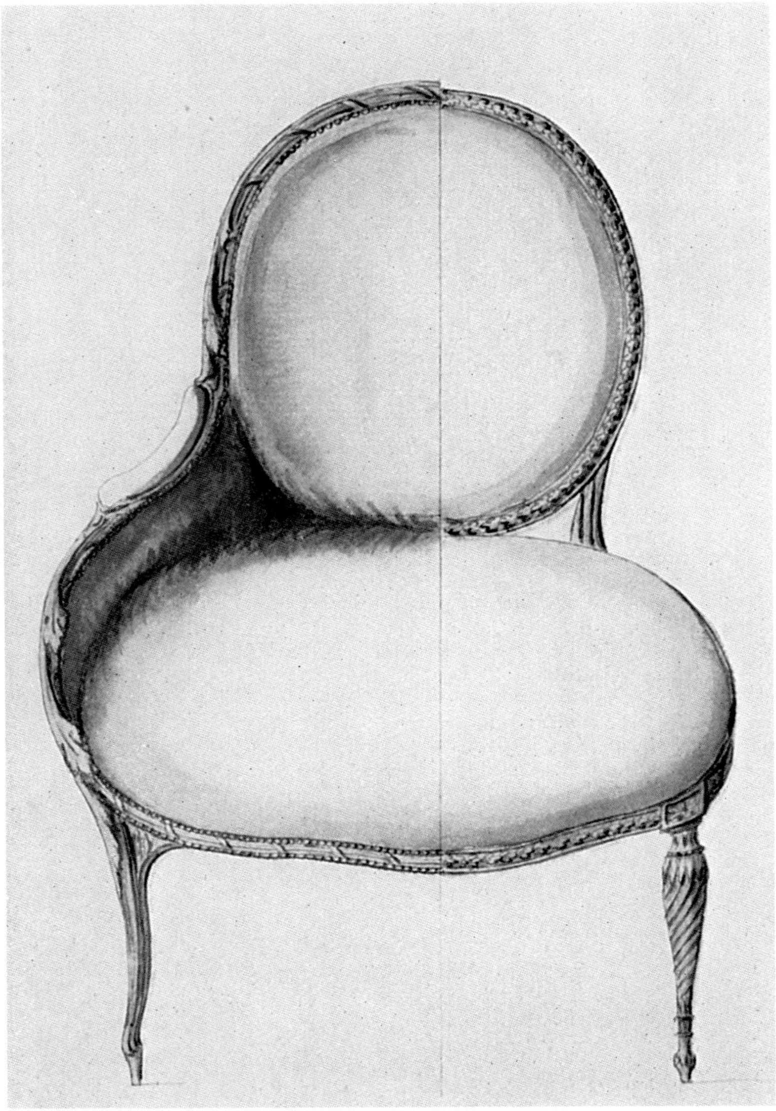

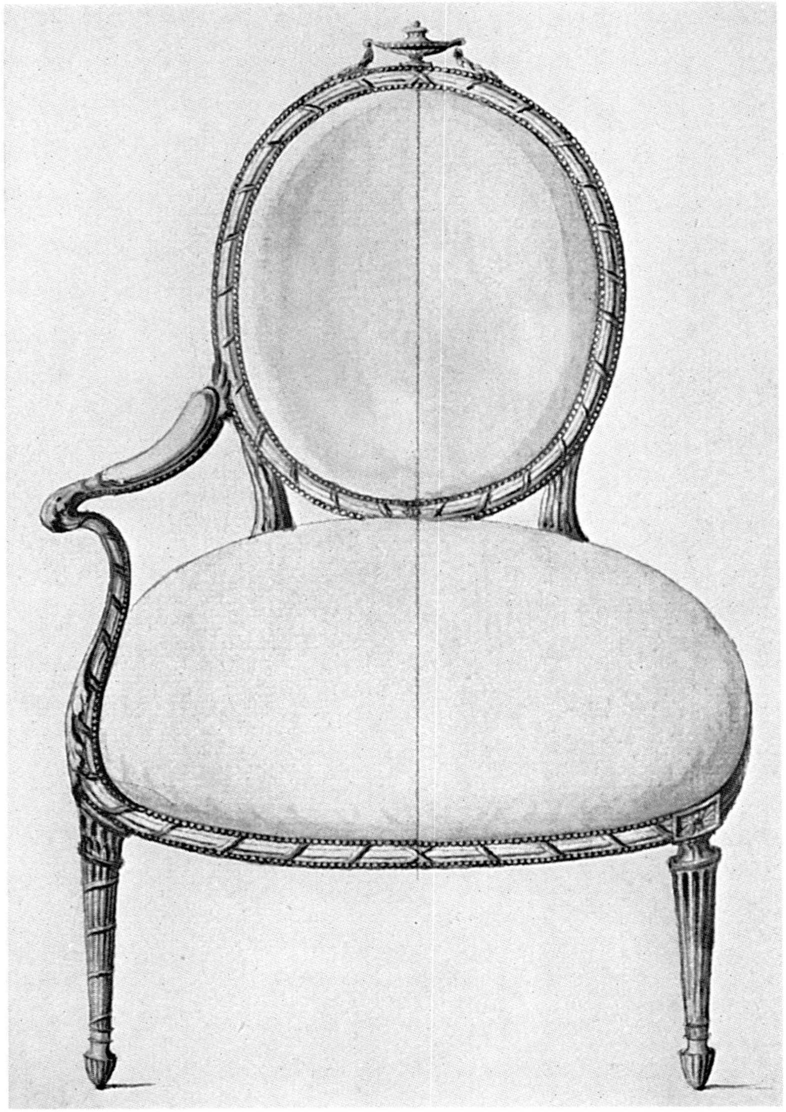

253. Matthias Lock: An arm-chair. Drawing, about 1770.

252. Matthias Lock: An arm-chair. Drawing, about 1770.

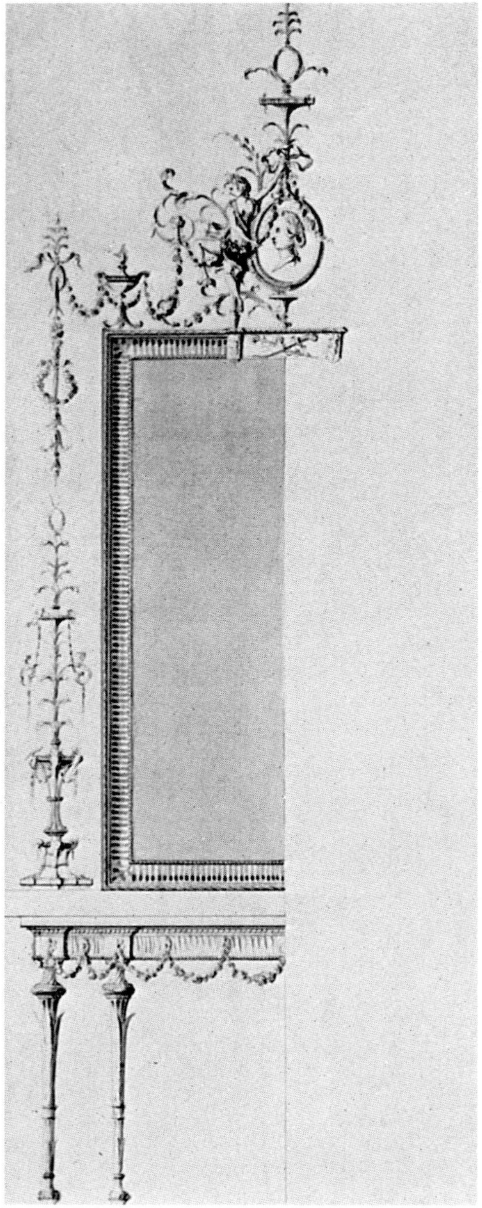

255. Matthias Lock: A looking glass. Drawing, about 1770.

254. Matthias Lock: Pier table and mirror. Drawing, about 1770.

256. Matthias Lock: Two tables. Etching, 1769.

257. Matthew Darly: Glass and picture frames. Etching, 1770.

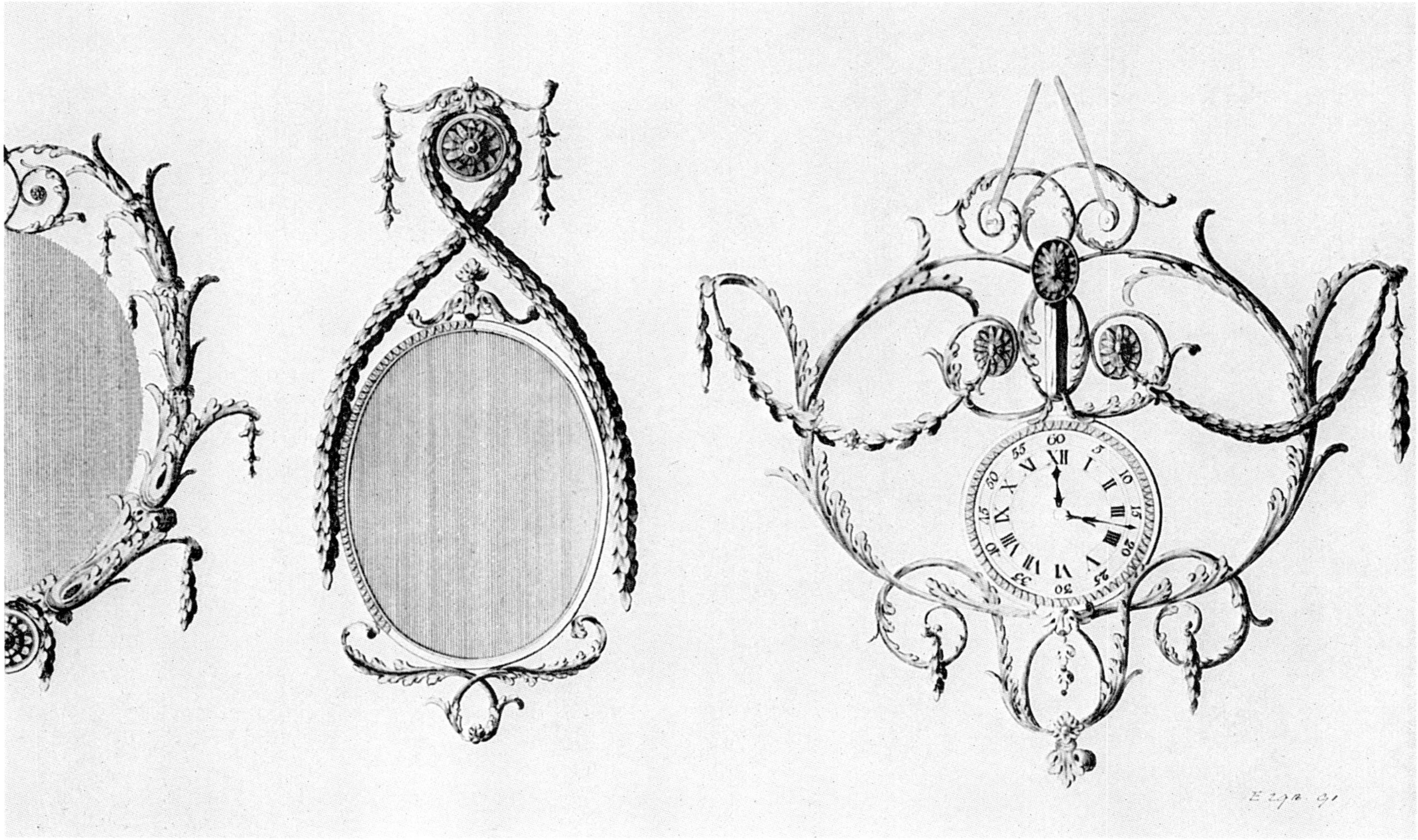

258. Matthew Darly: A clock and two mirrors. Etching, 1771.

259. Henry Keene: A cabinet. Drawing, about 1770.

260. Pergolesi: A table for the Duke of Northumberland. Drawing, about 1780.

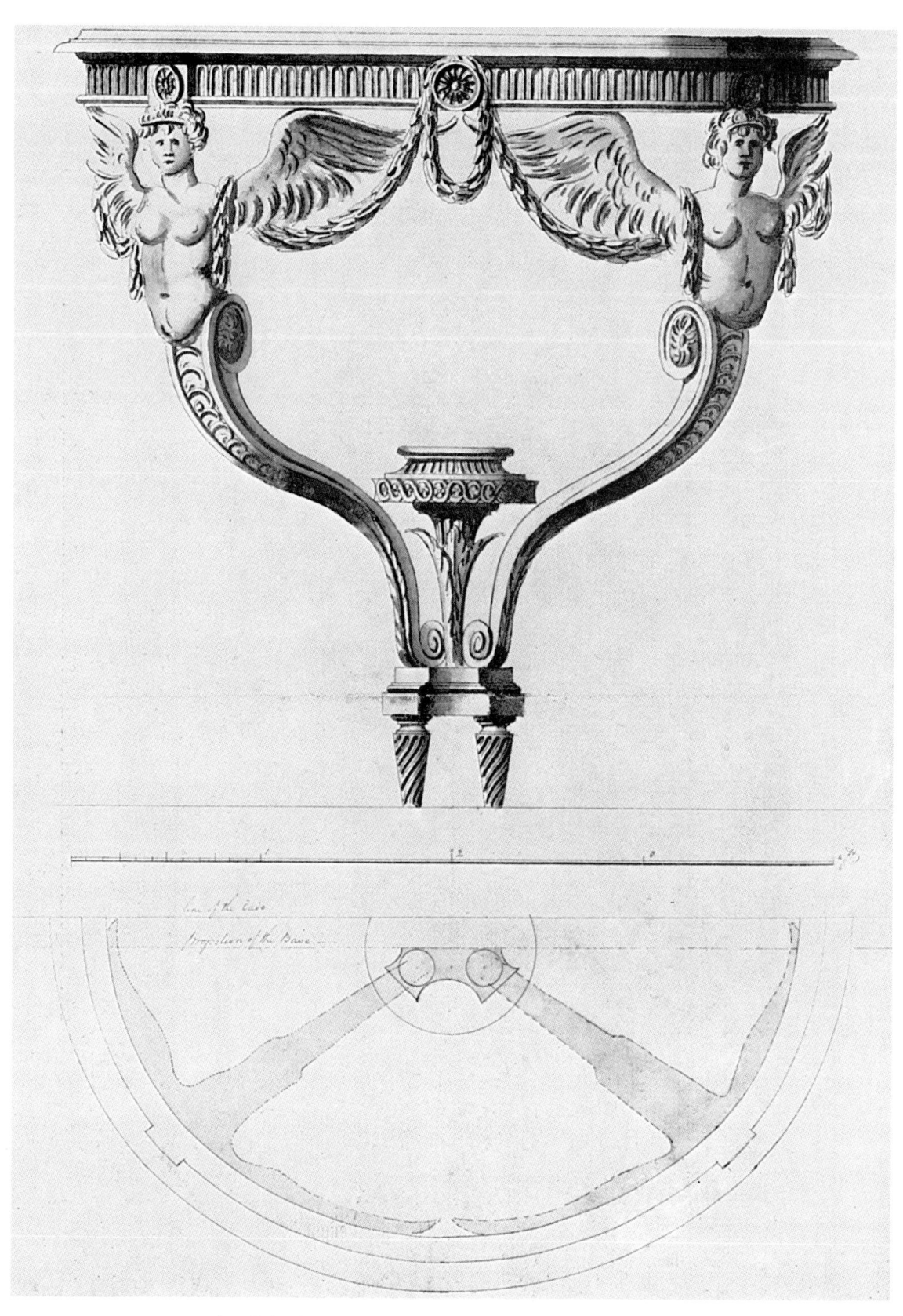

261. John Yenn: A console table. Drawing, about 1780.

262. John Yenn: A side-table. Drawing, 1780.

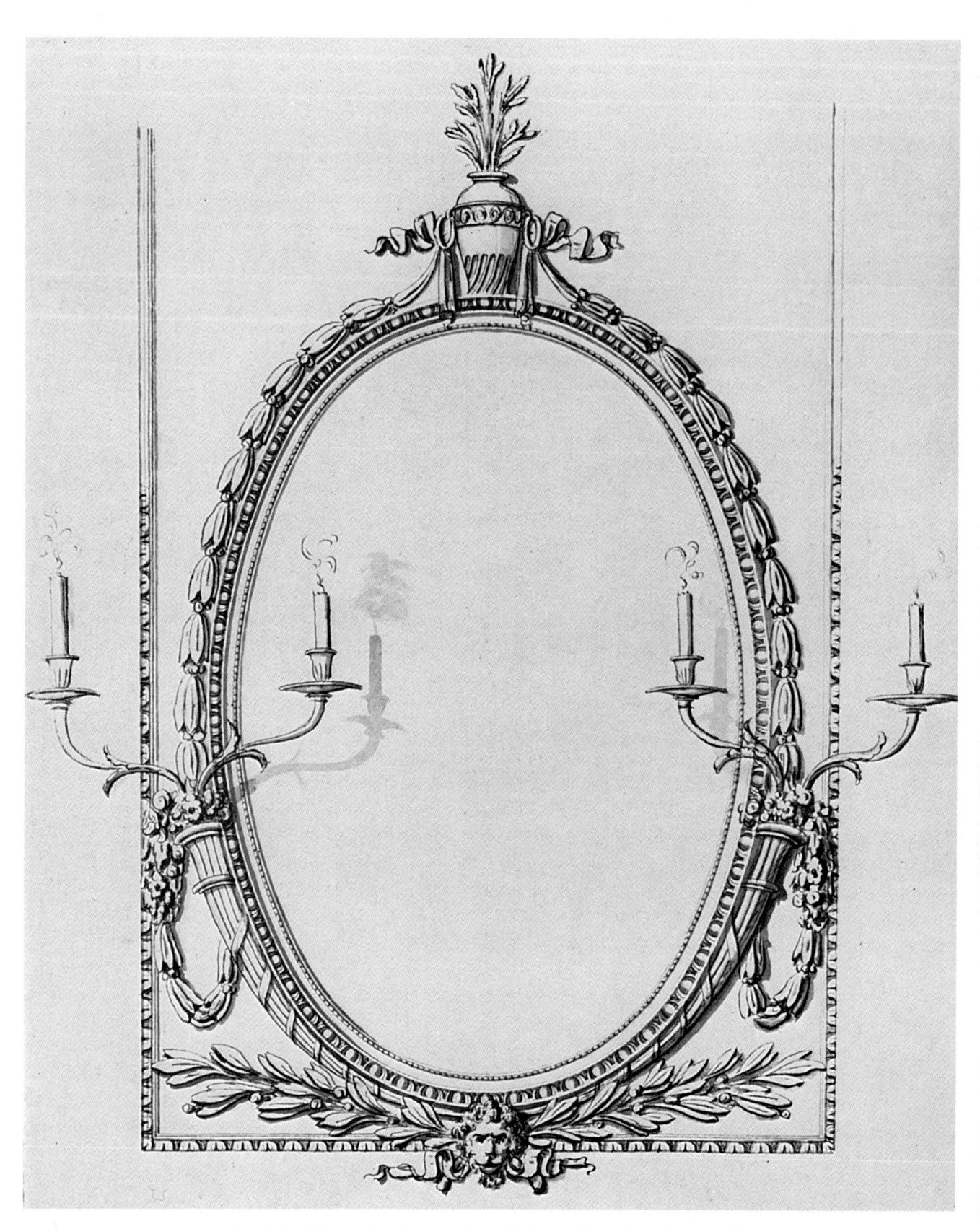

263. John Yenn: A mirror with candelabra. Drawing, about 1780.

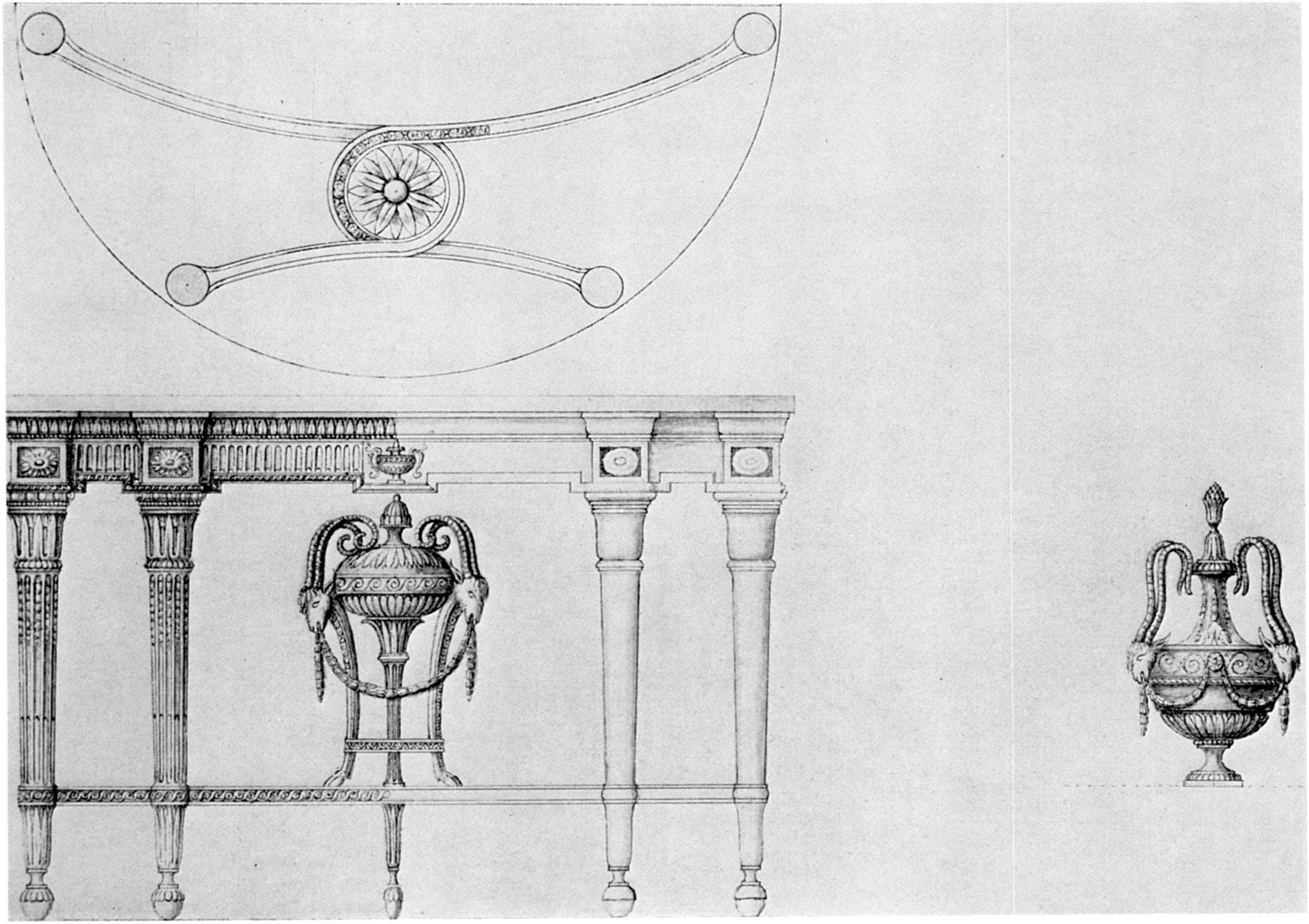

264. Anonymous drawing of a side-table. About 1780.

265. Anonymous drawing: Mirror and console table, about 1780.

266. Anonymous drawing: A side-table, about 1775.

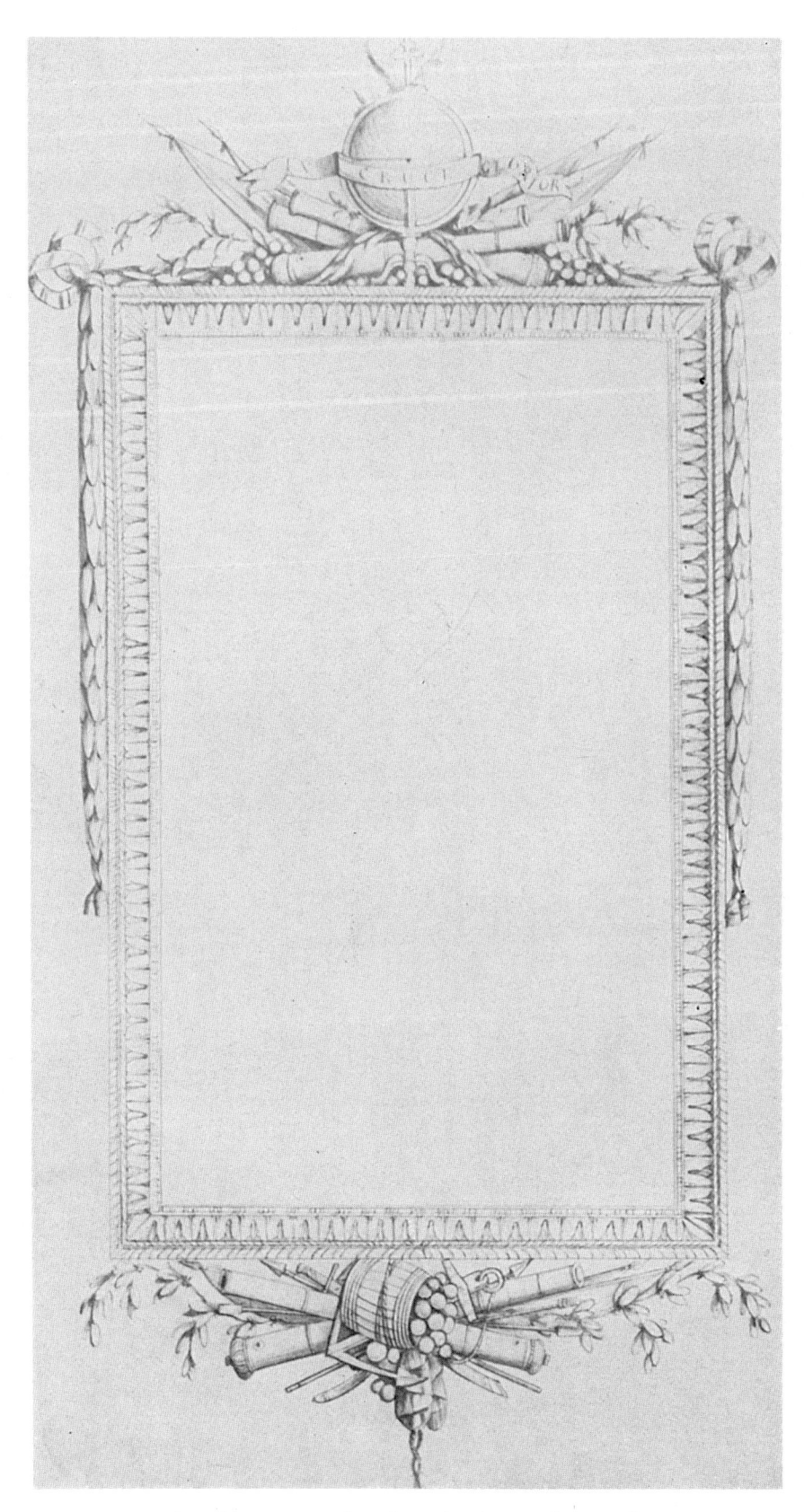

267. Anonymous drawing: A mirror, about 1780.

268. Anonymous drawing: Two mirrors, about 1780.

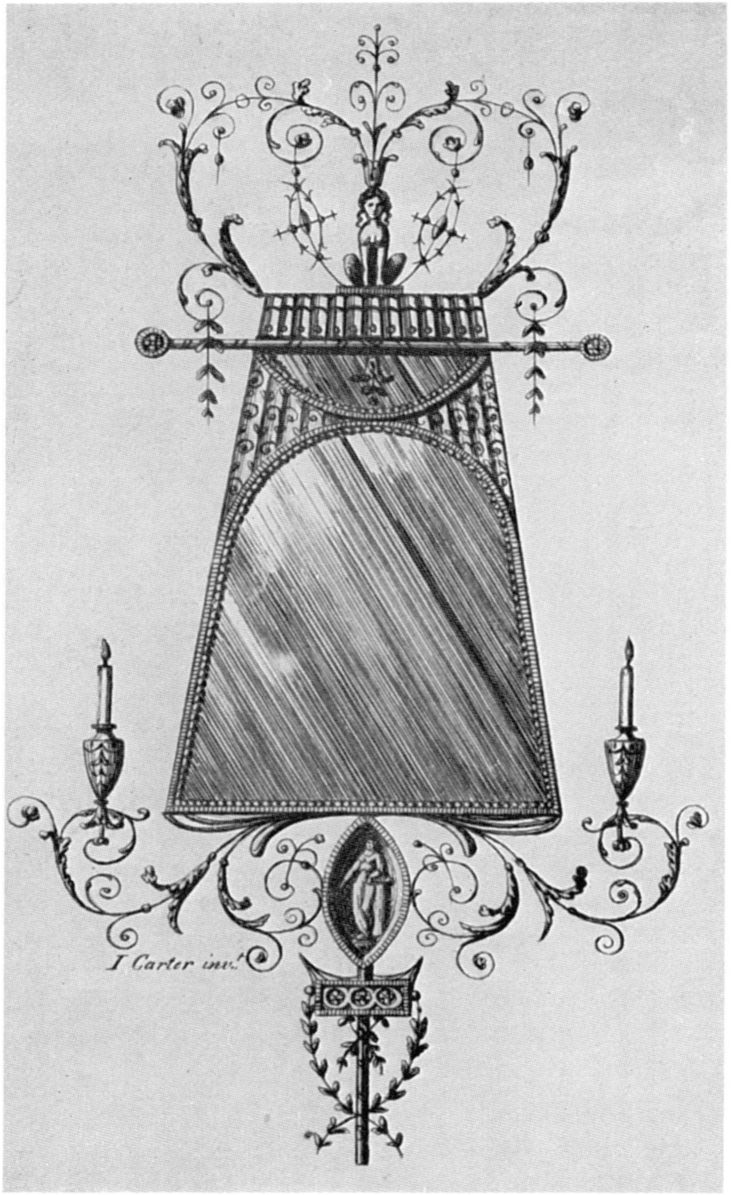

270. John Carter: A mirror. Etching, 1778.

269. John Carter: A girandole. Etching, 1776.

272. John Carter: A clock case. Etching, about 1775.

271. John Carter: A chandelier. Etching, 1777.

273. John Carter: A chair. Etching, 1777.

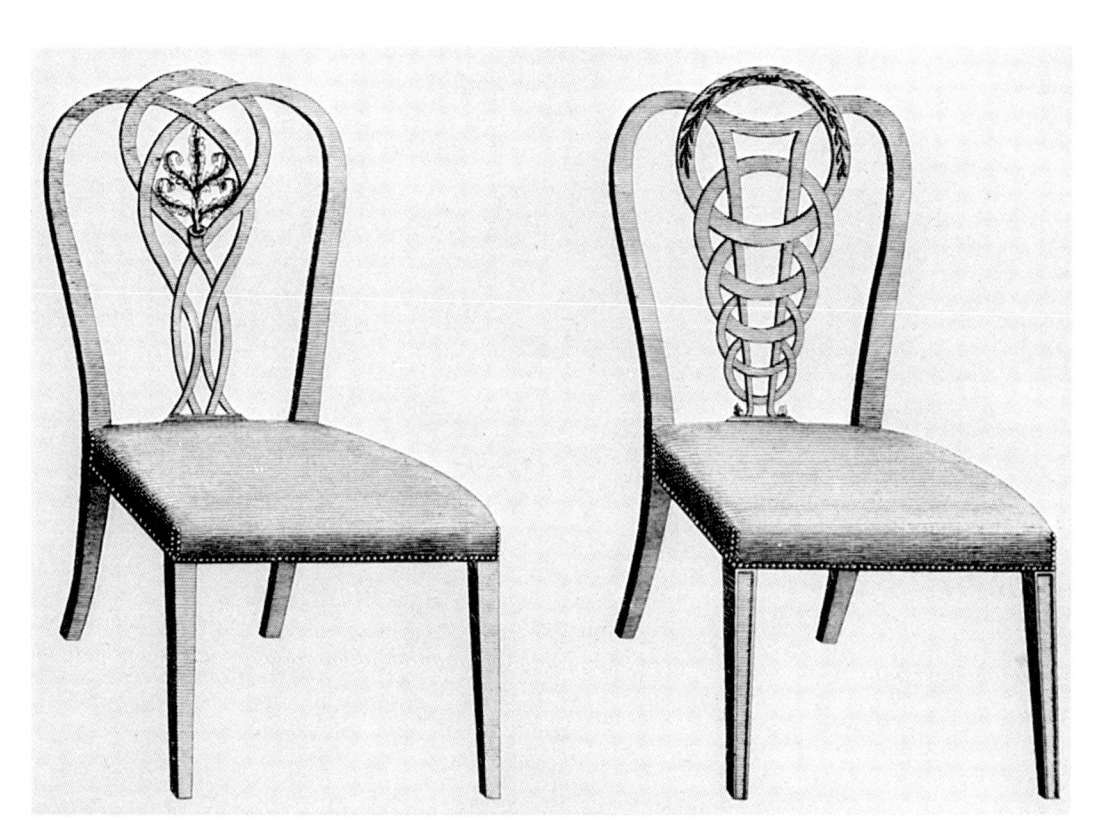

274. George Hepplewhite: Two chairs. Engraving, 1787.

275. Hepplewhite: Two state chairs. Engraving, 1787.

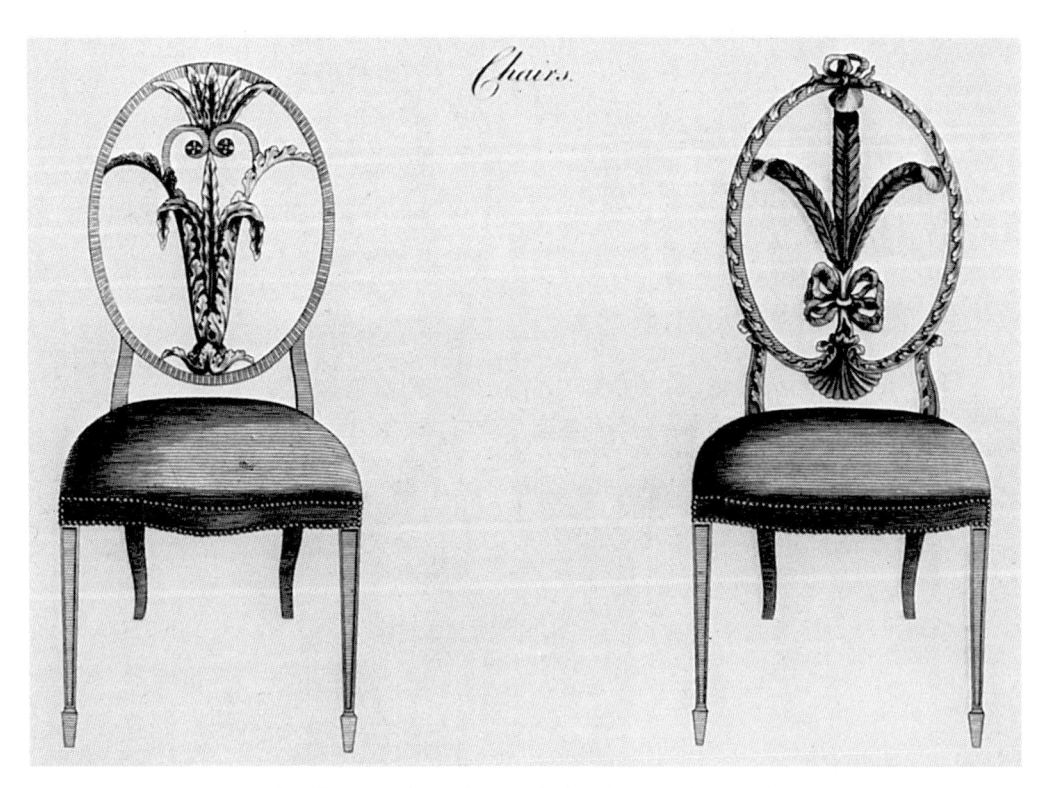

276. Hepplewhite: Two chairs. Engraving, 1787.

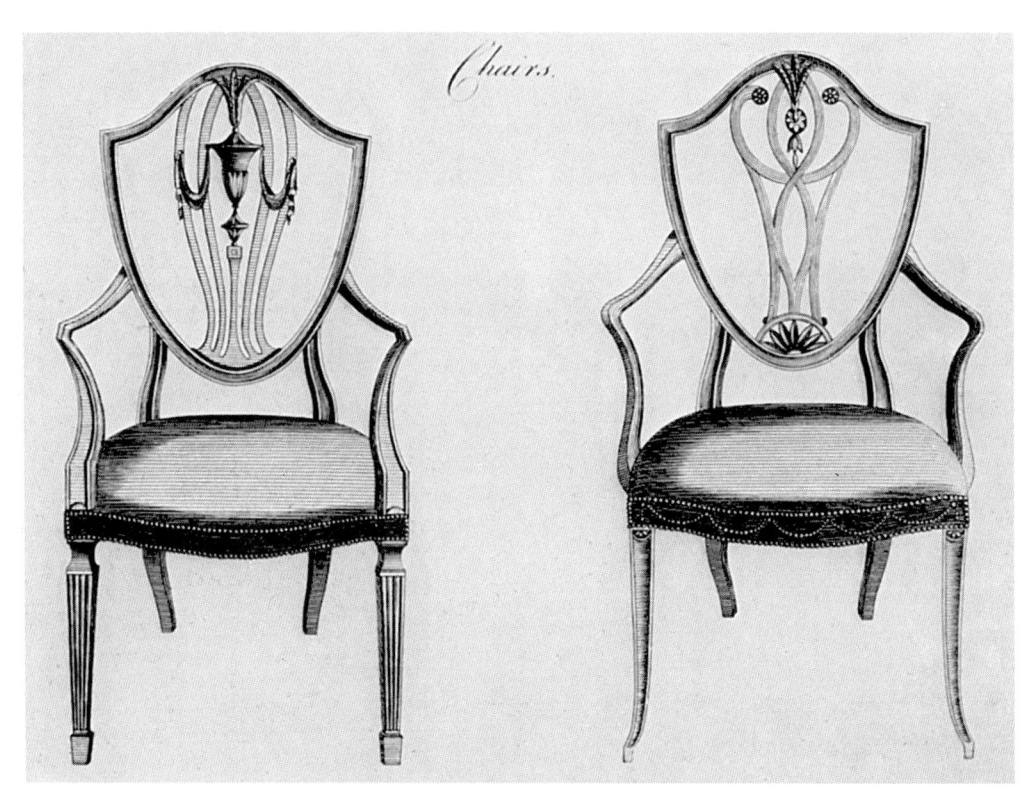

277. Hepplewhite: Two chairs. Engraving, 1787.

278. Hepplewhite: A bar back sofa. Engraving, 1787.

279. Hepplewhite: 'A Duchesse.' Engraving, 1787.

Window Stools.

280. Hepplewhite: Two window seats. Engraving, 1787.

281. Hepplewhite: 'An easy chair and gouty stool.' Engraving, 1787.

282. Hepplewhite: A wardrobe. Engraving, 1787.

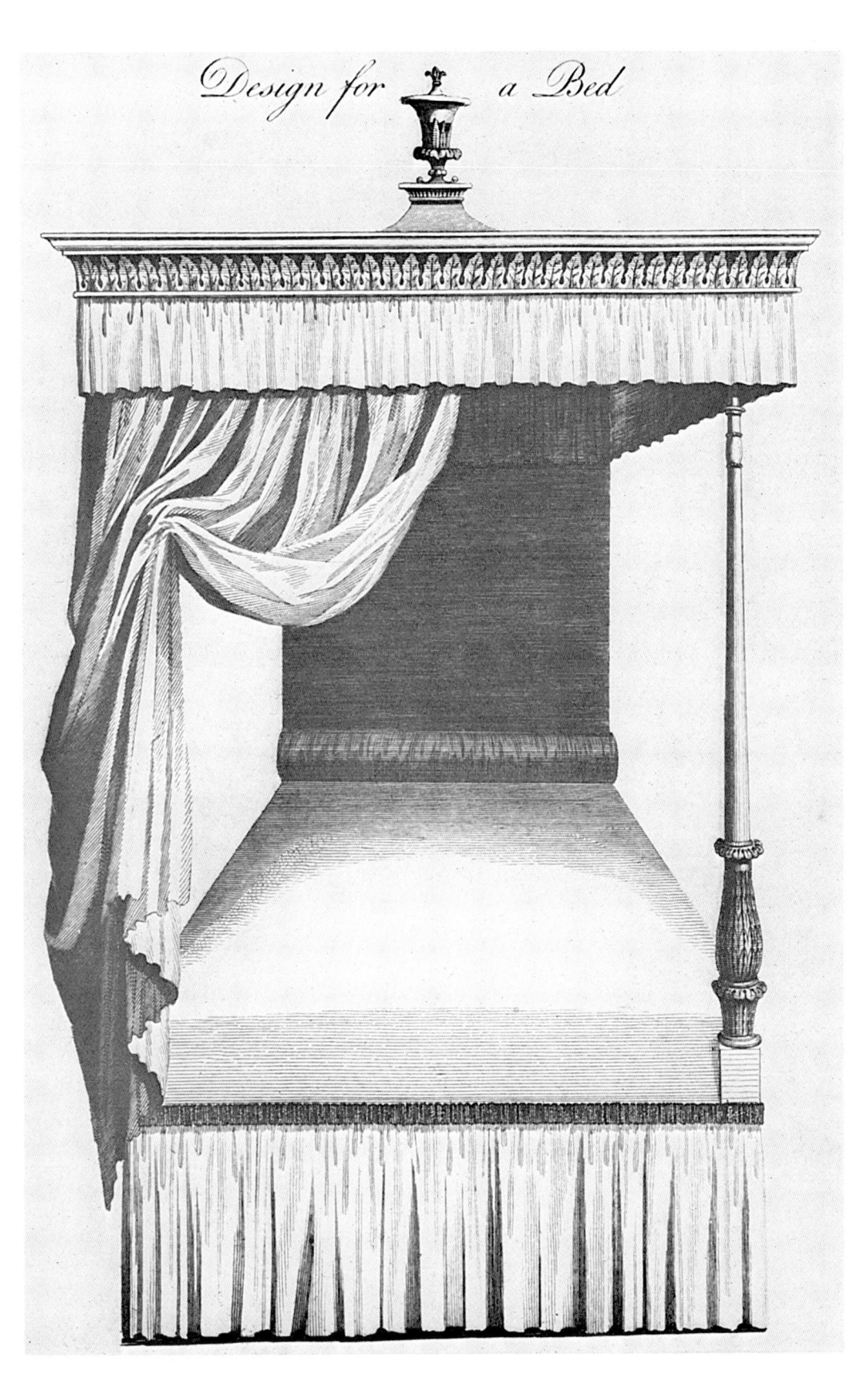

Design for a Bed

283. Hepplewhite: A bed. Engraving, 1787.

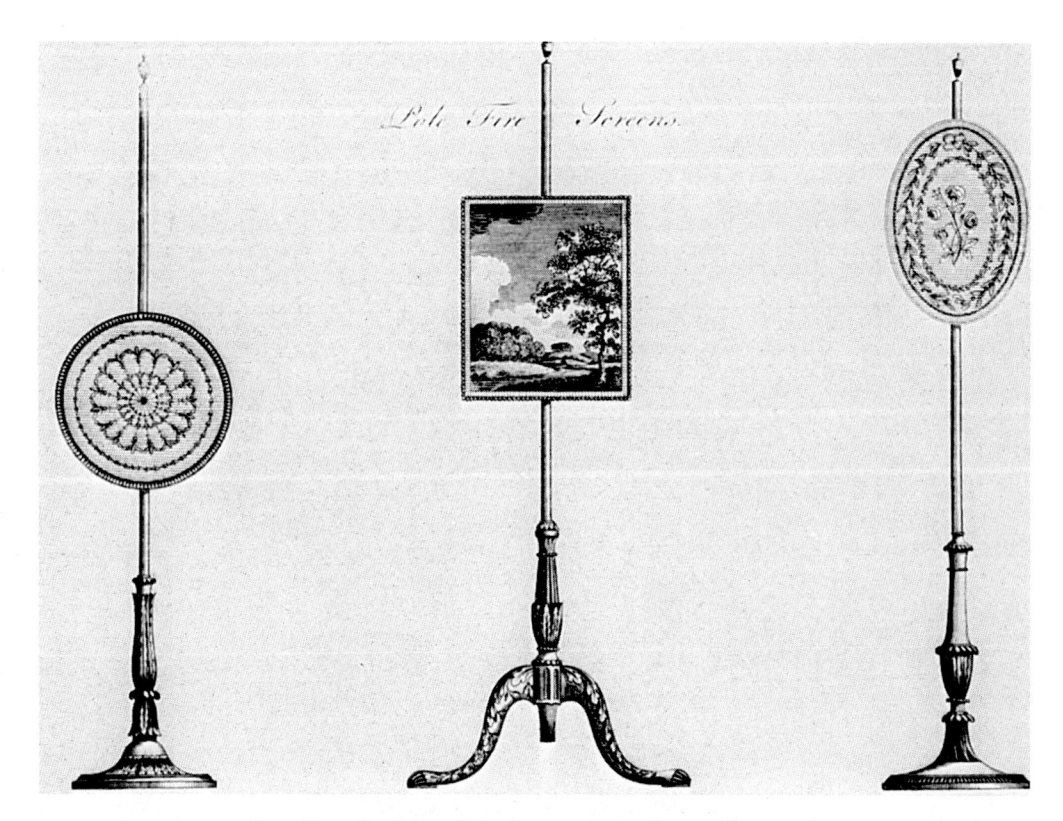

284. Hepplewhite: Pole fire screens. Engraving, 1787.

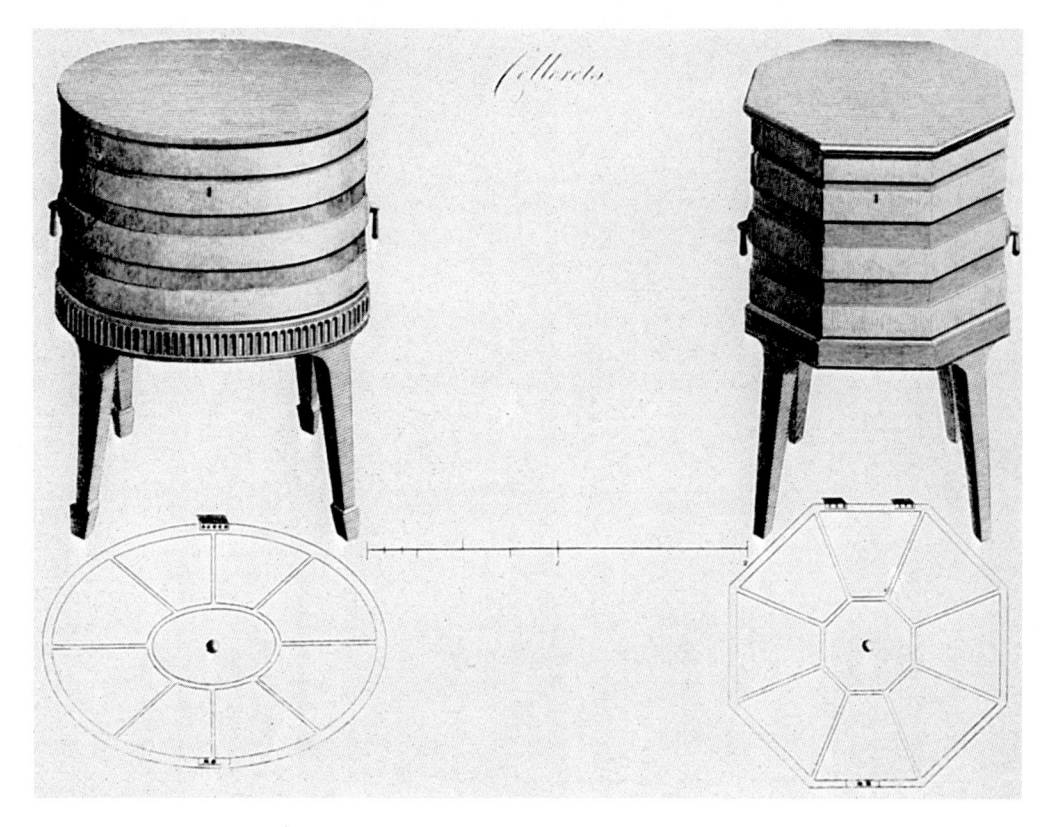

285. Hepplewhite: Two wine cases. Engraving, 1787.

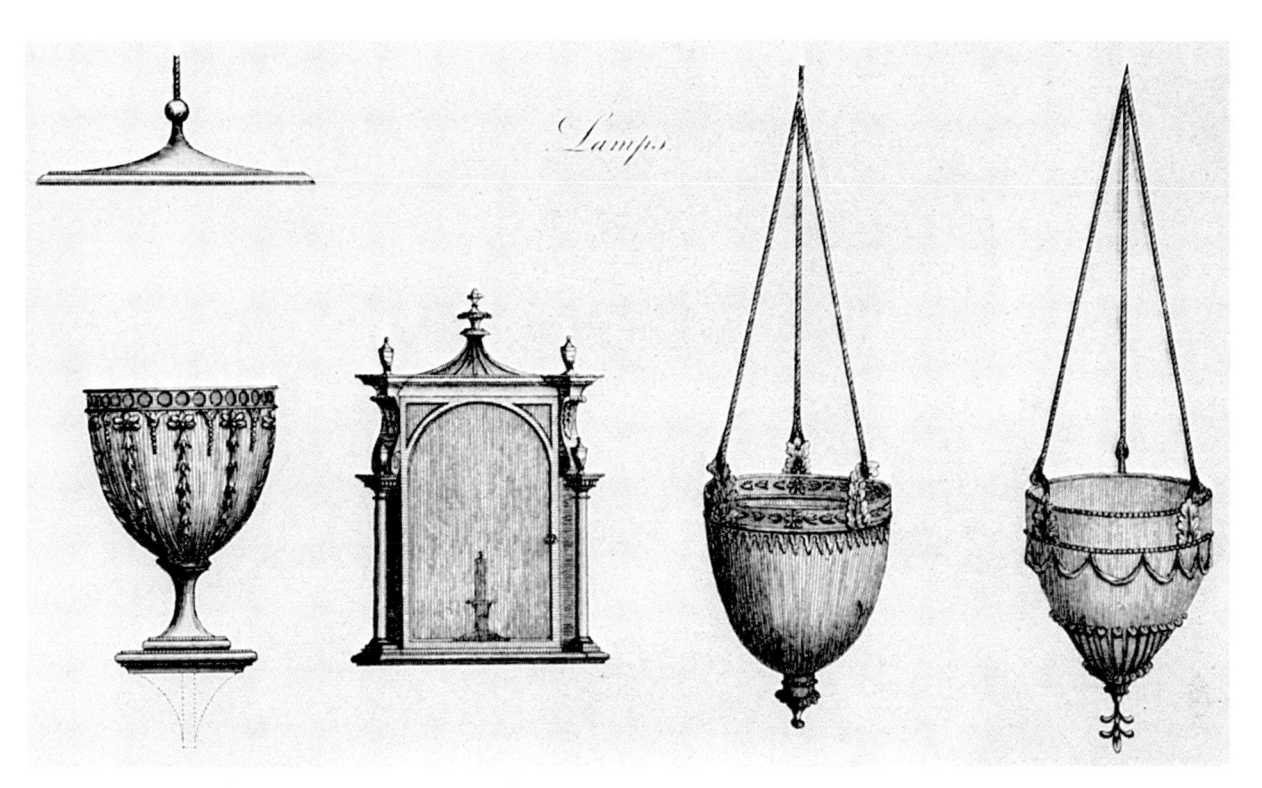

286. Hepplewhite: Four lamps. Engraving, 1787.

287. Hepplewhite: Four knife cases. Engraving, 1787.

Pier Tables.

288. Hepplewhite: Two pier tables. Engraving, 1787.

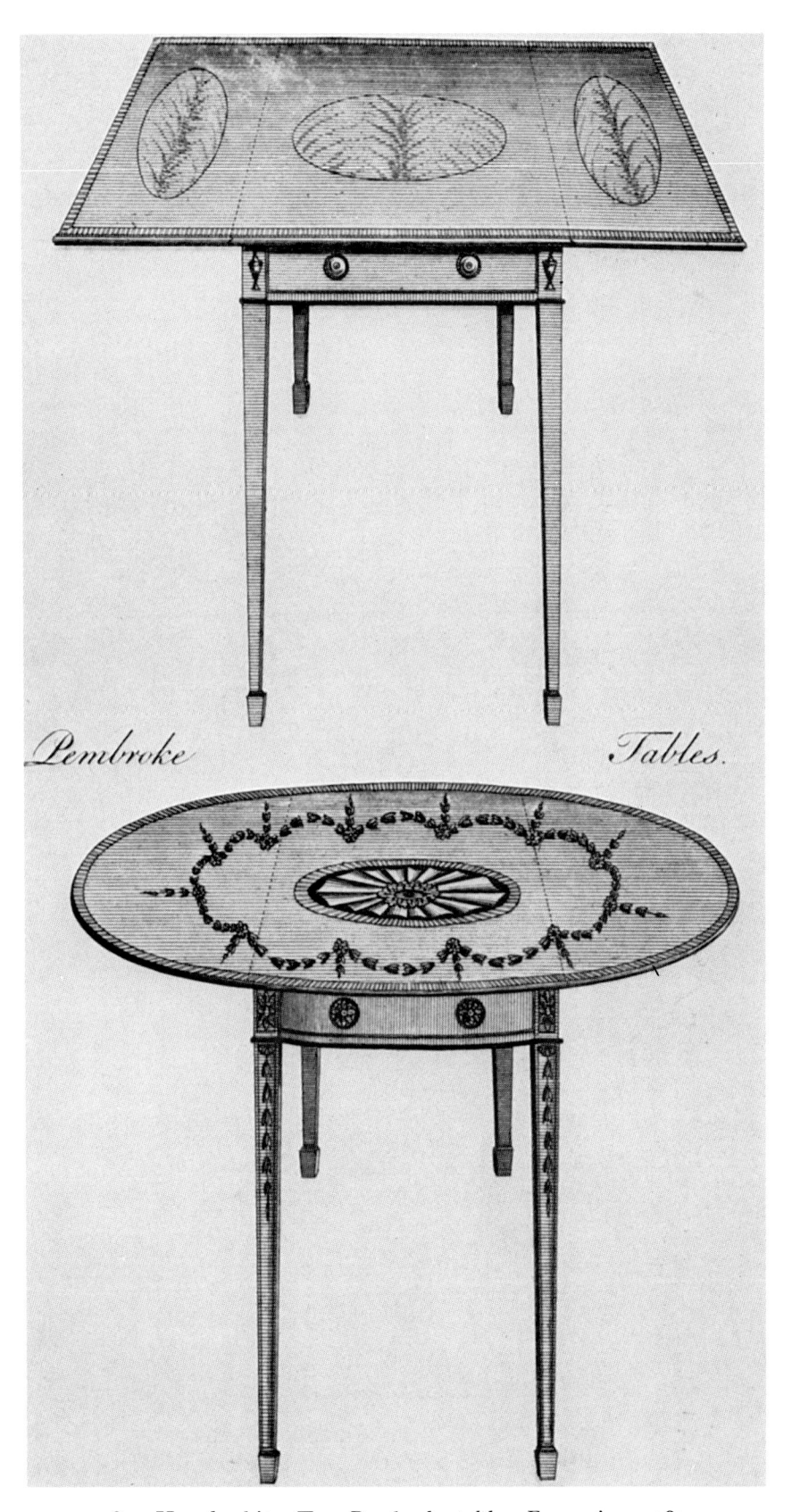

289. Hepplewhite: Two Pembroke tables. Engraving, 1787.

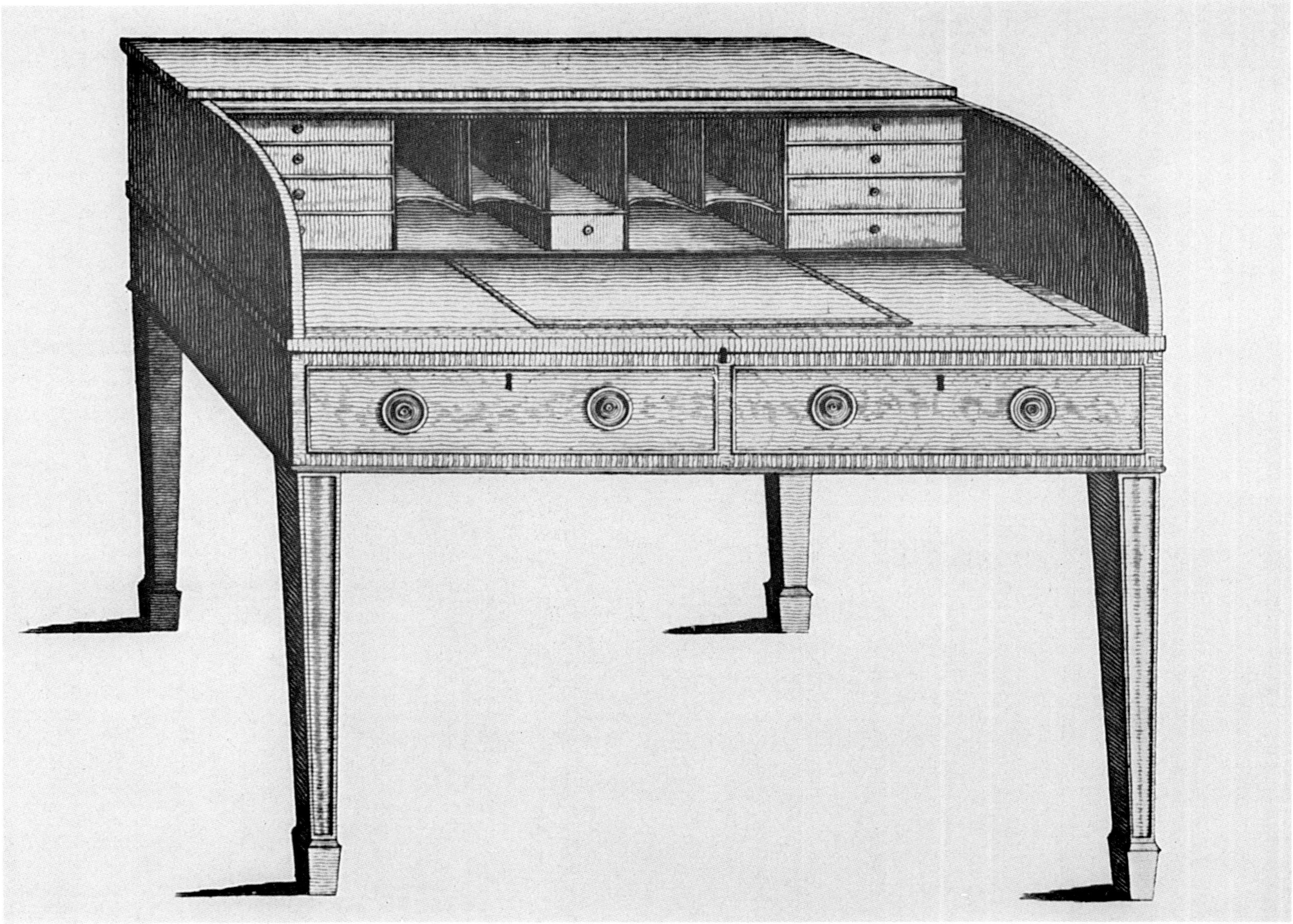

290. Hepplewhite: A tambour writing-table. Engraving, 1787.

291. Hepplewhite: A commode. Engraving, 1787.

292. Hepplewhite: A 'social table' and knee-hole writing-table. Engraving, 1792.

293. Hepplewhite: A 'serpentine cabinet.' Engraving, 1787.

294. Thomas Shearer: A library bookcase. Etching, 1788.

295. Thomas Shearer: A sideboard. Etching, 1788.

296. Thomas Shearer: Two bureau bookcases. Etching, 1788.

297. Thomas Shearer: A wardrobe. Etching, 1788.

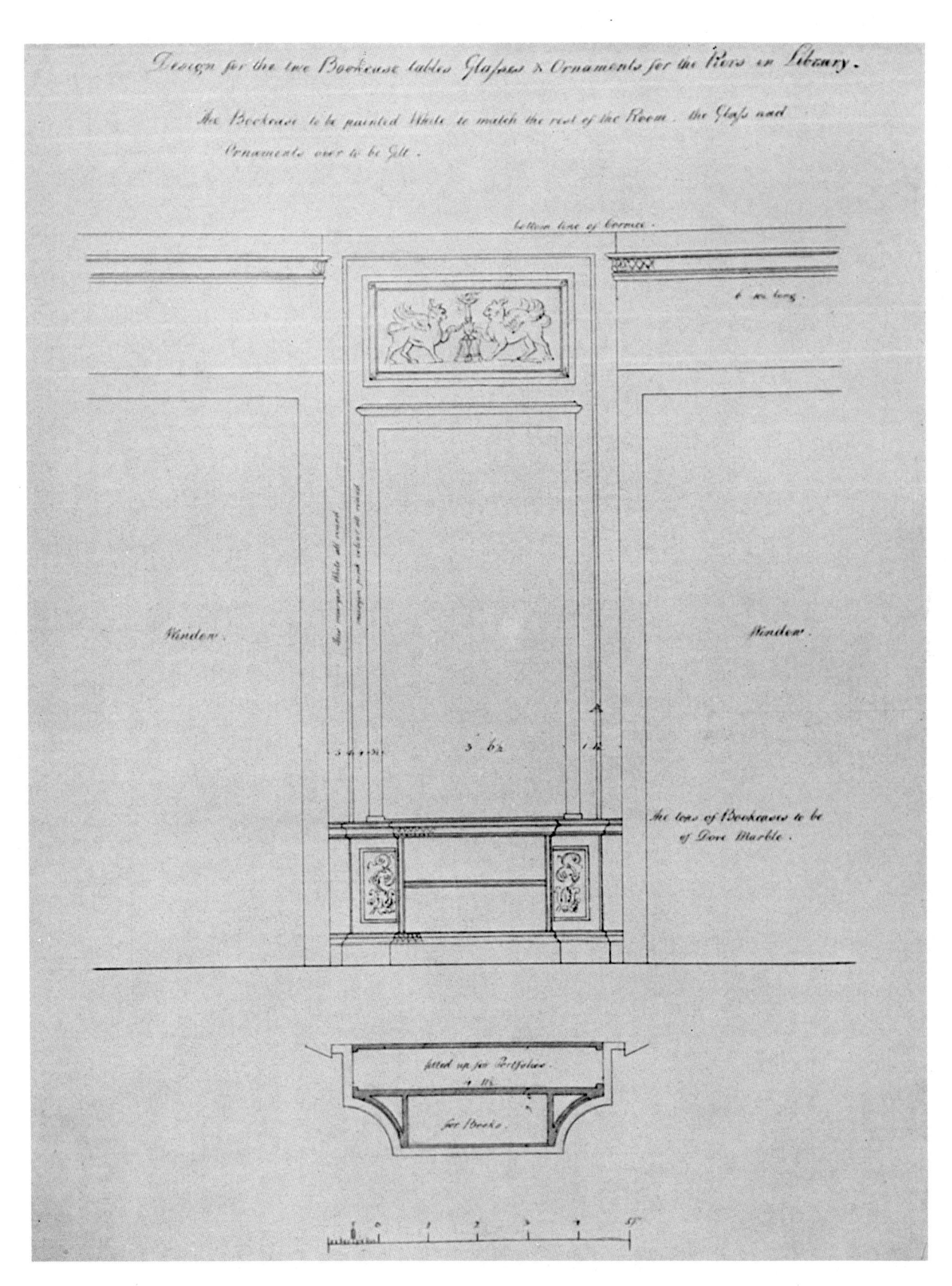

298. Henry Holland: A 'bookcase table' at Southill. Drawing, about 1800.

299. Henry Holland: A stand for a lamp. Drawing, about 1800.

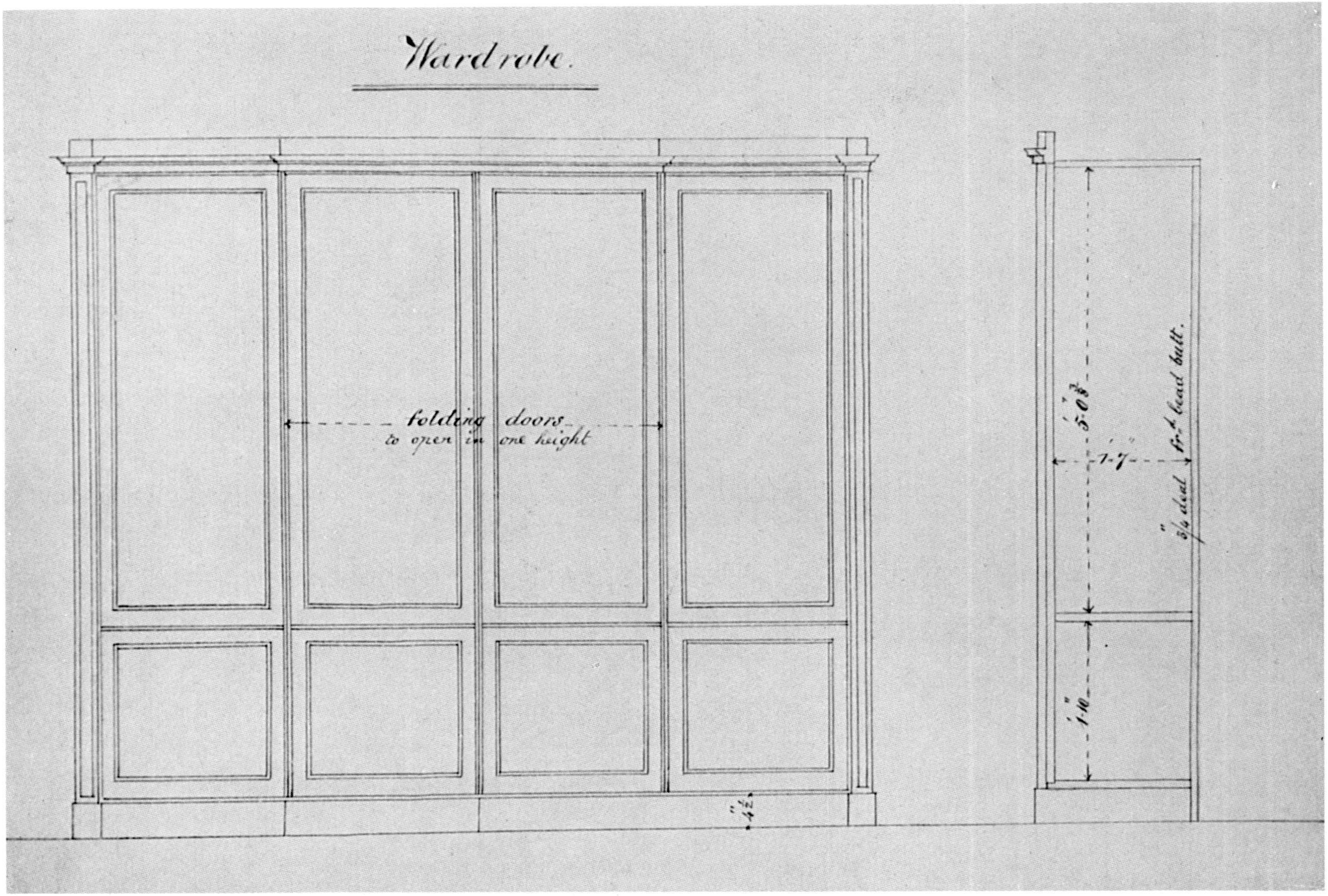

300. Henry Holland: A wardrobe. Drawing, about 1800.

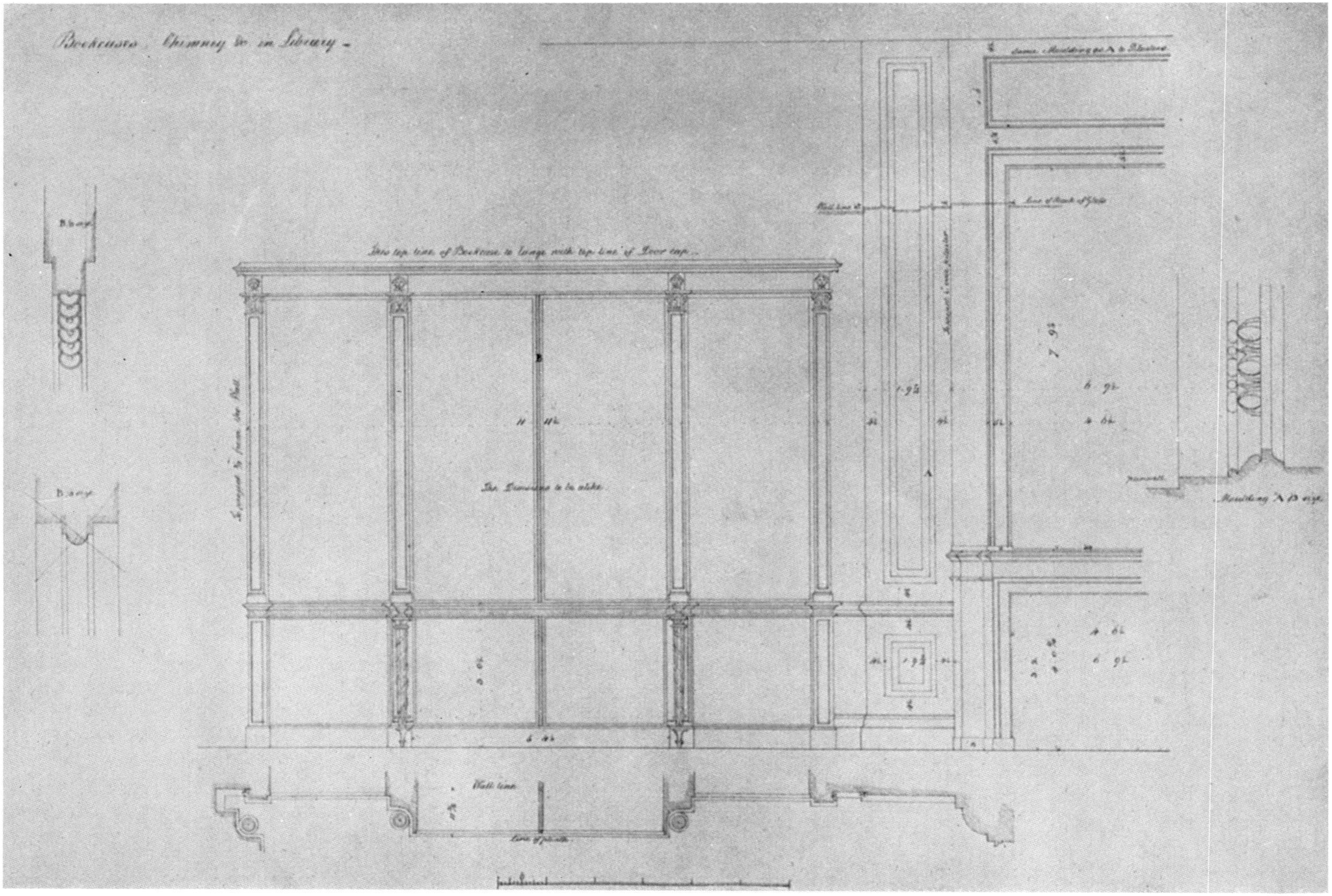

301. Henry Holland: A bookcase for Woburn Abbey, about 1788.

302. Henry Holland: A pier table and mirror for Woburn Abbey. Drawing, about 1788.

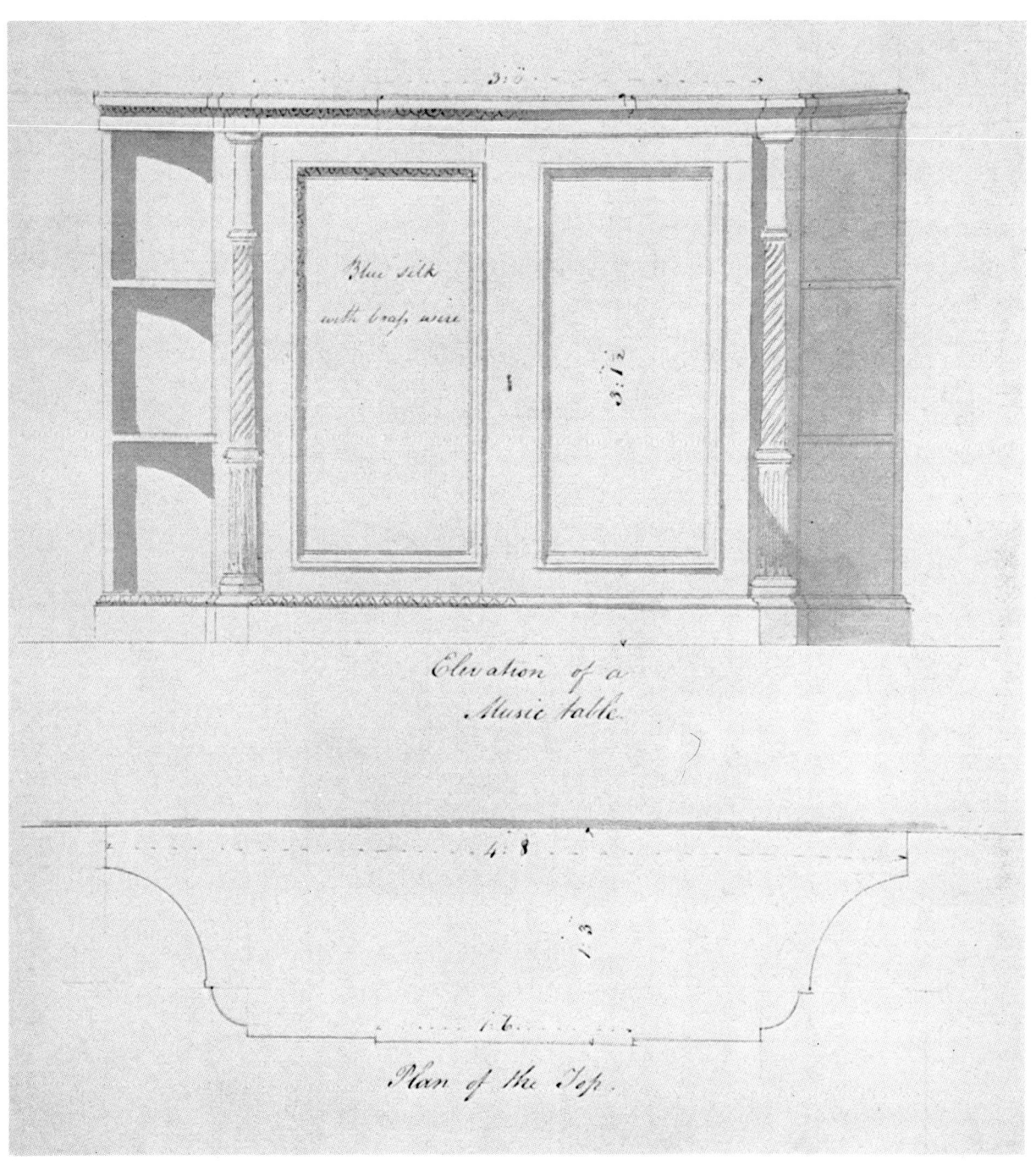

303. Sir John Soane: Music table for the Duke of Leeds. Drawing, 1797.

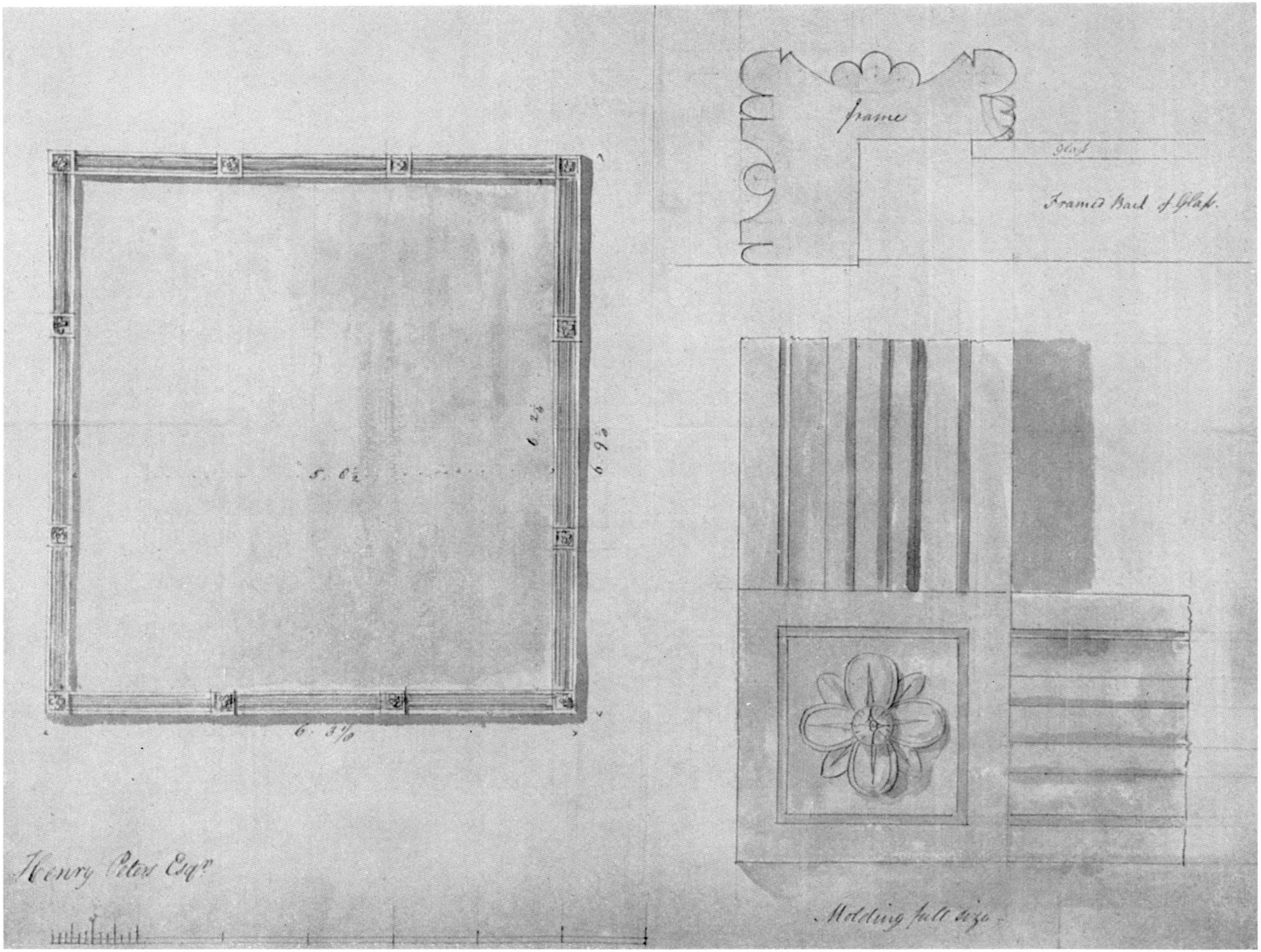

304. Sir John Soane: A mirror for Bletchworth Castle, Dorking. Drawing, about 1799.

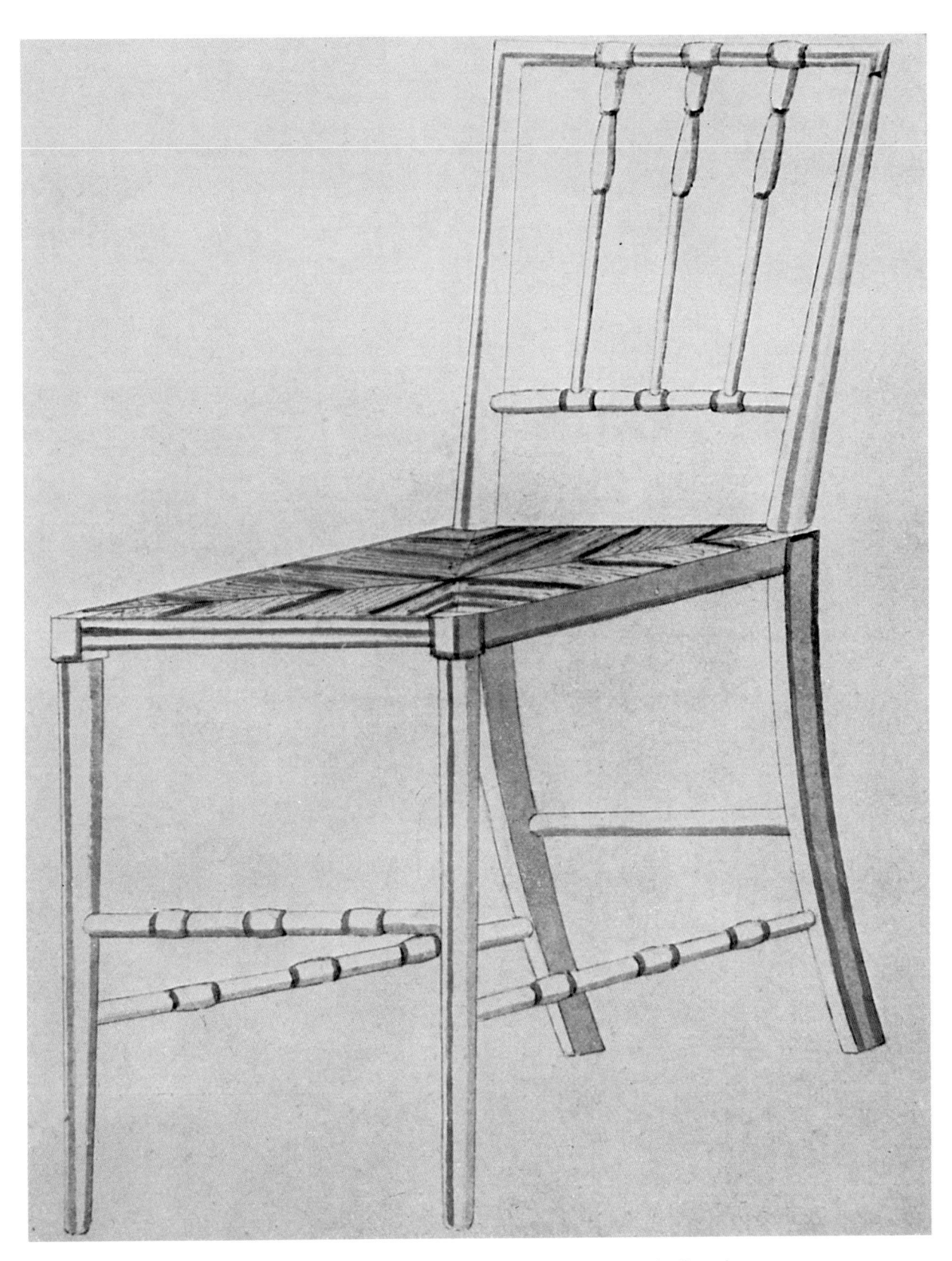

305. Sir John Soane: A chair for Shotesham Park, Norwich. Drawing, 1790.

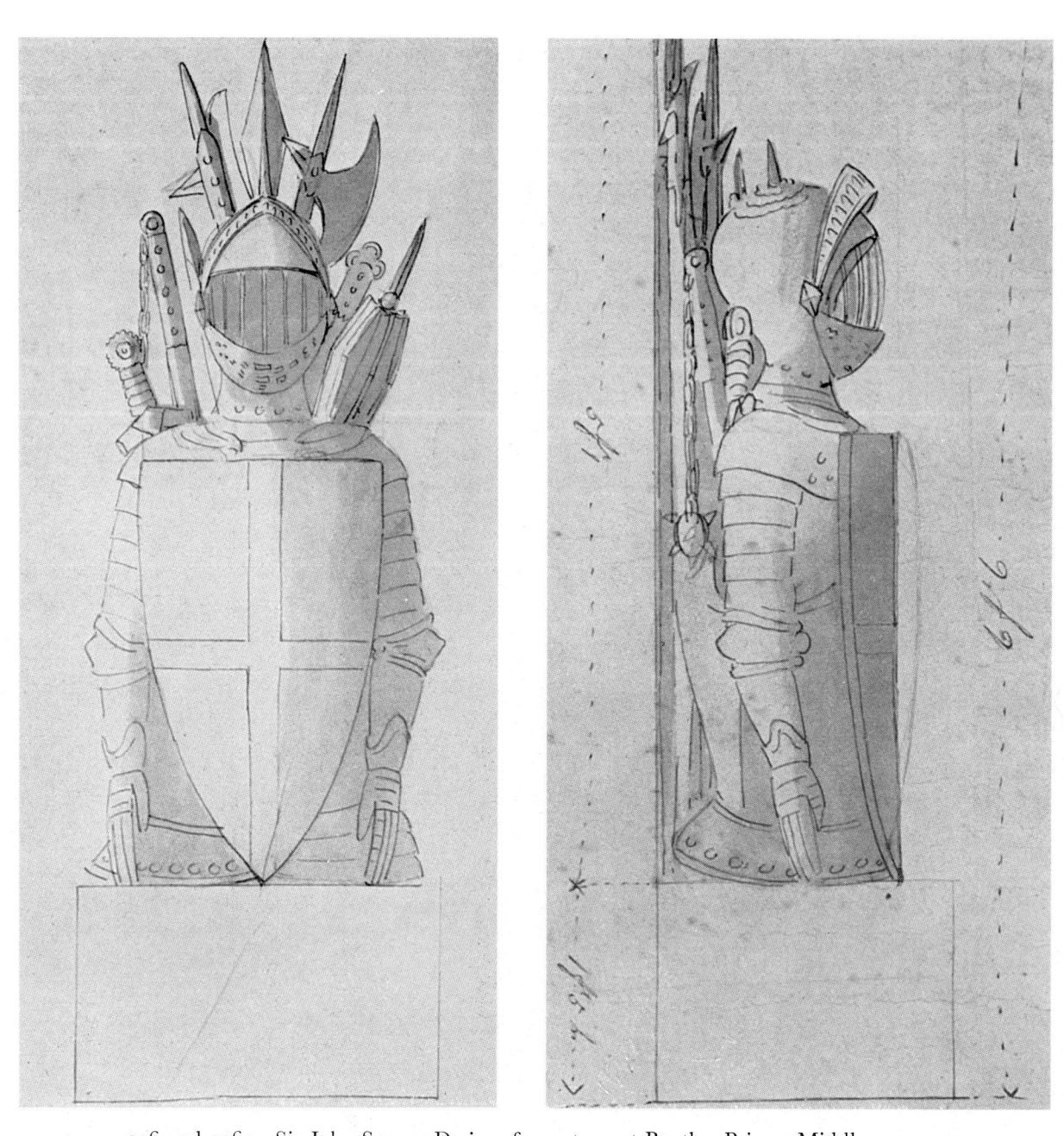

306 and 306A. Sir John Soane: Designs for a stove at Bentley Priory, Middlesex. 1799.

307. C. H. Tatham: A papal chair. Drawing, 1794.

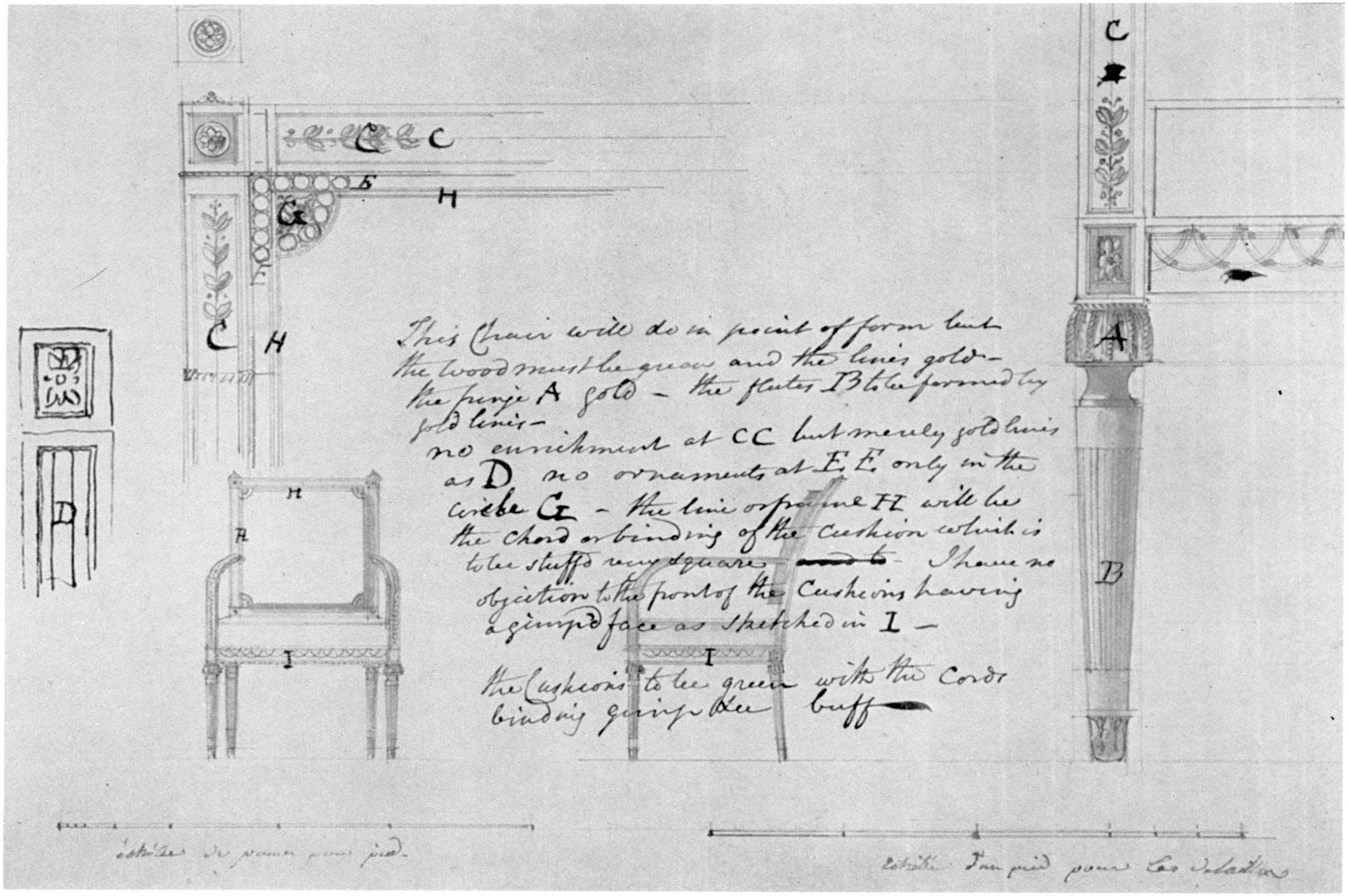

308. John Nash: An arm-chair. Drawing, about 1790.

309. Thomas Sheraton: A mirror frame. Drawing, about 1790.

310. Sheraton after Henry Holland: Furniture at Carlton House. Engraving, 1793.

311. Sheraton: A commode. Engraving, 1794.

312. Sheraton: Two dressing chests. Engraving, about 1793.

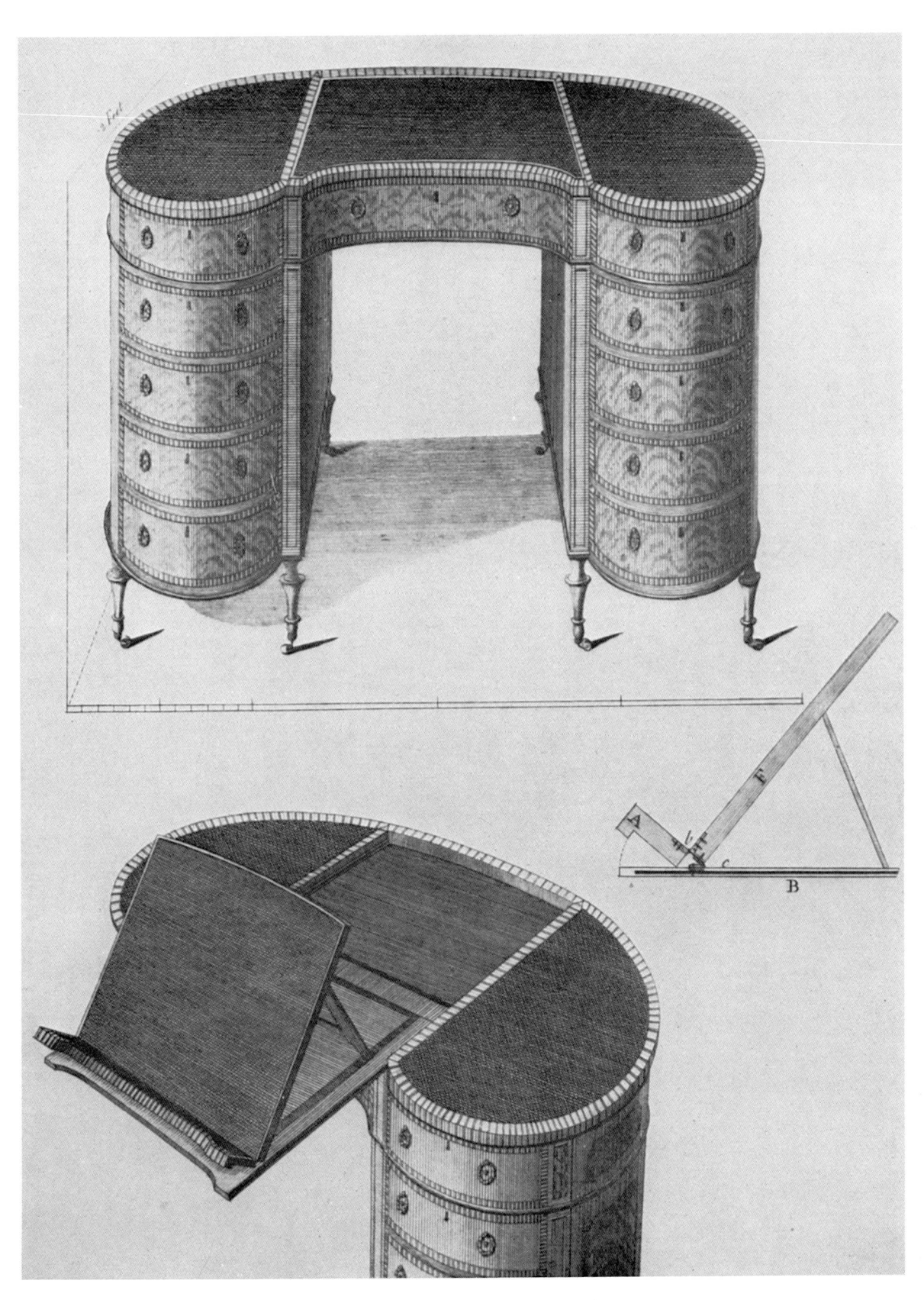

313. Sheraton: 'A kidney table.' Engraving, 1792.

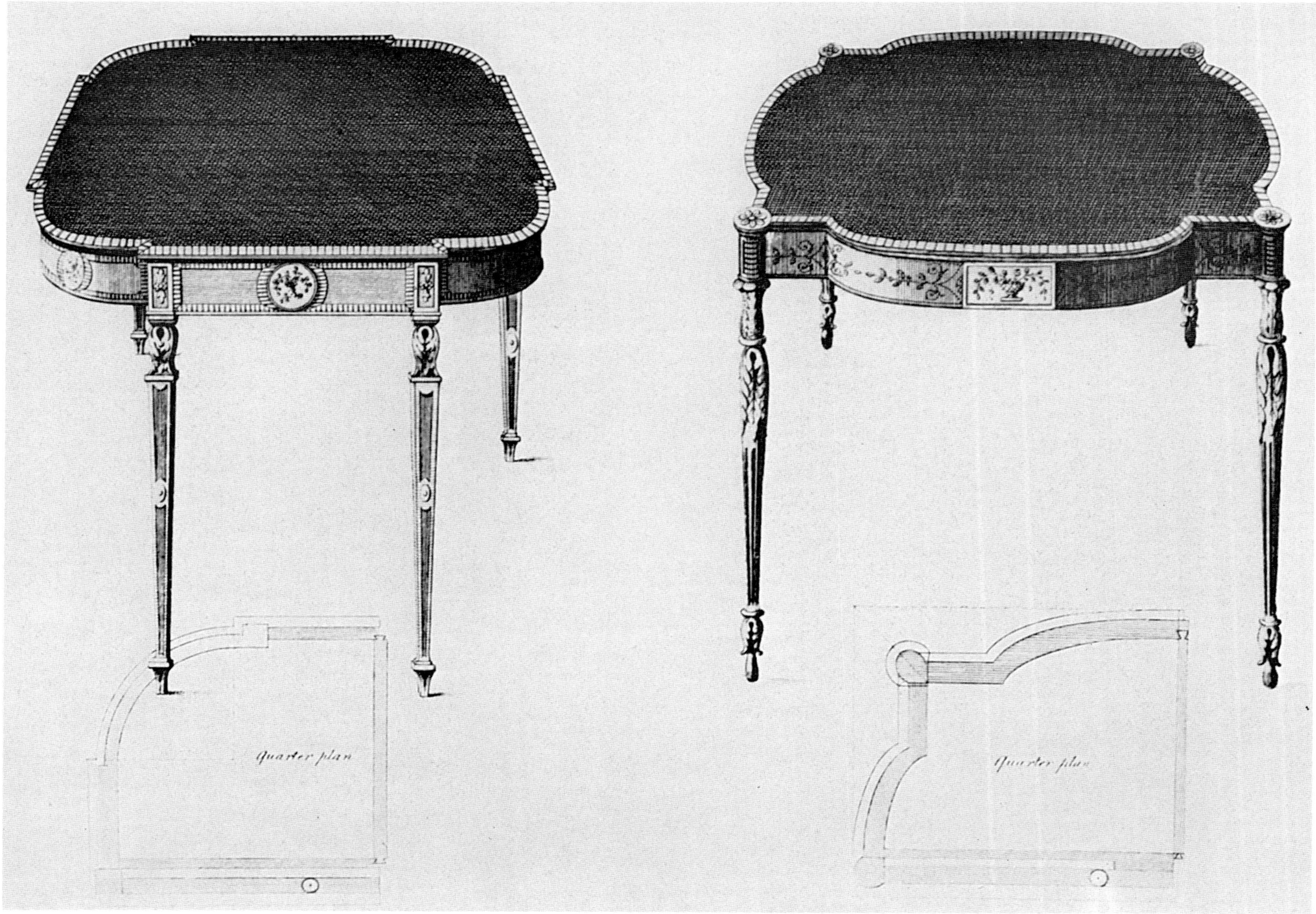

314. Sheraton: Two card tables. Engraving, 1793.

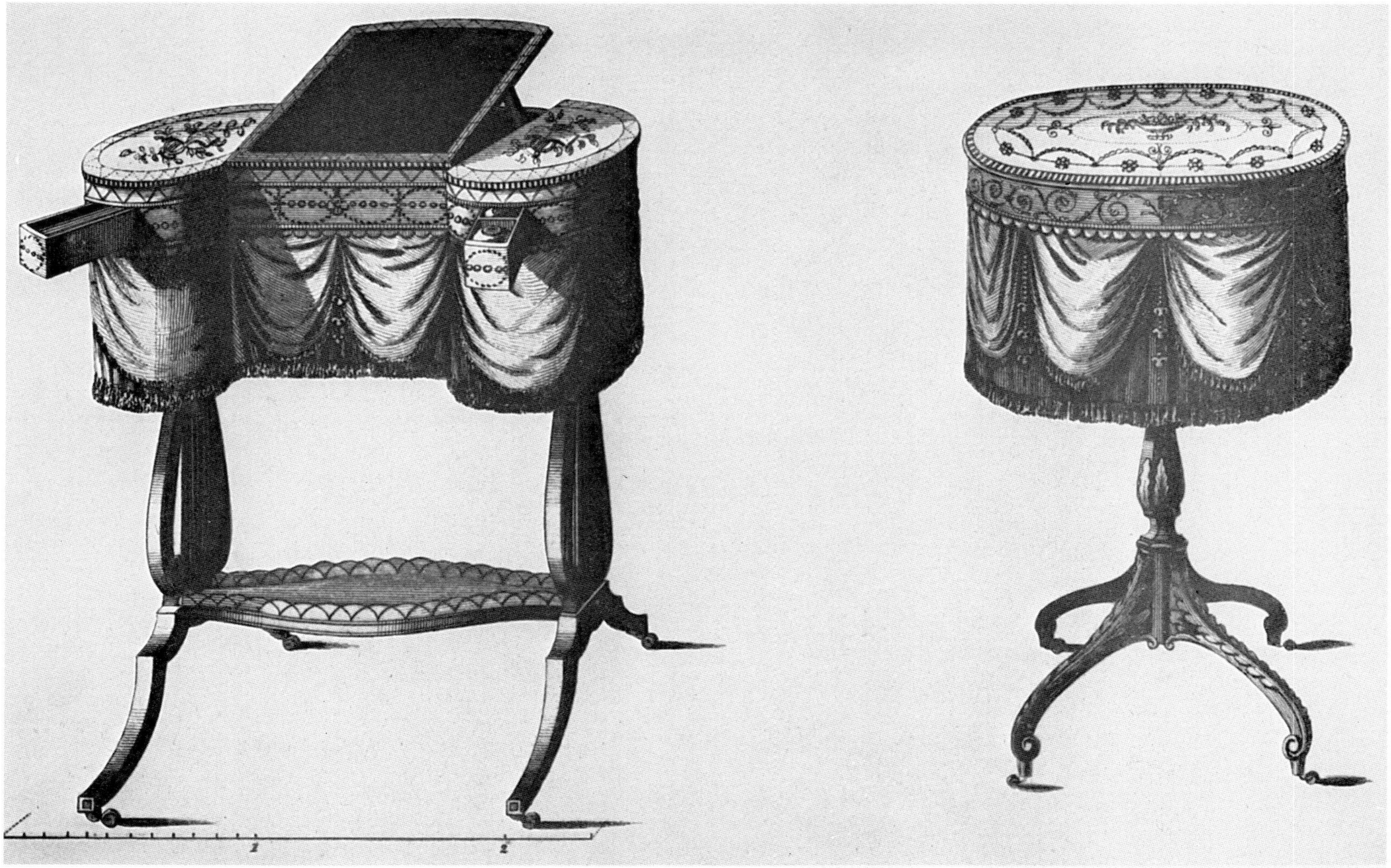

315. Sheraton: 'Ladies' work-tables.' Engraving, 1793.

A LIBRARY CASE

316. Sheraton: A bookcase. Engraving, 1793.

A SIDE BOARD. with VASE KNIFE CASES.

317. Sheraton: A sideboard. Engraving, 1793.

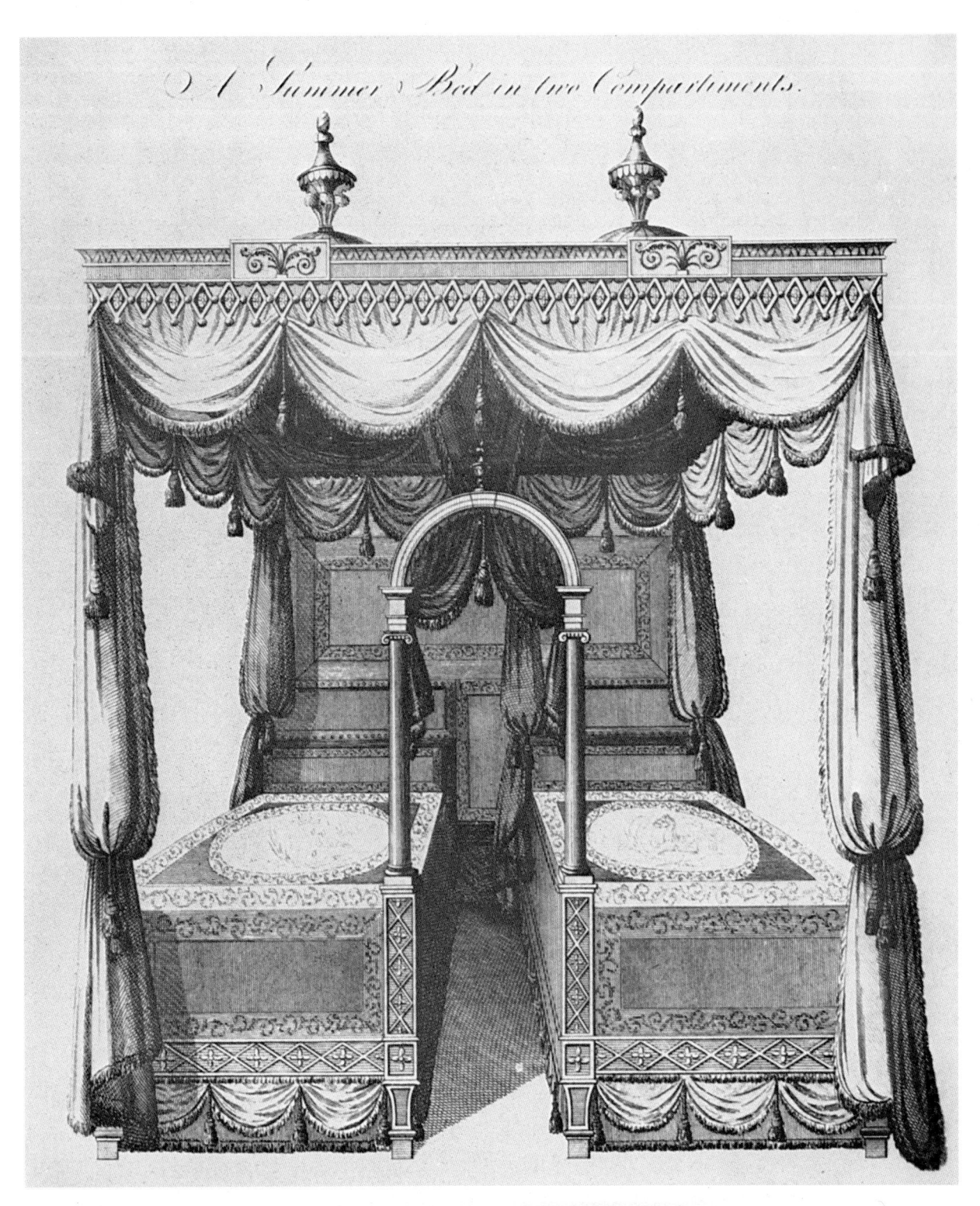

318. Sheraton: 'A summer bed in two compartments.' Engraving, 1792.

319. Sheraton: Basin stands. Engraving, 1792.

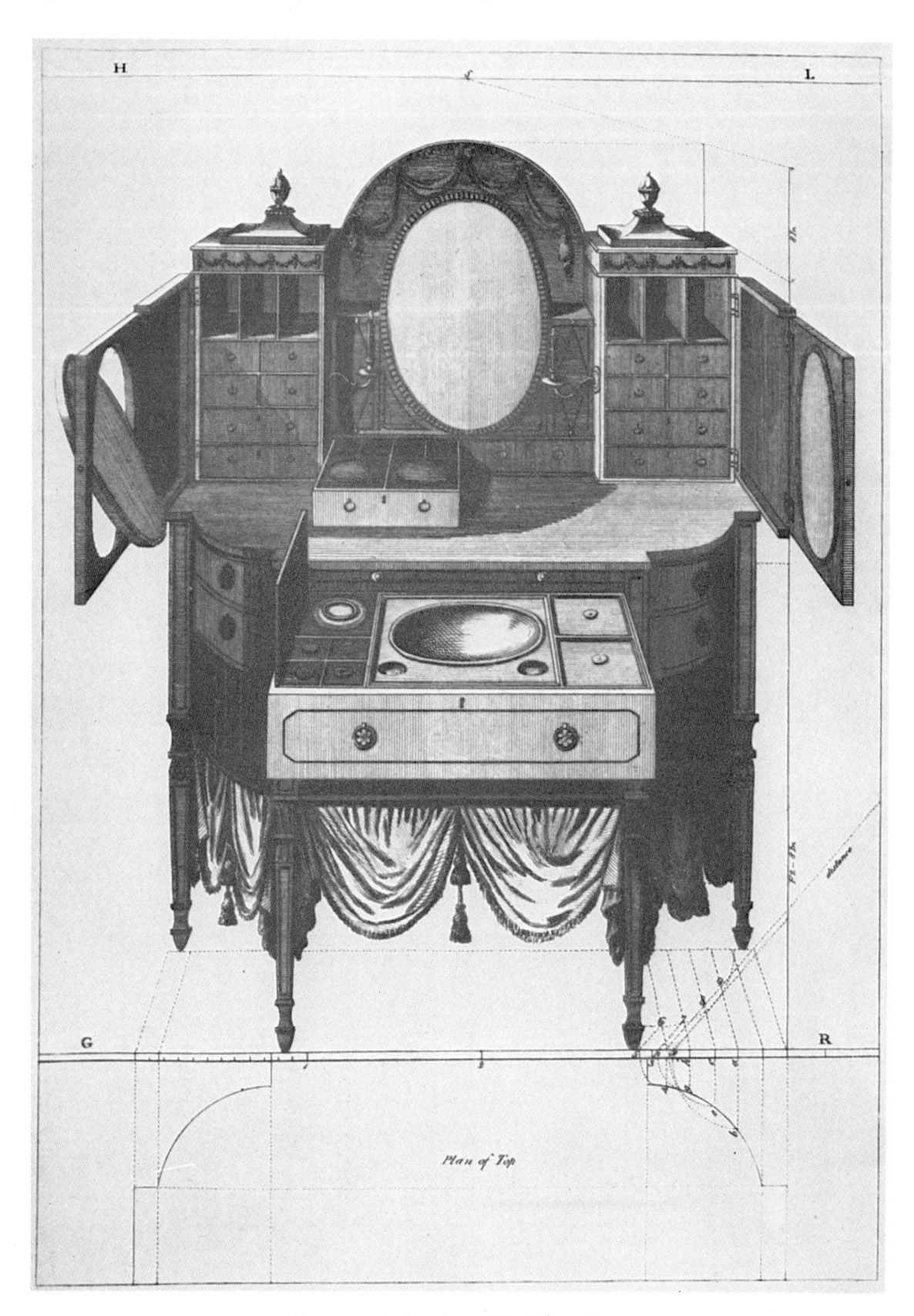

320. Sheraton: A dressing table. Engraving, 1792.

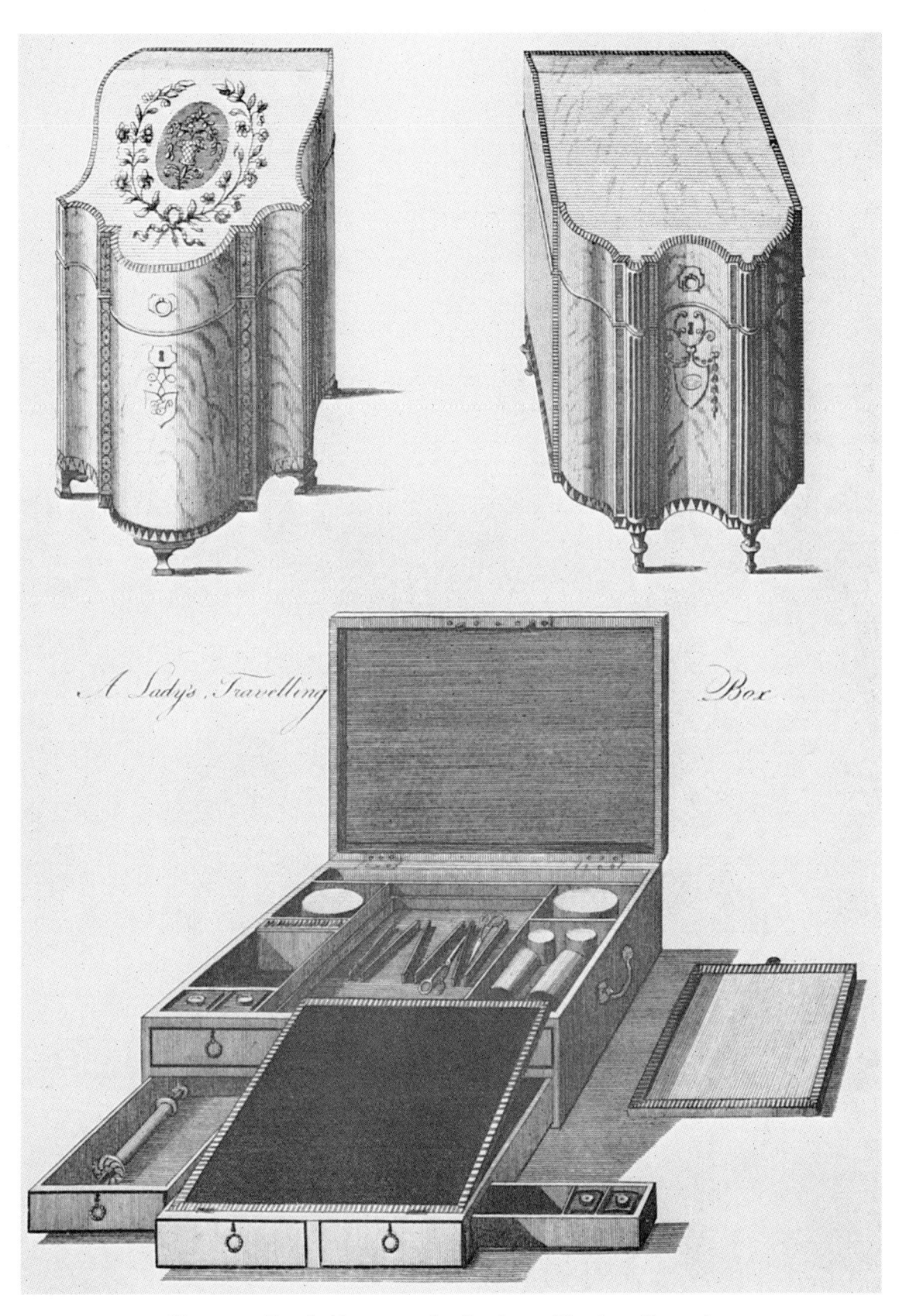

321. Sheraton: Two knife cases and a fitted travelling box. Engraving, 1792.

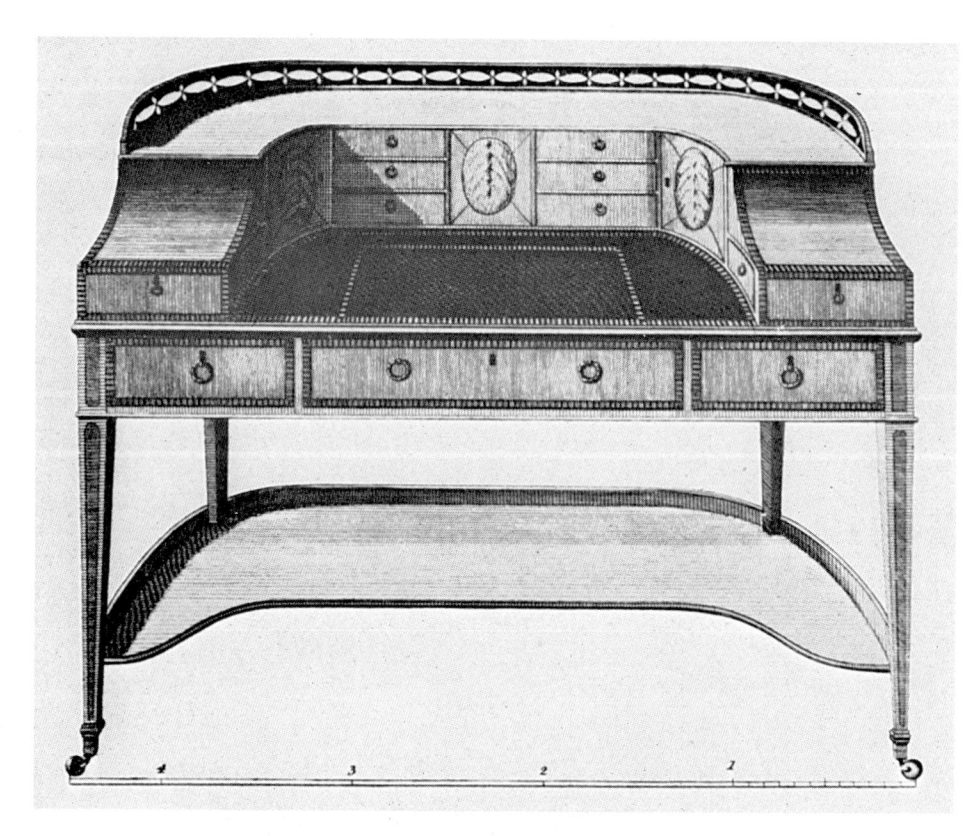

322. Sheraton: A Carlton House table. Engraving, 1793.

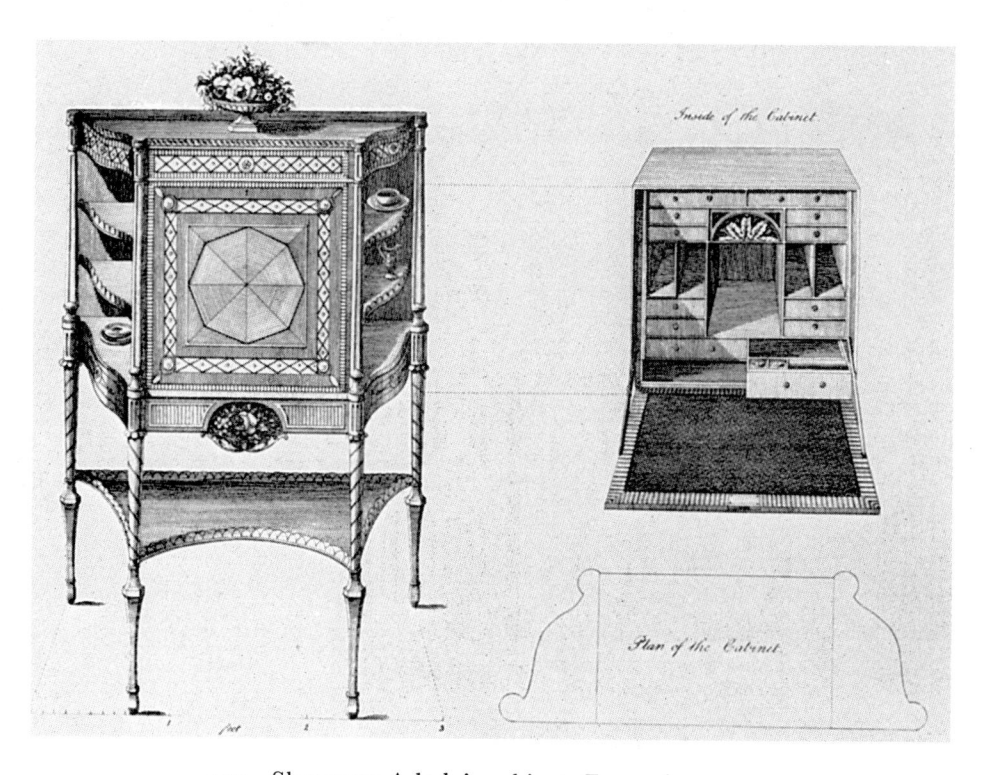

323. Sheraton: A lady's cabinet. Engraving, 1793.

324. Sheraton: A Pembroke table. Engraving, 1803.

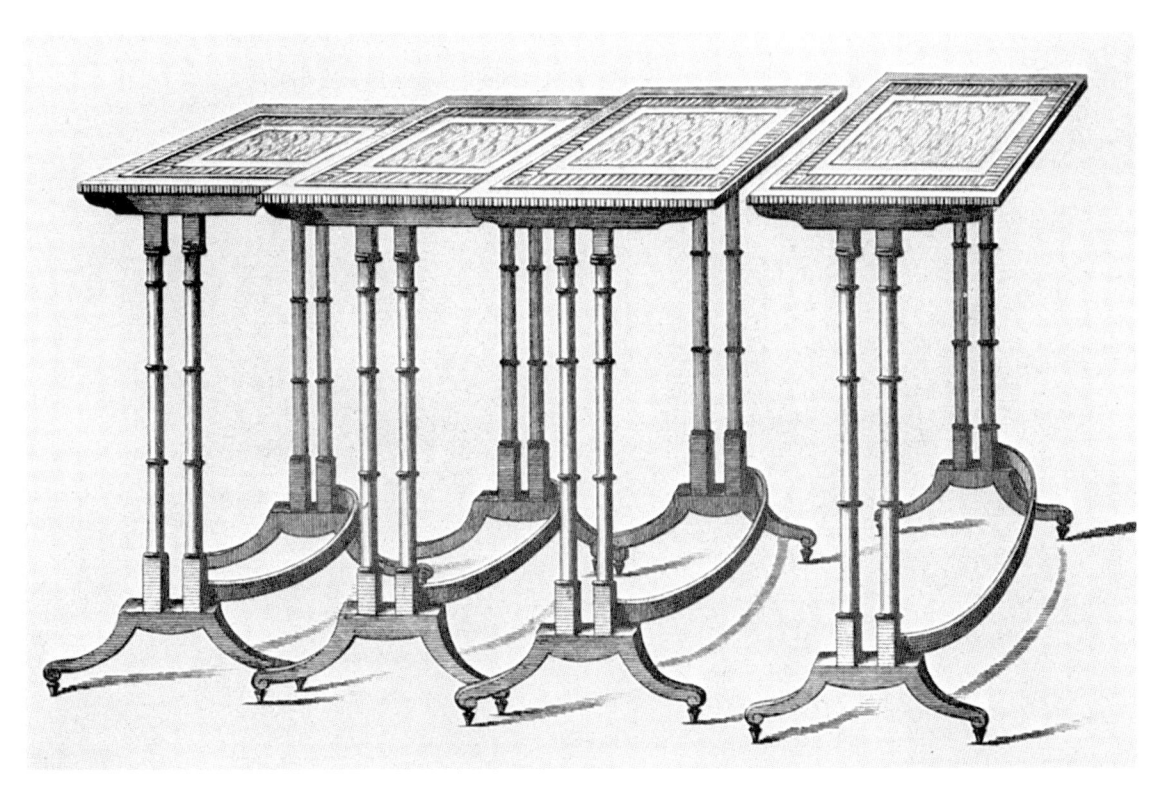

325. Sheraton: Quartetto tables. Engraving, 1803.

326. Sheraton: Sofa and conversation chairs. Engraving, 1793.

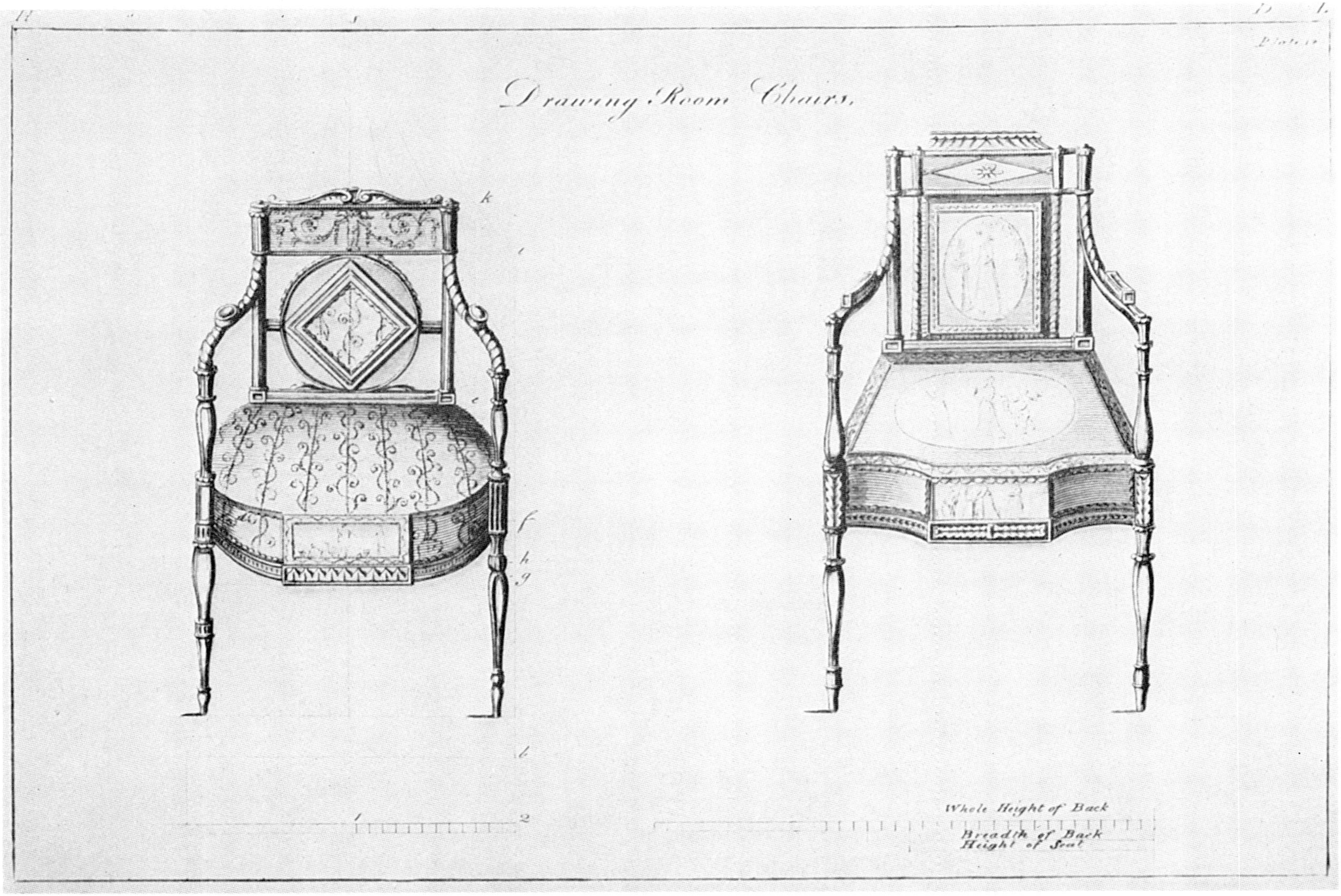

327. Sheraton: Drawing-room chairs. Engraving, 1792.

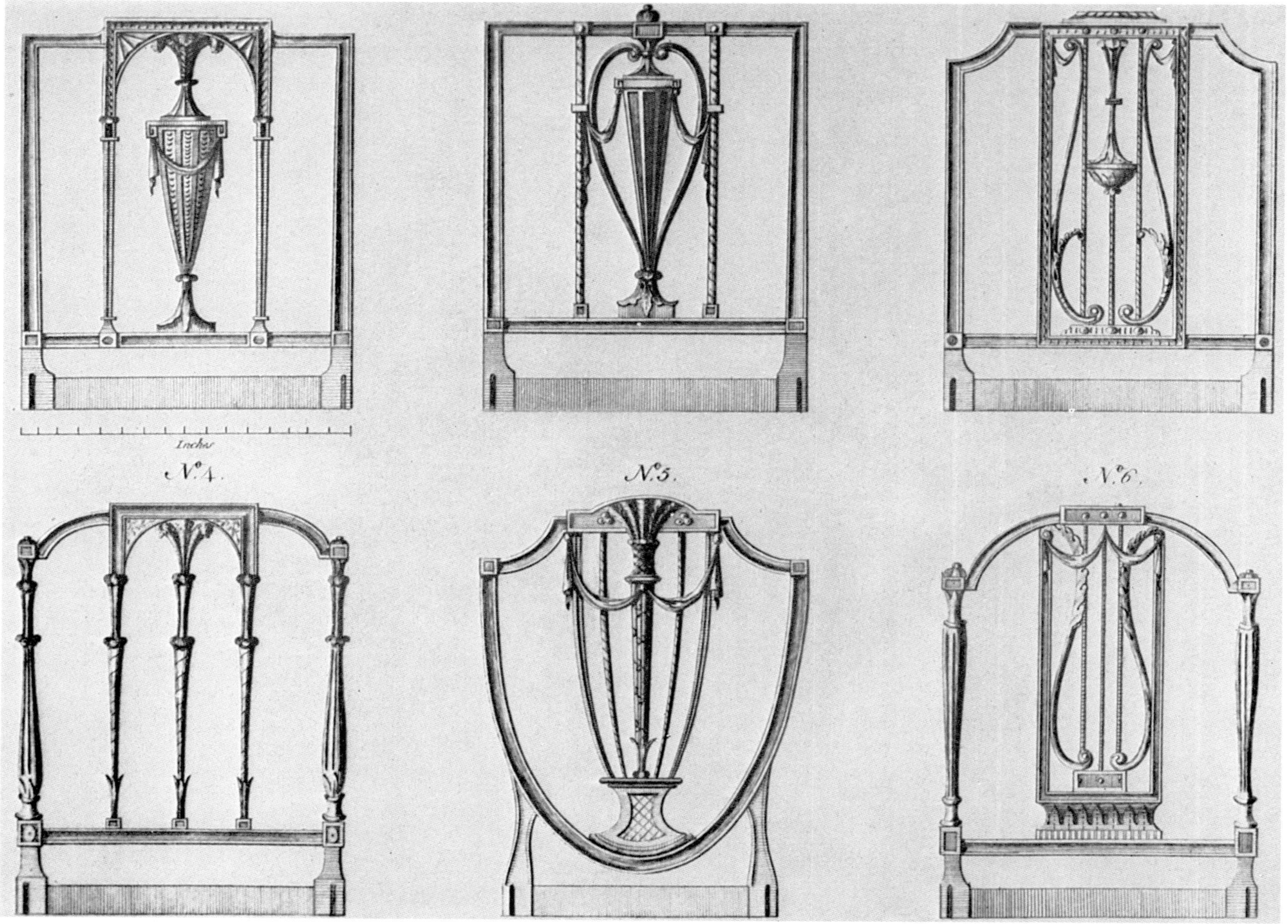

328. Sheraton: Six chair backs. Engraving, 1792.

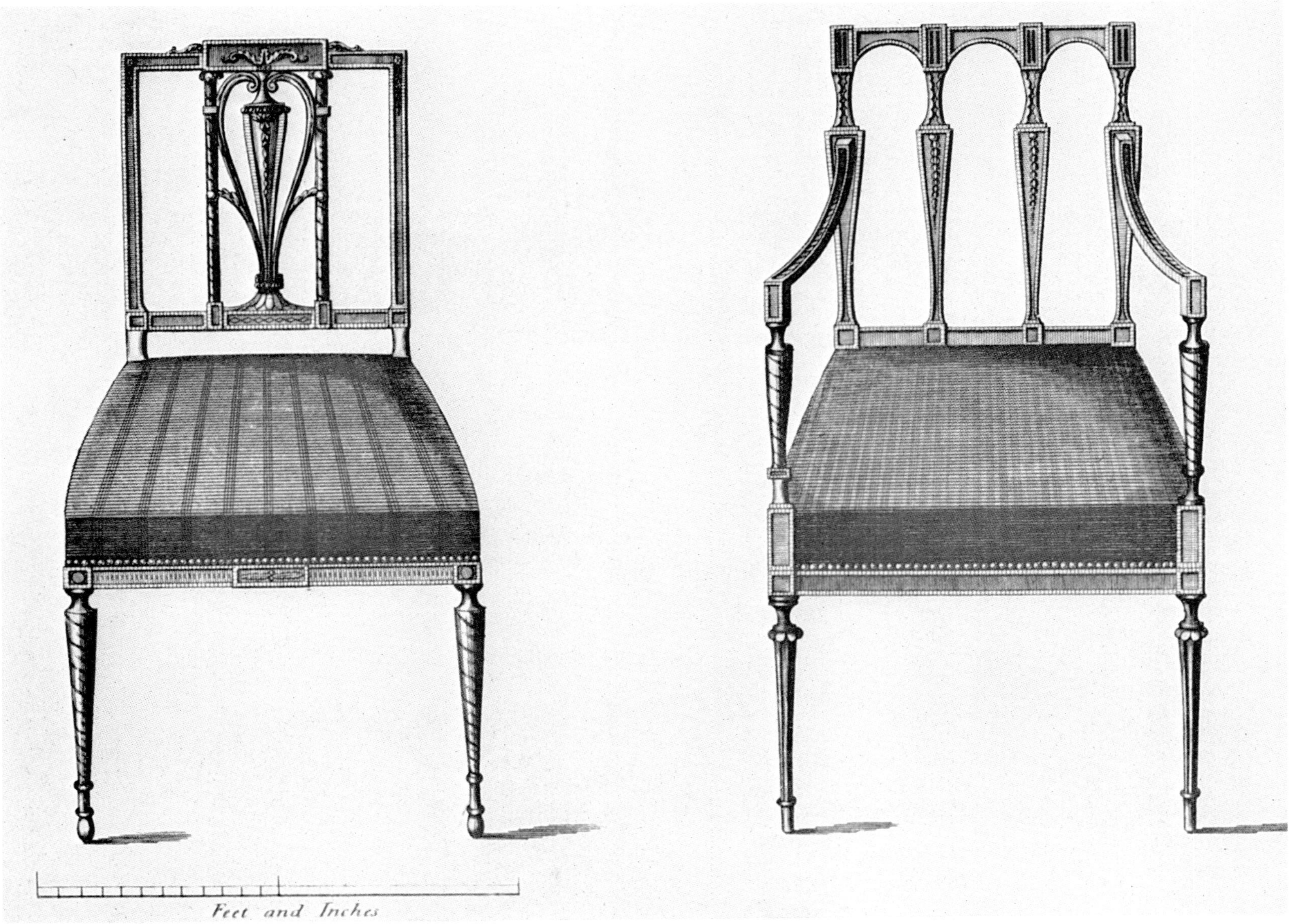

329. Sheraton: Two parlour chairs. Engraving, 1792.

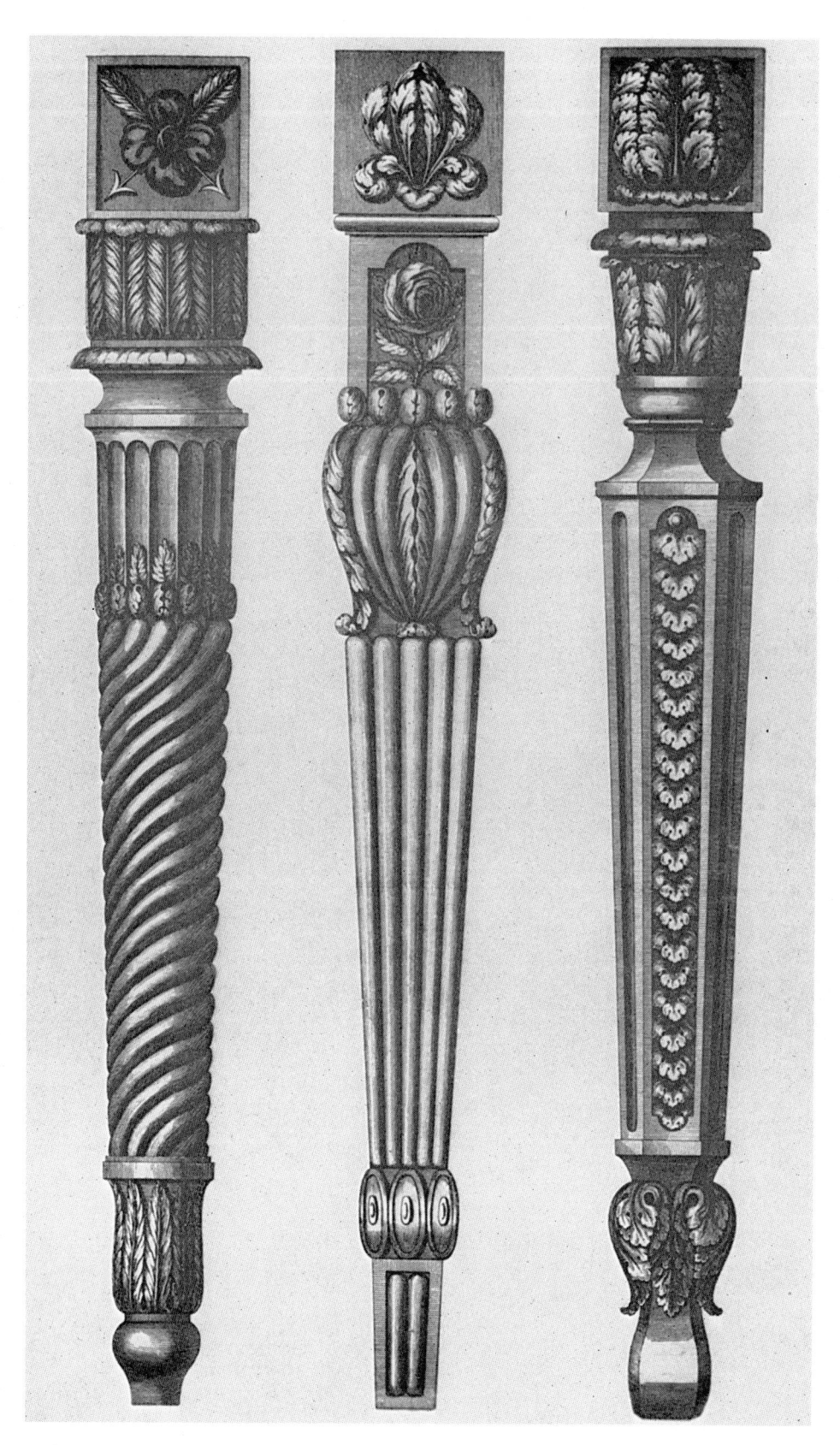

330. Sheraton: Designs for chair legs. Engraving, 1793.

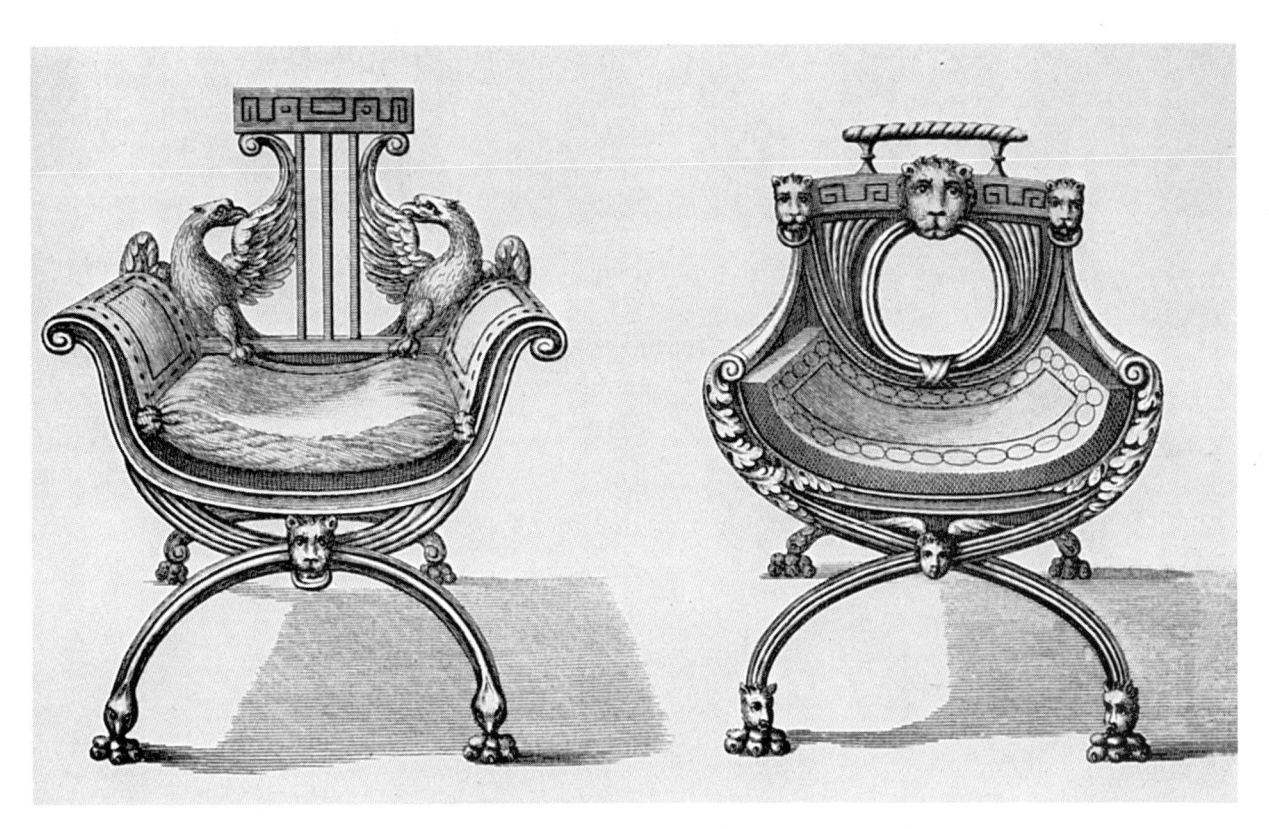

331. Sheraton: Drawing-room chairs. Engraving, 1803.

332. Sheraton: Two 'Herculaneums.' Engraving, 1802.

333. Sheraton: Two library tables. Engraving, 1802.

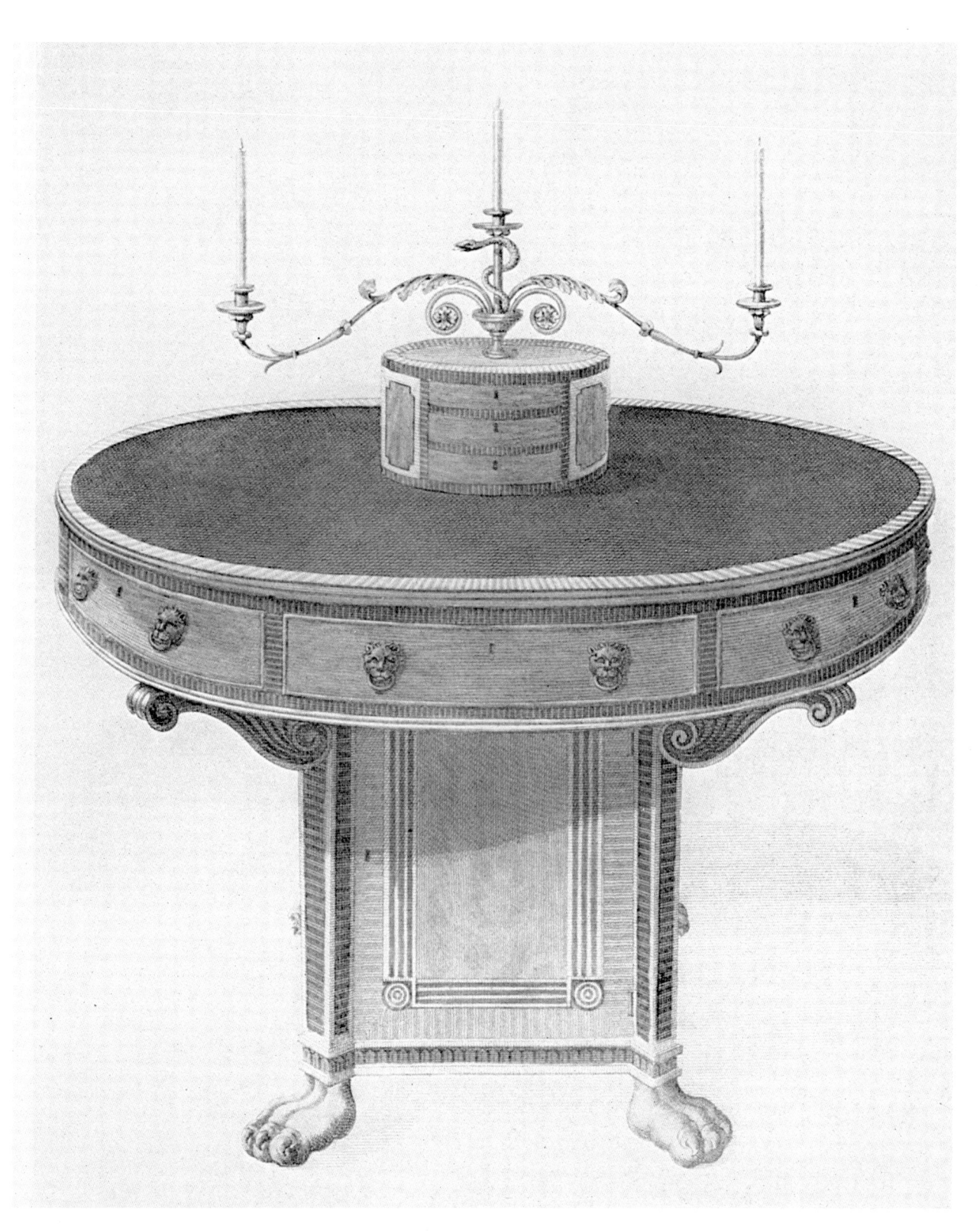

334. Sheraton: A library table. Engraving, about 1806.

335. Sheraton: A 'Grecian' dining table, etc. Engraving, 1803.

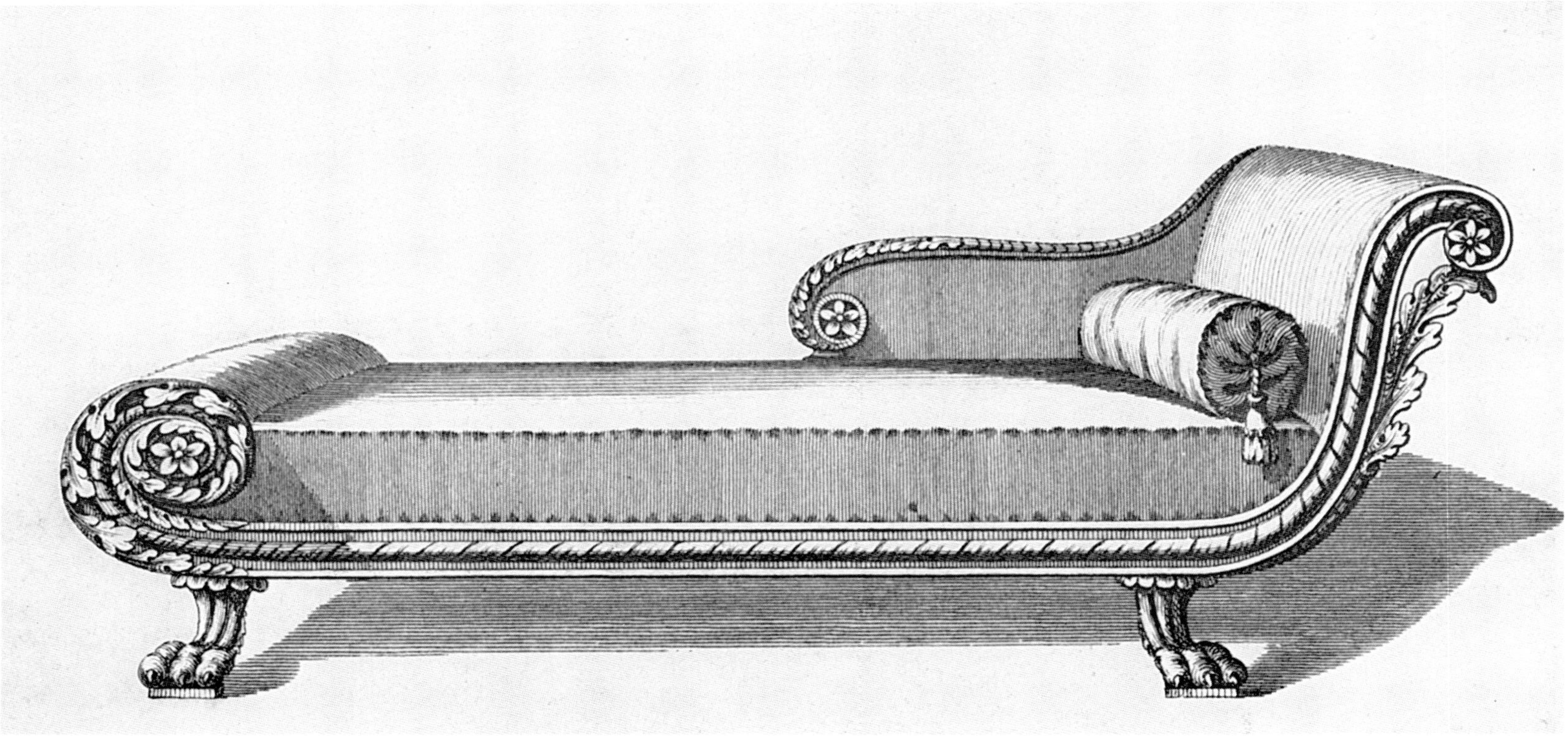

336. Sheraton: 'A Grecian squab.' Engraving, 1802.

337. Sheraton: A sofa. Etching, about 1806.

338. Sheraton: A 'Grecian' bed. Etching, about 1806.

APPENDIX

339. A chimney-piece at Wilton House, Wilts, designed by Inigo Jones. From J. Vardy's *Some Designs of Mr. Inigo Jones and Mr. Wm. Kent*, 1744. This type of architecture influenced furniture design during the second quarter of the eighteenth century. *cf.* Kent's design for an organ (No. 14) and see pages 7–8.

340. Design for a cartouche by an unidentified artist. A 16th century engraving, probably Italian. See page 10

341. Design for a cartouche by Agostino Mitelli (1609–1660); an early example of asymmetrical design. See page 10.

343. Design for a cartouche in the *style auriculaire* by Gerbrand van den Eeckhout (1621–1674). From a set entitled *Veelderhande Nieuwe Compartemente*, engraved by M. Mosyn.
See page 10.

342. Design for a cartouche by Stefano della Bella (1610–1664). Etching. See page 10.

344. Engraved design for an ink-stand by Juste-Aurèle Meissonnier; an example of completely abstract, asymmetrical rococo ornament. See pages 10–11.

345. Specimens of *rocaille* ornament by N. J. B. de Poilly (b. 1712). Etching. See page 11.

346. De la Cour. Title-page to his *First Book of Ornament*, 1741. An early example of *rocaille* decoration published in England. See pages 13 and 34.

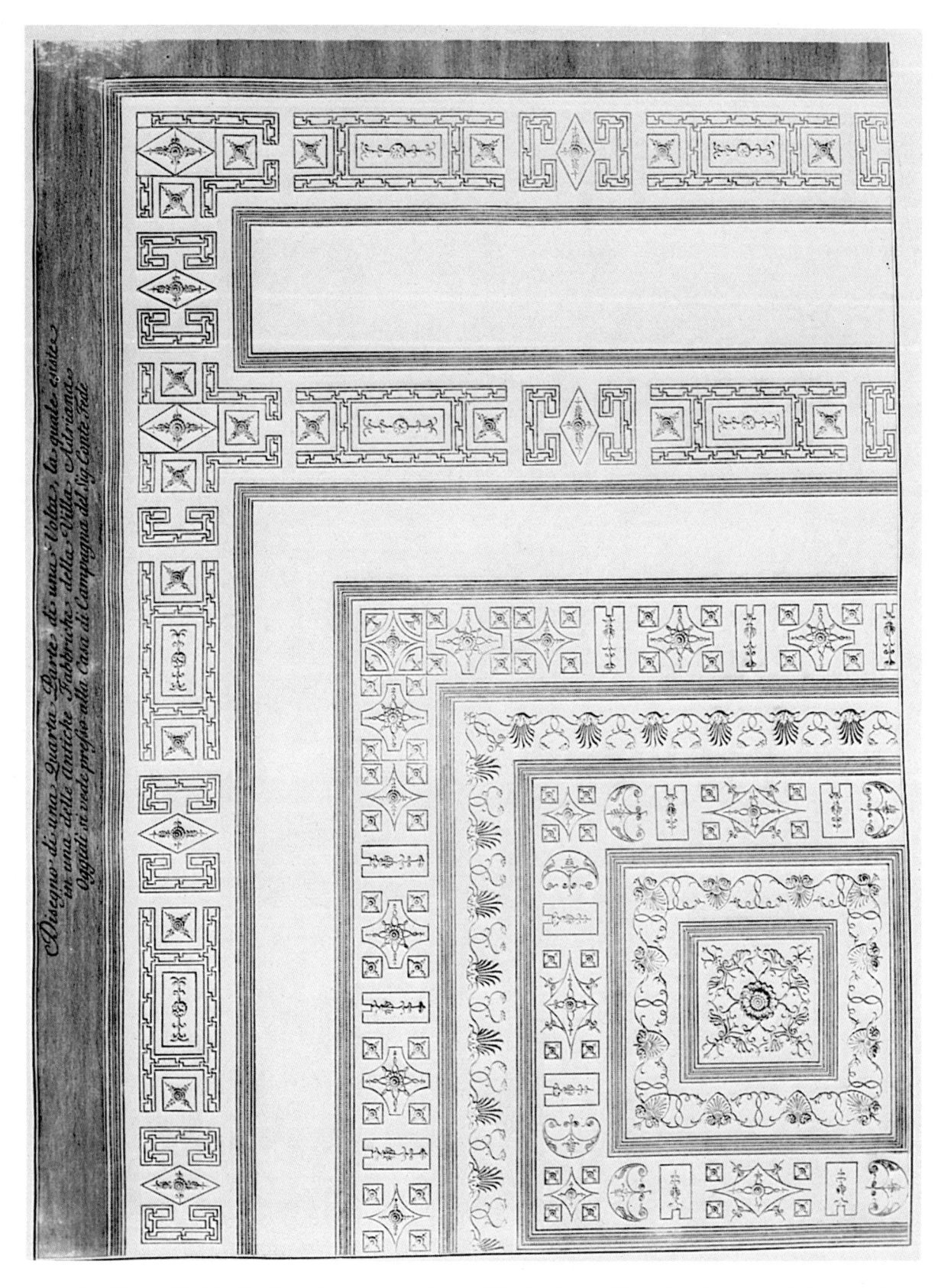

347. A ceiling in Hadrian's villa, after an engraving by Nicolas Ponce. From *Les Arabesques Antiques des Bains de Livie*, *etc.*, Paris, 1789. See page 11.

348. An ancient Roman ceiling painting of the type which inspired the grotesques of the sixteenth and eighteenth centuries. From P. S. Bartoli, *Recueil de Peintures Antiques*, Paris, 1783. *cf.* no. 349 and see page 11.

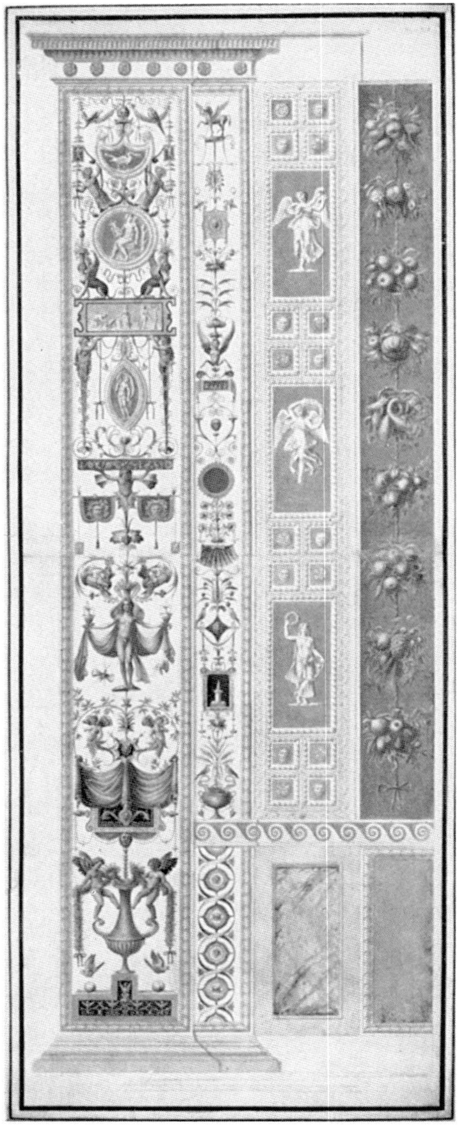

349. Panel of grotesque decoration by, or after, Raphael in the Vatican *loggie*. From an engraving by G. Savorelli and P. Camporesi. See page 11.

351. Design for an overmantel mirror by J. F. Blondel. From his book *De la Distribution des Maisons de Plaisance . . .*, Paris, 1738. See page 12.

350. Engraved design for a grotesque by Jean Bérain. (1637–1711). See page 12.

353. Design for a saloon by Thomas Lightoler. Plate 77 in *The Modern Builder's Assistant* by W. and J. Halfpenny, R. Morris and T. Lightoler, 1742 and 1757. See page 12.

352. Design for a wall panel and doorway by Nicolas Pineau. About 1735. After an engraving by J. G. Merz. See page 12.

354. Engraved designs for tables by François Cuvilliés. Compare the designs by Lock (No. 49), and Linnell (No. 193).

355. Engraved designs for tables by François Cuvilliés. Compare the designs by Lock (No. 49), and Linnell (No. 193).

357. Engraved designs for candle-stands and a bracket by François Cuvilliés. Compare the design by Thomas Johnson (No. 143) which was clearly inspired by the design on the left.

356. Engraved design for an ornamental frame by François Cuvilliés. Compare the design by Lock, No. 51.

358. Design for a 'Chinese cabinet', decorated with porcelain and panels of lacquer, by Daniel Marot. From the set entitled *Nouvelles Cheminee*. About 1700. See page 15.

359. The entablature of a 'Gothic Order' by Batty Langley. Plate 5 from his *Gothic Architecture Improved*, 1742. The frieze is decorated with a 'Gothic fret', an early example of a type of ornament much used on furniture during the 1750's and 60's. See pages 19 and 35–36.

360. A Roman chair. From C. H. Tatham, *Etchings of Ancient Ornamental Architecture*, 1799. The sweeping curves and scrolls were imitated by Sheraton and other designers at the end of the eighteenth century. See page 29.

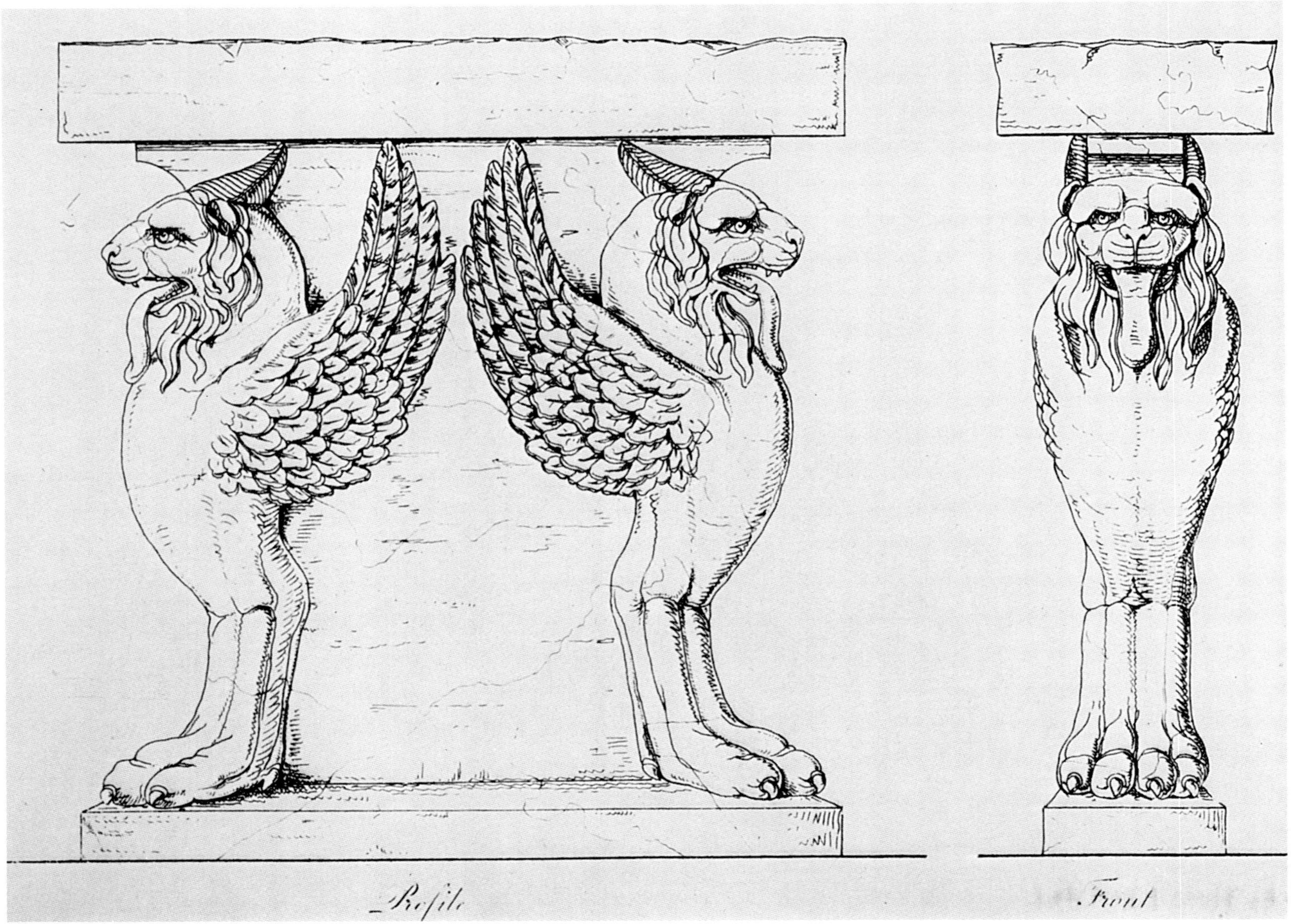

361. A Roman table with lion supports. From C. H. Tatham, *Etchings of Ancient Ornamental Architecture.* See pages 29–30.

362. A Roman table with paw feet and bowed legs. From C. H. Tatham, *Etchings of Ancient Ornamental Architecture*, 1799. See pages 29–30.

363 and 364. A Roman porphyry cistern. The form was closely copied by Adam in his design for a stool (No. 207). From C. H. Tatham, *Etchings of Ancient Ornamental Architecture*, 1799.

366. Designs for furniture in the neo-classical taste by J. F. de Neufforge from his *Recueil Elémentaire d'Architecture*, 1757–1772. The probable date about 1770.

365. Design for a clock by Johann Friedrich Lauch (active 1720–1760). Compare the plagiarized design by Thomas Langley, No. 30. See page 35.